A Political Companion to
Walt Whitman

POLITICAL COMPANIONS TO GREAT AMERICAN AUTHORS

Series Editor: Patrick J. Deneen, Georgetown University

The Political Companions to Great American Authors series illuminates the complex political thought of the nation's most celebrated writers from the founding era to the present. The goals of the series are to demonstrate how American political thought is understood and represented by great American writers and to describe how our polity's understanding of fundamental principles such as democracy, equality, freedom, toleration, and fraternity has been influenced by these canonical authors.

The series features a broad spectrum of political theorists, philosophers, and literary critics and scholars whose work examines classic authors and seeks to explain their continuing influence on American political, social, intellectual, and cultural life. This series reappraises esteemed American authors and evaluates their writings as lasting works of art that continue to inform and guide the American democratic experiment.

A POLITICAL COMPANION TO
Walt Whitman

Edited by John E. Seery

THE UNIVERSITY PRESS OF KENTUCKY

Copyright © 2011 by The University Press of Kentucky
Paperback edition 2014

Scholarly publisher for the Commonwealth,
serving Bellarmine University, Berea College, Centre
College of Kentucky, Eastern Kentucky University,
The Filson Historical Society, Georgetown College,
Kentucky Historical Society, Kentucky State University,
Morehead State University, Murray State University,
Northern Kentucky University, Transylvania University,
University of Kentucky, University of Louisville,
and Western Kentucky University.
All rights reserved.

Editorial and Sales Offices: The University Press of Kentucky
663 South Limestone Street, Lexington, Kentucky 40508-4008
www.kentuckypress.com

The Library of Congress has cataloged the hardcover edition as follows:

A political companion to Walt Whitman / edited by John E. Seery.
   p. cm. — (Political companions to great American authors)
  Includes bibliographical references and index.
  ISBN 978-0-8131-2654-8 (acid-free recycled paper)
  1. Whitman, Walt, 1819–1892—Political and social views. 2. Democracy in literature. I. Seery, John Evan.

PS3242.P64P65 2011
811'.3—dc22
                          2010030300

ISBN 978-0-8131-4737-6 (pbk. : alk. paper)

This book is printed on acid-free paper meeting
the requirements of the American National Standard
for Permanence in Paper for Printed Library Materials.

Manufactured in the United States of America.

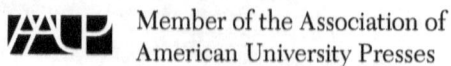

Member of the Association of
American University Presses

Contents

Series Foreword   vii

Acknowledgments   ix

Introduction: Democratic Vistas Today   1
  John E. Seery

PART I. INDIVIDUALITY AND CONNECTEDNESS

1. Walt Whitman and the Culture of Democracy   19
  George Kateb

2. Strange Attractors: How Individualists Connect to Form Democratic Unity   47
  Nancy L. Rosenblum

3. Mestiza Poetics: Walt Whitman, Barack Obama, and the Question of Union   59
  Cristina Beltrán

4. Democratic Desire: Walt Whitman   96
  Martha C. Nussbaum

5. The Solar Judgment of Walt Whitman   131
  Jane Bennett

PART II. CITY LIFE AND BODILY PLACE

6. "Mass Merger": Whitman and Baudelaire, the Modern Street, and Democratic Culture   149
  Marshall Berman

7. Promiscuous Citizenship   155
   Jason Frank

8. Walt Whitman and the Ethnopoetics of New York   185
   Michael J. Shapiro

9. Democratic Manliness   220
   Terrell Carver

PART III. DEATH AND CITIZENSHIP

10. Whitman as a Political Thinker   245
    Peter Augustine Lawler

11. Whitman, Death, and Democracy   272
    Jack Turner

12. Morbid Democracies: The Bodies Politic of Walt Whitman and Richard Rorty   296
    Kennan Ferguson

13. Democratic Enlightenment: Whitman and Aesthetic Education   310
    Morton Schoolman

Frontispieces from *Leaves of Grass*

1855 edition   340
1860 edition   341

Selected Bibliography   343

List of Contributors   353

Index   357

Series Foreword

THOSE WHO UNDERTAKE A study of American political thought must attend to the great theorists, philosophers, and essayists. But such a study is incomplete, however, if it neglects American literature, one of the greatest repositories of the nation's political thought and teachings.

America's literature is distinctive because it is, above all, intended for a democratic citizenry. In contrast to eras when an author would aim to inform or influence a select aristocratic audience, in democratic times, public influence and education must resonate with a more expansive, less leisured, and diverse audience to be effective. The great works of America's literary tradition are the natural locus of democratic political teaching. Invoking the interest and attention of citizens through the pleasures afforded by the literary form, many of America's great thinkers sought to forge a democratic public philosophy with subtle and often challenging teachings that unfolded in narrative, plot, and character development. Perhaps more than any other nation's literary tradition, American literature is ineluctably political—shaped by democracy as much as it has in turn shaped democracy.

The Political Companions to Great American Authors series highlights the teachings of the great authors in America's literary and belletristic tradition. An astute political interpretation of America's literary tradition requires careful, patient, and attentive readers who approach the text with a view to understanding its underlying messages about citizenship and democracy. Essayists in this series approach the classic texts not with a "hermeneutics of suspicion" but with the curiosity of fellow citizens who believe that the great authors have something of value to teach their readers. The series brings together essays from varied approaches and viewpoints for the common purpose of elucidating the political teachings of the nation's greatest authors for those seeking a better understanding of American democracy.

Patrick J. Deneen
Series Editor

Acknowledgments

MY DEBTS FOR THIS volume are many. My gratitude goes to Patrick J. Deneen, series editor, for entrusting me in the first place with the joyous task of coordinating this volume and for extending that trust for as long as I needed. I owe Stephen M. Wrinn, the director of the University Press of Kentucky, my overflowing appreciation (and maybe an overflowing drink, too) for his wise counsel, unbounded patience, and unfailing good cheer at every step of the way toward producing this book. Thanks as well to Ila McEntire, Susan Murray, Candace Chaney, and all of their other supportive and talented colleagues at the University Press of Kentucky. Peter Kurtz and Emily Saliba served as my able assistants over separate summers, and I heartily thank them and the Pomona College SURP program for sponsoring such research. My appreciation extends to Princeton University's Center for Human Values for its generous support. I also want to acknowledge the tremendously helpful advice of several reviewers for this volume. Finally, I feel profoundly thankful for the efforts of the contributors to this volume: they are the worthy expositors of Whitman, and I have been wonderfully privileged to serve as their collaborator.

Introduction: Democratic Vistas Today

John E. Seery

We have frequently printed the word Democracy. Yet I cannot too often repeat that it is a word the real gist of which still sleeps, quite unawaken'd, notwithstanding the resonance and the many angry tempests out of which its syllables have come, from pen or tongue. It is a great word, whose history, I suppose, remains unwritten, because that history has yet to be enacted.
—Walt Whitman, "Democratic Vistas"

A POLITICAL COMPANION TO Walt Whitman is the first volume to bring together political theorists to ponder Walt Whitman as a political writer. Such calculated, if rather belated attention surely behooves explanation.

The world of secondary literature devoted to the writings of Walt Whitman is already rich, extensive, and impressive. Scholars have scrutinized, it would seem, almost every line and verse of Whitman's poetry and prose. They have also deftly connected these gems to Whitman's personal and historical milieu. The sheer volume of such commentary almost overwhelms. The Library of Congress lists thirty edited collections of Whitman scholarship published in the last twenty years alone, along with more than one hundred single-authored book monographs on Whitman (all in addition to the ongoing *Walt Whitman Quarterly Review*). These learned analyses cover a wide assortment of topics, and almost all of them engage to some extent with what might be called "political" aspects of Whitman's work. Whitman's writings have been read through the lenses of race, history, class, religion, gender, sexuality, nationalism, and transnationalism. He has been called the gay poet, the poet of manliness, the woman poet, the black poet, the postcolonial poet, the poet of workers, the poet of the city, the poet of organicism, the poet of transcendence, the poet of individualism, the poet of connectedness, the poet of citizenship, the poet of outsidership, the war poet, the poet of sensuousness, the poet of the body, the poet of life, the poet of death, the poet of America, and, of course, the poet of democracy. All together, the scholarship would seem to confirm that Whitman, indeed, contains multitudes.

The extent to which one should read Whitman as a "political" poet at all is a matter of dispute in the literature. Some scholars remain embarrassed by Whitman's exuberant gesticulations regarding democracy, and they point out his lapses with respect to slavery, Native Americans, women, or foreigners. Such critics tend to insist on separating his best personalist poetry from the overtly political work, and to that end they also often distinguish artistic form from political content. Others, most notably Betsy Erkkila in *Whitman the Political Poet,* argue that Whitman realized, with the publication of *Leaves of Grass* in 1855, that a truly democratic America would require not simply a revolution in substantive practice but in literary form as well; thus, the poetry and the politics are inextricably intertwined.[1] Some find confirmation of these designs in Whitman's 1871 essay "Democratic Vistas," wherein Whitman famously calls for the emergence of American poets of democracy. That essay in particular touches on themes such as pluralism versus solidarity, the status of the democratic individual, voting rights, republican participation, women's suffrage, and political liberty. Yet, as Gary Wihl notes in a summary of Whitman's "politics": "Whitman's poetry and journalism offer evidence of his interest in these issues, but not a definitive political position."[2] Hence scholars find many places in Whitman's corpus that seem to invite greater elaboration on the politics thereof.

A curiosity, or more than that, to observe about that avalanche of Whitman commentary: Almost all of the authors of the above-mentioned one-hundred-plus books, and almost all of the contributors to the above-mentioned thirty edited volumes, are professors of literature, with an occasional historian or perhaps art historian, musicologist, or practicing poet chiming in. Political theorists, political philosophers, and political scientists are conspicuous by their absence: in all of the edited collections I've surveyed, reaching back past that twenty-year mark, I've found one and only one political philosopher as a contributor (a piece connecting Whitman to John Rawls).[3] This silence is surprising, especially in light of George Kateb's 1990 *Political Theory* piece on Whitman, republished in this volume, which begins thus: "I think that Walt Whitman is a great philosopher of democracy. Indeed, he may be the greatest. As Thoreau said, Whitman 'is apparently the greatest democrat the world has ever seen.' To put it more academically, he is perhaps the greatest philosopher of the culture of democracy. He writes the best phrases and sentences about democracy."[4] Or it is surprising, given Martha Nussbaum's 1995 call for Whitman-inspired "poetic justice" to be fully integrated into public conceptions of democratic judgment.[5] Or it is surprising, given Richard Rorty's 1997 claim that Whitman (along with Dewey) is the great prophet of American civic religion, offering, so says Rorty, an account of political freedom that ought to inspire us to this day.[6] Kateb is arguably one of America's greatest contemporary political theorists; Nussbaum is arguably one of America's greatest contemporary classicists; the late Rorty was arguably one of America's greatest contemporary philosophers. More than a decade ago, these three luminaries focused attention on Whitman, and yet few have followed their clarion leads.

We could venture a few wild speculations about why political theorists have simply not made Whitman a subject of sustained attention, let alone affection. That collective oversight is especially surprising since we've seen a resurgence of interest in the political-theoretical implications of the writings of fellow Transcendentalists Emerson and Thoreau. Stanley Cavell, along with Kateb, inaugurated a new generation of scholarly Emersonians and agonistic Nietzscheans, informing readers that Emerson had served as an American wellspring for much nineteenth-century continental thought. Thoreau, perhaps because of his "Civil Disobedience" essay, never went completely out of favor among political thinkers—Rawlsians, Arendtians, Gandhians, civil libertarians, war protesters, environmentalists, and others would always return to Thoreau as a touchstone or *locus classicus* for latter-day appropriations. But Whitman, while once popular with the Beats of the 1950s and the Peaceniks of 1960s, has not enjoyed any similar continuity or recuperation—perhaps because of his over-the-top "Americaness"? or his insistence on the literariness of politics? or his alternative erotics? or his maleness? or his whiteness? or his quasi-metaphysics? Once canonized (Ezra Pound said of Whitman: "He *is* America"), Whitman apparently ceased being the buoyant contrarian channeled by Langston Hughes, Allen Ginsberg, and Adrienne Rich. He fell out of favor. Few political theorists, perhaps in some part owing to their professional straits as situated within data-driven political science departments, were willing to risk their careers by investing studiously in such a once-indecorous yet now-imperious poet. Or maybe they were simply continuing a much older antagonism between philosophy and poetry.

Fads die, of course, and aging chestnuts crack. I propose that it is, in fact, a great time for political theorists and their students to read in and around Whitman. Many of our contemporary concerns seem to be echoic of Whitman's stirrings: democracy's discontents and aspirations; America's boundaries; nationalism, transnationalism, postcolonialism, and globalization; individualism versus aggregation; identity versus difference; gender, sexuality, race, and class concerns; civic religion; war; postmetaphysics; the pluralized subject; cultural politics. In many ways, political theorists in America have already been working for quite some time on manifold Whitmanesque themes, and it may be time to draw explicit attention to that unrhymed legacy.

Whitman was mostly a critic, and a caustic one at that, of the forms and practices of democracy in his own day, and he ostensibly deferred to an indefinite future any full realization of the very notion of democracy. Hence the political theorists in this volume take up that charge for brooding review. Such an assembly need not imply some kind of disciplinary privilege or territoriality about the concept, practice, or study of "politics." If anything, Whitman himself advocated an expanded and protean sense of the democratic self ("Did you, too, O friend, suppose democracy was only for elections, for politics, and for a party name?"). The English professors have done a great job in explicating Whitman's work, and they have been true to the interdisciplinary possibilities of his project. Instead, the operational spirit of the enterprise at hand is simply to offer an occasion for political theorists to look anew at Whitman's poetry and prose, and to see what comes forth, likely throwing into even sharper relief the issue of poetry's politics. The tone is critical and scholarly—which is to say, there isn't a hidden agenda insinuating that contributors (and readers) ought to become cheerleaders for a rehabilitated or vindicated Whitman. Whitman himself signaled the importance, or the inevitability, of a symbiotic relationship, a back-and-forth exchange over time, between creative poetry and the scholarly commentary it provokes:

> Poetry, largely consider'd, is an evolution, sending out improved and ever-expanded types—in one sense, the past, even the best of it, necessarily giv-

ing place, and dying out. For our existing world, the bases on which all the grand old poems were built have become vacuums—and even those of many comparatively modern ones are broken and half-gone. For us to-day, not their own intrinsic value, vast as that is, backs and maintains those poems—but a mountain-high growth of associations, the layers of successive ages. Everywhere—their own lands included—(is there not something terrible in the tenacity with which the one book out of millions holds its grip?)—the Homeric and Virgilian works, the interminable ballad-romances of the middle ages, the utterances of Dante, Spenser, and others, are upheld by their cumulus-entrenchment in scholarship, and as precious, always welcome, unspeakably valuable reminiscences.[7]

Whitman thus raises the matter of poetry's relationship to scholarship—and so prompted, we might bend that concern to our own purposes at hand. This volume implicitly poses the related inquiry: What claim—what authority, what expertise, what insight, what right—might the scholarly subfield known as political theory have on poetry? Or turning it around, what discernable benefits can the careful study of poetry possibly deliver to the organized understanding and, therewith, the practice of politics? Those questions speak to the need for positioning this unusual volume. The political theorists herein surely need to account for their forays into the literary strongholds on Whitman in the fields of English and American studies; but they also probably owe an account to their larger disciplinary home of political science, where devoting considerable resources to the serious study of a poet might be seen not just as a silly indulgence or distraction from the hard-minded enterprise of political research but, even more, as an utter waste of scholarly time and capital. Given that inhospitable climate, we ruefully concede that it may be far too facile or wistful to fancy that Whitman's poetic overtures toward democracy, even professionally mediated, could today be received as widely relevant rather than hopelessly quaint. Are we poetically inclined political theorists thus spinning our tops? I'd like to venture forth a few rejoining ruminations about the volume's position vis-à-vis various implicated constituencies: the English professors, the political scientists, and perhaps a democratically disposed readership at large.

First, it shouldn't come as a tremendous surprise that many political theorists have been operating as shadow literary theorists for some time now. Even as that subfield first started defining itself, political theorists were attracted to mixed and multiple genres of political authorship, inspiring or impelling them to acquire sundry skills and techniques of literary analysis. In addition to including formal political tracts, treatises, pamphlets, and manifestos, the political theory canon has always been replete with works and tropes of imaginative literature—dialogues, novels, plays, satires, sermons, dreams, confessions, meditations, utopias, hypotheticals, metaphors, allegories, and, yes, poetry, epic, lyric, and dramatic. A conscientious student of political theory necessarily reads the fictions of Homer, Sappho, Sophocles, Plato, Cicero, Virgil, Christine de Pizan, Augustine, Machiavelli, More, Shakespeare, Harrington, Montesquieu, Voltaire, Rousseau, Diderot, Nietzsche, and so on. It's also the case, aligning them even more closely with their literary colleagues, that a great number of contemporary political theorists have taken "the literary turn" in their studies,[8] attending thus scrupulously to the importance of language and textual interpretation in their quests for greater understanding of the politics of the human condition. Those literary turns have taken different twists and gone in different directions: scriptural midrash and exegesis; Heideggerian hermeneutics; Frankfurt school aesthetics; Wittgensteinian ordinary language analysis; Voegelinian noesis; Straussian esotericisim; Derridean deconstruction; or poststructuralist complexity. Above all, it's fair to say that many if not most political theorists have become highly attuned to *textuality*—and therefore turning one's full-on attention to poetry and poetic form doesn't seem quite out of the ordinary.

Call that comportment or propensity a literary sensibility, and those who share it constitute a community of sorts (absent, however, the nervous need to qualify such community as imagined). Allow me, for now, to push it as a dividing line between political theorists and political scientists.[9] Literature implicitly signals and sanctions its own performative dimension—performative in the sense used by Austin, Butler, and others—whereas didactic approaches to political science (if I may submit a sweeping provocation) are usually oblivious to their own rhetorical renderings. Customarily poets and novelists, while pursuing projects not mutually collapsible, all want to move or stir their audience in some way or ways, often unpredictably so; they are concerned with affect, plot, character, mood, style, and reception. Anyone who teaches literature knows that you cannot begin a classroom discussion by jumping to the bottom line and blurting out, "What is this book about finally, what's the main point?" That gambit kills conversation. You cannot just glance at the last page and get it. As a teacher, you must go through the process of reading and remarking, especially if it's an epic poem or bildungsroman. The texture of presentation, the dialogue, the possible irony, the character entanglements, the narrative twists and turns, the particulars, also the unstated, that which is inserted only between the lines as it were, the assumed, the imagined, or the invisible, may in fact be the point, a point that may elude prosaic recapitulation and reduction. Readers must *participate,* as it were, in and with the text. In other words, I dare say that many novelists and poets, and many readers of imaginative literature, better understand that there's a possible politics (and many variations thereabouts) to the back-and-forth interactions cued, feigned, projected, and carried on between writers and readers—a subtext to the text—whereas I suspect that many academic practitioners of normal political science see their own textual activity as unilaterally expository rather than complexly interactive. Their aim is accedence, not contestation. Yet that apparent presumption that their own scholarly activity is, or can be, neatly bracketed from the wider political condition is but an occupational fiction, a pretense under which many academics seem to labor. Political scientists—of all persons!—should be savvier and more attuned to this self-conceit about authorial power than they seem to be.

The point is: The performative dimension to literature (an awareness thereof) cries out for, that is, demands, requires, invites, and elicits, *interpretation* (the bugbear of all dogmatists). Academic writers, especially social scientists, typically want to prove their points, QED, and their ideal captive audiences presumably are to serve as rapt spectators to their hypotheses, adduced evidence, arguments, tables, graphs, equations, and conclusions. Literary writers and their writings can, of course, have tendentious agendas, but it usually requires readerly participation to tease them out, that is, if one can even settle upon a stable or privileged interpretation. Thus I suggest that much or most of literature embodies and promotes an implicitly participatory ethic, and one that is usually pluralistic as well, since most worthy works risk multiple interpretations and appropriations. My cartoon political scientist, in contrast, attempts to assume an autocratic relation to his or her audience, controlling and even attempting to dictate a singular relationship to the work, the one and only correct answer, the correct reading of the work as intended by the author. Our students understand very well this curricular divide (yes, overdrawn here) between pedants and poets—it's not just that novels, plays, poems, and films are more entertaining when we deploy them in our classrooms. Rather, our students know or sense intuitively that active and independent involvement in literary works is required of them, as opposed to finding themselves browbeaten into submission by an imperial author or lecturer. In short, I don't see many political scientists as thoroughgoing pluralists or republicans (with a small *r*), let alone democrats (with a small *d*); or if they affirm participatory pluralism on principle, they betray it in practice, where the form and content of their own activity necessarily diverge. Reading such works, students quickly surmise that the bottom line is actually political hypocrisy: Do as I say, not as I do. The literary sensibility, limned above, I see as a check against academic autocracy and as conducing toward the practical exercise of pluralism—in much the way that Hannah Arendt appealed to the "faculty of imagination" as the basis for representative thinking.[10] (Nothing of the above, I admit, addresses the concerns and meets the objections of those who shudder with contempt at the very prospect of a leveling pluralism. Poetry may win over hearts and minds, but can it convert hardened souls?)

Whitman throws down an ongoing challenge to his prospective readers: We moderns, he rudely reiterates, don't yet understand the sheer idea of democracy, let alone practice it. Professional political scientists, drawing on extensive polling data and/or game theory, might wish to dismiss Whitman's broadside out of hand, yet such museful ideas have a nagging way of sticking around. We still look to Homer as the poetic founder of Hellenism; we look to Virgil for political insights into imperial Rome; we look to Dante for pan Christendom; we look to Shakespeare, Faust, Zarathustra, or T. S. Eliot for coming tragedies of the modern. Whitman well knows this long-standing, time-tested, poetic-political lineage. Drawing upon it, unsettling it, adapting it, he calls for a new breed of poets—poets of democracy—to emerge:

> For the great Idea, the idea of perfect and free individuals,
> For that, the bard walks in advance, leader of leaders,
> The attitude of him cheers up slaves and horrifies foreign
>   despots.
> . . . .
> For the great Idea,
> That, O my brethren, that is the mission of poets.[11]

About that expanded, exalted, yet still elusive notion of democracy, Whitman doesn't simply *show* and *tell,* he also attempts to *do,* to perform it, to call it into being, to instantiate it via his forms of presentation, to rankle, inspire, admonish, and conjure it. The poet thus implicates his reader ("Thou Reader")[12] at almost every turn: "And what I assume you shall assume, / For every atom belonging to me as good belongs to you."[13] It's not enough to say— a commonplace—that Whitman's vision of political democracy exceeds the conventional terms of formal elections and institutional governance (which count to many, those apparently lacking in long-term touchstones, as "real politics"). Homer was the poet of epic heroes; Dante was the poet of epic pilgrims; Shakespeare was the poet of kingly types; the trick for democratic poets will be to sing the high praises of average individuals while merging them with the undifferentiated mass, conferring singular dignity upon the fungible, divinity of sorts upon the dispensable.[14] Democracy unbounded yet ennobled will require democratic practice, not just democratic preaching ("I say that democracy can never prove itself beyond cavil, until it founds and luxuriantly grows its own forms of art, poems, schools, theology").[15] The democratic writer, whether scholar or poet, must be capable of reaching out and engaging ordinary citizens, even when reproaching and exhorting them upward and onward (the receptive propensities for which are already in place, or, as Tocqueville writes: "I readily admit that the Americans have no poets; I cannot allow that they have no poetic ideas").[16] Clearly Whitman understands his own writing as an extended exercise in civic education, a peer-to-peer evangelism that somehow elides the elitist distinction between priestly poet and lowly supplicant; and such exemplary poetry is, or will be, the sine qua non for triggering and galvanizing an expansively democratic culture. To press the point of poetry's larger, if unrealized, political relevance, by invidious comparison: Could a poetry-free political science, a civics built mainly on regression analyses and quantitative methods, provide the necessary and sufficient conditions for generating a salutary and sustainable democratic culture? Will any *American Political Science Review* article ever emerge as truly memorable over time, our Homeric testament to the ages? Does the intensive reading of political science actually translate into making us better citizens? If one were to be shipwrecked and stranded on a deserted island with but one book, is there any noteworthy political science publication that any sane, sentient being would prefer to a tattered copy of *Leaves of Grass*? Granted, true enough, indeed: Poets, and Whitman in particular, are regarded as politically otiose in some cranky camps. But that plight may merely reflect poorly on our current state of affairs rather than providing good empirical proof against ever mixing politics and poetry. We may need this unusual volume to remind ourselves of, or to awaken anew, our subdued democratic inklings and outlooks. To that end, I might note to readers, as an editorial aside and quick insider's tip, that Whitman's unruly recommendations for democracy are often iconoclastic, not just iconicizing:

> To the States or any one of them, or any city of the States,
>   *Resist much, obey little.*
> Once unquestioning obedience, once fully enslaved,
> Once fully enslaved, no nation, state, city of this earth,
>   ever afterward resumes its liberty.[17]

A Political Companion to Walt Whitman includes three republished pieces and ten original essays penned specifically for this volume. Readers hoping for a neat, coherent, cumulative, or exhaustive treatment of everything political in Whitman's oeuvre are liable to be disappointed by the volume's organization, or lack thereof—call it the fluidity of presentation. Perhaps such editorial forbearance, resisting the academic temptation to carve up, define, contain, and deliver one's subject, is the best way to remain true to Whitman's free-form democratizing artistry (as Allen Ginsberg famously asserted, Whitman is too vast to be seen). The essays herein take up various themes, consider different aspects of Whitman's work, and emphasize finally different points. A careful reader will spot intersecting threads, recurrent motifs, notes of convergence, and nascent or outward disputes betwixt and between particular authors. The individual essays, however, really ought to be read on their own, in their own right, rather than as contributions mainly to a whole. As a concession to some kind of preview and overview, however, we offer the following advance teasers and tidbits, grouping essays into convenient clusters (but no more than that): We begin with George Kateb's pioneering essay "Walt Whitman and the Culture of Democracy," which introduced Whitman as a political philosopher and argued that Whitman is a great teacher of democratic individuality, whose final lessons are those of solitude, Kateb insisted, not connectedness. Yet Kateb finds in Whitman's poetry and prose the crucial idea that individual potentiality can translate into a democratic receptivity (call that the connectedness) toward others.

In a responding article published in the same volume of *Political Theory*, Nancy Rosenblum challenged Kateb for what she saw as an overly individualizing (and overly philosophizing) account of Whitman. For Rosenblum, Kateb's Whitman—who juggles and somehow conjoins individual separateness with equalizing association—would have a hard time parlaying such democratic receptivity into rights-based democratic institutions. Rosenblum contends that Whitman's poetry and his biography in fact reveal attractions and exclusions (for example, on the basis of property, race, and gender) that cannot be adequately explained via Kateb's conception of individuality. Instead, Rosenblum recommends that we look particularly at Whitman's poetic enchantments and dazzling inducements toward the spectacle of public diversity, which, she suggests on a discordant note, may not happily translate into sustainable civic forms and political practices. Cristina Beltrán assumes Rosenblum's appreciative critique of Kateb and then applies Rosenblum's notion of Whitman's spectacular embrace (and simultaneous elision) of diversity to Barack Obama's presidential campaign, with a special focus on Obama's allusive attempts to manage racial conflict. Beltrán contends that Whitman's poetry helps us to understand Obama's racial strategies, yet those efforts at aesthetic unity ought to be supplemented with a more agonistic ethos of racial crossing—a resource Beltrán finds in Gloria Anzaldúa's poetic idea of "mestiza consciousness" and an idea that might bring closer together aesthetic attraction with civic concerns for justice.

Martha Nussbaum finds in Whitman not only a poetic push toward democratic inclusion but also a prophetic call to this-worldly justice, and she locates that call in Whitman's democratically loving vision of "citizens as ends." But to understand how love can be combined with the demands for justice, we need to change our notions of love, she says following Whitman; and that altered understanding of love will require an erotic recuperation of the human body and, therewith, of human finitude. Far from deflecting or whitewashing troubling concerns about race, slavery, gender, and sexuality out of his poetry, Whitman, Nussbaum writes, incorporates his awareness of social hierarchy, exclusion, anger, and hatred into that eroticized poetry, the profoundly equalizing grittiness of which virtually compels political response. Jane Bennett shares Martha Nussbaum's fascination with Whitman as a latter-day Jesus figure, who espouses an ostensibly undiscriminating love as the basis for democracy's future; and yet such a broad affirmation raises Kateb's, Rosenblum's, and Beltrán's question of how one can extend democracy's embrace without abandoning all countervailing credulity. Both Nussbaum and Bennett think Whitman's pan-democratic love need not dissolve complicating judgments; but Bennett takes issue with Nussbaum's subject-centered theory of judgment (from another of her essays on Whitman). Bennett finds in Whitman explicit and repeated reference to "solar judgment," a curious phrase that seems to indicate a kind of impersonal and even nonanthropocentric form of nonjudgmental judgment, which might arbitrate the competing democratic claims of diversity and unity in new ways. Whereas some of our commentators seem to ascribe to poetry the tendency to attract or bind through alluring, dazzling, or sentimental wordplay or form, Bennett looks to Whitman's "middle-voiced" poetry as potentially disrupting the grammatical and normative landscape of the politics that are. One might observe that this section in the volume, from Kateb to Rosenblum to Beltrán to Nussbaum to Bennett, adumbrates a range or evolution from humanist to posthumanist responses to Whitman.

The next three essays—by Marshall Berman, Jason Frank, and Michael Shapiro—all focus on Whitman's fascination with city life: the city itself as a subject to be encountered and negotiated by the poeticized self. A fourth essay in that bloc, by Terrell Carver, investigates the imaging of democratic citizenship mapped onto another place, namely America. Marshall Berman writes that Whitman was trying to make people feel more at home in a modern city, responding to growing fears of noisy crowds and untamed democratic mobs. Whitman spun attractive fantasies of a great city as an emotionally complex sexual encounter. Whereas Berman sees Whitman as extending bedroom intimacy outward, relaxing the distinction between private versus streetwise encounters, Jason Frank shades Whitman's promiscuous urbanism toward a particularly "public" kind of love, a way of seeing anonymous strangers—uniquely nonintimates—as the basis for sensual attraction and collective identification. Michael Shapiro draws upon Whitman's poetic musicality—his references to the songs, voices, choruses, sounds, and rhythms associated with New York City—as a hook for understanding Whitman's way of dramatizing the individual subject's encounter with the collective city, especially on the matter of ethnic difference. Distinguishing between Kantian versus Deleuzian variations on the Whitman subject (Frank also draws from Deleuze), Shapiro pays special heed to Whitman's and Whitmanesque writers' accounts of ethno-poetic musicality, distinguishing such performances as monophonic, polyphonic, or cacophonic. Like Shapiro and Beltrán, Terrell Carver attends to the concern that Whitman's lofty rhetoric (or the reception thereof) might mask racialized exclusions and occlude (or engender, or renegotiate) other kinds of undisclosed invidiousness. Carver jointly questions American democracy qua icon and Whitman qua icon. In particular, Carver calls for an agonistic reading of Whitman's masculinized democracy, again inviting affinities with Beltrán's and Shapiro's essays.

The writers grouped into the final section—Peter Lawler, Jack Turner, Kennan Ferguson, and Morton Schoolman—all reflect upon Whitman's call for great democratic poets of death, along with the reimagined metaphysical and worldly commitments to be culled poetically from death's vantage. Peter Lawler, explicating Whitman as a political thinker, locates the poet's politics with respect to several authors in the political theory canon, particularly Tocqueville and Paine. Tocqueville and Whitman, he says, both associate democracy with the religious quest for personal immortality, the overcoming of death. Both seek to combine heroic individualism with democratic justice. But Lawler questions, now in a contrast with Tocqueville, whether Whitman's possible pantheism, scientism, historicism, and anti-ecclesiasticism impede his Homeric attempts to exalt the democratic individual. Following Lawler, Jack Turner similarly acknowledges Whitman's conflicting tendencies toward materialism versus immortality and heroism versus democracy; yet Turner identifies three different kinds of responses to death that he finds in Whitman's poetry. Whitman finally teaches, says Turner, agnosticism toward death, a cool Socratism that can enhance democratic citizenship. Kennan Ferguson agrees with Turner that Whitman did not fear death yet contends that the political implications may not be as futurist as some Whitman readers, such as Richard Rorty, assume. Ferguson compares his "presentist" reading of Whitman's poetics of death with Rorty's futurist left-patriotic pragmatist reading, and he contests the implication that Whitman's vision of death necessitates nationalist redemptions. Like Carver, Ferguson sees Whitman's poetic comradeship, drawing on death as an equalizing yet vitalizing force in the present, as transnationalist in spirit. Finally, in a close reading of the structure of "Democratic Vistas," Morton Schoolman agrees with many of Ferguson's threads: that Whitman views death not as an ending; that American democracy exceeds a nationalist frame;

that Whitman's call for a future poet seems to be auto-referential. Drawing upon death as a great unknown (akin to Turner's agnosticism), Whitman's poetry for Schoolman models an inclusive aesthetic that serves as a cultural barrier to converting the diversity of appearances into forms of Otherness. Whitman's political lessons—for us moderns, survivors of genocides and world wars—may be more to withstand evil widely than to erect a heroic culture of quasi-immortal peers. Schoolman's emphasis on evil-avoidance thus invites political comparison with Kateb's emphasis on rights-based individualism at the outset of the essays.

Notes

1. Betsy Erkkila, *Whitman the Political Poet* (New York and Oxford: Oxford University Press, 1989).

2. Gary Wihl, "Politics," in *A Companion to Walt Whitman,* ed. Donald D. Kummings (Malden, Mass., and Oxford: Blackwell, 2006), 77–86.

3. Wai Chee Dimock, "Whitman, Syntax, and Political Theory," in *Breaking Bounds: Whitman and American Cultural Studies,* ed. Betsy Erkkila and Jay Grossman, 62–79 (New York: Oxford University Press, 1996).

4. George Kateb, "Walt Whitman and the Culture of Democracy," *Political Theory* 18, no. 4 (November 1990).

5. Martha C. Nussbaum, *Poetic Justice: The Literary Imagination and Public Life* (Boston: Beacon Press, 1995).

6. Richard Rorty, *Achieving Our Country: Leftist Thought in Twentieth-Century America* (Cambridge and London: Harvard University Press, 1998).

7. Walt Whitman, "A Thought on Shakespeare," in *Walt Whitman: Complete Poetry and Collected Prose,* Library of America series (New York: Literary Classics of the United States, 1982), 1151.

8. Simon Stow, *Republic of Readers: The Literary Turn in Political Thought and Analysis* (Albany: State University of New York Press, 2008).

9. From John Steinbeck's *America and Americans* (New York: Viking Press, 1966), 135–36:

> Not long ago, after my last trip to Russia, I had a conversation with an American very eminent in the field of politics. I asked him what he read, and he replied that he studied history, sociology, economics, and law.
>
> "How about fiction—novels, plays, poetry?" I asked.
>
> "No," he said, "I have never had time for them. There is so much else I have to read."

I said, "Sir, I have recently visited Russia for the third time. I don't know how well I understand Russians; but I do know that if I had only read Russian history I could not have had the access to Russian thinking I have had from reading Dostoevski, Tolstoy, Chekhov, Pushkin, Turgenev, Sholokhov, and Ehrenburg. History only recounts, with some inaccuracy, *what* they did. The fiction tells, or tries to tell, *why* they did it and what they felt and were like when they did it."

My friend nodded gravely. "I hadn't thought of that," he said. "Yes, that might be so; I had always thought of fiction as opposed to fact."

But in considering the American past, how poor we would be in information without *Huckleberry Finn, An American Tragedy, Winesburg, Ohio, Main Street, The Great Gatsby,* and *As I Lay Dying.* And if you want to know about Pennsylvania of the last hundred years, you'll read O'Hara or you'll know less than you might.

This is no plea for fiction over history, but it does suggest that both are required for any kind of understanding.

10. Hannah Arendt, "Understanding and Politics," *Partisan Review* 20, no. 4 (July–August 1953): 377–92.

11. Walt Whitman, "By Blue Ontario's Shore," in *Walt Whitman: The Complete Poems*, ed. Francis Murphy (New York: Penguin Books, 1975), 369.

12. Walt Whitman, "Thou Reader," in *The Complete Poems*, 49.

13. Walt Whitman, "Song of Myself," in *The Complete Poems*, 63.

14. Bonnie Honig has inspired some of these formulations.

15. Walt Whitman, "Democratic Vistas," in *Prose Works 1892*, vol. 2, ed. Floyd Stovall (New York: New York University Press, 1964), 365.

16. Alexis de Tocqueville, "Of Some of the Sources of Poetry amongst Democratic Nations," in *Democracy in America*, ed. J. P. Mayer, trans. George Lawrence (Garden City, New York: Anchor Books, 1969), 485.

17. Whitman, "To the States," in *The Complete Poems*, 44.

PART I

Individuality and Connectedness

CHAPTER 1

Walt Whitman and the Culture of Democracy

George Kateb

I THINK THAT WALT WHITMAN is a great philosopher of democracy. Indeed, he may be the greatest. As Thoreau said, Whitman "is apparently the greatest democrat the world has ever seen."[1] To put it more academically, he is perhaps the greatest philosopher of the culture of democracy. He writes the best phrases and sentences about democracy. By democratic culture, I mean these things especially. First, democratic culture is (or can be) the soil for the creation of new works of high art—great poems and moral writings, in particular. Second, democratic culture is (or is becoming) a particularist stylization of life—that is, a distinctive set of appearances, habits, rituals, dress, ceremonies, folk traditions, and historical memories. Third, democratic culture is (or can be) the soil for the emergence of great souls whose greatness consists in themselves being like works of art in the spirit of a new aristocracy. All these meanings are interconnected and appear in Whitman's writings throughout his life. Perhaps they receive their most powerful expression in "Democratic Vistas." But, in my judgment, the central meaning when we study Whitman is democratic culture as the setting in which what I have elsewhere called "democratic individuality" (a phrase close to Whitman's usage) is slowly being disclosed. I believe that the setting for democratic individuality is a greatly more powerful and original idea than any of the other ideas of democratic culture that I have just mentioned.

In other places, I have tried to suggest that working together with Emerson and Thoreau, Whitman tries to draw out the fuller moral and existential significance of rights. These are the rights that individuals have as persons, and that the political system of democracy exists in order to protect, and also to embody in its workings. Democratic individuality is what rights-based individualism in a democracy could eventually become, once the political separation from the Old World was complete; and had already become, to some degree, in their time. I see the Emersonians as trying to encourage the tendency to democratic individuality, to urge it forward so that it may express itself ever more confidently and therefore more splendidly. In their conception of democratic individuality, I find three components: self-expression, resistance in behalf of others, and receptivity or responsiveness (being "hospitable") to others. My judgment is that for the Emersonians, the most important component of democratic individuality, by far, is receptivity or responsiveness. An individual's insistence on first being oneself expressively is valuable mostly as a preparation for receptivity or responsiveness: behavioral nonconformity loosens the hold of narrow or conventional methods of seeing and feeling (as well as preparing a person to take a principled stand in favor of those denied their rights).

This responsiveness or receptivity can also be described as a way—a profoundly democratic way—of being connected to others and to nature. As Whitman says in "Song of the Open Road": "Here the profound lesson of reception, nor preference nor denial."[2] It is a way that deepens the sort of connectedness already present in rights-based individualism, but that only time and a steady commitment to rights can call forth. Time is needed because rights-based individualism is such a strange idea, and so untypical of past human experience, that those who live it and live by it—even though imperfectly—have to keep remembering, or keep learning as if they never knew, both the basic meaning and the further implications of what they profess and enact. And the steady commitment therefore turns out to be not so steady after all, but only as steady as the strangeness permits.

I would like to explore the connectedness that emanates from democratic individuality, as Whitman perceives and perfects it. He knows, let it be said immediately, the extent of the strangeness, and the steadiness for what it is, in democratic society. He says in the Preface, 1876, to *Leaves of Grass:* "For though perhaps the main points of all ages and nations are points of resemblance, and, even while granting evolution, are substantially the same, there are some vital things in which this Republic, as to its individualities, and as a compacted Nation, is to specially stand forth, and culminate modern humanity. And these are the very things it least morally and mentally knows—(though curiously enough, it is at the same time faithfully acting upon them.)"

In the Preface, 1872, he looks back on what he has been doing since he began writing *Leaves of Grass*. He says: "'Leaves of Grass,' already published, is, in its intentions, the song of a great composite *democratic individual,* male or female. And following on and amplifying the same purpose, I suppose I have in my mind to run through the chants of this volume, (if ever completed,) the thread-voice, more or less audible, of an aggregated, inseparable, unprecedented, vast, composite, electric *democratic nationality.*" For me, Whitman's greatness does not lie in his pursuit of an image of a democratic American nationality, an image—in my phrase—of a particularist stylization of life. Such a notion strikes me as being of secondary importance at best. How important to the world is one more stylization? Even more, I do not think that the notion is consistent with the project of proposing "a great composite democratic individual." A "compacted Nation" (Preface 1876) is antithetical to a composite individual. Nationhood is too close to a conception of group identity: a shared pride in tribal attributes rather than in adherence to a distinctive and principled human self-conceptualization that may one day be available to persons everywhere in the world. As national poetry, "Drum-Taps" is full of a hateful belligerence: Whitman sees and exults in the indissociable bond between nationhood and war. No, Whitman's greatness lies in his effort, the greatest effort thus far made, to say—to sing—the democratic individual, especially as such an individual lives in receptivity or responsiveness, in a connectedness different from any other. Such connectedness is not the same as nationhood or group identity. (A later point in this essay is that it is not the same as "adhesiveness.")

I would like to suggest that his individualist effort attains its greatest height in the poem "Song of Myself." This is not to deny that everywhere in Whitman's work we will find resources for enriching or refining the poem's teaching. It is also true that he is sometimes less literal in this poem than he is elsewhere and later. But "Song of Myself" is of supreme value; it can organize one's reading of Whitman's body of writing. In thinking about this poem as the central work, one can make discoveries about the culture of democracy.

The poem is full of complexities. This democratic poem, like all of

Whitman's best work, is immensely difficult; it is only barely accessible. His characterization of his own poems (in "As Consequent, etc.") perfectly suits "Song of Myself":

> O little shells, so curious-convolute, so limpid-cold and voiceless,
> . . . .
> Your tidings old, yet ever new and untranslatable.

And if "Song of Myself" said—like any great work—unexpected things in its time, it remains—like any great work—altogether unexpected. So let us try to see what "Song of Myself" teaches. I mean to treat this poem as a work in political theory, which is what Whitman himself encourages (to say the least). Now and then, it is wise, however, to recall a line from "Myself and Mine": "reject those who would expound me, for I cannot expound myself."

Whitman makes major additions from version to version and omits a few lines here and there. We should be content, I think, with the last version, that of 1891–92, even though it is interesting to study Whitman's changes. One change, however, should be noticed. Whitman did not call the poem "Song of Myself" until 1881. In the first version of 1855, the poem, like all the poems in the first edition of *Leaves of Grass*, had no title. Thereafter, the poem is successively called "Poem of Walt Whitman," "Walt Whitman," and finally, "Song of Myself."

All of its various titles are odd—as, indeed, the title of the collection (*Leaves of Grass*) is odd. The poem's titles are odd because when we read it, we do not find the poem autobiographical, except in a few unimportant details. The egotistical titles are not the titles of an egotistical work. Nor is the work self-referring or self-revelatory in any usual sense. There is scarcely anything intimate in it. It tells no story about the writer. Perhaps it would be all the more odd if the poem were self-revealing: Until rather late in life, Whitman had little fame. Why should anyone have cared to hear an account of his life in 1855?

In the very first section of the poem, Whitman says:

> what I assume you shall assume,
> For every atom belonging to me as good belongs to you.

Notice the extreme rapidity of movement in mood in these two lines. "What I assume you shall assume" seems to indicate that the poet is demanding that his readers obey him in their thought: a sentiment worse than egotistical. But then, in the next line, he is telling us that the reason we are to assume what he assumes is that "every atom belonging to me as good belongs to you." It is not that we must obey him as we read him. Rather, if we understand the poem, we will see that the poet and his readers are alike, and therefore we will come to assume what the poet does. In telling of himself, the poet is telling us about ourselves: That is what is to be assumed. His words about himself are words about us. As he proclaims in the climax of one of his long and observant catalogs of expressive human roles and functions: "of these one and all I weave the song of myself" (sec. 15). In a Notebook entry (1855–56), Whitman says: "I have all lives, all effects, all hidden invisibly in myself. . . . [T]hey proceed from me."[3] In fact, if luck had made any of his readers democratic poets (and contingency is the thing that makes the greatest difference), we would have said or sung poems with the same purport as "Song of Myself":

(It is you talking just as much as myself, I act as the tongue of you,
Tied in your mouth, in mine it begins to be loosen'd.) (sec. 47)

We are alike in a certain way: Living in a rights-based democracy enables and encourages a certain recognition of likeness. What is the nature of this likeness? Whitman says that "every atom belonging to me as good belongs to you." Let us emphasize the word "atom." What does it mean in this poem? An atom is a potentiality, I think. Every individual is composed of potentialities. Therefore, when I perceive or take in other human beings as they lead their lives or play their parts, I am only encountering external actualizations of some of the countless number of potentialities in me, in my soul. These atoms are in everyone; hence "every atom belonging to me as good belongs to you." The difficult and important complication is that in one's experience of others, one encounters their personalities, not their souls. The world contains an amazing diversity of personalities. Contingency has a great share in realizing any potentiality. Souls, however, are the same: infinite potentialities.

At this point, I should try to say something about the categories that

Whitman uses or suggests in speaking of the different (so to speak, structural) aspects of the individual. I am guided to some degree by Roy Harvey Pearce and Harold Bloom.[4]

The key term is "soul"; it frequently occurs in "Song of Myself" and in all of Whitman's work. It has both a secular meaning and a religious one, while the boundaries of the two meanings are not always distinct. Whitman intends, I think, some fluidity of definition. In its secular meaning, the soul is what is given in the person, and in all persons the given is the same: the same desires, inclinations, and passions as well as aptitudes and incipient talents. The secular soul is made up of the unwilled, the unbidden, the dreamt, the inchoate and unshaped. It is the reservoir of potentialities. Its roots are wordless. It exists to be observed and worked on, to be realized. In its religious meaning, soul is unique and unalterable individual identity; one's genius or "eidolon"; the "real Me" (from "As I Ebb'd with the Ocean of Life"); the "actual me" (from "Passage to India"). It seems to be untouched by experience, and it survives death to find numberless incarnations. For me, the Whitman that matters is the one who believes in the secular soul, not the one who fancies he believes in the religious soul (toward which he does sometimes turn a skeptical glance).

The sharply contrasting term to "soul" is, of course, "body." Whitman sometimes speaks dualistically of the soul and the body. He means to proclaim that the rights of the body are as sacred as those of the soul. He celebrates not only sex but the senses, which take their turn in being praised in "Song of Myself." When he does this, he is defying those whose religious conception of the soul is more conventional than Whitman's own and who associate the body with sin and damnation. On the other hand, Whitman's secular soul is unthinkable without the body and conversely.

What, then, is the self, insofar as it is not a synonym for the whole individual? In "Pioneers! O Pioneers!" he says:

> I too with my soul and body,
> We, a curious trio.

From this verse and others, I would infer that the self (the I, the ego) is active self-consciousness and disciplined creative energy. It is a purely secular category that Whitman does not want us to confuse with soul, especially in its religious sense. The self does its great work when it observes its soul and body as from a distance and exploits the faculty of speech to tell as much of the truth as possible about them. The self is power that draws on its given resources of soul and body to become a poet: everybody is at least a partway poet. It is with the poet's virtues of receptivity (in whatever way or degree possible) that each self democratically connects to the world of persons, creatures, and things. "You be my poem" (from "To You") helps to define connectedness.

The other work that the self does is to put together a social persona, a personality, and thus enable the individual to lead a life. The creative energy of the self realizes one or another potentiality of the soul (and body). The personality is what is immediately recognizable by others: one's characteristics as they flow to and from one's work and social relations. Personality has surface and depths.

"Song of Myself" begins with "I celebrate myself." What the poem celebrates is soul, body, and self, but especially the inexhaustibility of the soul and the power of the self to observe the soul and make democratic poetical understanding. The poem does not really celebrate personality or social persona; it merely admires and praises it. Whitman depends on it to keep things going: he does not love society as society. He is neither a novelist nor a sponsor of novelists whose ultimate reality is well-rounded characters that appeal to our sense that each person is what he or she is, just like that.

One last point: The crucial meaning of "composite" is not the structural condition of having aspects (soul, body, self, and personality) but, rather, the indefinite multiplicity of the soul.

I have made Whitman's teaching cumbersome. Some less clumsy effort must nevertheless be faithful to its complexity. Whitman is not saying anything simple, and I think that despite occasional vagueness or inconsistency, he sustains his distinctions concerning the aspects of the individual throughout his work. William James's great and intricate writing on the consciousness of self bears some important resemblances to Whitman's understanding of aspects. The views of both stem from a will to democratize human self-conception.

In any case, Whitman is suggesting two main things. All the personalities that I encounter, I already am: That is to say, I could become or could have become something like what others are; that necessarily means, in turn, that all of us are always indefinitely more than we actually are. I am potentially all personalities, and we equally are infinite potentialities. Whitman's poetic aim is to talk or sing his readers into accepting this highest truth about human beings. Democracy covers it over less than all other cultures. If people take thought, they will have to acknowledge that, first, they have all the impulses or inclinations or desires (for good and for bad) that they see realized around them, even if they act on other ones, and consequently, second, that each of us is, in Emerson's word, an "infinitude," or, in another formulation of Emerson's, "an inner ocean." The deepest moral and existential meaning of equal rights is this kind of equal recognition granted by every individual to every individual. Democratic connectedness is mutual acceptance. Rejection of any other human being, for one reason or another, for apparently good reasons as well as for bad ones, is self-rejection. A principal burden of Whitman's teaching, therefore, is that the differences between individuals do not go as deep as the commonalities. Personality is not the (secular) soul. He explicitly says in "To You" that every endowment (talent) and virtue is latent in every individual, not merely every impulse or desire.

If I am right in the suggestions that I am making concerning the poetic aim of "Song of Myself," the result is rather strange (to use that word again). The great poem of individualism in a democracy is not individualist in any conventional sense. After all, to be individual originally meant to be indivisible. Clearly, "Song of Myself" is not asking us to pretend that we are indivisible. It is more than a matter of having aspects: soul, body, self, and personality. The (secular) soul itself is a crowded house. (Later on, in "One's-Self I Sing" [1867], he can refer to each of us as "a simple separate person." If he is still consistent with his earlier teachings, "simple" would have to connote unpretentious, yet precious, but not indivisible.) I read the odd and funny line, "It is time to explain myself—let us stand up" as a pleased reference to inner multiplicity (sec. 44). More famously, he says toward the end of the poem:

> Do I contradict myself?
> Very well then I contradict myself,
> (I am large, I contain multitudes.) (sec. 51)

Our potentialities are not only numberless but—and for that reason—conflicting. We are inhabited by tumultuous atoms. We are composite, not even composed. In "Crossing Brooklyn Ferry," he goes so far as to posit "myself disintegrated, everyone disintegrated." I think that Whitman would have admired Nietzsche's convolutedly Platonic saying that the body is "but a social structure composed of many souls."[5] Whitman's radicalism shows in his distance from Plato's dream of harmony among the aspects of the individual and of stillness in the house of the potentialities.

Yet, in abandoning in "Song of Myself" the idea that the individual is indivisible, he is not creating an altogether new sense of individualism. He sees that more than a few American individuals are aware of their own composite nature and of their own undefinability. The telling point is not so much that the United States is a pluralist society made up of all psychological and sociological types as it is that democratic individuals see (if only unsteadily) that each of them contains the raw material of all types, yet is more than any type or all types, and is even more than its special personality. (Of course, it counts for a good deal that the democracy is as expressively diverse as it is, and is so on a plane of equality rather than hierarchically.)

Let me now summarize provisionally what Whitman is doing in "Song of Myself." He is presenting a portrait of himself, but it is not a portrait of his social or everyday personality. It is not a story, either, of the things that he has done or the particular experiences that have shaped his personality or even shaped the course of his life. To tell these things is not to tell of what is most important about himself. "Song of Myself" is not like a photo or realistic drawing; but it is, nevertheless, the best and fullest account of himself—and, also, of course, of everyone else.

The question persists: Why does Whitman not give a conventionally realistic account of himself, on the assumption that somehow he could have interested the world in his personality? The answer must be that the portrait he gives is more truly himself than any realistic account could ever hope to be. How, then, to describe this portrait? Whitman's phrase is best: It is a portrait of "a great composite *democratic individual*." Everyone is composite, and in a democracy each one can and should see himself or herself as a "great composite *democratic individual*." If the (secular) soul is potentiality, an honest portrait of oneself will register one's ability to perceive, and to identify or sympathize or empathize with, all the actualized potentialities that one tries to take in, and will also impart the sense that no actualization is definitive of anyone. The net impression left by "Song of Myself" is oneself, as it were, simultaneously but vicariously actualized in all directions. Oneself democratically perfected is truly a collage; one is "stucco'd" all over with personalities (sec. 31). A person is also a Picasso-like concurrence of many perspectives within one frame. Whitman cannot talk about himself just by talking about himself; nor can anyone. If I talk honestly—that is to say, poetically—about myself, I must talk about others. Perhaps I must talk much more about them than about myself, as Whitman does. "Song of Myself" is—to use the title of one of Gertrude Stein's books—*Everybody's Autobiography*. As he put it in a draft, "I celebrate myself to celebrate you."[6]

Thus the poem seeks to teach that so far from being indivisible or even coherently multiple, one is, and should be glad to be, at any given moment, a composite—that is, ambiguous and ambivalent—and that in a timeless but mortal sense, one is an immense and largely untapped reservoir of potentiality. D. H. Lawrence has referred to Whitman's attempt to articulate an "accumulative identity."[7] One lifetime is not enough to realize more than a few potentialities, so that one lives many lives (on earth) only through the ability to perceive and identify with others, and thus, in an unarrogant sense, to become them, if only for a minute now and then. Whitman's emphasis on absorbing others is precisely, for him, the best way of letting them be, of not possessing them. In "A Song for Occupations," he provides a succinct account of what it means to connect to others by identifying with them:

> Neither a servant nor a master I,
> . . . .
> If you stand at work in a shop I stand as nigh as the nighest in the same shop,
> If you bestow gifts on your brother or dearest friend I demand as good as your brother or dearest friend,
> If your lover, husband, wife, is welcome by day or night, I must be personally as welcome,
> If you become degraded, criminal, ill, then I become so for your sake.

The individual demands to share the goods, the suffering, the fate of the stranger, and does so by imagining the stranger's life as a life he or she could lead and never feel out of place. As Whitman says in his earliest Notebook: "A man only is interested in anything when he identifies himself with it."[8]

Whitman wants to coax us into thinking that we can identify with anything if we try, and that if we try we show not presumption but democratic honesty.

"Song of Myself" teaches its lessons about the individual not only in what it says directly. Part of Whitman's poetic subtlety consists in saying much about himself and every person through the compositional and structural traits of the poem. The poet is talking about the nature of himself and of every individual in the formal qualities that he has chosen. I do not refer to the absence of rhyme, the uneven lines, or the variety of rhythms in "Song of Myself" (and almost all of his poetry). Free verse does, to be sure, make a cultural point. There can be beauty when the inherited forms are abandoned and new forms are created. New forms express a new sense of artistic beauty: the artistic beauty appropriate for a new world, for a democracy. On the other hand, it is undeniably relevant for understanding the meaning of self-disclosure that Whitman creates a poem that is made up of genres. "Song of Myself" contains, for example: anecdotes, not all of which lend themselves easily to emblematic uses; philosophical reflections on the nature of the person, but also on a full range of other questions that are made existential; descriptions of particulars that are observed with an eerie closeness; epic lists of localities and of human types; and lyrical passages of adoration and despair. This assortment of genres is a way of saying that adequate speech about oneself cannot be confined to any one genre.

My main interest, however, is rather that the *sequence* of passages and the poem's *texture* reflect the nature of the individual. These are the formal qualities that especially matter because they conduce to the feeling that our nature is strange (to use that word yet again), that oneself is a strange place. I believe that Whitman means to teach the lesson that if we are poetically persuaded of this strangeness, we will grow more in mutual recognition, in democratic acceptance. Feelings of superiority and other discriminations will exist, even exist intensely, but their validity will be challenged by a poetically enhanced awareness of the vastness of every individual equally.

By sequence (not plot or progression) and texture, I mean such qualities as the poem's discontinuities, abrupt transitions, and sudden eruptions into different tones; its overall indifference to the demand that a story about oneself be a story; the seeming disproportion of attention accorded in it to small matters; its startling conjunctions and almost arbitrarily associated matters; the blank spaces in it caused by the many things left unsaid but that a reader could have expected; its occasional hallucinatory quality; the dreamlike suddenness of emergences and vanishings in it; and the poet's dreamlike mobility of identity that consists in mobilities of foci (both grand and microscopic) and of tense and perspective.

These compositional and structural traits are needed to provide an accurate portrait of the whole person. If the direct teaching of the poem is that one is multiple, that one will find, if one looks honestly, others inside oneself, the formal qualities of the poem teach a related lesson: Namely, that one is (or should be) mysterious to oneself, as others are (or should be) to themselves. Exploring or examining oneself makes one less familiar to oneself. Knowing oneself is therefore knowing that there is no single, transparent entity to know. Hence knowing oneself is coming to know that one cannot really know oneself—at least not fully and not definitely. "As if I were not puzzled at myself!" he says (in an untitled poem excluded from the final edition).[9] The Socratic paradox of knowledge as ignorance is transferred by "Song of Myself" to self-knowledge. What mistily emerges from democratized self-examination is not so much inhibition as surprise. Montaigne's identification of self-contempt as the fruit of self-knowledge suffers a partial rebuke. The limits of self-knowledge are the limits of poetical speech, and Whitman says that though speech is the twin of his vision, speech "is unequal to measure itself." At any given moment, there is always more to know about oneself than one can say. He addresses these unpoetical words to the faculty of poetical speech:

> My final merit I refuse you, I refuse putting from me what I really am,
> Encompass worlds, but never try to encompass me,
> . . . .
> Writing and talk do not prove me, . . . (sec. 25)

If honest, one becomes almost another to oneself. By far the most important result would be that the passion to judge, condemn, and punish others is reduced and replaced, to a major degree, by the desire to accept or empathize or sympathize with them. If an individual is composite, it should become greatly more difficult to equate a person with any of his or her deeds, no matter how awful—perhaps, also, no matter how good. As he programatically says in "Great Are the Myths" (a poem that he dropped from the final edition):

> What the best and worst did, we could do,
> What they felt, do we not feel it in ourselves?
> What they wished, do we not wish the same?[10]

I believe that the direct and the indirect lessons of the poem are great democratic lessons in connectedness. The ideas of the individual as composite, and of the individual as honestly unfamiliar to itself, are ways of awakening all of us to human equality on the highest moral and existential plane. To admit one's compositeness and ultimate unknowability is to open oneself to a kinship to others that is defined by receptivity or responsiveness to them. It intensifies the mutuality between strangers that is intrinsic to the idea of rights-based individualism in a democracy.

Whitman's work is to encourage us to become ever more consistent in living the life of equal rights. He admits everyone and everything into his poem. His mode is intensification. "I am a look," he says in a fragment.[11] He poetizes everyone and everything. He invests them with beauty so that we may look at them, look as if for the first time, or look again and not look away, and then to feel instead of freezing. He freshens the beauty of beautiful persons (and beautiful natural and man-made things). He goes far—as far as Emerson and Thoreau—in trying to connect us to the world through a sense of beauty that dares to limit the ravenous appetite of the sense of moral virtue, because it easily turns (and for good reasons) world-despairing or even world-hating. But he is not content with doing only that. Whitman poetizes what is not conventionally thought beautiful: He tries to make wondrous the common, the commonplace, the everyday, "the plain landscape" (as he puts it in a Notebook).[12] Even more, he tries to have us think it possible that what is cheap or coarse or ugly or artless has its own beauty also—the beauty that any person or thing has just by being there, or has just by force of wanting to be looked at rather than turned away from. Even when he calls ugliness ugly, as in "Faces," and parades it, the depiction is so vivid that ugliness becomes humanly indispensable. As he says in an excluded poem, "Thoughts—: Visages": "Of ugliness—To me there is just as much in it as there is in beauty."[13]

Similarly, in order to encourage what he calls sympathy, or what we can also call empathy, he enhances the humanity of human beings, the creatureliness of animals, the quiddity of things. He shows poetically, and invites us to share, his sympathy with what is already quite sympathetic but what, in our hurry, we do not sympathize with enough. But more important, he poetically conveys the need to sympathize with what is unattractive or even repellent. He makes poetic room for the homely, the unimportant, the obscure, the overlooked, the despised, the wicked, and the diseased.

And all the while, of course, his constant appeal is for us to exercise recognition: to recognize that when one learns to perceive more beauty and feel more sympathy, one is only doing justice to *oneself*, to one's composite nature. Just as I am more than others can take in, so are they more. It is especially important to feel that the unbeautiful are not just unbeautiful and that the wicked are not just wicked, and to do so, as Whitman does enough of the time, without depending on any religious conception of the soul.

To live democratically, to live receptively and responsively, is risky, and therefore the invitation to it is easily resisted. Whitman knows that. This is why he understands life in a democratic culture as heroic. Intensified democratic connectedness is heroic. What makes it so is the extraordinary amount of self-overcoming that is required. Many things in oneself must be overcome. First is the disposition to think that one is one's personality, and that therefore it is all right to live one's life solely dedicated to the prohibitions and allowances of one's role or function or solely devoted to cultivating one's peculiarities and differences—what Mill favorably calls "eccentricity." Another thing that must be overcome is the inevitable desire to close oneself to experience by finding others, or aspects of nature, condemnable or horrible. The failure of recognition and hence of acceptance is a perpetual possibility and frequent occurrence. Self-overcoming as the overcoming of fear and disgust is the poet's constant message.

Unblinking attention to surfaces and depths is facilitated by the conviction that what one perceives or intuits or interprets is not exhaustively constitutive of the individuals one encounters or imagines. One can endure the surfaces and depths all the better when one knows that people could exceed, in all directions, the given, particular aspect we encounter. Or, one can exult in the surfaces or depths all the more when one knows that they are mere temporary manifestations of a residual and inexhaustible potentiality, that they are only promises. Whitman thus aims to attach us more tightly to others as they are, whatever they are, while, and because, he points to the undefinable soul which each is, to which we cannot attach ourselves, and which we can only revere.

In a very late poem, "Grand Is the Seen," he says lines that can be read, in spite of Whitman, in a strictly this-worldly and mortal way, and given a general relevance:

> Grand is the seen, the light, to me—grand are the sky and stars,
> Grand is the earth, and grand are lasting time and space,
> And grand their laws, so multiform, puzzling, evolutionary;
> But grander far the unseen soul of me. . . .
> . . . .
> More evolutionary, vast, puzzling, O my soul!
> More multiform far—more lasting thou than they.

The visible is inferior to the invisible, but Whitman manages to raise the inferior (mere personalities), yet make the superior (souls) appear real.

For example, the life of work elicits from Whitman, in "A Song for Occupations," the paradigmatic judgment that in it there is "far more than you estimated, (and far less also,)." His poetizing has thus a two-way motion. Life is poetically richer than is commonly assumed but also less real than the souls from which it emanates. Part of Whitman's mission is to awaken admiration of the surfaces and depths of social beings and their relations. But he wants admiration to be honestly aware of the contingent nature of actuality and the real nature of potentiality. This awareness can lead to a more poignant admiration of what is there and thus avoid the bad faith that makes the world falsely solid and falsely necessary. (I hope that I am not making Whitman too Sartrean.)

Of course, my reading of Whitman runs the risk of ending up in a paradox, namely that of suggesting that no single manifestation is good in itself but that an indefinite number of potential manifestations has infinite worth. In answer, I would say that Whitman builds the feeling that what gives indefinite potentiality its worth is precisely the reverence toward anyone that it may arouse and hence the acceptance of everyone that it should lead to. The doer is more than the sum of deeds.

I would like to notice just briefly an essential difference between Whitman and Emerson in the strategies that they adopt to overcome not only fear and disgust but also what Whitman calls, in "Song of the Open Road," "a secret silent loathing and despair." Both are troubled by the timidity and general melancholy that they find in American life, and both seem to suggest at times that the explanation is found in the rigors of economic pursuits and in the failure of economic rewards to gratify or even to compensate for the rigors.

In *Nature* and elsewhere, Emerson tries to effect a reconciliation between the despondent individual and what is outside him or her—the *"NOT ME,"* he calls it—by endeavoring to show that the processes of Nature are the emanation of God's mind, but that this mind is like our own and thus that whatever we see is only our intelligence projected and externalized. The proof of humanity's affinity to Divinity is that Nature supplies all sorts of humanly valuable lessons, practical and moral. It seems to have been designed by a mind intent on instructing other minds. Nature is God's language; we learn to read it when we learn to see correspondences between the natural and the mental. Emerson's ambition—some of the time, anyway—is similar to Hegel's: namely, to overcome alienation and achieve reconciliation by recognizing resemblance between the way in which one's mind works and the way in which natural processes meaningfully unfold. There are times, too, when Whitman follows Emerson in this design. Indeed, later on in life, Whitman pays tribute to Hegel.[14] There is actually a great Hegelian or Emersonian moment in "Song of Myself":

Dazzling and tremendous how quick the sun-rise would kill me,
If I could not now and always send sun-rise out of me. (sec. 25)

His sunrise is his power of poetical speech, a power to re-create the world as it is by articulating it. For all that, however, I think that he is doing something in "Song of Myself" that is divorceable from Emersonian metaphysics. Indeed, the preceding lines lend themselves to an existentialist rather than a Transcendentalist reading.

It is not a matter of detecting similarity in the processes of mind and nature, but of discovering kinship between oneself and others (and the rest of nature). The relationship is not analogical or symbolical, not a correspondence or reflection, but actual; it is independent of any reference to a Creator or to any assimilation to a Creator. I think that Whitman's general way in "Song of Myself" is much the better way of trying to effect reconciliation. Not only does it avoid theological metaphysics, it does not too insistently moralize. Whitman comes right out and says in the Preface, 1876, that "while the Moral is the purport and last intelligence of all Nature, there is absolutely nothing of the moral in the works, or laws, or shows of Nature." And Whitman's way expands the sense of strangeness while it expands the sense of sameness.

I do not deny that some of Whitman's beliefs ease the risk of accepting his teaching, that is, the risk of living democratically. He suggests now and then (especially in "Democratic Vistas," 1871) that the person has solidity, that one is no mere composite. It is as if he thinks that he has to give a guarantee that amid all the operations of perception and sympathy that he wants to encourage, and hence the connectedness of kinship that he wants to encourage, he is not urging us to dissolution. Courage and generosity in perception and sympathy will be more possible if one thinks that one has a core and that it always remains intact.

Whitman is not content with the limited stability that comes from memory, from the precarious continuity of consciousness, and from the moments—moments only—of self-concentration. Nor is he content to tie a person's constant identity to the simple fact that one's stream of consciousness—the mingling of self and soul on the terms of neither—is one's own and no one else's; that one has sole access to it; that, because of it, only I can live inside myself and know that I am I and not another. Whitman wants to affirm his faith that deep down in the person is something that is both distinctive and unchanging. What is involved is a religious conception of soul as unique and unalterable identity, whether immortal or not. In "Democratic Vistas," he refers to "that something a man is, (last precious consolation of the drudging poor,) standing apart from all else, divine in his own right, and woman in hers."[15] He also says: "The quality of *Being*, in the object's self, according to its own central idea and purpose, and of growing therefrom and thereto—. . . is the lesson of Nature. True, the full man wisely gathers, culls, absorbs; but if, engaged disproportionately in that, he slights or overlays the precious idiocrasy and special nativity and intention that he is, the man's self, the main thing, is a failure, however wide his general cultivation."[16] These passages seem to threaten the radicalism of "Song of Myself." They seem to locate individuality in each person's profound and permanent difference rather than in the flight from fixed identity and toward the generosities of perception and sympathy.

Whitman had been reading Mill's *On Liberty*. The first paragraph of "Democratic Vistas" refers to it. I think, however, that Mill's great (third) chapter on individuality may contaminate Whitman's thinking. He combines Mill's notion of the individual as exceptional, as eccentric (Whitman's word is "idiocratic") with his own belief in a substratum; but all the while he is doing his real work, which is to vivify the genuinely democratic idea that an individual should try not to acquire or retain an identity (in the wrong spirit). I mean that a democratic individual, if he or she is to be true to the spirit of democracy, should not (on one hand) aspire to become a shaped presence, like a work of art, resplendent in its integrity and unmistakable in its attainment, or (on the other hand) try to disclose one's true "genius."

I think that such substantialist talk about the person or the soul gets in the way of Whitman's most democratic teaching. I much prefer to stay with his idea that what is left inside oneself when one is filling a function or playing a part is an infinite reservoir or, better, repertoire. Unexpressed potentiality rather than an indestructible core (that must remain hidden or can show itself only specially) suits the idea of "a great composite democratic individual," which is the idea to be preserved.

It is undeniable that the heights of receptivity and responsiveness are impossible to live on continuously. To put it clumsily, one must have a personality. That is, one must do a job, fill a function, play a part—probably more than one. One must live a life that is made up mostly of ordinariness. In the Preface, 1876, Whitman says: "To the highest democratic view, man is most acceptable in living well the practical life and lot which happen to him as ordinary farmer, seafarer, mechanic, clerk, laborer, or driver." A person will perform his labors and also "his duties as a citizen, son, husband, father and employ'd person." Ordinariness becomes troubling only when it is rooted in unreflective conformity. Lines in "That Shadow My Likeness" tell us that Whitman wants us to be haunted by, and thus suspicious of, our conformity:

> That shadow my likeness that goes to and fro seeking a livelihood,
>   chattering, chaffering,
> How often I find myself standing and looking at it where it flits,
> How often I question and doubt whether that is really me.

Whitman's highest hope must be that there will be moods or moments in which an individual comes to and remembers or realizes the deep meanings of living in a rights-based democracy. These occasions of self-concentration may be rare, but they should have some more pervasive and longer-lasting effect, even if somewhat thinned out. Whitman's model for such moments is poetic inspiration, but his phrases about the mood of composition are interchangeable with those he uses in a Notebook to describe existential receptivity to the world: "the idea of a trance, yet with all the senses alert—only a state of high exalted musing—the tangible and material with all its shows—the objective world suspended or surmounted for a while and the powers in exaltation, freedom, vision."[17] The effect will show itself not only in solitary spiritual acts of perception or sympathy when "Appears aloof thy life, each passion, each event,"[18] but also in democratically inspired deeds from the most casual to the most disciplined. Attentiveness and empathy, even if not continuously strong, gradually build up the overt connectedness of a democratically receptive culture: its tolerance, its hospitableness, and its appetite for movement, novelty, mixture, and impurity.

It is better, however, not to pretend that receptivity can be a direct and continuous principle of public policy. Once everyone's rights and minimal needs are guaranteed, the aim of political action will remain undetermined by Whitman's teaching, except indirectly. The image of such indirectness is given in Whitman's "By Blue Ontario's Shore," when he speaks of the influence of good poetry: "Will it absorb into me as I absorb food, air, to appear again in my strength, gait, face?" Another image of indirectness is given in his powerful catalog of woe "I Sit and Look Out":

> All these—all the meanness and agony without end
> I sitting look out upon,
> See, hear, and am silent.

Attention and silence are not the final deeds, only the indispensable preliminary to a sane, ameliorative response, the content of which is inspired but not specified by Whitman's ideal of receptivity.

I would also like to suggest that this overt, acted-out connectedness is not well illustrated by Whitman's notion of adhesive love, or love of comrades. This is, in my judgment, too literal an application of receptivity and responsiveness. It is equality made too literal: One is dissolved in the "en masse" rather than remaining connected to others as an equal. It promises to exceed sympathy but must fall short of it and become gregariousness. The line used in a war poem, "Over the Carnage Rose Prophetic a Voice," is false: "affection shall solve the problems of freedom yet." Adhesiveness threatens to suffocate the very individualism of personality that Whitman is trying to promote, while it despiritualizes and falsifies the superior idea of oneself as composite, and hence as indefinite, and hence not properly amenable to an all-enfolding merger. It does not go with the spirit of rights-based individualism. It also serves the sinister project of nationalism. The comradely side of Whitman is not his most attractive because it is not the genuinely democratic one. Comradeship in a struggle and comradeship as a consolation for the griefs of a hierarchical or stigmatizing society are fine, but comradeship as the defining democratic bond is not good because it is not fine.

It is well to notice that adhesiveness does not figure in "Song of Myself," and that in "Song of the Open Road" (1856), close in time to "Song of Myself," Whitman does give, for once, a notion of adhesiveness that does not betray his most radical individualism:

> Here is adhesiveness, it is not previously fashion'd, it is apropos;
> Do you know what it is as you pass to be loved by strangers?
> Do you know the talk of those turning eye-balls?

The model is sexual cruising—momentary intensities, which are a sort of connectedness that is in the same family of sentiments as sympathy. If what I have just said is too glib, consider, instead, some lines (from "A Song of the Rolling Earth") that give one of Whitman's best definitions of sympathy:

> I swear I begin to see love with sweeter spasms than that which
>   responds love,
> It is that which contains itself, which never invites and never refuses.

Another lesson that Whitman teaches is that the composite individual will live for itself in a manner greatly different from the self-absorption of nondemocratic cultures. First, all that Whitman says about the individual is an instigation to act out more and more of one's potentiality. "Once more I enforce you to give play to yourself," he says in "So Long!" (in a line dropped from the final edition).[19] That means to lead a more experimental life. It may also mean to seek a heterogeneous accumulation of experiences, as if only in that way can numerous yearnings of one's soul be accommodated. Whitman's hope is that with so much to gain, there cannot be very much to lose. He says in "A Song of the Rolling Earth" that "undeniable growth" establishes the reality of soul. Second, and relatedly, in any given activity, the idea that one is always capable of more than what one is now doing should affect the quality of how one does what one is doing. Whitman's greatest formulation appears in the fourth section of "Song of Myself":

> Apart from the pulling and hauling stands what I am,
> Stands amused, complacent, compassionating, idle, unitary,
> Looks down, is erect, or bends an arm on an impalpable certain rest,
> Looking with side-curved head curious what will come next,
> Both in and out of the game and watching and wondering at it.

There is a whole ethic of action compressed in these five lines, and it is an ethic that peculiarly suits a democracy because of the consecration that democracy gives to the will to transform action into contentious play, to replace military combat by "saner wars, sweet wars, life-giving wars" ("The Return of the Heroes"). "In and out of the game" is democratic seriousness: "Nothing is for keeps" is a truth that should be embraced rather than resented.

Democracy has sometimes been associated with grossness, a plebeian, underbred grossness. Edmund Burke said in *Reflections on the Revolution in France* that under the system of aristocratic manners, "vice itself lost half its evil by losing all its grossness." Well, Whitman is trying to suggest that democracy has its own grace, the grace of being "both in and out," hence the grace of unsolemnity, of looseness, and that this grace is enabled finally by the understanding that those toward whom one acts are one's equals, are oneself in the most important respects. This is no mere stylization. It is easier to be graceful if we never feel that we are in the presence of aliens. Democratic grace is caught in Whitman's almost rhetorical questions about the democratic individual:

> The friendly and flowing savage, who is he?
> Is he waiting for civilization, or past it and mastering it? (sec. 39)

The ethic of "in and out of the game" Whitman dares to apply even to suffering, whether one's own or that of someone else. He is suggesting that if I stop my own momentum in order to observe others, their hurts can register more painfully on me. If I am not quite completely in my own game, I can have a chance to notice what is happening to others who may be caught up in my game or in some other. On the other hand, if I am not quite completely in my own game, I am able, perhaps, to observe my own hurts rather than merely suffering them, and they may, therefore, register less painfully on me.

It is at this point, perhaps, that even an appreciative reader of Whitman may think that his idealization of the composite individual asks too much and may, in addition, ask for the wrong thing. His poetic identification with all who suffer may seem forced. I would like to take up sketchily some of the difficulties that the overall aspiration to an intensified connectedness may encounter.

To begin with, one can ask, are there not inevitable and desirable limits on the ability to perceive beauty? How far can one go in seeing beauty when, by conventional standards of both taste and decency, what presents itself is trivial or shameless or hideous? Why not rather encourage a greater effort at aesthetic improvement? Whitman himself is eager to see a more aesthetically accomplished and vibrant culture.

There is good sense in this complaint, as Whitman's own more conventional aestheticism, as found especially in "Democratic Vistas," demonstrates. In response, I suppose one can say that what comes to characterize American art more and more in the twentieth century is the uncanny and persistent appetite to make art out of junk and thus to get us both to redefine what art is and to look again at what we are disposed to overlook or disdain or throw away as junk. This characteristic is faithful to the spirit of Whitman's work. It is a democratic characteristic; it is radical; it is heroic in a new way. And, for these reasons, it is best not to establish too quickly the limits on generous perception, and, instead, to anticipate that American art will frequently manage to redeem aesthetically the apparently unredeemable. What artists do professionally, others can do without planning. (This phenomenon exists apart from the insidiously attractive qualities of mass or popular art, attractive precisely to the well educated because they detect in some of this art a seriousness that repays generous perception.)

Greater difficulties are encountered in the matter of sympathy or empathy. Are there not both proper moral and inevitable mental limits to the ability to identify with human beings? Let us leave aside the admirable wish to establish kinship with animals and indeed with inanimate nature, as Whitman tries to do. Let us even grant Whitman the amazing mobility of identity that he poetically claims when, for example, he says:

> I turn the bridegroom out of bed and stay with the bride myself,
> I tighten her all night to my thighs and lips. (sec. 33)

and then immediately goes on to say:

> My voice is the wife's voice, the screech by the rail of the stairs,
> They fetch my man's body up dripping and drown'd. (sec. 33)

He moves from identity with the bridegroom to identity with the established married woman, that is, from consummation to loss. He is both sexes and many conditions. Let us allow that an individual, democratically prepared, can perform such feats of empathy, and should want to.

What does one say, however, when Whitman writes:

> I am the man, I suffered, I was there.
> . . . .
> I am the hounded slave, I wince at the bite of dogs,
> Hell and despair are upon me,
> . . . .
> Agonies are one of my changes of garments,
> I do not ask the wounded person how he feels, I myself become the
>   wounded person,
> My hurts turn livid upon me as I lean on a cane and observe. (sec. 33)

When encountering or imagining a hounded slave, what does it mean to become the hounded slave? Whitman amazingly says, "My hurts," not "His hurts." But is he encouraging us to feign transfers of identity? At the same time, one leans on a cane and observes. The extreme of empathy is claimed, and at the same time, the extreme of detachment is being admitted, and not only admitted but insisted on. The question arises as to whether there are sufferings so terrible that the lucky unsuffering individual, no matter how intensely democratic in reception, cannot share them in imagination. Similarly, are there not acts of criminality so atrocious that one should not be encouraged to try to understand the person who is responsible for them? Can one find the Hitler and the Stalin in oneself, if one only tried? Whitman insists a number of times that he is as evil as the worst person. It is not possible to believe him. Do not even the greatest tragedians and novelists take shortcuts in their impersonations of madness and criminality, and have to?

Furthermore, is it not the case that when we encounter people performing their deeds, they are often simply acting according to rules? There is no personality to understand. All that needs to be understood are the rules that people are following. Such understanding may be hard to come by, but empathy or sympathy may have no place in the attempt to achieve it. More generally, may it not be the case that people, even in one's culture, are just too different from each other? Is not what is most important about all of us not our potentiality but our divergent personalities, the sum of what, in each case, our particular culture has made us? Or, put more generously, what is perhaps best about us is the way in which we take one potentiality and realize or embody it fully and therefore achieve something definite and formed. What could be better than shaping a life by means of a voluntary and resourceful submission to a discipline or project? Sartre, the great theorist of bad faith, was also the great theorist of project. Is not reality found there and only there? Yet another question may arise. If Whitman means that one must try to see individuals from even the most dissimilar cultures as actualizations of one's own potentialities, is he not presuming to understand what he really cannot? Is not even the most democratically determined observer confined in his or her perspective?

To all these questions concerning moral and mental limits to sympathy or empathy (and there are more), one may be able to give only hesitant answers. I will not pretend to give any answers here. Is Whitman conscious of these problems? Does it matter whether we say that he is or is not? He certainly appears reckless. In "Song of the Answerer," he says, "Every existence has its idiom," but immediately insists that the poet "resolves all tongues into his own," without loss. Yet, in that remarkable poem "The Sleepers," Whitman raises the possibility that he understands that his radical empathy is only a dream, that mobile identity is only a dream (and that only in sleep or death are people alike and equal):

> I dream in my dream all the dreams of the other dreamers,
> And I become the other dreamers.
> I am a dance—
> . . . .
> I am the actor, the actress, the voter, the politician,
> . . . .
> I am she who adorn'd herself and folded her hair expectantly.

Does it help to enlist so austere a philosopher as Collingwood in defense of Whitman's effort at empathy? In *An Autobiography,* Collingwood characterizes the historian: "If he is able to understand, by rethinking them, the thoughts of a great many different kinds of people, it follows that he must be a great many kinds of man. He must be, in fact, a microcosm of all the history he can know. Thus his own self-knowledge is at the same time his knowledge of the world of human affairs."[20] Could it be that unless a claimed kinship is the basis of observation, all appreciation of "otherness" tends to turn into a mere patronizing aesthetic of the picturesque or into a paternalist anthropological solicitude? Human beings will be denatured, in either case, by being seen or imagined only as surfaces. More likely, otherness will arouse fear and disgust.

Finally, I would only say again that, at the least, it is democratic not to draw the limits too narrowly and not to give up too quickly or complacently in epistemological defeat. Whitman is straining to extend the limits of knowing, and it is democratically better to err on the side of presumptuousness than on the side of bafflement. Implied in Whitman's idea of the burden of perception and sympathy that the spirit of democracy means to impose is the will to activate the feeling of contingency: It is a matter of chance that any person has been born and then been raised in one way rather than another. Further, every life is interwoven with chance, with good and bad luck. Things could easily have turned out differently. The proper way of acknowledging contingency is to realize that the same biological being that I am could have been culturally situated in an indefinitely great number of places and acquired a different personality and outward life in each case. And all the time, if I look inward, I can see the beginnings of other possibilities that I do not act on or act out and that make me indefinitely more than my socially shaped personality.

Now, Nietzsche, the great theorist of helpless and bounded perspective-seeing and of the pathos of distance, can nevertheless say: "[T]o *want* to see differently, is no small discipline and preparation of the intellect for its future 'objectivity'—the latter understood not as 'contemplation without interest' (which is a nonsensical absurdity), but as the ability *to control* one's Pro and Con and to dispose of them, so that one knows how to employ a *variety* of perspectives and affective interpretations in the service of knowledge."[21] Or, as Wallace Stevens—great heir of both Whitman and Nietzsche—says about the aim of poetical perception and feeling:

> It is a visibility of thought,
> In which hundreds of eyes, in one mind, see at once.[22]

Whitman has his own perspectivism, and it corresponds to a person's inner multiplicity in a double sense. On one hand, the composite individual has many eyes to see diversity appropriately. On the other hand, he or she, like anything else, needs to be seen by many eyes—not only by the many sets of eyes of many individuals, but also by any one individual's many eyes.

But Whitman's final lesson is solitude, not the adventures of human connectedness. He would not be a defender of individuality if he taught otherwise. His work urges each of us back to a solitary relation with something unconceptualizable—perhaps the sheer fact of existence, of one's being and the being of anything else, even and especially when "cheaper, easier, nearer" ("A Song of the Rolling Earth"). What makes this solitude democratic—a democratic transcendence of democratic culture—is the, as it were, philosophical self-respect (what Tocqueville saw as natural Cartesianism) that democracy encourages in each person and that Whitman's work tries so profoundly and so desperately to make convincing. Democratic culture therefore opens the possibility for each to take himself or herself seriously as directly connected to whatever is irreducible, to that around which the mind can never close. In "Song of Myself," he gives a perfectly secular indication (induced by musical passion):

> to feel the puzzle of puzzles,
> And that we call Being.
> To be in any form, what is that? (secs. 26–27)

One's culmination is impersonal contemplation of the puzzle. For the sake of this, one must be one and only one. One's end is found alone.

As he puts it matchlessly, though still too religiously, in "Democratic Vistas": "Alone, and identity, and the mood—and the soul emerges, and all statements, churches, sermons, melt away like vapors. Alone, and silent thought and awe, and aspiration—and then the interior consciousness, like a hitherto unseen inscription, in magic ink, beams out its wonderous lines to the sense it is exclusively for the noiseless operation of one's isolated Self, to enter the pure ether of veneration, reach the divine levels, and commune with the unutterable."[23]

Notes

Originally published as George Kateb, "Walt Whitman and the Culture of Democracy," *Political Theory* 18, no. 4 (November 1990): 545–71. Reprinted by permission of Sage Publications.

1. Quoted in F. O. Matthiessen, *American Renaissance: Art and Expression in the Age of Emerson and Whitman* (New York: Oxford University Press, 1941), 649.
2. I have used throughout Walt Whitman, *Leaves of Grass,* ed. Sculley Bradley and Harold W. Blodgett (New York: Norton Critical Editions, 1973). Section numbers of "Song of Myself" are given in the text.
3. Ibid., 707.
4. Roy Harvey Pearce, introduction [to the facsimile edition of the 1860 text of] *Leaves of Grass* (Ithaca, N.Y.: Cornell University Press, 1961), vii–li; Roy Harvey Pearce, *The Continuity of American Poetry* (Princeton: Princeton University Press, 1977), 69–83; Harold Bloom, *Poetics of Influence,* ed. John Hollander (New Haven, Conn.: Schwab, 1988), 297–307.
5. Friedrich Nietzsche, *Beyond Good and Evil,* trans. Walter Kaufmann (New York: Vintage 1966), sec. 19, p. 26.
6. Quoted in Matthiessen, *American Renaissance,* 555.
7. D. H. Lawrence, "Whitman" (1921), in *Leaves of Grass,* ed. Bradley and Blodgett, 845.
8. Quoted in Matthiessen, *American Renaissance,* 518.
9. Whitman, *Leaves of Grass,* 595.
10. Ibid., 585.
11. Ibid., 694.
12. Ibid., 672.

13. Ibid., 597.

14. See especially the section "Carlyle from American Points of View," in "Specimen Days," in *Leaves of Grass and Selected Prose,* ed. John Kouwenhoven (New York: Modern Library, 1950), 729–36.

15. Whitman, *Leaves of Grass and Selected Prose,* ed. Kouwenhoven, 471.

16. Ibid., 487.

17. Whitman, *Leaves of Grass,* 672.

18. An uncollected poem, ibid.

19. Ibid., 638.

20. R. G. Collingwood, *An Autobiography* (London: Oxford University Press, 1939), 115.

21. Friedrich Nietzsche, *On the Genealogy of Morals,* trans. Walter Kaufman (New York: Vintage, 1969), essay 3, sec. 12, p. 119.

22. Wallace Stevens, "An Ordinary Evening in New Haven," sec. 30, in *The Collected Poems* (New York: Vintage, 1982), 488.

23. Whitman, *Leaves of Grass and Selected Prose,* ed. Kouwenhoven, 491.

CHAPTER 2

Strange Attractors: How Individualists Connect to Form Democratic Unity

Nancy L. Rosenblum

FOR SEVERAL YEARS, GEORGE Kateb has been spinning out a glittering line of thought: Democracy exists *for* individualism—our unique and shining selves are democracy's whole purpose and end, and individualism is the real force preserving democracy. He reiterates the theme of earlier work, that individualists offer the strongest resistance to statism in its various oppressive guises: nationalism, groupism, civic republicanism, and communitarianism. Here, Kateb adds a new, more brilliant thread: Individualists can create democratic unity; individualism itself is the answer to atomism and other, worse forms of pathological disconnection. He takes Walt Whitman as his guide.

Kateb is not the only contemporary political theorist to confer on Whitman's poetry the status of teachings about the sources of democratic unity. Writing about the national idea in American politics, Samuel Beer appealed to Whitman's picture of America as an organic whole.[1] Like Durkheim's division of labor, only vastly more comprehensive, Whitman sees solidarity emerging from a rich complementarity of excellences and social exchange. For Beer, Whitman is a great sociological imagination. For Kateb, Whitman is a philosopher who illuminates the self's true nature and how, in the chaos of unique and separate identities, individuals act on one another as "strange attractors" to create democratic unity.

This focus is severely selective. Whitman the lover of comradeship, for whom union evoked "adhesive" homoerotic attraction and who saw nakedness and sexual merging everywhere, barely makes an appearance.

Nothing much is said about the historical Whitman, either. We associate him with the crisis of the Civil War, sometimes forgetting that Whitman was just one generation away from those for whom "the sacred purpose of 1776" was an immediate, personal purpose. His father knew and admired Thomas Paine; he was a grown man in 1826, the year the last signer of the Declaration of Independence died. It is not surprising that he echoed Paine, and Michelet too, in deprecating Christianity as destructive myth and apotheosizing the people. Nor is it strange, given how unstable republican political ideas had become by the time of secession, that one aspect of Paine—the nation as a personification of the genius of humanity—threatens to displace the Paine of governments made and *dissolved* by a sovereign people as a matter of right.[2] Whitman was typically unsettled about who "the people" includes, even at its most radical: He deplored slavery, deplored abolitionist "ranting," thought free blacks unfit for "amalgamation," and would deny them every civil right. His idea of democratic unity is distressed and politically elusive for grim historical reasons.[3]

Kateb also says very little about the peculiar way that poetry teaches philosophy (if it can be said to teach at all). Most surprising, he does not appeal to Whitman's visionary aesthetic, in which democracy appears as a dazzling spectacle of diversity. Yet for men and women susceptible to it, the extraordinary aesthetic experience of the sublime may be the most powerful force attaching them to democracy, and I return to this point at the end.

Instead, Kateb presents Whitman as a philosopher who comes closest to conveying the truth about the self. The self is defined as *a* reservoir of possibilities, as the I who has "all lives, all effects, all hidden invisibly in myself." Since poetry captures our "startling conjunctions . . . almost arbitrarily associated matters, blank spaces; occasional hallucinatory quality," I would not have been surprised to find a deconstruction of *Leaves of Grass* in this connection. Whitman was the exemplary self, after all, who called the volume his literal corpus and told his readers: "It is I you hold and who holds you." But Kateb directs us away from texts and bodies down a different interpretive path. Inventing his own apt analogy to visual art, he characterizes the self as a "Picasso-like concurrence." Because the capacity for democratic connection is said to follow directly from the self's inessential nature, Kateb's analogy is worth pursuing.

The revolutionary works of Picasso's cubist phase portray our relationship to objects as constantly changing. An infinite number of perspectives is possible; there is no view from nowhere but *only* perspectives on seeing and knowing; and there is no single way of combining every possible standpoint into a final composition—a representation could always have been otherwise (for example, *Girl with Mandolin* painted by both Picasso and Braque). In order to point up the falsification of static naturalist representations, cubism imposed this view of reality on familiar everyday objects, so the analogy successfully evokes "startling combinations" as the truth about every individual. The analogy also underscores the fact that we are always presenting ourselves to the view of others, and at the same time that no self-presentation is definitive. It does not follow from perspectivism, however, that in terms of internal structure or felt experience, the self really is a composite rather than an organic unity; paintings and drawings do not obviously provoke the question whether the concurrent self is decentered rather than identified with a core heart or will, reason or drive. That is why a stronger visual parallel to the philosophy of the self as potentiality is Picasso's constructivist sculpture made of found objects, like the piece in which handlebars and bicycle seat become a horned bull.[4] These constructions tell us that nothing *is* essentially or exclusively as it presents itself to us. Everything is a fragment. And instead of referring back to some original authoritative whole, fragments can be given renewed coherence.

This conception of a composite self has implications for contemporary discussions of ontology in political philosophy; certainly, it expands the range of terms for characterizing the self and its dynamic of development. Built up from an eclectic array of "found objects," the self is neither a passive product of Foucauldian discipline nor a pure, arid, existential creation. The composite self also speaks plainly to critics of individualism who see only atomistic men and women rigidly bounded and impermeable, or narcissistic selves negligibly connected to others. For on this analogy to constructivism, self-creation is oddly unself-absorbed and firmly world-oriented. Everything impinges on us and has constitutive potential. Fragmentation and contingency do not signal baleful alienation but opportunity to "accept, fuse, rehabilitate."

The analogy between self and Picasso-like composite suffers a serious limitation, though: Works of art, particularly sculptures, have form and boundary, but plainly the most formidable characteristic of Whitman's self is its boundlessness. It is elastic and permeable. *Nothing* need be other, or "not me." We are familiar with the double-edged character of fluid identity: Proponents of the labor theory of value are challenged to show that mixing one's labor results in an addition to what one has, in ownership, rather than losing one's labor; mystic merging may be self-abnegation or divine self-enlargement; in psychoanalytic theory, the process of identification is sometimes part of ego development and other times an inflation of superego fatal to personal identity. Whitman's unbounded self has been called imperial: in his own "convertible terms," Walt Whitman is all history, all America, and "contains multitudes." On the other side, D. H. Lawrence most famously took Whitman's limitless "I" for terrible dissolution: "Walt" was leaking out into the universe, on the verge of disappearing altogether.

Kateb is confident that the Whitmanesque self strikes a balance. It is receptive, yet preserves its separateness. It has no fixed social identity, yet it can enter into relations of mutuality. Before discussing just how contingent selves adhere to create democratic unity out of radical individualism, I want to consider Kateb's broader underlying proposition that part of the truth about this self is that it bears a special relation to democracy. For it is not obviously the case that Whitman's eye is steadily on individuals rather than wholes or that from the perspective of individualism, his democracy is dependably benign.

In a provocative passage, Kateb quotes Whitman's boast that the self as it has emerged in the United States "culminate[s] modern humanity." The phrase invokes Whitman's confessed Hegelianism, which once invoked is hard to set aside or to reconcile with democratic individuality. Whitman was plainly attracted to the thought that in the movement of history in which nothing is lost, he stands at the culminating moment, when America and the poet personally encompass in themselves the entire European past.[5] Whitman also adopted the Hegelian formula of crisis leading to higher unity, in which the self-defeating forces of sectional, economic, and ethnic differences and even bloody civil war are resolved in a system big enough to contain them. Whitman got his Hegel piecemeal and secondhand and used Idealist concepts metaphorically, but he is responding to the genuine philosophical problem of reconciling ourselves to the point to which we have come. Poetry's responsibility may be to effect this therapeutic reconciliation. Certainly for Whitman, America is the culminating Idea, the vindication of a gruesome past and all the dead.

The political implications of this Hegelian strain in Whitman are not individualistic. There is the righteous, militant, annexationist tendency of his nationalism: "Yes: Mexico must be thoroughly chastised!" Whitman is no statist and does not exalt political obligation over liberty, but he is indifferent to the standard political dangers of holism; certainly his grandiose "National Union will" eclipses rights-bearing, consenting, dissenting individuals. Literary elements of the poetry reinforce this impression of all-absorbing union. There is Whitman's characteristic long line—aggregating and insistently inclusive. His rhythms register, marshal, and enroll human *types,* so that his counting Americans in is physiologically palpable. And nothing casts the solidity of Whitman's political commitment to individualism more in doubt than his repetition of misty, encompassing ideas.

Kateb pushes quickly past the thought that the emergence of the self in America is "the culmination of modern humanity" and avoids getting caught in this Hegelian undertow. Instead, the special relationship between self and democracy that he finds in Whitman recalls the Platonic correspondence between soul and political order. What, then, is the defining characteristic of democratic culture corresponding to the self as a reservoir of potentiality? Kateb is committed to keeping rights and representative government firmly in view, but faithful to Whitman, what emerges most clearly is not the institutional apparatus of democratic politics at all but pluralist democratic culture, in particular, Whitman's vast urban vista with its widely dissonant "en masse." Of course, social pluralism per se is not contingency's complement, since pluralism may refer to a social and institutional structure that is complex, yet settled and traditionalist. There is no correspondence so long as diversity is arranged in hierarchies or balanced federations, or if membership in parties and spheres is ascribed, inherited, or severely constrained. Democratic culture must be sufficiently diffuse, seething, and "oceanic" that even "society" with its defined advantages and interests dissolves away. That is why Whitman's self spinning along the open roads (or idly riding the Brooklyn ferry) is so unlike Stendhal's calculating Julien Sorel or any other upwardly mobile individual exploiting modern society and careers open to talent.

In the face of this picture of fractured, pluralist democratic culture, Robert Penn Warren described the correspondent self as a "diminished self" and the poet's relation to democracy as alienation.[6] We can appreciate even more, then, the originality and importance of Kateb's argument that "moderate alienation" is beneficial and that composite selves can enjoy a strange sort of intimacy with fragmented democratic culture; he helps us to see how Whitman could say that he found the "million-headed city," New

York, "comforting."[7] For Kateb, democracy provides the eclectic materials and the setting in which individuality is disclosed. He is at his best here, discussing the creative possibilities of contingency.

Kateb does not stop with the existential correspondence between contingent self and democratic culture, however. He wants not only correspondence but adherence, claiming that democratic unity arises from the mutual attraction of unique individuals. But he is less successful when he argues that the unity created by individuals is political, that their receptivity translates into even the irreducible minimum of beliefs and actions in support of democratic institutions. As I see it, Kateb's account of how selves aware of their contingency may be drawn to one another is complex; indeed, it contains two closely intertwined but psychologically independent dynamics by which the self moves from awareness of contingency to receptivity and union. One is eclectic and the other skeptical. The question in each case is whether either one can take us beyond the existential benefits of moderate alienation, and beyond responsiveness simply, to a convincing explanation of democratic unity?

In one version, connection to others arises from the self's exploratory, imaginative identification with every "not me." Because I am aware that I could be other than what I am, people are interesting to me as possibilities. This recalls William James's wonderful portrait of Whitman as the rare open sensibility who is able to really see others' lives, particularly their joys.[8] The spirit of identification here is eclectic.

Moral philosophy often assigns sympathy a central part, of course, but identification with others is not thought to depend on a particular theory of the self as potentiality or on an interest in others as "not me." On the contrary, this ethic is usually essentialist. Identification is with the universal attributes of men and women rather than with others in respect of their strangeness. Rousseau's pity involves recognition of the common suffering of sentient beings, and the imperative that follows is to avoid deliberate cruelty. For some moralists, acknowledging this basic commonality and refraining from causing pain is enough, or at least a good beginning. But it is not the sort of responsive attachment that Kateb looks for in Whitman.

He wants active mutuality, for one thing. But the spirit of eclecticism that makes us look on others with genuine, nonegoistic interest is rare, as William James said. And openness does not ensure reciprocity. It is likely to be unrequited. Certainly, Whitman loved America more than Americans loved him or one another (or, most likely, themselves). It is not enough, then, for Kateb to show the possibility of correspondence between democratic culture and feelings of contingency and receptivity. There is the further question whether the personal experience of pluralism that activates feelings of contingency is actually available to everyone in democratic culture. We know it is not. Constraining economic and social conditions inhibit the experience of "potentiality": race, gender, and the forces of socialization operate as formidable internal and external obstacles to imaginative identification with others. Whitman himself is particularly sensitive to the way in which property, and even more occupation, acts in America as necessary protections against humiliation and disenfranchisement with their attendant isolation.[9] In short, whether what lies behind mutual responsiveness is Whitman's eclecticism or something more orthodox like "respect for persons," the circumstances of justice that make receptivity psychologically tenable simply must be taken up.

Kateb also expects responsiveness to translate into actions to secure individual rights in democracy. But the path from awareness of contingency to interest in "not me" and from there to political action is not clearly marked. There is no reason to conclude that the permeable self is a principled and concerned citizen rather than an anarchist, say, or merely indifferent to politics and just a good (or not so good) neighbor. The line of thought that takes us from eclecticism to action in support of civil liberty and democratic representation is not compelling. In fact, Kateb worries that indiscriminate openness does not rule out sympathetic identification with evil or with some collectivity rather than separate selves. He also wonders whether being responsive to any- or everyone is not asking too much, in which case the bright spirit of eclecticism threatens to turn into a sober and demanding universal obligation. (For some philosophers, of course, the problem is not demanding too much but too little: "deep ecologists," for example, think that genuine imaginative identification will extend to animals and inanimate nature—as indeed it did for Whitman.)

A different path from self to democratic unity depends, like the first, on activating feelings of contingency and on the lack of ordinary egoism. It is distinguished from the first by severe philosophical self-consciousness, for one thing. It involves detachment rather than identification. And its ethos is skeptical and reserved rather than brightly eclectic. Here, heightened feelings of contingency result in self-distancing, and individuals are suspended in a state of awareness of potentiality, what Whitman described as "being in uncertainties, mysteries, doubts, without any irritable reaching after fact and reason."[10] Kateb claims that the effect is to reduce the passion to judge and condemn—particularly if, as he also insists, awareness involves the thought that others are to themselves as I am to me. Alexander Nehamas spoke in just these terms about the possible beneficial effect of perspectivism in Nietzsche's thought:

> What we need to do, one might urge at this point (having taken the view that untruth is a condition of life) is to become more self-conscious and less arrogant about our practices and modes of life, to become aware of their contingent bases, and perhaps to abandon the goal of ever representing the world as it really is.[11]

Political theorists have indicated a route to tolerance and moderation like this one before. The idea is that philosophical skepticism inclines to religious liberty and political restraint because in the absence of certainty, rulers (and subjects) are likely to rest content with peace and safety in a lawful order. This position is usually associated with liberalism and not democracy, however, still less with individuals' strong mutual connection in democratic unity. In any case, the psychological logic of skepticism is not borne out in historical practice. Dampening the ferocity and braking the finality of judgment do not by themselves inhibit political authoritarianism. We do not have to be convinced of our infallibility (or sure of the solidity of our own or others' identity) to find a variety of perfectly pragmatic, politically justifiable reasons to oppress, dismiss, discipline, and exclude others. In philosophy, too, as we know from conventional interpretations of Nietzsche's will to power, the heroic exploitation of contingency supplants humility and tolerance.

Moreover, reducing self-certainty and abstaining from final judgments of others, in which Kateb places great hope, have other sources besides insight into the truth about the self and are even less likely to result in affective unity. Self-loathing is another strong reason for focusing on potentiality. We learn about deliberate exhibitions of self-distancing in Whitman's own life as Justin Kaplan narrates it. In poetry, photographic self-presentations, and confessions to friends, Whitman created a gallery of views of himself. In a spirit of concealment, he reshaped his past and kept the "long foreground" of *Leaves of Grass* in mystery. This was just as plausibly a reaction to bruising disappointment as an expression of a philosophy of identity. The distinctive form that misanthropy takes when it is aroused by democratic culture produces distancing, too, as it did for Thoreau, who sought his correspondent infinitude in nature and frankly preferred it to men and women as he found them. For Thoreau, the political accompaniment of detachment was the radical individualism of conscientious objection and threatened disassociation. Whitman was not immune to this sort of "negative receptivity." He wondered whether there were "indeed, men here worthy of the name . . . or perfect women?"; and in revulsion rivaling Thoreau's, he described "a sort of dry and flat Sahara," cities "crowded with petty grotesques, malformations, phantoms, playing meaningless antics."[12] Whitman's diagnosis is startling only because he points to the "depletion" of women as the chief symptom of democracy's failure to produce people who are at once "average, limitless, and free."

Kateb's account of the self, its heightened feeling of contingency and its capacity for receptivity (if we add negative as well as positive receptivity) is psychologically acute. The problem, as I have argued, comes in trying to see this as the basis for a political philosophy of democratic unity. The self that Kateb describes emerges from experiences that have democratic culture as their medium, but it does not obviously produce support for democratic institutions, much less anything as active as commitment to political principles or setting out concrete political aims. The individualist can be perfectly at home floating high off democracy's mundane political surface. In fact, awareness of contingency and receptivity to others require just that. Whitman said as much: "There is, in our sanest hours, a consciousness, a thought that rises, independent, lifted out from all else, calm, like the stars, shining eternal. This is the thought of identity—yours for you, whoever you are, as mine for me. Miracle of miracles."[13]

In place of an account of democratic unity in which contingent selves are drawn to one another, I propose an alternative thesis that preserves Kateb's focus on the self as potentiality and its special relation to democratic culture but sees the force of attraction differently. On my view, the adhesive power that Whitman sets at work in readers of his poetry and in American thought is distinctively aesthetic, and the object of attraction is a peculiarly poetic vision of democracy.[14]

Despite his appeal to Whitman, Kateb never expands on why poetry is better than philosophy in providing insights into the self or whether poetry is essential to democracy. But it is clear enough that he means to assign poetry a different part than most moral and political philosophers writing on the subject today, for whom literature's function is to bring ethical conduct home to us in the form of concrete stories. I cannot expand here on the thought that neither position—poetry as self-illumination or storytelling as moral education—gives sufficient independent weight to aesthetics or to distinctively aesthetic responses. I will simply assert in this connection that discussions of these questions could be enriched if political theorists expanded their range, for example by adding Schiller to Plato and Aristotle as authorities on art and morality. For now, the point is that Whitman's poetry is significant for political theory because it activates strong feelings of attraction to democracy, and it does so by creating a poetic vision of democracy as a spectacle of diversity. The attraction, then, is not to other men and women personally and individually, as Kateb has it, but to the extravagant spectacle in which unique individualists exhibit themselves in a dazzling display. Whitman evokes the experience of democracy as a genuine experience of the sublime. For him, the experience is compelling; it is motivation for attachment to democratic culture, real energetic glue.

Whitman's extravagant picture of democratic culture was nourished by his immersion as a journalist in the parades, marches, oratory, and conventions of electoral activity in New York in the mid-nineteenth century. But institutions, laws, agreements, and arms have no special part in his poetic vision of the spectacle of diversity; when they appear at all, they simply make their appearance as elements among others in the awesome array. Democratic *politics* recedes into the background. The democratic spectacle is an invitation to exhibitionism, so the ethos of freedom is public but not civic. The spectacle is anarchic, antihierarchic, and antiauthoritarian, but his is not the sort of political egalitarianism that translates nicely into defense of rights or representative government. The experience of the spectacle is aesthetic, and aesthetic appreciation is ephemeral and has no direct outcome in political beliefs or in regular support for the political machinery of constitutions, or organized parties, or voting.

Yet Whitman's spectacle of diversity *does* have significance for political theory if we are willing to acknowledge the binding power of aesthetic response, and the fact that Burkean traditionalists have no monopoly on this force for attachment. In Whitman's vision, the plain face of democracy takes on its own enchantment; he loved the spectacle of diversity in the same way that Burke loved monarchical plumage. He speaks for those for whom the ability to experience democracy as sublime makes them feel at home there and for whom it is the only experience that does. Whitman also portrays the dynamic of attraction. Other romantic sensibilities thought of themselves as reservoirs of potentiality and looked to nature to find the external plenitude that "fits" their sense of infinite possibility. Whitman is explicit about finding just this perfectly satisfying correspondence in the spectacle of diversity:

> Here at last is something in the doings of man that corresponds with the broadcast doings of day and night. Here is not merely a nation but a teeming nation of nations. Here is action untied from strings necessarily blind to particulars and details, magnificently moving in vast masses. Here is the hospitality which forever indicates heroes.[15]

Notes

Originally published as Nancy L. Rosenblum, "Strange Attractors: How Individualists Connect to Form Democratic Unity," *Political Theory* 18, no. 4 (November 1990): 576–86. Reprinted by permission of Sage Publications.

    1. Samuel Beer, "Liberty and Union: Walt Whitman's Idea of the Nation," *Political Theory* 12, no. 3 (1984): 362.

    2. See Robert D. Richardson Jr., *Myth and Literature in the American Renaissance* (Bloomington: Indiana University Press, 1978); Daniel Rodgers, *Contested Truths* (New York: Basic Books, 1987).

    3. More unsettled than most, given the way that Whitman's workingman's radicalism was at odds with his antislavery (see Sean Wilentz, *Chants Democratic* [New York: Oxford University Press, 1984]).

    4. It is not hard to see Whitman's poetry as prefiguring constructivism in art. He builds up lines and verses from found objects like Picasso's objects from an industrial world. The analogy applies particularly to the unprecedented structure of *Leaves of Grass*, an assemblage of leaves or fragments, which Whitman continually added to and subtracted from so that it is characterized by self-conscious unfinish, not perfection.

    5. "Specimen Days," in *The Portable Whitman* (New York: Penguin, 1973), 608–10. Unless noted, references from Whitman are to this volume. As George Kelly shows, this was not Hegel's expectation for chaotic America (see *Hegel's Retreat from Eleusis* [Princeton: Princeton University Press, 1978], 151–52).

    6. Robert Penn Warren, *Democracy and Poetry* (Cambridge: Harvard University Press, 1975).

7. Kateb introduced the idea of "moderate alienation" in *Hannah Arendt* (Totowa, N.J.: Rowman and Allanheld, 1984), 178; "Specimen Days," 531.

8. William James, "On a Certain Blindness in Human Beings," in *The Writings of William James* (New York: Random House, 1967), 629–45.

9. "Democratic Vistas," 337–39.

10. Quoted in Justin Kaplan, *Walt Whitman: A Life* (New York: Simon and Schuster, 1980), 190.

11. Alexander Nehamas, *Nietzsche: Life as Literature* (Cambridge: Harvard University Press, 1985), 57.

12. "Democratic Vistas," 327–28.

13. Quoted by Nancy L. Rosenblum, *Another Liberalism: Romanticism and the Reconstruction of Liberal Thought* (Cambridge: Harvard University Press, 1987), 120.

14. Rosenblum, "Heroic Individualism and the Spectacle of Diversity," ibid.

15. From 1855 Preface to *Leaves of Grass,* quoted ibid., 119.

CHAPTER 3

Mestiza Poetics: Walt Whitman, Barack Obama, and the Question of Union

Cristina Beltrán

WHEN IT CAME TO identifying with famous antebellum figures, Barack Obama chose early. Declaring his candidacy for the presidency from the steps of the Old State Capitol in Springfield, the junior U.S. senator from Illinois assumed the mantle of one of America's greatest presidents: Abraham Lincoln. Delivered in Lincoln's hometown on the weekend of Lincoln's birthday, Obama's speech was audacious in its use of analogy and allusion. The candidate described Lincoln as "a tall, gangly, self-made Springfield lawyer" who showed America that "there is power in words." Invoking Lincoln's famous "house divided" speech at the start of his announcement,[1] Obama spoke of the "unfinished business of perfecting our union" before concluding with echoes of the Gettysburg Address ("Let us finish the work that needs to be done, and usher in a new birth of freedom on this earth").[2]

The candidate strongly linked the appeal to Lincoln and his legacy to questions of union. For Obama, "Lincoln's legacy was his effort to bring the country together." Despite governing during a time of slavery, civil war, and secession, Lincoln "had an unyielding belief that we were, at heart, one nation, and one people."[3] Running to be the first African American to lead a major-party ticket, Obama sought to redeploy Lincoln's vocabulary of union, challenging the idea of divided America and claiming instead that "beneath all the differences of race and region, faith and station, we are one people."[4]

Obama's paeans to union appeared to be more than the usual platitudes of a candidate running for national office. Indeed, his campaign and election seemed to spark genuine moments of civic unity and national euphoria—from the massive campaign rallies to the spontaneous election-night street celebrations across the nation to the unprecedented crowds that flooded Washington, D.C., for his January 20 inauguration. Yet in Obama's first few months in the White House, the ideological conflicts and bitter partisanship that gave rise to such unitary rhetoric engulfed his administration. By the first anniversary of his election, the language of unity that once charmed an electorate no longer inspired. Instead, anger and frustration over the bank bailouts, the continuation of two wars, and compromises over health care, immigration, energy, and civil rights for gays and lesbians led voters to respond to invocations of unity with anger, disappointment, cynicism, and despair. Whether Obama can emerge from his presidency as a Lincolnesque figure who leaves the nation more united than when he began remains to be seen.

Much has been made of the Lincoln-Obama connection—with, doubtless, much more to follow in the coming years. Yet in trying to understand Barack Obama as both a political phenomenon and a figure of union, this essay recommends shifting our gaze away from Lincoln and toward a different figure of the antebellum era, the poet Walt Whitman—a man whose own relationship to Lincoln has already been the site of an enormous body of scholarship and analysis.[5] In trying to understand the political implications of Obama's attachment to union, I find Whitman to be a particularly valuable interlocutor. Like Lincoln, he was deeply committed to the idea of national unity, but his poetic vision also emphasized democracy as a spectacle of diversity.[6] It's my contention that this synthesis of union and democratic spectacle offers important insights into the power of collective display and the significance of aesthetic response to the election of America's first black president.[7] In this essay, I argue that a deeper understanding of the 2008 presidential election requires such enhanced attention to the event's aesthetic and affective dimensions.

In suggesting that the 2008 election can best be understood as a political and sensory event, I draw on Nancy Rosenblum's reading of Whitman and her claim that political theorists often give insufficient weight to the binding power of aesthetics.[8] In contrast to democratic theory's often-moralistic and procedural logic, Rosenblum argues that the significance of Whitman's poetry for political theory lies in its ability to activate "strong feelings of attraction to democracy"; this creates "a poetic vision . . . in which democracy appears as a dazzling spectacle of diversity."[9] Extending Rosenblum's thesis, I argue that the mass gatherings surrounding Obama's campaign and election can be understood as "Whitmanesque" spectacles of diversity whereby participants experienced their collective heterogeneity as a form of democratic enchantment. The massive rallies that became characteristic of the Obama campaign both produced and exhibited a relationship to the African American candidate that was unusually expressive, communal, and performative. Moving between global narratives of migration and dueling American narratives of slavery and immigration, Obama's rhetoric drew on both autobiography and the politics of visibility in order to embody America's tangled racial past while simultaneously uniting disparate elements of the American story.

As Betsy Erkkila notes, in Whitman's poetry, we see a desire "to balance and reconcile major conflicts in the American body politic: the conflicts between 'separate person' and 'en masse,' individualism and equality, liberty and union, the South and the North, the farm and the city, labor and capital, black and white, female and male, and religion and science."[10] At its best, Whitman's conjoining language of juxtaposition and fusion articulates new practices of identification that support democratic forms of equality, identification, and solidarity. Yet Whitman's adhesive voice also neutralizes conflict, transforming diversity into the aesthetic experience of the sublime while turning serious differences into "mere variation."[11] We see this in Whitman's well-known use of catalogs—his "epic lists" creating equivalences and wholeness through the naming of things next to each other. In a similar vein, I want to suggest that part of Obama's unifying appeal lies in his tendency to create a sense of community through what I call a *poetics of equivalence*. In this essay, I argue that such poetics offered Obama and his campaign powerful civic resources that led to an unprecedented victory. Yet in analyzing Obama's aggregative practices and their impact on the 2008 election, I also want to draw our attention to the limitations of such Whitmanesque gestures. Ultimately, I want to suggest that the poetics of equivalence falters as an approach to governing.

In using the term "poetics," I am drawing on Allen Grossman's depiction of Whitman as a poet whose work thrives on forms of contradiction and inclusion.[12] Such forms of poetic pluralization are usually seen as anathema to the practice of governing. However, I would argue that given America's brutal racial past (and complicated racial present), Obama's recourse to a poetics of equivalence should come as little surprise. Nevertheless, such contradictory yet inclusive political claims regarding national unity often involve historical erasures and the suspension of judgment. It is this impulse to privilege union over justice that makes the poetics of equivalence so powerful—and so unsettling.

Forged through language and confirmed through democratic spectacle, Obama sought to create a sense of civic unity by making his unique individuality serve the democratic common. To put it another way: Racial diversity was not so much a barrier to unity as it was productive of it. It was the explicit (though often unstated) encounter with Obama's racial embodiment that allowed citizens to experience the sensation of national unity. Such forms of racial affect stand in contrast to previous presidential elections, suggesting that a serious analysis of the 2008 election must go beyond discussions of institutions, ideology, and party that typically characterize the relationship between a president and his public.

While Whitman's poetics provide valuable insights into Barack Obama's political appeal, it is also clear that Obama's poetics are more than merely Whitmanesque. While both poet and president engage in questions of embodiment and the relationship between the body and national unity, Obama's racialized subjectivity creates a politics of union distinct from Whitman's. More specifically, Obama invokes his status as a black man of mixed-race ancestry as a productive form of decentered subjectivity capable of uniting a diverse nation. In this way, Obama's approach to identity echoes the Chicana poet Gloria Anzaldúa and her discussion of "mestiza consciousness." I want to suggest that such "mestiza poetics" represents a form of democratic connectedness that challenges the sorts of dangerous equivalences and violent forgettings to which Obama's more Whitmanesque approach to union is sometimes susceptible.

This essay is divided into three parts. In the first, I discuss Whitman's poetics of union and its relationship to individuality by looking at George Kateb's discussion of *potentialities* and the relationship between individuality, receptivity, and democratic connectedness. Discussing Whitman's approach to the slavery question and his concerns regarding black suffrage following the Civil War, I complicate Kateb's reading by suggesting that Whitman's poetics of union ask both too much and too little from its citizen-readers. In the second section, I turn to Obama and his rhetorical efforts to reframe contemporary questions of national unity and democratic connectedness, exploring his racialized subjectivity through the poetry of the Chicana feminist Gloria Anzaldúa. In the paper's final section, I juxtapose Whitman's catalogs with Obama's memoirs, speeches, and mass gatherings, highlighting their shared ability to neutralize ideological differences and transform political contradictions into a poetics of equivalence and spectacle. Together, Whitman and Anzaldúa help us understand how questions of race and history complicate the desire for evanescent moments of union in the political (and poetical) era of Barack Obama.

Whitman and the Politics of Union: Potentialities and Democratic Connectedness

> I celebrate myself, and sing myself,
> And what I assume you shall assume,
> For every atom belonging to me as good belongs to you.
>   ("Song of Myself," sec. 1)

According to Stephen Black, Walt Whitman's "Song of Myself" reflects an "unconscious ambivalence" toward the self. Discussing the uncertainty he sees established by the poem's third line, Black writes: "If the atoms that belong 'as good' to others as to himself comprise his body, is it fair to ask who is the *me* to whom the atoms belong?" For Black, Whitman's celebration of self evolves into a troubling question: "who and what *am* I?"[13]

In contrast to Black's rather despairing depiction of Whitman's ambivalent subjectivity, George Kateb has argued that Whitman's poetry speaks more to the question of democratic *potentialities* and "the connectedness that emanates from democratic individuality, as Whitman perceives and perfects it."[14] In Kateb's reading, Whitman is exceptional in his capacity to show that "individuality's meaning is not fully disclosed until it is indissociably connected to democracy."[15] As Whitman writes in "By Blue Ontario's Shore":

> Underneath all, individuals,
> I swear nothing is good to me now that ignores individuals,
> The American compact is altogether with individuals,
> The only government is that which makes minute of individuals,

> The whole theory of the universe is directed unerringly to one single individual—namely to You. (sec. 15)

By emphasizing the status of individuals to "the American compact," Whitman's account of democratic individuality emphasizes the recognition that "each moral idea needs the other."[16]

For Kateb, Whitman's greatness lies in his effort to celebrate the democratic individual, "especially as such an individual lives in receptivity or responsiveness."[17] For Kateb, the "atom" in "Song of Myself" is "a potentiality." As he describes it, "to live receptively" is to understand that "every individual is composed of potentialities. . . . All the personalities that I encounter, I already am: That is to say I could become or could have become something like what others are; that necessarily means, in turn, that all of us are always indefinitely more than we actually are."[18] As Stephen Cushman notes in his discussion of Whitman and patriotism, Whitman's depiction of himself as a "kosmos" in section 24 of "Song of Myself" ("Walt Whitman, a kosmos, of Manhattan the son") suggests a description of himself as "an entire world or universe of feelings, sensations, impulses, and thoughts that constitute any self, once it realizes its own vast capacities."[19] This amazing mobility of identity produces a democratic poetics capable of identifying across lines of gender, region, race, and class:

> The city sleeps and the country sleeps,
> The living sleep for their time, the dead sleep for their time,
> The old husband sleeps by his wife and the young husband sleeps by his wife;
> And these tend inward to me, and I tend outward to them,
> And such as it is to be of these more or less I am,
> And of these one and all I weave the song of myself.
>
> I am of old and young, of the foolish as much as the wise,
> Regardless of others, ever regardful of others,
> Maternal as well as paternal, a child as well as a man,
> Stuff'd with the stuff that is coarse and stuff'd with the stuff that is fine,
> One of the Nation of many nations, the smallest the same and the largest the same,

> A Southerner soon as a Northerner, a planter nonchalant and
>   hospitable down by the Oconee I live,
> A Yankee bound my own way ready for trade, my joints the
>   limberest joints on earth and the sternest joints on
>   earth,
> A Kentuckian walking the vale of the Elkhorn in my deer-skin
>   leggings, a Louisianian or Georgian . . . (secs. 15–16)

We see in these lines what Ed Folsom has described as "the essentially absorptive nature" of Whitman's work.[20] Through his catalogs, Whitman enacts a form of connectedness that Kateb describes as democratic receptivity —the realization that "Things could easily have turned out differently. . . . [T]he same biological being that I am could have been culturally situated in an indefinitely great number of places and acquired a different personality and outward life in each case"[21] By pushing his readers to explore what it might mean to be "ever regardful of others," Whitman presents a portrait of the individual self as "a great composite democratic individual." Writing in "Starting from Paumanok":

> Dweller in Mannahatta my city, or on southern savannas,
> Or a soldier camp'd or carrying my knapsack and gun, or a miner
>   in California,
> Or rude in my home in Dakota's woods, my diet meat, my drink
>   from the spring . . . (sec. 1)

Describing Whitman's self as "a Picasso-like concurrence of many perspectives within one frame," Kateb understands Whitman's insight to be that speaking honestly about oneself requires talking about others.[22] Such a poetics of connectedness exceeds the logic of nationalism and group identity. As Whitman writes in "This Moment Yearning and Thoughtful":

> It seems to me there are other men in other lands yearning and
>   thoughtful,
> It seems to me I can look over and behold them in Germany,
>   Italy, France, Spain,
> Or far, far away, in China, or in Russia or Japan, talking other
>   dialects,

> And it seems to me if I could know those men I should become
> attached to them as I do to men in my own lands,
> O I know we should be brethren and lovers,
> I know I should be happy with them.

Yet Whitman's depiction of identification through our composite selves (defined through multiplicity rather than tribalism) also exposes a more uncomfortable realization—that "[o]ur potentialities are not only numberless but—and for that reason—conflicting."[23] Writing in "Crossing Brooklyn Ferry":

> It is not upon you alone the dark patches fall,
> The dark threw its patches down upon me also,
> The best I had done seem'd to me blank and suspicious,
> My great thoughts as I supposed them, were they not in reality
>   meagre?
> Nor is it you alone who know what it is to be evil,
> I am he who knew what it was to be evil,
> I too knitted the old knot of contrariety (sec. 6)

For Whitman, recognition of one's own unknowability and inconstancy (those "dark patches") reflects Kateb's claim that "oneself is a strange place"—that we are never fully knowable, even to ourselves. Yet for Whitman, such uncertainty represents a democratic resource rather than a problem to be solved. His ability to acknowledge fragmentation and contingency serves as a powerful resource for balancing democratic receptivity and individuality. For Kateb, "if we are poetically persuaded of this strangeness, we will grow more in mutual recognition, in democratic acceptance. Feelings of superiority and other discriminations will exist, even exist intensely, but their validity will be challenged by a poetically enhanced awareness of the vastness of every individual equally."[24]

In celebrating Whitman's insistent efforts at identification, individuality, and mutuality, Kateb acknowledges that such attempts can sometimes seem presumptuous. Discussing Whitman's depiction of himself as "the hounded slave" in "Song of Myself," Kateb asks: "Are there not both proper moral and inevitable mental limits to the ability to identify with human beings? . . . Is not even the most democratically determined observer confined in his or her perspective?"²⁵ Yet despite such questions and concerns, Kateb ultimately takes issue with those whose recognition of difference leads them to resist practices of democratic receptivity and connectedness. Such "appreciation of 'otherness' tends to turn into a mere patronizing aesthetic of the picturesque or into a paternalist anthropological solicitude." Instead, Kateb suggests we take inspiration from Whitman's efforts to extend the limits of knowing: "it is democratically better to err on the side of presumptuousness than on the side of bafflement."²⁶

I find much to appreciate in Kateb's reading of Whitman and the democratic refusal to "give up too quickly or complacently in epistemological defeat." Yet Kateb's focus on the self as potentiality (and its connection to democratic culture) downplays two important aspects of Whitman to which I want to turn. One is Whitman's distinctly aesthetic vision of democracy, and the second concerns race, for it is precisely around the question of race where Whitman's practice of receptivity and democratic individuality sometimes falters. In the following section, I want to suggest a deeper attentiveness to the tragic logic of race and to the aesthetics of democracy than Kateb's reading of Whitman offers. Increased attentiveness to the tragic reveals more complicated political lessons regarding the power of democratic receptivity, aesthetic response, and the relationship between race and the politics of union. As scholars have argued, Whitman's ideas regarding democratic unity are sometimes "distressed and politically elusive for grim historical reasons."²⁷ I want to turn to those "grim" reasons now.

Whitman and the Politics of Union: Ambivalence, Speed, Evasion

As many readers of Whitman have noted, although the poet hated slavery, his views on social and political equality between the races were far more complicated. Like many anti-extensionists opposed to the extension of slavery into the western territories, Whitman was "more concerned about preventing the spread of slavery than about getting rid of it."²⁸ In the lead-up to the Civil War, Whitman denounced both "proslavery Southern fire-eaters" as well as northern abolitionists—whom he described as "a few and foolish red-hot fanatics" and as an "angry-voiced and silly set."²⁹ Whitman's main concern was not the slaves themselves but the South's willingness to put their own interests above those of the nation. For him, the South's actions "threatened the delicate balance between state and national interests."[30]

Yet despite his moderate stance on the slavery question, abolitionists and radical Republicans strongly identified with Whitman's celebration of brotherhood and equality in poems such as "I Sing the Body Electric," "Song of Myself," and "Salut au Monde!" Since then, Whitman's work has often been praised for its stance on gender and racial equality. As Natasha Trethewey notes, because of his "open-armed enthusiasm, his inclusiveness and celebration of everyone, even the lowliest prostitute or degraded slave, Whitman's work has come to represent a poetics of democracy, a humane tradition of anti-racism."[31] Yet as Trethewey also reminds us, this same Whitman did not believe blacks capable of exercising the vote.[32] Whitman's all-encompassing ethic sometimes faltered as the poet associated slaves, blacks, and blackness with that which was repellent and/or corrupt. Writing in "Song of Myself":

> I will not have a single person slighted or left away,
> The kept-woman, sponger, thief, are hereby invited,
> The heavy-lipp'd slave is invited, the venerealee is invited;
> There shall be no difference between them and the rest. . . . (sec. 19)
>
> Through me many long dumb voices
> Voices of the interminable generations of prisoners and slaves,
> Voices of the diseas'd and despairing and of thieves and
>   dwarfs. (sec. 24)

Similarly, in "Song of the Open Road," Whitman announces his capacity to welcome all: "The black with his wooly head, the felon, the diseas'd, the illiterate person, are not denied."[33] As such moments make clear, Whitman's democratic receptivity is not without its racial contradictions.

According to David Reynolds, during the political turmoil of the 1850s, "the conflict between states' rights and centralized power fed directly into what Whitman saw as the central paradox of American life—the relation between the individual and the mass."[34] As the nation teetered on the brink of collapse, Whitman increasingly came to believe that poetry was the balancing agent capable of healing the nation and holding society together.[35] As

Reynolds notes, "with the possibility of resolution through normal political channels now dead," Whitman saw an even greater necessity to forge a new resolution in his poetry.[36] Issues of union and slavery "demanded especially careful literary treatment." According to Reynolds, "thus began what would become a long-term strategy of his: resolving thorny political issues by linguistic fiat."[37] Whitman's unifying, all-encompassing voice can be seen in his celebration of southern and northern states in "Starting from Paumanok":

> The Pennsylvanian! the Virginian! the double Carolinian!
> O all and each well-loved by me! my intrepid nations! O I at
>   any rate include you all with perfect love!
> I cannot be discharged from you! not from one any sooner than
>   another! . . .
>
> Of and through the States, as during life, each man and woman
>   my neighbor,
> The Louisianian, the Georgian, as near to me, and I as near to
>   him and her,
> The Mississippian and Arkansian yet with me, and I yet with any
>   of them . . . (sec. 14)

In his effort to rebind the nation through his aggregative voice, Whitman displays here what Ed Folsom has described as his "strong democratic affection," his eagerness "to sing the parts of the world into a massive juxtaposition," producing a poetry that "creates its world by naming things next to each other."[38] Here, Pennsylvania is depicted alongside Virginia and the Carolinas—all neighbors, each equally close, all equally loved. Similarly, Whitman begins "Our Old Feuillage" by using what Karen Sanchez-Eppler has described as the poetics of merger and embodiment in order to gather the union into his all-inclusive embrace:[39]

> Always the free range and diversity—always the continent of
>   Democracy;
> Always the prairies, pastures, forests, vast cities, travelers,
>   Kanada, the snows;
> Always these compact lands tied at the hips with the belt
>   stringing the huge oval lakes

The poem goes on to depict southern scenes of regional life wherein men and women of different races and status live and work in a state of affection and tranquility:

> There are the negroes at work in good health, the ground in all
>   directions is cover'd with pine straw;
> In Tennessee and Kentucky slaves busy in the coalings, at the forge,
>   by the furnace-blaze, or at the corn-shucking,
> In Virginia, the planter's son returning after a long absence,
>   joyfully welcom'd and kiss'd by the aged mulatto nurse.

Yet alongside such appealing depictions of the South, Whitman's efforts to heal the union also required a poetry that could identify with slaves as well as their masters. In this well-known passage from "Song of Myself," Whitman's democratic receptivity moves him to identify with the suffering of others (in this instance, the runaway slave):

> I am the hounded slave, I wince at the bite of the dogs
> Hell and despair are upon me, crack and again crack the
>   marksmen.
> I clutch the rails of the fence, my gore dribs, thinn'd with the
>   ooze of my skin,
> I fall on the weeds and stones,
> The riders spur their unwilling horses, haul close,
> Taunt my dizzy ears and beat me violently over the head with
>   whip-stocks.
>
> Agonies are one of my changes of garments,
> I do not ask the wounded person how he feels, I myself
>   become the wounded person,
> My hurts turn livid upon me as I lean on a cane and observe. (sec. 33)

Intriguingly, while identifying with various forms of suffering, Whitman makes little or no reference to an enemy or perpetrator. In "First O Songs" and other poems in *Drum-Taps*, this absence is on display in his celebration of the Union army and its martial display of Manhattan's men taking up arms:

> From the houses then and the workshops, and through all the
> doorways,
> Leapt they tumultuous, and lo ! Manhattan arming.
> . . . .
> Manahatta a-march—and it's O to sing it well!
> It's O for a manly life in the camp.
>
> And the sturdy artillery,
> The guns bright as gold, the work for giants, to serve well the guns,
> Unlimber them! (no more as the past forty years for salutes for
> courtesies merely,
> Put in something now besides powder and wadding.)[40]

As M. Wynn Thomas notes, it's no accident that "there is scarcely a mention of the enemy" in the poet's early wartime poems: "Whitman's feelings about the South were so mixed and so complicated that he found it much easier to construct a positive rhetoric (in favor of union, democracy, liberty, etc.) rather than a negative rhetoric."[41] Instead, Whitman's poetry can often be characterized by its celebration of heterogeneity while sidestepping disagreement. As Doris Sommer notes, Whitman's poetry does not so much deny conflict as neutralize it on the page.[42] Similarly, James Perrin Warren argues that Whitman's rhetorical strategy often involves not resolving contradictions so much as evading them.[43] Yet, as Sommers suggests, it is precisely through Whitman's catalogs that "the most extreme differences of social class, profession, origin, and gender level out through the steady and ardent incantation that melts differences into mere variation."[44] Writing again in "Song of Myself":

> The deacons are ordain'd with cross'd hands at the altar,
> The spinning-girl retreats and advances to the hum of the big
> wheel,
> The farmer stops by the bars as he walks on a First-day loafe
> and looks at the oats and rye,
> The lunatic is carried at last to the asylum a confirm'd case,
> (He will never sleep any more as he did in the cot in his
> mother's bed-room;)

> The jour printer with gray head and gaunt jaws works at his case,
> He turns his quid of tobacco while his eyes blurr with the
>   manuscript;
> The malform'd limbs are tied to the surgeon's table,
> What is removed drops horribly in a pail;
> The quadroon girl is sold at the auction-stand, the drunkard
>   nods by the bar-room stove,
> The machinist rolls up his sleeves, the policeman travels his
>   beat, the gate-keeper marks who pass,
> The young fellow drives the express-wagon, (I love him, though
>   I do not know him;)
> The half-breed straps on his light boots to compete in the race (sec. 15)

In this equalizing aesthetic, ideological conflicts and contending interests are brought together in what seems to be an almost random assemblage. Yet here, Whitman's listing also reveals signs of the tragic. The "malform'd limb" that "drops horribly in a pail" can be read in this vein—as the disfiguring element that is central to one's existence yet must be removed. It's telling that the vision of that which "drops horribly" is immediately followed by an equally abhorrent image: the "quadroon girl . . . sold at the auction-stand." Here, Whitman confronts us with a gendered image of rape and miscegenation that reminds the reader of both the sexual violence endemic to chattel slavery and the blood connections that bind Americans who exist as both slaves and masters. If slavery is the evil distorting the American body politic, then this malformation requires removal—a removal that might save the body politic, but whose removal will be horrible in its bloodiness.

Yet even here, evasions remain. Despite such allusions to suffering and tragic alternatives, we are faced with an image of suffering deprived of explicit agents. This absence runs through Whitman's poetry. Depicting the suffering of Civil War soldiers in "The Wound-Dresser," he again produces a confrontation with the bloody consequences of war that simultaneously shifts the reader's gaze away from the fact of political fratricide:

> To sit by the wounded and soothe them, or silently watch the dead;
> Years hence of these scenes, of these furious passions, these chances,
> Of unsurpass'd heroes (was one side so brave? the other was equally
>   brave (sec. 1)

Mestiza Poetics

Refusing to identify an institution or agent as the cause of such suffering, "The Wound Dresser" instead emphasizes heroism and sacrifice—the "equally brave" men who fought and died on both sides. Committed to a poetry capable of healing the nation and binding its wounds, Whitman engages in his own reparative cutting: excising adversaries and references to those who bear responsibility for the conflict and its consequences.

As John Mason notes, readers sometimes struggle with Whitman's seemingly endless lists, noting that "many (most) readers . . . skim the catalogs." In seeking to understand why Whitman adopted the catalog technique, Mason argues that readers must first accept skimming as "legitimate reading strategy," that the reader skims a Whitman catalog "to get an overview, a single image of a varied, polychromatic universe." Mason equates Whitman's catalogs with the turn-of-the-century "flipbook"—a book with a series of pictures that vary gradually from one page to the next, so that when the pages are turned rapidly, the pictures appear to animate by simulating motion. Flipbooks require speed, for "if the reader flips too slowly, the illusion is lost." For Mason, while "each item in a Whitman catalog is fully realized, for there to be motion, there must be speed."[45] In a similar vein, Stanley Coffman insists that Whitman's catalogs "convey meaning by their form." Describing the catalog technique in "Crossing Brooklyn Ferry," Coffman argues that "the words become effective as they function in the context of other words, which is to say they become effective aesthetically."[46] For both Mason and Coffman, the catalogs produce union as form of democratic spectacle—a distinctly aesthetic event. Moving quickly from one item to another, reading the catalogs transforms heterogeneity into the sensation of unity. Here, as Nancy Rosenblum notes, "the adhesive power that Whitman sets at work in readers of his poetry and in American thought is distinctively aesthetic, and the object of attraction is a peculiarly poetic vision of democracy."[47] At its most troubling, such a poetics is particularly capable of sustaining contradictions while sidestepping questions of racial justice, ideology, and interest.

Reading Whitman's postwar poem "Reconciliation," the question arises: Is anything lost in such an inclusive poetics? Are there any costs to Whitman's undifferentiated representation, catalogs, empty spaces, fragments? What happens when reconciliation requires absence?

> For my enemy is dead, a man divine as myself is dead,
> I look where he lies white-faced and still in the coffin—I draw near,

> Bend down and touch lightly with my lips the white face in
> the coffin.⁴⁸

As Natasha Trethewey notes, Whitman's emphasis on "the white face in the coffin" leaves out the reality of the many dead soldiers "whose faces were not white."⁴⁹ In her essay on Civil War memory and the South, Trethewey argues that such erasures represent the *lost* war—the betrayal of Reconstruction and "the narrative of black Americans whose stories were often subjugated, lost, or left out of public memory" while across the North and South, America's white citizenry were drawn together beneath the banner of reconciliation.⁵⁰

At his best, Whitman's inclusive language of democratic receptivity and connectedness encourages readers of his poetry not only to identify with that which is dissimilar from ourselves, but also to recognize that the unfamiliar and unknowable lies inside each of us—that each of us represents unknown potentialities. Rather than trying to supply a definite critical position, Whitman creates a powerfully affecting poetry of union defined by "epic lists" as well as gaps and silences. Yet this achievement comes at a cost. Whitman's inclusive logic of union can succeed poetically only by absorbing (rather than confronting) the racial violence and hierarchies that characterize democratic individuality in America. But what sort of democratic receptivity can exist in the context of such contradictions and historical evasions? Like Kateb, I, too, take inspiration from Whitman's efforts to "extend the limits of knowing" to include even the "hounded slave."⁵¹ But how is one to identify with the potentialities of oneself and others if questions of racial justice have been bypassed? As a practice of democratic theory, what are the risks of choosing absorption over agonism?

Ultimately, in reading Whitman, we are reminded that the creation of democratic connectedness inevitably involves dangerous equivalences. The poet's work highlights this risk, since his greatest poetic moments occur when rhetorically transcending the moments of division he seeks to heal.

Barack Obama's Allusive Poetics of Union

There's not a black America and white America and Latino America and Asian America; there's the United States of America.
—Barack Obama

According to Allen Grossman, "Whitman's poetry thrives on forms of contradiction and inclusion that governing cannot."[52] Discussing the poetics and policy of union in Whitman and President Lincoln, Grossman argues that Whitman's artistic brilliance exists precisely at the crisis of contradiction where Lincoln found only "disintegrative instability."[53]

While Grossman is correct in his reading of the politics of slavery and the Civil War, I want to suggest that at other historical moments, Whitman's poetics of union may have a great deal to teach us about leadership and the politics of governing. More specifically, the 2008 election of Barack Obama displayed a poetic concern for union that was "Whitmanesque" in its tendency to neutralize conflict through the rhetoric of unity and inclusivity. In an effort to avoid agonistic encounters on issues of racial justice, Obama (like Whitman) engaged our affection for the country by creating a poetic vision of national life. Reading Whitman helps us gain a better understanding of how Obama approaches race both metonymically and as an aesthetic event.

Barack Obama appeared on the national public stage in 2004 as a figure of union. Delivering the keynote address at the Democratic National Convention in Boston, he opens with the story of himself. Born to a Kenyan father and an American mother, Obama begins his autobiography by narrating differences of race and nation that ultimately result in "a common dream born of two continents." By highlighting the distinctiveness of his racial background alongside core American values of hard work, perseverance, and sacrifice, Obama's keynote speech begins as the particular story of exotic individuals and moves toward the universal in its effort to reaffirm the idea of American exceptionalism. Stating that "in no other country on Earth is my story even possible," he evokes a vision of unity and national greatness produced through the very diversity he embodies. Rather than framing his origin story in terms of America's divisive history of slavery and segregation, Obama constructs himself as a figure of fusion and integration. His subjectivity seems to embody the democratic principle he later invokes—"E pluribus unum"—out of many, one.

Throughout the 2004 speech, Obama frames the role of government in ways that challenge the liberal-conservative divide: "The people I meet in small towns and big cities and diners and office parks, they don't expect government to solve all of their problems.... Go into the blue-collar counties around Chicago, and people will tell you: They don't want their tax money wasted by a welfare agency or by the Pentagon."[54] Later, in what would become the speech's most famous section, Obama challenges presumed divisions of ideology and identity that characterize contemporary discussions of partisanship. Instead, his speech offers a democratic poetics capable of identifying across lines of ideology, race, religion, and sexuality:

> Now even as we speak, there are those who are preparing to divide us, the spin masters and negative-ad peddlers who embrace the politics of anything goes.
>
> Well, I say to them tonight, there's not a liberal America and a conservative America; there's the United States of America.
>
> There's not a black America and white America and Latino America and Asian America; there's the United States of America.
>
> The pundits like to slice and dice our country into red states and blue states: red states for Republicans, blue states for Democrats. But I've got news for them, too. We worship an awesome God in the blue states, and we don't like federal agents poking around our libraries in the red states.
>
> We coach Little League in the blue states and, yes, we've got some gay friends in the red states.
>
> There are patriots who opposed the war in Iraq, and there are patriots who supported the war in Iraq.
>
> We are one people, all of us pledging allegiance to the Stars and Stripes, all of us defending the United States of America.[55]

In declaring that "there's not a black America and white America and Latino America . . . there's the United States of America," the speech both simplifies and complicates America's politics. On the one hand, the statement can be read as the conservative claim that America has arrived at a "postracial politics." Yet by situating this claim within unexpected juxtapositions of social location and policy preference (religious citizens in blue states, gay Americans in the red states), Obama complicates the homogenizing assumption that a shared racial identity implies common policy preferences and a shared worldview. Instead, Obama describes a diverse citizenry of individuals whose values and political preferences crosscut the nation and exceed easy categorization. Again, Obama's depiction of the *United* States is forged not simply through claims of sameness (coaching Little League, attending church) but also alongside claims regarding our shared political differences (opposing and supporting the invasion of Iraq).

Obama grounds his form of democratic receptivity in a larger communitarian ethos that seeks to reconcile individual initiative and personal responsibility, with government action and mutual responsibility, stating:

> [A]longside our famous individualism, there's another ingredient in the American saga, a belief that we are all connected as one people.
>
> If there's a child on the south side of Chicago who can't read, that matters to me, even if it's not my child.
>
> If there's a senior citizen somewhere who can't pay for their prescription and having to choose between medicine and the rent, that makes my life poorer, even if it's not my grandparent.
>
> If there's an Arab-American family being rounded up without benefit of an attorney or due process, that threatens my civil liberties.
>
> It is that fundamental belief—I am my brother's keeper, I am my sister's keeper—that makes this country work.[56]

Like Whitman's claim in "One's-Self I Sing," Obama seeks to reconcile the individual with the community—the "simple, separate Person" alongside the democratic "En-masse." Both Whitman and Obama harmonize these values by offering a positive rhetoric that sidesteps the contradictions and inherent tensions that exist within these sometimes contending values.

In his 2006 book *Audacity of Hope*, Obama argues that "rightly or wrongly, white guilt has largely exhausted itself in America; even the most fair-minded of whites, those who would genuinely like to see racial inequality ended and poverty relieved, tend to push back against suggestions of racial victimization—or race-specific claims based on the history of race discrimination in this country."[57] One can see in this passage an interesting combination of confidence in the good intentions of white liberals combined with a rather disparaging critique of the political strategies being offered by race-conscious multiculturalists. Instead, like Whitman, Obama is a political moderate articulating an alternative form of connectedness that "tends outward" toward others—at the child unable to read, the senior citizen without means, the Arab American denied his legal rights. In order to "sing himself," Obama finds it necessary to talk about others.

Although Barack Obama's ambivalence about race differs from that of Walt Whitman, both men rely on a poetics of allusion to sustain democratic unity while acknowledging racial inequality. For Obama, such allusiveness is grounded in the politics of racialization. Notwithstanding discussions of him as a "postracial" candidate, it was impossible not to realize that a powerful politics of racialized embodiment surrounded Obama as a political phenomenon. The combination of personal appeal alongside his status as an African American political figure breaking down racial barriers has led to a rich politics of the visual, defined by tee shirts, calendars, and the ubiquitous HOPE poster by street artist Shepard Fairey. (Of course, Whitman is also a powerfully iconic figure. As Ed Folsom notes, the 1855 frontispiece portrait opposite the title page of *Leaves of Grass* has become the most familiar of all the images of Whitman.)[58] Understandably, while poet and president understand their individual embodiment as central to their politics, only Whitman speaks explicitly about the relationship between sexuality, eroticism, and union. Characterizing himself as "Turbulent, fleshy, sensual, eating, drinking, and breeding," Whitman is the poet of adhesive love, the poet of homoerotic attraction who openly celebrated "the body's capacity for multiple and varied pleasures."[59] By contrast, Obama's racial status as a black man has led him to downplay his sexuality even beyond that of previous presidents. Despite the fact that miscegenation is central to Obama's political and personal biography and that he is the product not only of an "an improbable love" but interracial sex, the connections between the political and the erotic generally went unspoken during the presidential campaign.[60]

The issue of race and sexuality speaks to the Obama campaign's awareness that the candidate's status as an African American was an ongoing site of both political danger and opportunity, requiring subtle negotiation. To harness the power of race while downplaying its risks, Obama sought to assuage white anxiety through a compelling combination of allusion and embodiment. Cognizant of his own visual and aural appeal, Obama's campaign speeches often allude to larger racial themes while avoiding explicit references to race. Drawing on a sense of the imagined and the unspoken, Obama's speeches display a mastery of space and silence, creating a politics that (while unsettling to some) can rightly be characterized as "poetic." Like Whitman's poetics of union, Obama's speeches often suggest an imagined future rather than an explicit critical position. Examples of this strategy abound. In his speech following his victory in the Iowa Democratic caucuses, Obama declares:

> Thank you, Iowa.
>
> You know, they said this day would never come. . . .
>
> They said this country was too divided; too disillusioned to ever come together around a common purpose.
>
> But on this January night—at this defining moment in history—you have done what the cynics said we couldn't do. . . . In lines that stretched around schools and churches, in small towns and big cities, you came together as Democrats, Republicans, and Independents to stand up and say that we are one nation, we are one people, and our time for change has come. . . .
>
> We are choosing hope over fear. We're choosing unity over division, and sending a powerful message that change is coming to America. . . .
>
> This was the moment when we tore down barriers that have divided us for too long. . . .
>
> Years from now, you'll look back and you'll say that this was the moment, this was the place, where America remembered what it means to hope.[61]

In his speech to Iowa voters, Obama combines allusion and racial visibility in ways that exploit textual space. Speaking to voters in this largely white and rural state, Obama makes no explicit reference to race. Yet the speech calls upon a shared awareness of his racialization in the opening claim that "they said this day would never come." Using an almost preacherly cadence, Obama speaks of tearing down "barriers that have divided us for too long." Implicitly congratulating his white audience for taking part in the historic effort to elect the first African American president, Obama tells Iowa voters that, "Years from now, you'll look back and you'll say that this was the moment, this was the place, where America remembered what it means to hope." Throughout the Democratic primaries, Obama's campaign speeches presumed a consciousness about his blackness that remains powerfully present, yet rarely spoken. In yet another example of this approach, Obama accepted the Democratic Party's nomination for president on the forty-fifth anniversary of Martin Luther King Jr.'s "I have a dream" speech—yet he made no overt mention of his own race in the speech. Through most of the election, such allusive strategies proved successful with the American electorate.

Obama's Mestiza Poetics and the Crisis of Race

> I am the son of a black man from Kenya and a white woman from Kansas. I was raised with the help of a white grandfather who survived a Depression to serve in Patton's Army during World War II and a white grandmother who worked on a bomber assembly line at Fort Leavenworth while he was overseas. I've gone to some of the best schools in America and lived in one of the world's poorest nations. I am married to a black American who carries within her the blood of slaves and slaveowners—an inheritance we pass on to our two precious daughters. I have brothers, sisters, nieces, nephews, uncles, and cousins of every race and every hue, scattered across three continents. . . . It's a story that hasn't made me the most conventional candidate. But it is a story that has seared into my genetic makeup the idea that this nation is more than the sum of its parts—that out of many, we are truly one.[62]

In March 2008, Barack Obama faced a political crisis that required moving beyond the allusive approach to race that had sustained him during earlier portions of the primary. Earlier that month, controversial sound bites from sermons given by Obama's longtime pastor, the Rev. Jeremiah Wright, began to appear in the national media.[63] Saying that blacks should not sing "God Bless America" but "God damn America," and that the United States had brought the September 11, 2001, attacks on itself through its own "terrorism," Wright placed the issue of black anger squarely at the center of Obama's presidential campaign. From then on, the candidate would face accusations of being a secret militant, unpatriotic and sympathetic to the radical separatism of black nationalists.

On March 18, Obama responded to the growing controversy by delivering a major speech on race that sought to place Wright's comments in historical and political context. More significantly, in the speech's initial refusal to disown the pastor outright, Obama sought to move the discussion on race toward a theory of affiliation that was complex, tragic, and restorative. While retaining a unitary impulse, the speech was explicit in its references to its author's racial identity. Throughout the speech, Obama invokes his mixed-race ancestry as a productive form of decentered subjectivity capable of uniting a racially divided country. He seeks to explicitly name and claim a series of multiple and shifting identities that challenge the claims of both cultural nationalists and color-blind conservatives. I want to suggest that Obama's approach here has important resonances with the Chicana poet Gloria Anzaldúa and her discussion of "mestiza consciousness." Approaching Obama through Whitman *and* Anzaldúa allows us to better observe the ways Obama's political impulses seem to veer between a politics of union that disavows conflict versus a more agonistic ethos of crossing.[64]

Obama's Philadelphia speech was the first time during the 2008 election where the candidate sought to publicly confront—rather than ameliorate—America's difficult racial past and our complicated racial present. Such emotive and potentially contentious language regarding race had not been seen since the publication of his 1995 memoir, *Dreams from My Father*. In both *Dreams* and the Philadelphia speech, Obama is less concerned with creating equivalences than with complicating his audience's assumptions regarding race and subjectivity. In both these texts, Obama uses his personal story to challenge the idea of a singular self—a subject able to fully occupy a single, unproblematic category. In this way, Obama maintains a Whitmanesque concern with democratic potentiality and receptivity while cultivating an understanding of racial identity appreciative of its fluidity, multiplicity, and contradictions.

In *Dreams from My Father*, this concern with potentiality can be seen in depictions of Obama's own youthful alienation and disaffection. Trying to "raise myself to be a black man in America," the author describes himself as "engaged in a fitful interior struggle." Recounting his anger and frustration in high school, Obama considers possible consequences of black identity:

> I had begun to see a new map of the world, one that was frightening in its simplicity, suffocating in its implications. We were always playing on the white man's court. . . . In fact, you couldn't even be sure that everything you had assumed to be an expression of your black, unfettered self . . . had been freely chosen by you. Following this maddening logic, the only thing you could choose as your own was withdrawal into a smaller and smaller coil of

rage, until being black meant only the knowledge of your own powerlessness, of your own defeat. And the final irony: Should you refuse this defeat and lash out at your captors, they would have a name for that, too, a name that could cage you just as good. Paranoid. Militant. Violent. Nigger.[65]

Later, criticizing an assimilated black college student from the suburbs who seemed to avoid her fellow black students, Obama admits: "The truth was that I understood her, her and all the black kids who felt the way she did. In their mannerisms, their speech, their mixed-up hearts, I kept recognizing myself."[66] In his capacity to acknowledge contingency, these passages reflect what George Kateb might understand as a Whitmanesque understanding of democratic individuality wherein "all of us are always indefinitely more" than we seem and that each us could have been "culturally situated in an indefinitely great number of places and acquired a different personality and outward life."[67] Moreover, by imagining himself occupying such varied subject positions, Obama echoes Kateb in his recognition that our potentialities are not only "numberless" but "conflicting."[68]

While attentive to the fact that democratic connectedness is not the same as "group identity," *Dreams from My Father* reflects Obama's deep understanding that America's racial divide represents a central barrier to our collective ability to live receptively and responsively with one another. Cultivating such democratic connectedness requires supplementing Whitman's poetics of union—a poetics whose aesthetic appeal often relies on Whitman's capacity to elide rather than confront divisions of race. By contrast, in *Borderlands/La Frontera*, Gloria Anzaldúa puts forward a mestiza poetics whose aesthetic power lies in its capacity to cultivate a "tolerance for ambiguity." In her poem "To Live in the Borderlands Means You," Anzaldúa describes a metaphorical and literal region where worlds blend and cross:

> To live in the Borderlands means knowing
>   that the *india* in you, betrayed for 500 years,
>   is no longer speaking to you,
>   that *mexicanas* call you *rajetas*,
>   that denying the Anglo inside you
>   is as bad as having denied the Indian or Black;
> *Cuando vives en la frontera*
>   people walk through you, the wind steals your voice,

> you're a *burra, buey,* scapegoat,
> forerunner of a new race,
> half and half—both woman and man, neither—
> a new gender;
> To live in the Borderlands means to
> put chile in the borscht,
> eat whole wheat tortillas,
> speak Tex-Mex with a Brooklyn accent;
> be stopped by *la migra* at the border checkpoints;
> To live in the Borderlands means you fight hard to
> resist the gold elixir beckoning from the bottle,
> the pull of the gun barrel,
> the rope crushing the hollow of your throat;
> In the Borderlands
> you are the battleground
> where enemies are kin to each other;
> you are at home, a stranger,
> the border disputes have been settled
> the volley of shots have shattered the truce
> you are wounded, lost in action
> dead, fighting back;
> To survive the Borderlands
> you must live *sin fronteras*
> be a crossroads.[69]

For Anzaldúa, the borderlands are always home and not home. Rather than a dream of origins and belonging, Anzaldúa's "home" is characterized by strangeness—a discontinuous and unstable region. Living in such a state of transition (belonging and not belonging) is risky, with Anzaldúa describing how hard it is to resist "the gold elixir beckoning from the bottle, the pull of the gun barrel, the rope crushing the hollow of your throat." Obama describes his own youthful struggle to negotiate this discontinuous and ruptured terrain ("Junkie. Pothead. That's where I'd been headed: the final, fatal role of the young would-be black man").[70] Yet as Romand Coles observes, despite its challenges, Anzaldúa recognizes this situation as "not simply tragic, but also *generative* of the highest possibilities and transfigurations of democratic engagement." In other words, "mestiza consciousness" is more than simply a depiction of hybridity and racially mixing. Rather than simply a crossed breed, Anzaldúa offers an ethos of crossing and being crossed.[71] In this politics of encounter, she refuses to "deny the Anglo" (or the black, or the Indian) within her. In this way, the new *mestiza* not only "sustains contradictions, she turns the ambivalence into something else."[72]

Throughout the Philadelphia speech, we see Obama struggling to convince his listeners of the value in such receptivity and crossings, in cultivating a democratic tolerance for ambiguity and contradiction. Within his condemnation of Wright, he also expresses a mestiza poetics that simultaneously refuses to reject the reverend and his church:

> I can no more disown him than I can disown the black community. I can no more disown him than I can my white grandmother—a woman who helped raise me, a woman who sacrificed again and again for me, a woman who loves me as much as she loves anything in this world, but a woman who once confessed her fear of black men who passed by her on the street, and who on more than one occasion has uttered racial or ethnic stereotypes that made me cringe. These people are part of me. And they are part of America, this country I love.[73]

In comparing Wright's bigotry with that of his white grandmother, Obama created a democratic correspondence capable of acknowledging that in America's racial crucible, "enemies are kin to each other." In doing this, Obama went beyond the usual communitarian platitudes articulated during campaign season to argue for a more agonistic conception of community—one enmeshed in a web of contending loyalties and commitments. Like the new *mestiza*, Obama works here to cultivate a more sophisticated ethos of union, defined by radical pluralism in which "nothing is thrust out, the good the bad and the ugly, nothing rejected, nothing abandoned."[74] In contrast to a strategy of union that relies on metonym and juxtaposition, Anzaldúa's poetics are defined by a more oppositional understanding of community.

Dreams from My Father is a memoir characterized by such complex identifications. Throughout the memoir, we encounter numerous examples of Obama refusing to simply demonize and repudiate the more nationalist and Afrocentric portions of the black community.[75] Instead, like his description in *Dreams* of first meeting Rev. Wright, Obama seeks to "hold together, if not reconcile, the conflicting strains of black experience."[76] Yet while Obama seeks to bridge the various communities of which he is a part, he does not share Anzaldúa's willingness to "be a crossroads." Instead, as the political philosopher Simon Critchley notes, Obama yearns to *belong*.[77] Rather than celebrating the political possibilities of never being "fully at home in any one group," *Dreams* is the story of a young man seeking to overcome his sense of alienation and estrangement.

Anzaldúa's mestiza poetics helps us recognize Obama's struggle between the less politically demanding politics of *union* versus a more difficult democratic ethos of "crossing and being crossed." In the Philadelphia speech on race, we see him working to reconcile these two impulses in ways both successful and unsuccessful.[78] For example, at one point in the speech, Obama compares Wright's anger at generations of violence and legalized discrimination with the racial resentments of white America. Describing the pitfalls of such equivalences, Lawrie Balfour writes: "Obama's comparison of Wright's grievances with the racial grievances of white Americans is a brilliant—and troubling—rhetorical move. If it accurately reflects the reality of white resentment, this reflection comes at the cost of flattening historical differences and radically understating the scale and effects of racial hierarchy from the colonial era through the present."[79]

Ultimately, while Obama displays certain promising affinities with the "*mestiza* poetics" of Gloria Anzaldúa—particularly in *Dreams from My Father*—his own inclination to reconciliation and closure has increasingly led him in more politically palatable directions. And while we are likely to see future moments where President Obama argues for an agonistic "ethos of crossing," the political constraints of the office—combined with his own desire to neutralize conflict—are likely to make such appearances rare.

Mass Rallies and the Democratic Sublime

As we've seen in this discussion of the Philadelphia speech on race, Obama's rhetoric often draws on the power of personal experience. Yet this is not the only way he makes his unique individuality serve the democratic common. In this final section, I consider how Obama draws on the power of public display and how such forms of democratic spectacle lead citizens to experience the sensation of union.

Accepting the Democratic Party's presidential nomination in Denver, Barack Obama transformed the traditional conclusion of his party's convention into an enormous spectacle of diversity. Speaking at Invesco Field, a crowd of nearly eighty thousand filled the open-air stadium.[80] Such mass gatherings were a staple of Obama's campaign, making the Denver rally a fitting end to the long primary season. Over the past fifteen months, massive rallies had become crucial to Obama's claim to be a figure of union. Drawing on Nancy Rosenblum's reading of Whitman, I consider Obama's mass gatherings as part of visual aesthetic wherein individuals exhibited their support of a nonwhite candidate through a conscious display of bodies.

As with my earlier discussion of Mason and his comparison of flipbooks to Whitman's catalogs, the sensation of union requires a certain amount of *speed* in order to sustain the illusion of coherence and continuity. Similarly, it is my contention that Obama's rallies also must be understood in terms of their temporality. Rallies' immediacy and short duration are crucial elements to their success, generating a sense of unity and fellow-feeling while also sidestepping the difficult work of living together. Here in the crowd, we can take pleasure in our diversity without confronting our differences in a sustained way.

Whitman's appreciation of the suggestive and temporal aspects of democratic union helps us see how the experience of democratic union is as necessary as it is evanescent. As Whitman observes in "I Sing the Body Electric":

> There is something in staying close to men and women and
> > looking on them, and in the contact and odor of them,
> > > that pleases the soul well,
> All things please the soul, but these please the soul well. (sec. 4)

By gathering together in massive rallies, participants appear to themselves as a kind of unified collective. The pleasure and ongoing desire for such mass gatherings can be seen in the spontaneous street celebrations that took place across the country on election night 2008—as well as in the extraordinarily large turnout for Obama's inauguration.[81] In all of these instances, participants experienced the heterogeneous crowd as a form of democratic enchantment. The crowds' size and diversity were precisely what produced a sense of unity among the participants. Unlike the Philadelphia speech, these mass events did not ask participants to grapple with questions of racism, privilege, or divided loyalties. Instead, supporters were invited to experience their heterogeneity as a kind of democratic sublime.

While there is much to value in the fleeting pleasures of the democratic crowd, such short-lived delights stand in stark contrast to the requirements of governing. If politics is the strong and slow boring of hard boards, then perhaps we need to more deeply consider the tensions between Obama's aggregative and evasive poetics of transience versus the protracted work of legislating. Like the flipbook that is turned too slowly, in the realm of governing, illusions of unity and momentum are easily lost.

In the speech in which he accepted the Democratic Party's nomination for president, Obama relied on the power of spectacle alongside a form of aggregative speech that situated voters within a historical trajectory gathering together disparate and sometimes opposing movements into a common narrative of progress. Describing the "American spirit" at Invesco Field, Obama stated:

> [I]t is that American spirit, that American promise, that pushes us forward even when the path is uncertain, that binds us together in spite of our differences, that makes us fix our eye not on what is seen but what is unseen, that better place around the bend.
>
> That promise is our greatest inheritance. It's a promise ... that has led immigrants to cross oceans and pioneers to travel west, a promise that led workers to picket lines and women to reach for the ballot.
>
> And it is that promise that, forty-five years ago today, brought Americans from every corner of this land to stand together on a Mall in Washington, before Lincoln's Memorial, and hear a young preacher from Georgia speak of his dream.[82]

By depicting the immigrants alongside western pioneers, labor organizers alongside suffragettes and civil rights activists, Obama is engaging in a poetics of equivalence. Here, Obama echoes Whitman in his capacity to "sing the parts of the world into a massive juxtaposition," producing a poetry that "creates its world by naming things next to each other."[83] Reading Obama through Whitman, we see how this unifying poetics of equivalence relies not only on allusion and metonym but on fragments, evasions, and silences. The "American spirit" that Obama references here draws upon American civic and religious traditions while evading the complicated history of empire, racism, sexism, and segregation that also influenced these political actors. In this tale of the American spirit, clashing interests are excised. Like Whitman, Obama's speech gives us heroes without enemies, American progress without American adversaries.

Obama's metonymic and racially allusive speech is an important reason why he has often been characterized as politically opaque. In his analysis of "Obama's subjectivity and how it forms his political vision and . . . extraordinary popular appeal," Simon Critchley writes:

> [P]erhaps this opacity is Obama's political genius: that it is precisely the enigmatic, inert character of Obama that seems to generate the desire to identify with him, indeed to love him. Perhaps it is that sense of internal distance that people see in him and in themselves. Obama recognizes this capacity in an intriguing and profound remark when he writes, "I serve as a blank screen on which people of vastly different political stripes project their own views." He is a mirror that reflects back whatever the viewer wants to see. . . . Obama's desire for union with a common good becomes unified with ours. For that moment, and maybe only for that moment, we believe, we hope. It is a strangely restrained ecstasy, but an ecstasy nonetheless.[84]

While he is right to recognize Obama's capacity to serve as a political "blank screen," Critchley fails to connect Obama's opacity with the question of race and the anxiety of white voters. Put somewhat differently, Obama's reluctance to name ideological opponents and clearly identify those he holds politically responsible for our national crises may well represent an approach to conflict shaped by race. Without a reading of whiteness and its own political investments in innocence and redemption, the relationship between Obama's popular appeal and his lyrical allusiveness remains unintelligible.

Conclusion

> Does poetry know anything that policy does not?
> —Allen Grossman, "The Poetics of Union in Whitman and Lincoln"

As I suggested at the beginning of this essay, the election of Barack Obama can best be understood as both a political *and* a sensory event. Like Walt Whitman, Obama sparked our attraction to democracy through the binding power of aesthetics. His success remains astounding: In a country still deeply divided by identity and ideology, Americans enthusiastically elected a progressive black man to represent them to the world, to be the public face of the United States. Understanding such an event—one that runs counter to so many historical precedents and prejudices—requires thinkers to go beyond the usual categories, institutions, and practices of American politics and democratic theory.

Thinking poetically about democracy and the presidency helps make sense of far more than merely the 2008 election. In exploring Obama's civic resources and tendencies, we can better understand how he has chosen to govern from the Oval Office. Reading Whitman helps us see how poetic pluralizations helped Obama win the election and frame progressive policies; at the same time, Whitman aids our understanding of why these same poetics have been less successful as Obama has moved from campaigning to governing. The uniting rhetoric that left adversaries unnamed helped Obama forge an electoral majority. Yet today, these same evasions are creating new challenges and posing new questions for an administration that must now privilege successful legislation over aggregative inclusion. What happens when the rhetoric of bipartisanship and compromise outweighs the commitment to equity and fair play? Or when the Obama administration weakens Miranda rights while signaling reluctance about pursuing investigations into alleged crimes of the Bush administration? At such moments of aggregative governing where acts of injustice go unnamed, what is being sacrificed to sustain the national fantasy of union? What happens when the rights of marginalized communities (gays and lesbians, undocumented immigrants, etc.) are put on the back burner because advancing the rights of such subjects is simply too "divisive" in our current political climate? At such moments of evasion, what has unity wrought? When poised at such moments of decision, citizens need more than a poetics of inclusion—they need policies that value transparency, accountability, and the rule of law.

Reading Whitman, we are reminded that democratic connectedness inevitably involves dangerous equivalences and violent forgettings. These risks appear in the policies of Barack Obama, even as his poetics of union give citizens a deeper understanding of the evanescent power of democracy. Such aesthetic moments achieve what traditional politics and policy cannot. Yet as our president negotiates his political future, we can only hope that he cultivates a poetics capable of reconciling the needs of union with the demands of justice.

Notes

I am grateful to the Haverford students who participated in my 2007 political theory seminar "Walt Whitman and the Democratic Arts." Particular thanks to Jillian Bunyan, Sean Stambaugh, and Fay Strongin for their deep engagement and critical insights into all things Whitman. Special thanks to Matthew Budman for his editorial acumen and keen advice on earlier drafts of this essay.

    1. Obama's precise wording is telling here: "And that is why, in the shadow of the Old State Capitol, where Lincoln once called on a divided house to stand together, where common hopes and common dreams still live, I stand before you today to announce my candidacy for President of the United States" (see "Illinois Sen. Barack Obama's Announcement Speech [As Prepared for Delivery]," *Washington Post,* February 10, 2007).

    2. Ibid. Following the 2008 election, Obama continued to reference Lincoln. In explaining his selection of former primary opponents Joe Biden and Hillary Clinton as his running mate and secretary of state, President-elect Obama approvingly cited Doris Kearns Goodwin's book *Team of Rivals,* an account of Lincoln's election and assembly of his cabinet. And finally, on January 19, Barack Obama was sworn in as president of the United States on the same Bible that Lincoln used to take the oath of office (see Janie Lorber, "Another Lincoln Moment for Obama," *New York Times,* January 10, 2009).

    3. See Katharine Q. Seelye, "The Abraham Lincoln Analogy," *New York Times,* February 12, 2009.

    4. See "Illinois Sen. Barack Obama's Announcement Speech."

    5. Whitman's deep admiration for Lincoln is well known and resulted in some of his most celebrated and well-known poems ("When Lilacs Last in the Dooryard Bloom'd," "O Captain! My Captain!"). Some works that explore the Whitman-Lincoln connection: William Coyle, ed., *The Poet and the President: Whitman's Lincoln Poems* (New York: Odyssey Press, 1962); Allen Grossman, "The Poetics of Union in Whitman and Lincoln: An Inquiry toward the Relationship of Art and Policy," in *The American Renaissance Reconsidered,* ed. Walter Benn Michaels and Donald E. Pease (Baltimore: Johns Hopkins University Press, 1985); "The Eighteenth Presidency!" in Clifton Joseph Furness, *Walt Whitman's Workshop* (Cambridge: Harvard University Press, 1928); George M. Fredrickson, *Inner Civil War: Northern Intellectuals and the Crisis of the Union* (New York: Harper, 1965);

Daniel Aaron, *The Unwritten War: American Writers and the Civil War* (New York: Knopf, 1973); Edmund Wilson, *Patriotic Gore: Studies in the Literature of the American Civil War* (New York: Oxford University Press, 1962).

6. Lincoln, Whitman, and Obama also share a commitment to biblical language. As George Shulman notes, both Obama and Lincoln "draw on biblical language to call a special nation to its higher and redemptive purpose, and thus name common purposes" that mobilize nation-building (see George Shulman, "Civil Religion, Prophecy, and Obama," The Immanent Frame, http://blogs.ssrc.org/tif/2009/06/11/civil-religion-prophecy-and-obama/). Although the question of religion is an intriguing aspect of Whitman's poetics, this essay does not explore the linkages between biblical language and the politics of union.

7. Of course, as Ed Folsom notes, one astonishing aspect of Whitman's legacy is how he keeps emerging in the terms of various presidents in the century-plus after his death. (Folsom cites the role *Leaves of Grass* played in the Monica Lewinsky scandal, as well as the way *Leaves* was invoked after September 11, 2001, and at the lead-up to the Iraq War.) Moreover, Whitman himself "admired and disdained presidents with unusual passion, rising to some of his most sublime language to evoke Lincoln ('the sweetest, wisest soul of all my days and lands') and descending to some of his coarsest to describe Benjamin Harrison ('the scalawag who was and is . . . the shit ass! God damn 'im')" (see Ed Folsom, "'What a Filthy Presidentiad!' Clinton's Whitman, Bush's Whitman, and Whitman's America," *Virginia Quarterly Review* 81, no. 2 [Spring 2005]: 96–113).

8. See Nancy L. Rosenblum, "Strange Attractors: How Individualists Connect to Form Democratic Unity," in this volume, 47–58.

9. Ibid., 48, 56.

10. Betsy Erkkila, "'Song of Myself' and the Politics of the Body Erotic," in *Approaches to Teaching Whitman's Leaves of Grass*, ed. Donald D. Kummings (New York: Modern Language Association of America, 1990), 57.

11. See Doris Sommer, "The Bard of Both Americas," in *Approaches to Teaching Whitman's Leaves of Grass*, 163.

12. See Allen Grossman, "The Poetics of Union in Whitman and Lincoln: An Inquiry toward the Relationship of Art and Policy," in *The American Renaissance Reconsidered*, ed. Michaels and Pease.

13. See Stephen A. Black, *Whitman's Journeys into Chaos: A Psychoanalytic Study of the Poetic Process* (Princeton: Princeton University Press, 1975).

14. George Kateb, "Democratic Individuality and the Claims of Politics," *Political Theory* 12, no. 3 (August 1984): 332. See also George Kateb, *The Inner Ocean: Individualism and Democratic Culture* (Ithaca: Cornell University Press, 1992).

15. Kateb, "Democratic Individuality and the Claims of Politics," 332.
16. Ibid., 333.
17. George Kateb, "Walt Whitman and the Culture of Democracy," in this volume, 21.
18. Ibid., 549, 551.
19. Stephen Cushman, "Whitman and Patriotism," *Virginia Quarterly Review* 81, no. 2 (Spring 2005): 168.
20. Ed Folsom, "'Scattering It Freely Forever': Whitman in a Seminar on Nineteenth-Century American Culture," in *Approaches to Teaching Whitman's Leaves of Grass*, ed. Donald D. Kummings (New York: Modern Language Association of America, 1990), 42.
21. Kateb, "Walt Whitman and the Culture of Democracy," 43.
22. Ibid., 28.
23. Ibid., 26.
24. Ibid., 29.
25. Ibid., 41–42.
26. Ibid., 43.
27. Rosenblum, "Strange Attractors," 48.
28. David W. Reynolds, *Walt Whitman's America: A Cultural Biography* (New York: Vintage, 1995), 125.
29. Ibid., 118–19.
30. Ibid., 112.
31. Natasha Trethewey, "On Whitman, Civil War Memory, and My South," *Virginia Quarterly Review* 81, no. 2 (Spring 2005): 51.
32. Ibid., 55.
33. "Song of the Open Road," p. 127 (sec. 2).
34. Reynolds, *Walt Whitman's America*, 112.
35. Ibid., 119.
36. Ibid., 146.
37. Ibid., 119.
38. Ed Folsom, "Scattering It Freely Forever," 140.
39. Karen Sanchez-Eppler, "To Stand Between: Walt Whitman's Poetics of Merger and Embodiment," in *Touching Liberty: Abolition, Feminism, and the Politics of the Body* (Berkeley and Los Angeles: University of California Press, 1993).
40. "First O Songs for a Prelude," *Leaves*, 235–36.
41. M. Wynn Thomas, "Fratricide and Brotherly Love: Whitman and the Civil War," in *The Cambridge Companion to Walt Whitman* (New York: Cambridge University Press, 1995), 28.
42. Sommer, "The Bard of Both Americas," 162.

43. James Perrin Warren, "Reading Whitman's Postwar Poetry" in *The Cambridge Companion to Walt Whitman*, 51.

44. Sommer, "The Bard of Both Americas," 163.

45. John B. Mason, "The Poet-Reader Relationship in 'Song of Myself,'" in *Approaches to Teaching Whitman's Leaves of Grass*, 47.

46. Stanley K. Coffman Jr., "'Crossing Brooklyn Ferry': A Note on the Catalogue Technique in Whitman's Poetry," in *Modern Philology* (May 1954): 226, 227.

47. Rosenblum, "Strange Attractors," 55.

48. "Reconciliation," in *Leaves*, 270.

49. Trethewey, "On Whitman, Civil War Memory, and My South," 53.

50. Ibid., 53.

51. Kateb, "Walt Whitman and the Culture of Democracy," 43.

52. Grossman, "The Poetics of Union in Whitman and Lincoln," 876.

53. Ibid.

54. Barack Obama, "The Audacity of Hope," Democratic National Committee keynote address, Tuesday, July 27, 2004.

55. Ibid.

56. Ibid.

57. Barack Obama, *The Audacity of Hope: Thoughts on Reclaiming the American Dream* (New York: Three Rivers Press, 2006), 247.

58. Ed Folsom, "Appearing in Print: Illustrations of the Self in *Leaves of Grass*," in *The Cambridge Companion to Walt Whitman*, 139.

59. See "Song of Myself," sec. 24. For an engaging account of Whitman's "distinctly phallic sexuality," see David Haven Blake, "Reading Whitman, Growing up Rock 'n' Roll," *Virginia Quarterly Review* 81, no. 2 (Spring 2005): 34–47. While there is much to say about Whitman's sexuality and the eroticism of *Leaves of Grass*, because this essay focuses on the insights Whitman offers for analyzing the presidency of Barack Obama, my discussion of sexuality and union are more implicit than explicit in this essay.

60. While public discussions of Obama's sexual appeal occasionally emerged during the campaign (the YouTube video "I Got a Crush . . . on Obama," for example, was named the biggest Web video of 2007 by *People* magazine, the AP, *Newsweek*, and AOL), the Obama campaign worked to downplay the candidate's sexual appeal to voters. Instead, Obama's eroticism has been defined solely in terms of his marriage to his wife.

61. Remarks of Senator Barack Obama, Iowa Caucus Night, Des Moines, Iowa, January 3, 2008.

62. Barack Obama, "A More Perfect Union," Constitution Center, Philadelphia, Pa., March 18, 2008.

63. Wright had been Obama's pastor for the last twenty years at the Trinity

United Church of Christ on Chicago's South Side. Wright had married Obama and his wife, Michelle, baptized their two daughters, and was credited by Obama for the title of his book *The Audacity of Hope* (see "Obama's Pastor: God Damn America, U.S. to Blame for 9/11," ABC News, March 13, 2008).

64. Of course, in turning to Anzaldúa, I'm not suggesting her work is free of contradictions and pitfalls. As I've discussed elsewhere, Anzaldúa's tendency to invoke epistemic privilege as a queer woman of color leads her toward forms of essentialism that undermine her power as a democratic theorist. For more on this critique of Anzaldúa, see Cristina Beltrán, "Patrolling Borders: Hybrids, Hierarchies and the Challenge of *Mestizaje*," *Political Research Quarterly* 57, no. 4 (2004): 595–607.

65. Barack Obama, *Dreams from My Father: A Story of Race and Inheritance* (New York: Three Rivers Press, 2004), 85.

66. Ibid., 100.

67. Kateb, "Walt Whitman and the Culture of Democracy," 25, 43.

68. Ibid., 26.

69. Gloria Anzaldúa, *Borderlands/La Frontera: The New Mestiza* (San Francisco: Spinsters/Aunt Lute Press, 1987), 194–95.

70. Obama, *Dreams from My Father*, 93.

71. Romand Coles, "TRADITIO: Feminists of Color and the Torn Virtues of Democratic Engagement," *Political Theory* 29, no. 4 (August 2001): 496, 494, 506.

72. Anzaldúa, *Borderlands/La Frontera*, 80.

73. Barack Obama, "A More Perfect Union," Philadelphia Convention Center, Philadelphia, Pa., March 18, 2008.

74. Anzaldúa, *Borderlands/La Frontera*, 79.

75. For more on this aspect of Obama's character, see Obama's discussion of black nationalism and his "uneasy alliance" with Rafiq al Shabazz, president of the Roseland Unity Coalition in Chicago; his depiction of the Afrocentric school counselor Asanta Moran; and his analysis of his Muslim half-brother, Roy (Obongo) Obama, in *Dreams from My Father*, 180, 196, 441–42.

76. Ibid., 282.

77. Simon Critchley, "The American Void," *Harper's Magazine*, November 2008, 17–20.

78. Tellingly, the fact that Wright's later remarks ultimately led Obama to denounce his former pastor and resign his membership from Trinity Church points to the political complexities of the situation.

79. See Lawrie Balfour, "Remembering Obama," The Immanent Frame, http://blogs.ssrc.org/tif/2009/05/21/remembering-obama/.

80. See Mark Leibovich, "Politics, Spectacle and History under Open Sky," *New York Times*, August 28, 2008.

81. See Amanda Melillo, Frank Rosario, and Dan Mangan, "New York Cheers Agent of Change," *New York Post,* November 5, 2008.
82. Barack Obama's Acceptance Speech, Denver, Colo., August 28, 2008.
83. Folsom, "Scattering It Freely Forever," 140.
84. Critchley, "The American Void," 17–20.

CHAPTER 4

Democratic Desire: Walt Whitman

Martha C. Nussbaum

WALT WHITMAN IS A political poet, a poet who holds that poetry has an essential role to play in the life of the American democracy.[1] This is so because the poet knows what it is to see men and women as ends, and to see the boundless and equal worth of each and every one of them:

> He sees eternity in men and women, he does not see men and
>   women as dreams or dots.
>
> For the great Idea, the idea of perfect and free individuals,
> For that, the bard walks in advance, leader of leaders,
> The attitude of him cheers up slaves and horrifies foreign despots.
>   (BO 153–56)

The vision of democracy is in itself, for Whitman, a poetic vision, and citizens are those who "have left all feudal processes and poems behind them, and assumed the poems and processes of Democracy" (BO 185).

For Whitman, the democratic vision is, ultimately, a vision of love. In a poem entitled "Recorders Ages Hence," Whitman tells the future what to say about him: "Publish my name and hang up my picture as that of the tenderest lover / . . . / Who was not proud of his songs, but of the measureless ocean of love within him." But this idea of love is not cozy or bland. It will require a radical reform, he argues, in common religious and secular understandings of love. The poet-speaker considers American ideals of equality and freedom, and concludes:

> Underneath all is the Expression of love for men and women,
> (I swear I have seen enough of mean and impotent modes of
>   expressing love for men and women,
> After this day I take my own modes of expressing love for
>   men and women.) (BO 266–69)

Whitman's "own ways" of expressing love were not congenial to conventional American society. Although the 1855 first edition of *Leaves of Grass* was greeted with much praise, including a remarkable public letter from Emerson, denunciation began at that time and escalated gradually, Emerson himself eventually joining the chorus. The book was called "a mass of stupid filth," a "heterogeneous mass of bombast, egotism, vulgarity, and nonsense," whose author must be "some escaped lunatic, raving in pitiable delirium." Whitman "should be kicked from all decent society as below the level of a brute."[2] In large part, these reactions are addressed to the poems' treatment of sexual and bodily themes. Whitman insistently pursues these themes throughout his career, holding that the appropriate conception of democratic love cannot be articulated without forging a new attitude toward both the body and its sexuality. The poetry of equality must also be erotic, and erotic in a bold and defiant manner. And the erotic must be frankly sexual. What are these connections? What is the new conception of love that Whitman claims to bring to America? And why must this democratic love be erotic, and erotic in a sexual sense?

"I Am He Attesting Sympathy"

Before we can approach these questions, we must understand the context and historical motivation of Whitman's project. The first edition of *Leaves of Grass* was published in 1855, just before the Civil War. Subsequent editions cover the period of the war, the second presidency of Abraham Lincoln, the death of Lincoln, and Reconstruction.[3] The great political theme of this poetry is the overthrow of slavery; the democracy Whitman addresses with love is the preserved Union; and racial hatred is the central problem to which Whitman's new conception of love is addressed. The 1871 epitaph for Lincoln, one of Whitman's simplest and most eloquent statements, leaves no doubt of Whitman's intense feeling on this matter:

> This dust was once the man,
> Gentle, plain, just and resolute, under whose cautious hand,
> Against the foulest crime in history known in any land or age,
> Was saved the Union of these States.

It is because the poet-speaker lacks confidence that conventional forms of religious morality can deal effectively with the question of racial hatred—and other related hatreds and exclusions—that he has concluded that his own mission requires a radically reformulated idea of love, one that cannot be straightforwardly derived from religion. In a remarkable poem of 1855,[4] "Now Lucifer Was Not Dead," the speaker, a black slave, imagines that he must be the dark angel Lucifer, excluded as he is from Heaven, and even from the Earth, by the pious Christians who surround him:

> Now Lucifer was not dead—or if he was, I am his sorrowful terrible heir;
> I have been wrong'd—I am oppress'd—I hate him that oppresses me,
> I will either destroy him, or he shall release me.
>
> Damn him! how he does defile me!
> How he informs against my brother and sister, and takes pay for their blood!
> How he laughs when I look down the bend, after the steamboat that carries away my woman!
>
> Now the vast dusk bulk that is the whale's bulk, it seems mine;
> Warily, sportsman! though I lie so sleepy and sluggish, the tap of my flukes is death.

Inverting traditional metaphors of blackness and whiteness, of God and Devil, hunter and huntsman, Whitman shows the white Christian as an informer, a callous sportsman making a game of human flesh, a defiler of the true dignity of humanity, which in the poem is represented by its darkness. Whiteness becomes a metaphor for brutality, the angelic a metaphor for disdain and contempt of humanity; humanity itself is represented by the metaphors of the dark angel and of the animal, the whale's bulky dusky body. Identifying himself with the hunted dark body, Whitman writes a powerful prophecy of revenge—not as an endorsement of hatred over love, but as a warning cry for justice, an injunction to show real love before it is too late.

Whitman omitted this poem from the last two editions of *Leaves of Grass,* perhaps simply for structural reasons, perhaps feeling that the "charity" of which Lincoln spoke entailed, so many years later, a deemphasizing of anger and revenge.[5] But Lincoln's forgiveness was never without teeth. In the Second Inaugural Address, the famous exhortation to show "malice toward none and charity toward all" is immediately followed by an exhortation to "firmness in the right as God gives us to see the right"—and preceded by a damning criticism of those who imagine that God could ever have sanctioned the cause of slavery: "It may seem strange that any men should ask a just God's assistance in wringing their bread from the sweat of other men's faces."

Whitman, similarly, sets out to create a love that is just and firm in the right, and yet capable of forgiveness and reconciliation. We will be on the right track if we ask at every point in the poetic argument, how does this phrase, this image, bear on the task of creating a new and transfigured America—an America that truly practices equality and inclusion, that is free from the poisonous hatred of the outsider? And also, how does this poetic strategy bear on the more immediate task of binding together an America riven by the waste and horror of a war fought for the most basic and elementary starting point of justice, a war that has destroyed generations of citizens for the sake of establishing what should never have been in question?

> And I saw askant the armies,
> I saw as in noiseless dreams hundreds of battle-flags,
> Borne through the smoke of the battles and pierc'd with missiles I saw them,
> And carried hither and yon through the smoke, and torn and bloody,
> And at last but a few shreds left on the staff, (and all in silence,)
> And the staffs all splinter'd and broken.
>
> I saw battle-corpses, myriads of them,
> And the white skeletons of young men, I saw them,

> I saw the debris and debris of all the slain soldiers of the war . . .
> The living remain'd and suffer'd, the mother suffer'd,
> And the wife and the child and the musing comrade suffer'd,
> And the armies that remain'd suffer'd. ("Lilacs," 171ff.)

It is in this tragic and yet still hopeful context that we should hear the poet's announcement, "I am he attesting sympathy" (SM 22.461). It is a cry for radical social change to move the nation beyond this time of cruelty, guilt, waste, and mourning. We are put on notice that this is not a facile sympathy, but, like Lincoln's, a sympathy with teeth, coupled with a prophetic call to this-worldly justice. Seeing eternity in men and women entails working for a society that treats every one of them as an end, and none as a mere tool for the ends of others.

I have mentioned men and women. And a second great historical development that Whitman witnesses and makes his own is the growing movement for women's equality. Whitman was a contemporary of the early suffragists. He was directly and deeply involved in the women's rights movement, both as journalist and as poet. In his journalism he spoke out against domestic violence and other forms of misogyny. Underlining the link between prurience and puritanism, he criticized the representation of women in pornography; he called for respect for prostitutes and a reform of their living conditions. Nor did he ignore inequalities internal to marriage: well before J. S. Mill's *The Subjection of Women* (1869), Whitman made most of its central arguments, calling for the democratization of marriage and of opportunities and duties within marriage, for new ideas of sexual attractiveness that did not eroticize domination on the one side, submission on the other. And he went further than Mill, advocating equality and mutuality in sexual pleasure itself as a sine qua non of a healthy society. He even advocated premarital sex for women as an avenue toward women's full sexual equality.[6]

Given this journalistic background, it is not surprising that, from the first, women's issues were given a central place in *Leaves of Grass*. In an 1847 draft, he wrote: "I am the poet of women as well as men. / The woman is not less than the man." In the preface to the 1855 edition, he continues in the same vein: "A great poem is . . . for a woman as much as a man and a man as much as a woman." In "Song of Myself," these words become the poetic lines: "I am the poet of the woman the same as the man, / And I say it is as great to be a woman as to be a man, / And I say there is nothing greater than the mother of men" (SM 21.425–57). And although Whitman continued to stress the importance of the woman's role as mother, it was in the context of a radical rethinking of the family structure in which the household would not divide functions by sex and in which there would be a true equality of respect: "The wife, and she is not one jot less than the husband, / The daughter, and she is just as good as the son, / The mother, and she is every bit as much as the father" ("A Song for Occupations," 33–35).

Whitman took issue with some strategies of the women's suffrage movement for he felt that the narrow focus on voting rights would be unlikely to ameliorate problems of misogyny and unequal respect. He believed that women could gain full equality only through a radical change in relations between the sexes. In a prose article, he writes: "To the movement for the eligibility and entrance of woman amid new spheres of business, politics, and the suffrage, the current prurient, conventional treatment of sex is the main formidable obstacle. The rising tide of 'women's rights,' swelling every year advancing farther and farther, recoils from it in dismay."[7] And, in a related fragment: "[O]nly when sex is properly treated, talked, avowed, accepted, will the woman be equal with the man, and pass where the man passes, and meet his words with her words, and his rights with her rights."[8] Among our central tasks will be to uncover his reasons for making these connections.

Finally, there is a political issue that emerges in Whitman's work in a more indirect and yet insistent manner: the issue of homosexual love. Whitman's highly erotic poems about love between males were found controversial in his own time, a time in which, as the historians George Chauncey and Martin Duberman have shown,[9] there was in many respects less intrusive opposition to same-sex activity than we have frequently supposed. Nonetheless, there was opposition, and Whitman suffered greatly from it. It now appears likely, on the basis of new evidence marshaled by the literary historian David Reynolds, that in his youth Whitman was dismissed from a teaching position in Southold, on the eastern end of Long Island, for a suspected sexual relationship with a student or students.[10] Twenty-one years old at the time, he was apparently, as a boarder in the schoolmaster's home, required to share a bed with other males, whether students or sons of the master we do not know. All details of the living arrangements, including the ages of Whitman's possible roommates, are pure conjecture.

At any rate, given Whitman's well-known lack of sexual interest in women and his keen interest in men, rumors began to circulate. They reached a notoriously aggressive local Presbyterian preacher, the Reverend Ralph Smith. (Smith was trained at Princeton University—a fact that would have been meaningful to Whitman, since Princeton, though in the North, made a specialty at this time of training the elite gentlemen of the South, allowing them to bring their slaves with them, as slaves, to its New Jersey campus.)[11] Smith alleged in a sermon that sexual acts had been committed and that Whitman should be punished. Members of the congregation, whipped up into a frenzy of hostility, apparently formed a furious mob, hunted Whitman down where he hid, cowering under a neighbor's mattress ticking, seized him, plastered tar and feathers all over him, and rode him out of town on a rail. Severely injured by the attack, he took a full month to recover.

We have no way of knowing whether there was any truth in the accusations; Whitman's perceived preferences would have sufficed to explain them, even without any other foundation; such assaults have been known to occur, not least in America. What is clear is that the incident was an exceedingly painful one that very likely shaped Whitman's attitudes both toward established religions and toward America's dominant moral views.

In the aftermath of the event, which he carefully shrouded in secrecy, Whitman in later years frequently approached the topic of same-sex relations, writing very passionately and erotically about male-male love—but, at the same time, publicly denying that explicit sexuality was really what he had in mind. John Addington Symonds, finding in the poems of the "Calamus" sequence in *Leaves of Grass* a prophecy of homosexual liberation, wrote to Whitman asking pointedly about their sexual meaning. When Whitman denied any such meaning, calling Symonds's inferences "morbid" and "damnable," Symonds refused to give up and wrote again. At this point, Whitman replied with confusion: perhaps the "Calamus" sequence "means more or less what I thought myself—means different: perhaps I don't know what it all means—perhaps never did know. . . . I maybe do not know all my meanings."[12] This same idea of hidden meanings can be found in a poem in a later edition of the "Calamus" sequence itself, entitled "Here the Frailest Leaves of Me" (1860):

> Here the frailest leaves of me and yet my strongest lasting,
> Here I shade and hide my thoughts, I myself do not expose them,
> And yet they expose me more than all my other poems.

In a related poem near the beginning of the "Calamus" sequence, he darkly hints at the danger his readers incur in following him. Given the suggestive title "Whoever You Are Holding Me Now in Hand" (1860), the poem begins as follows:

> Whoever you are holding me now in hand, . . .
> I give you fair warning before you attempt me further,
> I am not what you supposed, but far different.
>
> Who is he that would become my follower?
> Who would sign himself a candidate for my affections?
>
> The way is suspicious, the result uncertain, perhaps destructive . . .
>
> The whole past theory of your life and all conformity to the lives
>   around you would have to be abandon'd . . . (1–6, 9)

Although the ensuing account makes it plain that the "follower" is a follower of Whitman's poetic vocation, in fact his devoted reader, the erotic imagery continues:

> Here to put your lips upon mine I permit you,
> With the comrade's long-dwelling kiss or the new husband's kiss,
> For I am the new husband and I am the comrade.
>
> Or if you will, thrusting me beneath your clothing,
> Where I may feel the throbs of your heart or rest upon your hip,
> Carry me when you go forth over land or sea . . . (19–24)

Thus the reader, who is for the most part imagined as male (voyaging on the sea, walking in the woods, putting a book on his hip), but who can by turns also become the bride awaiting her "new husband," becomes the recipient of Whitman's intense erotic attentions. I think Whitman's warnings, these suggestions of danger and of hidden painful matter, are far too deliberate for us to take at face value his claim to Symonds that he does not know what he means.

Consider, finally, the remarkable poem about sexual shame that Whitman published in editions of *Leaves of Grass* between 1855 and 1867, "O Hot-Cheek'd and Blushing":

> O hot-cheek'd and blushing! O foolish hectic!
> O for pity's sake, no one must see me now! my clothes were stolen
>   while I was abed,
> Now I am thrust forth, where shall I run?
>
> Pier that I saw dimly last night, when I look'd from the windows!
> Pier out from the main, let me catch myself with you, and stay—I will
>   not chafe you,
> I feel ashamed to go naked about the world.
> I am curious to know where my feet stand and what this is flooding
>   me, childhood or manhood—and the hunger that crosses the
>   bridge between.
>
> The cloth laps a first sweet eating and drinking,
> Laps life-swelling yolks—laps ear of rose-corn, milky and just ripen'd;
> The white teeth stay, and the boss-tooth advances in darkness,
> And liquor is spill'd on lips and bosoms by touching glasses, and the
>   best liquor afterward.

The poem begins with a powerful evocation of primal sexual shame, shame about the body and its naked exposure. The speaker imagines fleeing for shelter to the shadows of a "pier" at nighttime: and the piers of New York were even then, as they are now, associated with homosexual encounters. The speaker associates his flight to the pier with a shame at being seen by the world. But then the poem shifts. Together with the shame there is an insistent sexual curiosity and desire. Indeed, sexual desire is seen as a hunger that bridges the gap between the condition of childhood (the helpless powerlessness of the body) and manhood (adult pleasure). It would appear that knowledge of this hunger might possibly dissipate the childlike panic and the condition of helpless shame. The speaker is standing on unknown ground, flooded with arousal.

In the remarkable final stanza, the speaker now permits himself to map the aspects of himself that the stolen clothes had covered. The clothing itself now becomes erotic, a cloth that not only covers the lap, but also "laps" the body as waves lap at the shore. First, the fabric caresses the sweetness of arousal, "a first sweet eating and drinking." Next, it touches "life-swelling yolks" and "ear of rose-corn, milky and just ripen'd."[13] Although one should not overliteralize these striking erotic images, it is hard not to see them as, inter alia at least, suggestive of penis and testicles. The poet both has these (his clothes cover them) and views them with erotic desire. And as so often in Whitman,[14] the image of male genitalia is followed by an image of fellatio, as the teeth of the poet, the white teeth, open around the "advancing" swelling of a bodily organ.[15] In the poem's conclusion, shame is overcome, and liquid pleasure ensues.

The poem combines homoerotic imagery with an intensity of pleasure in a way that we may associate with the important lines in "Song of Myself," 5, where the poet's mystical vision of the unity of all creation in love is prefaced by a fantasy of erotic oral contact between the poet's body and his soul.[16] Whether it is a commentary on Whitman's unhappy experience must remain uncertain. It is certain, at any rate, that his own experiences of exclusion, shame, and the longing for fulfilled love and pleasure powerfully color Whitman's writing, not only here but also more generally, providing him with ways of understanding other social exclusions and hatreds, and giving him powerful incentives toward the rethinking of society's moral and sexual norms.[17]

A Counter-Cosmos: The Democratic Body

From its beginning, Whitman's poetry announces its intention to subject traditional religion and morality to searching critical scrutiny, by the light of norms of equality, reciprocity, and human freedom. Whitman presents himself as, in a sense, a deeply religious poet, a follower of the life of Christ and a believer in a God who is the source of love. And yet he also arrogates to himself the right to interrogate all traditional systems of religious understanding to see how well they come up to his democratic ideal. What is important in both philosophical and religious teaching is not the authority of the teaching's source, but the quality of the love that is its content. In a poem entitled "The Base of All Metaphysics," Whitman, rather in the manner of Mahler—who, we recall, looked all through world literature including the Bible for his "redeeming word," only to conclude that words of love had to emerge from his own imagination—announces that he has looked all through the major metaphysical texts of his tradition, only to conclude that what really counts is human love, and one's own ability to articulate that love and live it:

> Having studied the new and antique, the Greek and Germanic systems,
> Kant having studied and stated, Fichte and Schelling and Hegel,
> Stated the lore of Plato, and Socrates greater than Plato,
> And greater than Socrates sought and stated, Christ divine having studied long,
> I see reminiscent to-day those Greek and Germanic systems,
> See the philosophies all, Christian churches and tenets see,
> Yet underneath Socrates clearly see, and underneath Christ the divine I see,
> The dear love of man for his comrade, the attraction of friend to friend,
> Of the well-married husband and wife, of children and parents,
> Of city for city and land for land.

Accordingly, Whitman sets out to create his own counter-metaphysical system of love that will express what he sees as religious metaphysics' true basis. Setting himself in the tradition of the cosmological writing of both Greek and Christian philosophy, he attempts to create a democratic counter-cosmos, in which hierarchies of souls are replaced by the democratic body of the United States, which he calls the "greatest poem."[18]

> Walt Whitman, a kosmos, of Manhattan the son,
>   . . . No sentimentalist, no stander above men and women or apart from them,
>   . . . In me the caresser of life wherever moving, backward as well as forward sluing,
> To niches aside and junior bending, not a person or object missing,
> Absorbing all to myself and for this song. (SM 13.232–34)

Here is the new cosmology that Whitman offers us, to stand over against the cosmologies created by philosophical and religious systems: the finite mortal individual, democratic citizen, equal to and among others, who contains the world within himself by virtue of his resourceful imagination and his sympathetic love. "I am he attesting sympathy" (SM 22.461), the poet announces. And "whoever walks a furlong without sympathy walks to his own funeral drest in his shroud" (SM 48.1272). The defects in earthly love are to be overcome not by any established system of belief—for the poet speaks holding "creeds and schools in abeyance" (SM 1.10)—but by the capacity of the individual to extend the circles of sympathy outward to embrace everything in the world with equal love. The poetry itself is democratic, in its freedom of form and line, in its inclusion of slang words such as "sluing" that were usually taken to be inappropriate to the dignity of literature.

Religious sources of love are not scorned in this poetry—"I do not despise you priests" (SM 43.1096), the poet writes; the poet's faith, he continues, is "the greatest of faiths" as well as "the least of faiths" (1097). But on the way to Whitman's America, some remarkable changes have taken place in religion. First of all, as we have already seen in the poem about Plato and Christ, it is deprived of its claims to authority. "Now I re-examine philosophies and religions" (OR 6.83), announces the citizen. His reader is told, "You shall no longer take things at second or third hand, nor look through the eyes of the dead, nor feed on the spectres in books" (SM 2.35). And lest this appear to be the prelude to a new claim to quasi-religious authority, the speaker immediately adds: "You shall not look through my eyes either, nor take things from me, / You shall listen to all sides and filter them from your self" (2.36–37). The agency of democratic love is not, like Dante's will, "upright, pure, and whole" on account of its relation to a religious authority. Its integrity is itself and its own.[19]

Second, religion no longer promises transcendence of our needy mortal condition. God is imagined as immanent in the world and its energy—indeed, in one passage, as an erotic partner of the poet himself.[20] The speaker announces his mortality and hopes for no immortality. He is the poet of life and he is the poet of death. "There will never be any more perfection than there is now, / Nor any more heaven or hell than there is now" (SM 3.42–43). There is just life, renewing itself; and the only continuity for the human being is the continuity of nature and of human civilization. The transcendence it makes sense to strive for is the transcendence of partiality and faction in sympathy, of hierarchy in equal respect, of oppression in citizenship and voting, of hatred in love. Indeed, this is the reason why the poet, not the religious thinker, not the legal thinker, not the economist, is the "equable man,"[21] the model of rational judgment required by a democratic nation: for, as we shall later see, it is in the poetic imagination, far more than in the modes of thought proper to these other professions, that narrow sympathies are transcended.

Third, as we have begun to see from the very beginning, this poetry affirms the body and its sexuality as has no other account of love's ascent that we have examined. Right from the beginning of "Song of Myself," with its daringly erotic depiction of the relationship between the poet and his God, and between his body and his soul, it is plain that the rehabilitation of sex is a central feature of Whitman's counter-cosmology. And I think one of the central questions posed by this poetry, one of the insistent obstacles to its understanding and full reception, still must be: Why is this theme so central? Why does Whitman believe that a new attitude toward sex and the body is involved in the solution to problems of hierarchy and racial hate?

The Reclamation of the Body

Whitman takes on a double task, its two parts closely related: the restoration to human beings of interest in and love for the blood and guts and bones that they are; and the restoration of sexual desire to the center of the account of ethical value. The two tasks are in some obvious ways connected, since sex leads attention to the stuff of the body, and sexual interest will become furtive and tinged with shame and disgust if that stuff is the object of disgust. By contrast, the idea that blood and guts are the scene of a great wonder and mystery, closely connected to the most valuable sort of sympathy and love, itself infuses sexuality with beauty.

Taking on this twofold task—above all in the poems that comprise the volume *Children of Adam*—Whitman represents himself as Adam before the Fall, and beckons to his reader, in language of noble simplicity, to join him in acceptance and delight:

> As Adam early in the morning,
> Walking forth from the bower refresh'd with sleep,

> Behold me where I pass, hear my voice, approach,
> Touch me, touch the palm of your hand to my body as I pass,
> Be not afraid of my body.

Notice that it does not matter whether the reader is male or female, or, indeed, whether the reader's caress is or is not specifically sexual. What stands at the center of the stage is loving acceptance of the flesh, and the innocence of the flesh.[22] In Eden there is no shame at any part of the body, no fear of its touch. In that innocence no pleasure of the flesh is marked off as specially problematic; none is a sphere of moral guilt or suspicion more than any other. The poem connects this absence of shame, obscurely, with an open acceptance of Adam's personhood. There is something about Adam's attitude toward his body that will make it possible for the reader, if he or she shares it, to walk right up to him and look him in the eye. This looking in the eye, which Whitman connects with the absence of the bodily shame of "O Hot-Cheek'd and Blushing," is seen by him as a crucial element in democratic inclusiveness, which cannot, he suggests, be built on disgust and self-concealment. "Was it doubted," the poet asks, "that those who corrupt their bodies conceal themselves?" (BE 1.5). By "corrupt their bodies," he means, however, not what conventional morality means—by "corrupt" he means "refuse to honor and respect."[23]

The central text of Whitman's counter-cosmology of the body is the remarkable poem "I Sing the Body Electric," in which the poet affirms the Aristotelian view that the body is the soul, coupling it with the view that the body is itself a poem and the theme of poems. Since what is remarkable about this counter-poem can only be seen in its unlikely detail, its bulky comic incongruities, its thrusting into verse of the most apparently prosaic, we need to have before us a substantial portion of its final section:

> O my body! I dare not desert the likes of you in other men and
>   women, nor the likes of the parts of you,
> I believe the likes of you are to stand or fall with the likes of the soul,
>   (and that they are the soul,)
> I believe the likes of you shall stand or fall with my poems, and that
>   they are my poems,
> Man's, woman's, child's, youth's, wife's, husband's, mother's, father's,
>   young man's, young woman's poems,

> Head, neck, hair, ears, drop and tympan of the ears,
> Eyes, eye-fringes, iris of the eye, eyebrows, and the waking or
>   sleeping of the lids,
> Mouth, tongue, lips, teeth, roof of the mouth, jaws, and the
>   jaw-hinges, . . .
> Strong set of thighs, well carrying the trunk above,
> Leg-fibres, knee, knee-pan, upper-leg, under-leg, . . .
> The lung-sponges, the stomach-sac, the bowels sweet and clean,
> The brain in its folds inside the skull-frame, . . .
> The voice, articulation, language, whispering, shouting aloud,
> Food, drink, pulse, digestion, sweat, sleep, walking, swimming,
> Poise on the hips, leaping, reclining, embracing, arm-curving and
>   tightening,
> The continual changes of the flex of the mouth, and around the eyes,
> The skin, the sunburnt shade, freckles, hair,
> The curious sympathy one feels when feeling with the hand the
>   naked meat of the body, . . .
> The thin red jellies within you or within me, the bones and the
>   marrow in the bones,
> The exquisite realization of health;
> O I say these are not the parts and poems of the body only, but of
>   the soul,
> O I say now these are the soul! (BE 9.129-35, 144-45, 153-58, 161-64)

This unlikely and irregular cosmology, this cosmology of our finitude and imperfection,[24] is Whitman's replacement for Plato's world of transcendent forms, for the Christian cosmology of Hell, Purgatory, and Heaven. Traditional metaphysicians, he suggests, do not know "the curious sympathy one feels when feeling with the hand the naked meat of the body"; or, if they do, they have aggressively eliminated it from their accounts of human love. And they hasten, too, in their different ways, to disengage their art from the sense of bodily weight conveyed in this bulky line, with its awkward human grace. All have disengaged themselves from the comic clumsy joyful enumeration of the parts of which poets and other citizens are made. But, says Whitman, this means that they avoid the soul. For all our acts are bodily acts, and all our art is naked meat, and all our sympathy is blood.

Particularly striking is the poem's thoroughgoing opposition to both shame and disgust. This body, the poet-speaker's own, has no urge to cover itself. It stands forth confidently as what it is. And it gazes at the bodies of other men and women with interest and joy. Parts of the body that are typically found disgusting, and that certainly do not figure as objects of praise in lyric poetry, are now seen as beautiful. Bowels, lungs, stomach, brain, "thin red jellies," all are parts of human health, to be admired along with flowing hair and muscular thighs. In the soft and organic, the poem discovers an "electric" vitality and dynamism.[25]

The political significance of this recuperation of the body is, Whitman claims, vast. For the body is the evident basis of human equality: "Have you ever loved the body of a woman? / Have you ever loved the body of a man? / Do you not see that these are exactly the same to all in all nations and times all over the earth?" (BE 8.121–23). This question, placed immediately after the narrative of a slave auction, comments upon it: for what the poet sees is not the auction of a slave, it is "a woman's body at auction" (118). And that is the crime of it, since all bodies are equally worthy of respect. Focusing on the body, we reveal ourselves to ourselves as equally needy and finite and mortal, and also equally noble and beautiful; we find a foundation for both equal support and equal respect and love. We then understand the ugliness and irrationality of treating some bodies as mere meat and others as spirits. We see that slave and free, laborer and manager, immigrant and native, rich and poor, "Each has his or her place in the procession" (BE 6.88).[26] Very much in the manner of Rousseau in *Émile*, Whitman connects a perception of common bodily humanity and vulnerability with the genesis of a highly critical and morally aggressive sympathy: thinking our humanity means realizing that hierarchies of power that subordinate some groups and treat them as mere things are artificial and indefensible.

And when we take as the focus of our love and sympathy not only the body but also its sexual organs, we will derive one further critical insight: we will see, Whitman argues, that the woman is of equal dignity and importance as the man. Misogyny, he repeatedly insists, derives from a disgust with our sexual organs and acts, the corollary to which is the evident desire to blame someone for inciting those acts. The female body has been seen as impure and unclean, the origin of our sinfulness. But when we think as Whitman urges, we no longer see the woman as flesh and the man as spirit, we come to see both as complementary agents in a democratic process, both spirit and body. "The male is not less the soul nor more, he too is in his place, / . . . / The man's body is sacred and the woman's body is sacred" (BE 6.75, 83).

Caressing Death

But what has this rehabilitation of the body to do with erotic love and desire? We might so far see Whitman's project as, in effect, one of returning us to Eden before the Fall, to a state in which (at least as Augustine imagines it) our bodies were indeed pure and holy, including their sexual organs and acts—but only because these acts were imagined to be free from desire, pleasure, and erotic longing; they were undertaken at the direction of the will for the purposes of reproduction. Whitman evidently does not seek to return us to Eden: he persistently represents his transfigured America as one that accepts, indeed is built on, passionate erotic desire as well as bodily health, one in which our deepest spiritual experiences are erotic, where sexual fulfillment is both among the deepest experiences and a model for others. We therefore now must ask: What does desire have to do with democracy, with racial equality, with the equality of men and women?

We may begin answering our question by returning to the initial reception of *Leaves of Grass*. Whitman's public was sorely divided about the merit of his more erotic poems. They were in agreement, however, about one thing: If Whitman was really speaking about sexual passion, his poems were vile. Thus the defenders against the charge of filth proceeded by denying the poems' erotic content: "I extract no poison from these leaves," wrote one Fanny Fern, contrasting Whitman's poems with popular romances in which "the asp of sensuality lies coiled amid rhetorical flowers." Edward Everett Hale, praising the book's "freshness and simplicity," insisted that "there is not a word in it meant to attract readers by its grossness."[27] What is striking about these reviews is their total inability to talk about deep sexual longing other than in the language of corruption, poison, and filth. These Americans all seem to be in the grip of a profound disgust-misogyny and misanthropy, linked to an aggressive shame about the fact of desire. Apparently all will be well if sex is regarded as merely a set of clean body parts in motion. It is the desire in it that is deeply threatening, that is seen as tinged with the disgust of decay. It is the art in the complex poetry of it that would be a snake coiled in the Garden. The reviews reveal an America in which prurience and puritanism live side by side and take their nourishment from one another.

Both prurience and puritanism are nourished, it appears, by an urgent desire for total control. What seems intolerable is the deep exposure of self to other in real passion. What seems acceptable is a cleaned-up and superficial sex in which nobody looks very deeply into anyone else. Whitman's task, then, is not simply to get his audience to accept clean bodily parts. It is the far more difficult task of getting them to accept real longing. Let us now examine a pivotal sequence in "Song of Myself," in which Whitman begins to make his case for the relationship between democracy and a more profound eroticism.

Immediately after a section in which the poet's body, talking to his soul, concludes that the cement of the universe is love, we find the following sequence:[28]

> A child said *What is the grass?* fetching it to me with full hands;
> How could I answer the child? I do not know what it is any more than he.
>
> I guess it must be the flag of my disposition, out of hopeful green
>   stuff woven.
>
> Or I guess it is the handkerchief of the Lord,
> A scented gift and remembrancer designedly dropt,
> Bearing the owner's name someway in the corners, that we may see
>   and remark, and say *Whose?*
> Or I guess the grass is itself a child, the produced babe of the
>   vegetation.
>
> Or I guess it is a uniform hieroglyphic,
> And it means, Sprouting alike in broad zones and narrow zones,
> Growing among black folks as among white,
> Kanuck, Tuckahoe, Congressman, Cuff, I give them the same, I
>   receive them the same.
>
> And now it seems to me the beautiful uncut hair of graves.
>
> Tenderly will I use you curling grass,

> It may be you transpire from the breasts of young men,
> It may be if I had known them I would have loved them,
> It may be you are from old people, or from offspring taken soon out
>   of their mothers' laps,
> And here you are the mothers' laps.
>
> This grass is very dark to be from the white heads of old mothers,
> Darker than the colorless beards of old men,
> Dark to come from under the faint red roofs of mouths.
> O I perceive after all so many uttering tongues,
> And I perceive they do not come from the roofs of mouths for
>   nothing. (SM 6.99–120)

The poet looks at a simple natural object, which a literal-minded scientific physiologist would describe in literal terms: some blades of grass. His imagination, however, sees so many other and further shapes in the blades of grass before him: images of hope, of divinity, of human equality. We are reminded that the vision of human equality is just that, a vision, an imagining, a seeing of something in something. As we go around the world, we see what is before us—but also, insofar as we are at all human, so much that is not straightforwardly before us. Shapes in motion do not by themselves announce their meaning. It is only through the generous work of the imagination that we people the world around us with life, going beyond what is straightforwardly present in perception to suppose the presence of life and growth in the grass, of thought, feeling, and dignity in our fellow citizens. This exercise of imagination is already itself erotic—a reaching into the inside of a thing beneath its perceived surface, an insertion of oneself into the thing to explore its hidden recesses. Whitman shortly makes this eroticism explicit, caressing tenderly, in fancy, the bodies of the soldiers dead in the war, the lost children. If we refuse this probing, he suggests, we doom ourselves to the surfaces of things, to seeing nature, and one another, merely as a set of shapes in motion. This objectlike vision of people he connects with slavery, mentioning the topic of race for the first time in the poem. To think the equality of black and white is to cast aside the idea that a human being can be a mere object, an "animate tool," as Aristotle defined the slave. It is to think, instead, that the black person has an inner world and a depth; it is to probe into this depth. But this thinking requires the poetic imagination; and this imagination, he now suggests, involves a form of erotic touching.

In the lines that follow the mention of democratic equality, the poet's imagination reaches deeper still, into the mystery of our mortality itself, the "beautiful uncut hair of graves." In the link between eroticism and the mystery of death, he finds a very basic ingredient of democratic citizenship—for it is not so much in the shape and configuration of our bodies that we stand before one another as equal. Nor is it only in the dignity of our living acts. It is, as well, in our darkness, in the faint redness of our mouths, in the fact that we will be buried in the earth and give nourishment to the grass that comes after us.

Shortly after the section that answers the child's questions about the grass, we find the poem's first extended discussion of slavery. A runaway slave comes to the poet's house and stops outside. He hears "his motions crackling the twigs of the woodpile." The poet comes out and sits with him on a log; finding him weak and injured, he fills a tub "for his sweated body and bruis'd feet"—a clear reference to Christ's humility and service. He gives him a room "that enter'd from my own"—indicating thereby that he has no hesitation about bodily proximity in the night. He gives him clothes, puts plasters on the sores on his neck and ankles. The slave stays with the poet for a week before he goes farther north. "I had him sit next me at table," the poet concludes, "my fire-lock lean'd in the corner." We see equality, but feel, as well, the external menace and pressure of hate.

We might now expect a general philosophical rumination on racial equality and the hatred of the black man. We do find it, but in an extraordinary form. The next section of the poem is called by Whitman a "parable," drawing attention to its importance and its religious significance. But it is a parable that would not be found in the sermons of conventional religion.

> Twenty-eight young men bathe by the shore,
> Twenty-eight young men and all so friendly;
> Twenty-eight years of womanly life and all so lonesome.
>
> She owns the fine house by the rise of the bank,
> She hides handsome and richly drest aft the blinds of the window.

> Which of the young men does she like the best?
> Ah the homeliest of them is beautiful to her.
>
> Where are you off to, lady? for I see you,
> You splash in the water there, yet stay stock still in your room.
>
> Dancing and laughing along the beach came the twenty-ninth bather,
> The rest did not see her, but she saw them and loved them.
>
> The beards of the young men glisten'd with wet, it ran from their
>   long hair,
> Little streams pass'd all over their bodies.
>
> An unseen hand also pass'd over their bodies,
> It descended tremblingly from their temples and ribs.
>
> The young men float on their backs, their white bellies bulge to the
>   sun, they do not ask who seizes fast to them,
> They do not know who puffs and declines with pendant and bending
>   arch,
> They do not think whom they souse with spray. (SM 11)

These lines depict female sexual longing, and the exclusion of the female, by morality and custom, from full sexual fulfillment, and from public recognition as a sexual being. They link this exclusion with the confinement of the female to the domestic, rather than the public, sphere. The placement of the section, and Whitman's announcement that it is a parable, invite us to link it to the story of the slave that has preceded it, seeing the woman as a figure for the excluded black man, who must also hide his desire from the white world, who also runs the risk of being seen as a metaphor for the feared intrusion of the sexual. But there is another excluded party who also hides behind the curtains. In the depiction of the woman's imagined sexual act, linked, as it is, to other oral-receptive imagery in other poems about the allure of the male body, Whitman also refers to the exclusion of the male homosexual, whose desire for the bodies of young men must be concealed even more than female desire must be. The easy joy of these young men depends on their not knowing who is watching them with sexual longing;

and this is true of the situation of the homosexual male in society at least as much as it is of the black man gazing erotically at the white woman, or the female gazing erotically at the male. As he says in "Calamus": "Here I shade and hide my thoughts, I myself do not expose them, / And yet they expose me." The woman, then, is also the poet, caressing in fancy bodies that in real life shun his gaze.

The woman's gaze, like the gaze of the poet's imagination in the earlier section, is tenderly erotic, caressing the bodies in ways that expose their naked vulnerability, their soft bellies turned upward to the sun. And she caresses something more at the same time. The number twenty-eight signifies the days of the lunar month and also of the female menstrual cycle. The female body, in whose rhythms Whitman sees the rhythms of nature itself, is immersed in finitude and temporality in a manner from which the male body and mind at times recoils. (Havelock Ellis, writing eloquently about this passage, cites the elder Pliny's remark that "nothing in nature is more monstrous and disgusting than a woman's menstrual fluid.") In caressing the twenty-eight men, the woman caresses her own temporality and mortality, and at the same time sees it in them, approaches and makes love to it in them.

Why must the woman's gaze be hidden? And why, we still need to know, is the woman an appropriate figure for the black man, as well as for the male who desires men? We now must talk about gazing in America. In the South, in Whitman's time and later, there were certain offenses that could be committed with the eyes. Taking their cue, perhaps, from the biblical idea that to look at a woman with lust is already to commit a sin, white men in the Jim Crow South prosecuted black men for gazing with desire at a white woman. This crime was colloquially known as "reckless eyeballing,"[29] and it resulted in at least some prosecutions. In 1951, in Yanceyville, North Carolina, a black man named Mark Ingraham was prosecuted for assault with intent to rape for looking at a seventeen-year-old white girl in a "leering manner." The prosecution claimed that he "undressed this lovely little lady with his eyes." Thurgood Marshall sardonically characterized the so-called crime as "highway looking and attempting to want."[30] In 1953, in Atmore, Alabama, a black man named McQuirter was convicted of the same crime, apparently after simply walking too close to a white woman. The state court of appeals held that racial factors might be considered in assessing the defendant's state of mind.[31]

Beyond the impact of such convictions on individual lives, such uses of the criminal law set the tone for "a stigmatizing code of conduct"[32] for black men, which made mandatory downcast eyes, and a shame-filled concealment of desire.[33] Black men must wear their bodies with shame rather than with pride, in effect becoming a walking metaphor for the shamefulness of sexuality. For despite the lowered gaze, the black man by his very presence was, and frequently is, taken to be a threatening emblem of sexuality, emanating from a fictive Africa that has typically been represented by white America as a wild place of unfettered eroticism.[34] Whitman understands that the black man is hated and feared in part because he is seen as an image of sexual longing and of the depth and power of the sexual; his gaze is itself, therefore, a contamination. And refusal of his sexuality is a central way of refusing him full equality.

Let us now consider the desiring gaze of a woman. Had the young men seen the twenty-ninth bather, we may conjecture that they would have scattered in shame and confusion. In Whitman's world, and surely not only there, the female was not supposed to look with desire, any more than was the black man; there was felt to be something monstrous, threatening, defiling, in the assertive and aggressive sexuality of a woman, something that threatened to sully the simple clear world of male control. (Recall Mr. Lockwood, in whom the gaze of desire prompted both fear and cruelty.) For Rousseau, human women (unlike the females of all animal species) have "unlimited desires"—and therefore must learn shame as a "brake," lest desire lead to disorder. "If woman is made to please and to be subjugated, she ought to make herself agreeable to man instead of arousing him."[35] Her modest concealment of desire was thus a crucial part of social order. Out of a related fear of disorder, Thomas Jefferson insisted that full citizenship for women was impossible, because they simply could not mingle freely with men: "Were our state a pure democracy, there would still be excluded from our deliberations women, who, to prevent depravation of morals and ambiguity of issue, should not mix promiscuously in gatherings of men."[36] Denial of erotic agency and relegation to a sphere ruled by patriarchal power go hand in hand. Whitman, we sense, has identified an issue deeply lodged in America's founding conceptions of the citizen.

Let us consider, finally, the gaze of the homosexual. In the recent extremely fraught discussions of the admission of openly homosexual soldiers to the U.S. Army, the central issue, which keeps on surfacing, is not that of forced sexual conduct or even of sexual harassment: for all agree that those are practices that should be forbidden no matter who engages in them. Nor, given recent scandals about the ubiquitous harassment of women in the armed services, do people argue that male-male harassment would be a greater problem. The central issue is, once again, the gaze. The scenario that is most feared is, once again, that of being seen naked in the shower by someone who desires or might possibly desire you—when you are aware of that possible desire and it does not hide behind the curtains. The desiring gaze of the open homosexual is at present the central reason advanced for denying these would-be soldiers jobs for which they are in other respects acknowledged to be qualified.

Whitman is on to something deep, then, when he focuses on the relationship between exclusion and erotic gazing, and when he links this issue of the gaze to all three of the forms of exclusion that preoccupy him. What is this something? Whitman suggests that the willingness to be seen by desire entails a willingness to agree to one's own mortality and temporality, to be part of the self-renewing and onward flowing currents of nature. It is because it touches us in our mortality that sex is deep and a source of great beauty. In the final poem of *Leaves*, he imagines embracing a male comrade, and says, "Decease called me forth." The deep flaw in Whitman's America, then, the flaw that for him lies at the heart of hatreds and exclusions, is a horror of one's own softness and mortality, of the belly exposed to the sun; the gaze of desire touches that, and is for that reason to be repelled. Over against this flawed America, Whitman sets the America of the poet's imagination, healed of self-avoidance, fear, and cruelty, and therefore able truly to pursue liberty and equality.

Whitman's rehabilitation of sex does not involve, as his critics frequently allege, an endorsement of "free love," a casual and promiscuous approach to sex. On the contrary, both in his prose writings and in his poems, he is a stern moralist, inveighing against promiscuity and the commercialization of sex, and especially against the treatment of persons as objects in pornography, which he views as highly subversive to democratic goals and processes. But, very much like D. H. Lawrence, he sees the prurient attitude toward sex expressed in pornography, and the commercialization of sex represented in the sex industry, not as inevitable features of erotic desire, but rather as features of the puritanical refusal of desire, of a piece with America's horror at the truly erotic gaze. Whitman persistently links these forms of false relation to persons with other American deformations, especially with an exploitative attitude toward nature, which cannot be seen in its awesome continuity of death and life by one who refuses his own mortality. Linking the poet's love of nature with the acknowledgment of the humanity of the sexual female, Whitman addresses these lines in 1860 to a common prostitute: "Not till the sun excludes you do I exclude you, / Not till the waters refuse to glisten for you and the leaves to rustle for you, do my words refuse to glisten and rustle for you."

Where, in all this, is the poet? In answering the child's questions, Whitman has depicted the poet as the one whose imagination does not shrink from caressing reality—including the reality of death and decay. In now depicting the poet as a being in hiding, whose fantasies must lurk behind the curtains, he connects American puritanism and prurience, in turn, with American philistinism, the refusal of the erotic imagination of the poet. The best way to defeat the power and depth of sex is to render it superficial, commercial, and unpoetic; the best way to defeat the gaze of the female is to pretend that she is just a thing to be bought and sold, like the slave at auction. But the poet threatens these structures of denial, and is for that reason a being to be feared and shunned. It is precisely for this reason that the poet is required as the public voice of democracy. "He judges not as the judge judges, but as the sun falling round a helpless thing"—seeing its every nook and crevice, seeing its helplessness sharply but with the illumination of love.

Mourning the Sun

The ascent of love enacted in this work, like several others we have examined, links the overcoming of hatred with the attainment of an inclusive and impartial love, and both of these with an overcoming of an excessive fear of one's own softness and neediness. In the process of attaining these goals, Whitman, very much like Mahler, has insisted on the power of compassion to bind a community together, and insisted, too, on the importance of democratic equality and reciprocity to the successful reform of love. Like Mahler, he insists that the love that can accomplish these goals must be erotic and must view its own this-worldly striving as an end in itself. Both, though in their own way religious, reject conventional religion in favor of a more personal spirituality that lays great stress on the role of the artist's imagination. While Whitman's poetic execution of this project is in many respects more uneven than Mahler's musical execution, in Whitman there is at the same time, obviously, a greater concreteness of relation to the particular hatreds and vices of a real social world. Anger at the very conditions of human life—and at humans who symbolize those conditions—is replaced by anger against injustice and social hierarchy.

It seems plausible to think that Whitman's cosmos has solved the problems that motivated love's ascent while retaining an inclusive compassion, while creating a plausible picture of democratic reciprocity, and while embracing every distinct individual with delight.

There remain, however, several problems with this new cosmos. First, there are flaws of execution. Whitman's poetry is highly uneven, veering from the extraordinary to the embarrassing. Sometimes the all-encompassing presence of the poet figure seems to defeat the project: for he seems so omnipresent, so sure of himself, so all-inclusive, that the realities of need and pain about which he speaks vanish from view. We receive at many moments an impression of self-sufficient and rather complacent egoism, and this certainly subverts the poetic design. Especially problematic are many passages dealing with women and with heterosexual love. Not surprisingly, we find here a forced bravado, an aggressive phallic muscularity, that seems entirely at odds with the poetry's deeper purposes. It seems like what it is, a form of self-concealment; and self-concealment is precisely what this poetry regards as the core political sin. Take, for example, this passage, in "A Woman Waits for Me," perhaps the most embarrassingly bad of all of Whitman's poems, in which the poet imagines himself making love to all the women of America:

> It is I, you women, I make my way,
> I am stern, acrid, large, undissuadable, but I love you,
> I do not hurt you any more than is necessary for you,
> I pour the stuff to start sons and daughters fit for these States, I
>   press with slow rude muscle,
> I brace myself effectually, I listen to no entreaties,
> I dare not withdraw till I deposit what has so long accumulated
>   within me.[37]

These are words of someone who does not want to be seen into; and this is a person who, insofar as he takes that stance, cannot see well the equality of others.

This flaw of execution seems, then, a deep one, connected with avoidance of a vulnerability in the poet himself. Another problem lies even closer to the core of the project. This is the grand sweep of the poetry, its refusal of the messiness of everyday life, even while it is precisely everyday life that it claims to be loving. The emphasis on mystical erotic experiences of fusion and oneness are a large part of this problem. For bodies just don't fuse. Elbows and knees, and even the genital organs to which Whitman attaches so much importance, tend to get in the way. As Lawrence wrote of Whitman:[38]

> Even if you reach the state of infinity, you can't sit down there. You just physically can't. You either have to strain still further into universality and become vaporish, or slimy: or you have to hold your toes and sit tight and practice Nirvana; or you have to come back to common dimensions, eat your pudding and blow your nose and be just yourself; or die and have done with it. . . . [E]ven at his maximum a man is not more than himself. When he is infinite he is still himself. He still has a nose to wipe. (846)

Lawrence is a little unfair, for Whitman speaks of caressing far more often than of fusing, of feeling the surface of the body far more than of merging with it. He is, in fact, frequently very preoccupied with the body's separateness and the obstacles it poses to unity; and in many passages he treats that separateness as a source of joy, rather than as a falling off from the sublime state. But there is something right in Lawrence's criticism. For Whitman does indeed often grandly shun the messiness of the everyday, in favor of a highly romantic account of American life that may in some respects serve to alienate us from our daily lives and bodies. One symptom of this is the utter lack of humor in the poetry; another is the sense we often have that aggressive athletic energy is being deployed to pick up things from where they are and put them on a map of the cosmos.

Finally, there is a complex problem at the very heart of Whitman's project. For his mission is, as I have suggested, to show the way to an acceptance of mortality, finitude, and loss, to enable us to mourn and therefore adequately to love. But that effort is to at least some extent compromised by his constant emphasis on the mysterious unity of all things in nature, the continuity and therefore immortality of all life. Frequently Whitman suggests that this continuity, somewhat mystically experienced, negates the finality of death: "I know I am deathless, / I know . . . I shall not pass like a child's carlacue[39] cut with a burnt stick at night" (SM 20.406–8).

But to teach that death is not really a loss, or not really death, is to undercut the entire attitude toward eroticism and loss that the poetry, at its finest, has been promoting. This problem goes deep, I think; for Whitman is increasingly enamored of mystical views of oneness derived from Indian philosophy; and he does not seem to grasp how much at odds these ideas are with his project of teaching America and Americans to accept death. We should not say that this causes his erotic project to fail; but it does create an air of confusion that periodically mars its expression. It means, among other things, that the individual does not have his or her full weight as an object of love in this poetry, or, what comes to the same thing, as an object of grief and mourning. All individuals are seen as curiously continuous with one another.

This confusion does not run straight through the work. Let us consider, by contrast, a moment when Whitman leaves his dalliance with the obscure metaphysics of unity and shows what the finitude of a human being really is, and what the mourning for the finite individual really is. Lincoln is the only truly individual object of love in Whitman's poetry, and his death inspired Whitman to express the tragedy of death and longing as nowhere else in the work. "When Lilacs Last in the Dooryard Bloom'd," the remarkable elegy on Lincoln's death, depicts the procession of Lincoln's coffin through the cities and towns of America. The poet imagines the grief of all who see it pass by, and mourn as for someone utterly irreplaceable. The whole of the nation is tinged with death. He now asks himself what he can give his dead president, to adorn the walls of his burial chamber. He answers that it must be pictures of the land they both love, pictures made in his poetic words.

> Lo, body and soul—this land,
> My own Manhattan with spires, and the sparkling and hurrying tides, and the ships,
> The varied and ample land, the South and the North in the light, Ohio's shore and flashing Missouri,
> And ever the far-spreading prairies covered with grass and corn.
>
> Lo, the most excellent sun so calm and haughty,

> The violet and purple morn with just-felt breezes,
> The gentle soft-born measureless light,
> The miracle spreading bathing all, the fulfill'd noon,
> The coming eve delicious, the welcome night and the stars,
> Over my cities shining all, enveloping man and land.

We see the beauty of the land under the form of mortality, with the sharper sense of splendor, with the shiver down the spine, that signals the nearness of death. The poet gives his president the land they both loved—and, also, this very poem of the land, a poem of the way the nation is seen by someone who knows about his own end. Air, light, and words, hanging on the walls of a tomb.

In these lines, as in the poem's larger picture of the nation mourning its leader, we see the vision of a transfigured America, an America grown up to adulthood, no longer making infantile claims to self-sufficiency and immortality, this nation that so much likes to believe that it can have and do anything without cost. The poet gives his dead president a portrait of the nation from the point of view of a citizen of this transfigured democracy, a place of truly free and equal individuals, where all, capable of mourning, can let go of hate and disgust, and pursue a truly inclusive love.

Isn't there still, one might ask, a characteristic American optimism in these proceedings? Whitman, even in the process of acknowledging tragedy, has performed a characteristically American conjuring trick, turning tragedy into good news, mortality into a hope of justice. Death is not just the horror of death, it is also an opportunity for social progress. We don't defeat death, but in assuming a more honest relationship to it we enable ourselves to live better with one another. To this question or charge one can only reply, yes, it is so. Does this determination to turn bad news into good show that Whitman in particular, and America in general, lacks a full-fledged sense of tragedy?[40] If a full-fledged sense of tragedy entails giving up the hope that things can become better in this world, the answer to this question must be yes. But why should we accept this account of tragedy? For a confrontation with the reality of our condition should be just that, a confrontation with reality. And the reality was and is that there is both bad news and good news: things are in many ways bad, but they do get better sometimes, when people fight for justice. The situation of African Americans and of women

Democratic Desire

has changed greatly since 1855. The situation of homosexuals has changed, though somewhat less greatly. Whitman's poetry, with its sui generis combination of tragedy and optimism, has played its part in inspiring those who were working for all of these changes. One need not have the unrealistic fantasy that America could ever lack hate and disgust completely, in order to join Whitman in the project of pushing it back a little, day by day.

In one way, resignation without optimism would be far easier. To recognize that change is possible is, for Whitman, to assume the burden of working for change the whole of one's life. In that way, as he sees it, the recognition of mortality has as its natural corollary a redoubled attention to our duties in the world:

> I dare not shirk any part of myself,
> Not any part of America good or bad,
> Not to build for that which builds for mankind,
> Not to balance ranks, complexions, creeds, and the sexes, . . .
>
> I will not be outfaced by irrational things,
> I will penetrate what it is in them that is sarcastic upon me, . . .
> I will make cities and civilizations defer to me,
> This is what I have learnt from America—it is the amount, and it I
>   teach again. (BO 17.282–85, 292–96)

In other words, realizing that we cannot make ourselves or our nation immortal, we can, and must, try for the available goal of making it equal and free.

Postscript

During the very hour on May 20, 1996, during which this essay was being presented publicly for the first time,[41] as a Weidenfeld Lecture at Oxford University, the U.S. Supreme Court announced its decision in *Romer v. Evans,* declaring unconstitutional a Colorado law, Amendment 2, that denied local communities the right to pass nondiscrimination laws protecting the rights of gays, lesbians, and bisexuals. I quote from Justice Kennedy's majority opinion, in which one may possibly discern Whitman's spirit:

> We find nothing special in the protections Amendment 2 withholds. These

are protections taken for granted by most people either because they already have them or do not need them; these are protections against exclusion from an almost limitless number of transactions and endeavors that constitute ordinary civic life in a free society. . . . It is not within our constitutional tradition to enact laws of this sort. Central both to the idea of the rule of law and to our own Constitution's guarantee of equal protection is the principle that government and each of its parts remain open on impartial terms to all who seek its assistance. "Equal protection of the laws is not achieved through indiscriminate imposition of inequalities." . . . A law declaring that in general it shall be more difficult for one group of citizens than for all others to seek aid from the government is itself a denial of equal protection of the laws in the most literal sense.

Or, as Whitman puts it—and we read these lines aloud later, to mark the occasion and honor the poet:

> Whoever degrades another degrades me,
> And whatever is done or said returns at last to me. . . .
> I speak the pass-word primeval, I give the sign of democracy,
> By God! I will accept nothing which all cannot have their counterpart
>   of on the same terms. . . .
>
> For the great Idea, the idea of perfect and free individuals,
> For that, the bard walks in advance, leader of leaders,
> The attitude of him cheers up slaves and horrifies foreign despots.
>
> Without extinction is Liberty, without retrograde is Equality,
> They live in the feelings of . . . men and . . . women. (SM 24.503–4,
>   506–7; BO 10.154–58)

Notes

Originally published as Martha C. Nussbaum, "Democratic Desire: Walt Whitman," in *Upheavals of Thought: The Intelligence of the Emotions* (New York and Cambridge: Cambridge University Press, 2001), 645–78. Reprinted with the permission of Cambridge University Press.

1. All citations to Whitman's poetry are to the Norton Critical Edition: Walt Whitman, *Leaves of Grass* (New York: Norton, 1973). I use the following abbrevia-

tions: "SM" for *Song of Myself,* "BO" for "By Blue Ontario's Shore," and "BE" for "I Sing the Body Electric."

2. See D. S. Reynolds, *Walt Whitman's America* (New York: Knopf, 1995), 346.

3. See the Norton Critical Edition, xxvii–lv. The first edition of *Leaves of Grass* (LG) of 1855 contained "Song of Myself" and eleven other poems. The 1856 edition added twenty more poems and gave them all titles. The 1860 third edition brought the total number of poems to 156. *Drum-Taps* was published separately in 1865, and a *Sequel* in 1865–66. The fourth edition of *Leaves of Grass* (1867) included 236 poems, incorporating the separately published items. An edition of 1871 contained only nine new poems, and an 1876 edition only a few. The edition of 1881 gave the work its final arrangement, and the "deathbed" edition of 1891–92, the final authorized text, added a few more poems, keeping the structure intact. A number of Whitman's published poems were excluded from *Leaves of Grass,* and some that found a place in earlier editions are not in the final edition. Other uncollected poems and manuscript fragments are also gathered in the Norton edition, with a detailed discussion of their history.

4. This poem appeared in the first edition of *Leaves of Grass,* and in subsequent editions until 1881, when it was excluded, along with the fascinating "O Hot-Cheek'd and Blushing," to be discussed later. Whitman's reasons for the exclusion are unclear; the Norton editor attributes it to a lack of fit with the context (in "The Sleepers," a visionary lyric). Whitman may have felt that the efforts of reconciliation after the war suggested deemphasizing anger and revenge—see the following text. As for the shame poem, he may possibly have felt that it was superseded by the completion of "I Sing the Body Electric"—embryonic and incomplete in the first edition, not in its present form until 1851.

5. See the previous note.

6. See the good discussion in Reynolds, *Walt Whitman's America,* chap. 7. Mill's *Subjection* is greatly indebted to some American writers about women affiliated with the abolitionist movement (see J. E. Hasday, "Contest and Consent: A Legal History of Marital Rape," *California Law Review* 88 [2000]: 1373–503). It is likely that Whitman had similar sources.

7. Quoted in Reynolds, *Walt Whitman's America,* 233, from Walt Whitman, *Prose Works, 1892,* ed. F. Stovall (New York: New York University Press, 1963–64), 2:494.

8. Quoted in Reynolds, *Walt Whitman's America,* 213, from Whitman, *Notes and Fragments,* ed. Richard M. Bucke (1899; repr., Ontario: A. Talbot, n.d.).

9. George Chauncey, *Gay New York* (New York: Basic Books, 1994); M. B. Duberman, *About Time: Exploring the Gay Past* (New York: Meridian, 1991).

10. Reynolds, *Walt Whitman's America,* 70–80.

11. The slaves were typically freed on the graduation of their "owners"; the black population of the town of Princeton still contains many descendants of these freed slaves.

12. Quoted in Reynolds, *Walt Whitman's America*, 396, from Horace Traubel, *With Walt Whitman in Camden*, 7 vols. (1905; rpt., New York: Rowman and Littlefield, 1961), 77.

13. The Norton editors write that the popcorn popular at that time had a rose-colored ear.

14. For other examples, see my discussion of "Song of Myself."

15. See the Norton edition, ad loc: "'[B]loss' originally designated a swelling or extension of an internal organ; later, any protuberance of 'embossed' book covers, metal ornaments, armor, etc."

16. "I mind how once we lay such a transparent summer morning,! How you settled your head athwart my hips and gently turn'd over upon me, / And parted the shirt from my bosom-bone, and plunged your tongue to my bare-stript heart, / And reach'd till you felt my beard, and reach'd till you held my feet."

17. Not, however, in every respect: Reynolds shows that taboos against masturbation are still endorsed by the poet, who had strong affiliations with antebellum purity reformers on this topic (see Reynolds, *Walt Whitman's America*, 199–200).

18. Preface to *Leaves of Grass* (1855); "The United States themselves are essentially the greatest poem."

19. In this sense, Whitman announces, animals are frequently better off than human beings—for they have escaped that subservience to institutionalized religion, that encasement in self-abasement, that has led to so much misery in the world: "They do not lie awake in the dark and weep for their sins, / . . . Not one kneels to another, nor to his kind that lived thousands of years ago" (SM 32.687–88, 690).

20. Whitman seduces the reader, inviting him to "stop this day and night with rue" (SM 2.33). Even so, and in very similar terms, he issues an invitation to God. In one of the most audacious gestures in "Song of Myself," Whitman imagines God as a male companion who accepts the invitation to spend the night in his bed, only to leave his side in the morning: "As God comes a loving bedfellow and sleeps at my side all night and close on the peep of day" (SM 3, 60). Later editions make the line less explicit: "As the hugging and loving bed-fellow sleeps at my side through the night, and withdraws at the peep of day with stealthy tread."

21. BO 10.137. On this section of the poem, see Martha Nussbaum, *Poetic Justice: The Literary Imagination and Public Life* (Boston: Beacon Press, 1995).

22. Compare Nietzsche's phrase "*das Unschuld des Werdens.*"

23. Here we discover another defect in Reynolds, *Walt Whitman's America*,

for he takes these remarks at face value and out of context, as evidence that "Whitman condemns masturbation." In context, they cannot possibly bear this meaning.

24. Cf. Aristotle, *De Caelo* I.12, which argues that the most perfect bodily shape, the shape among bodily shapes most suited to express perfection, is the sphere, and the most perfect motion revolution in a spherical orbit; the lumpy and irregular shapes of human and other animal bodies, and their corresponding movements, are signs of their distance from this perfection.

25. Contrast Jünger's "man of steel": his dynamism is purchased at the price of becoming a machine, rather than a creature of flesh and blood.

26. Notice Whitman's recognition of the importance of varying pronouns in this context, already in 1855: if what is being said is that there is no unmarked and no marked, then pronouns, too, must take their place in the procession.

27. See Reynolds, *Walt Whitman's America*, 346ff.

28. See also Nussbaum, *Poetic Justice*, chap. 2.

29. See Ishmael Reed's grimly funny novel of this title: *Reckless Eyeballing* (New York: St. Martin's Press, 1986).

30. See the discussion in J. Greenberg, *Crusaders in the Courts* (New York: Basic Books, 1994), 101. Though Ingraham was convicted and sentenced, the North Carolina Supreme Court eventually reversed the decision because it was evident that blacks had been excluded from the jury.

31. *McQuirter v. State*, 63 So. 2d 388, 1953, affirming the conviction on appeal. See the excellent discussion of this and related cases in R. Kennedy, *Race, Crime, and the Law* (New York: Pantheon, 1997), 89–90. McQuirter was fined five hundred dollars, a sentence that suggests a deterrent and symbolic purpose to the charge of attempted rape.

32. Kennedy, *Race, Crime, and the Law*, 88; the code "demanded exhibitions of servility and the open disavowal of any desire for equality."

33. Consider this description from Richard Wright's *Native Son* (New York: HarperCollins, 1993):

> He wanted to wave his hand and blot out the white man who was making him feel this. If not that, he wanted to blot himself out. He had not raised his eyes to the level of Mr. Dalton's face once since he had been in the house. He stood with his knees slightly bent, his lips partly open, his shoulders stooped; and his eyes held a look that went only to the surface of things. There was an organic conviction in him that this was the way white folks wanted him to be when in their presence; none had ever told him that in so many words, but their manner had made him feel that they did. (53–54)

And see also Wright's "The Ethics of Living Jim Crow," in *Uncle Tom's Children*

(New York: HarperCollins, 1993). Especially significant is the description of Wright's employment as a hall boy in a hotel frequented by white prostitutes and their johns, where he was often asked to bring refreshments to the rooms. "'Nigger, what in hell you looking at?' the white man asked me, raising himself upon his elbows. 'Nothing,' I answered, looking miles deep into the blank wall of the room. 'Keep your eyes where they belong, if you want to be healthy!' he said. 'Yes, sir.'"

34. See the acute analysis in Elisabeth Young-Bruehl, *The Anatomy of Prejudices* (Cambridge: Harvard University Press, 1996), drawing on the treatment of this theme in such writers as James Baldwin, Calvin Hernton, and Eldridge Cleaver.

35. *Émile* 5:359, 358 (Bloom translation).

36. Quoted in Susan Moller Okin, *Women in Western Political Thought* (Princeton: Princeton University Press, 1979), 249.

37. "A Woman Waits for Me" (25–30), Norton edition, 102–3.

38. "Whitman," from *Nation and Athenaeum* 29 (1921), Norton edition, 842–50.

39. A variant of "curlicue": a flourish in writing, easily erased.

40. See the related observations in my preface to the updated edition (2001) of Martha C. Nussbaum, *The Fragility of Goodness: Luck and Ethics in Greek Tragedy and Philosophy* (Cambridge: Cambridge University Press, 1986).

41. Whitman was part of the plan for the Gifford Lectures from the beginning, and a first draft of this material was completed before I delivered those lectures; but since there were to be only ten lectures, only four devoted to the material that is now part 2, I decided to give one lecture on the contemplative ascent, one on the Christian ascent, one on the Romantic ascent, and the final one entirely on Joyce. Thus there had been no occasion to present the Whitman material before 1996.

CHAPTER 5

The Solar Judgment of Walt Whitman

Jane Bennett

Discernment

ACCORDING TO HENRI BERGSON, perceiving is subtractive, an act of screening off: our bodies "allow to pass through them, so to speak, those external influences which are indifferent to them; the others isolated become 'perceptions' by their very isolation."[1] Perception is a "discarding of what has no interest for our needs," where the "interest" or principle of (de)selection is a pragmatic or action-oriented one.[2] In short, to be conscious of a percept is to "attain" only to "certain parts and to certain aspects of those parts" of all the "influences" of matter; "consciousness—in regard to external perception—lies in just this choice. But there is, in this necessary poverty of our conscious perception, something that is positive, [i.e.,] . . . discernment."[3]

Bergson presents perception as discernment, selection, or, one could say, as a kind of judgment. In what follows, I inflect the term "judgment" in this way, as the biocultural act of discriminatory discernment. I say "biocultural" because, as Bergson acknowledges, perception cannot be described in purely physiological terms: "In fact, there is no perception which is not full of memories. With the immediate and present data of our senses we mingle a thousand details out of our past experience. In most cases these memories supplant our actual perceptions, of which we then retain only a few hints, thus using them merely as 'signs' that recall to us former images."[4] Within this semantic frame, the act of *moral* judgment can be defined as those occasions when the practice of perceptual discernment is accompanied by this particular image or memory: the figure of the self as a potentially responsible agent, as, that is, a body able to control its fate because it is an active subject amid (more or less) passive objects.

Walt Whitman, it seems to me, commends to us a practice of judgment unaccompanied by this image/memory. In the 1855 Preface to *Leaves of Grass* and again in "By Blue Ontario's Shore," he celebrates the poet who has learned how to judge "not as the judge judges but as the sun falling around a helpless thing."[5] I will read this striking line as expressive of Whitman's concern about the unethical aspects of the practice of moral judgment and its ideal of the responsible human subject. "Judgmentalism" names several of these unethical aspects. To be judgmental is to apply to life a satisfying but falsifying logic of either/or, good/evil, friend/enemy, and it is to take a certain pleasure in exposing and punishing the sins of others.

The affinity between moral judgment and judgmentalism, between simplification, pleasure, and punitiveness, was the point of Nietzsche's critique of ressentiment, that vengeful demand that there exist someone to hold responsible and to pay for one's suffering, even though an indeterminate amount of pain stems from the impersonal condition of being a mortal being in an undesigned cosmos. I admire Nietzsche's (Zarathustran) quest to learn how to suspend the will to punish and create the alternative pleasures of art, science, philosophy. And I will be presenting Whitman as an ally in this project: How can "solar" judging forestall the unethical tendencies of moral judgment? How might such a solarity be extracted from one's own body? What techniques and exercises—literary, grammatical, aesthetic—does Whitman use or recommend? I will also be contending that solar judging entails for Whitman a special kind of perception, the capacity to discern the voices of (so-called) inanimate things. Thus Whitman's call for poets who take on the posture of falling sunlight is linked to his materialism, or to the way he conceives materiality—both human and nonhuman—as a living force.

I turn now to Whitman's poem.

Solarity

> He [the poet] is no arguer, he is judgment, (Nature accepts him absolutely,)
> He judges not as the judge judges but as the sun falling round a helpless thing,
> As he sees the farthest he has the most faith,
> His thoughts are the hymns of the praise of things,

> ....
> He sees eternity in men and women, he does not see men and women as
> dreams or dots. (sec. 10, 137–50)

The poet who judges not as the judge judges becomes as magnanimous and generous as the sun, as accepting of the things he encounters as Nature is of him—and "Nature accepts him *absolutely*." The poet receives without prejudice all types of bodies, "whoever you are!"—enslaved man at auction; farmer's wife; workman; Jew; son or daughter of China, Slavic empire, Damascus, Rome, Naples, Persia, or Greece; prisoner; helpless infant or old person; tires of carts, boot-soles, horses, snow-sleighs, rous'd mobs, and impassive stones.[6] Solar judging must also be farsighted, both in the sense of anticipating that things will become otherwise than they are and in the sense of taking a big-picture or wide-angled point of view. When the poet looks out on the world, he sees not fixed entities or "dots," but an "eternity" of fibers stretched out over time. This is not a landscape of individuals but of pulsating threads that are always interacting, tangling, joining, and snapping off. The poet's very self is also one of those durational threads: no longer aspiring to become a sovereign agent or even an exclusively organic entity, the poet calls forth from the various potentials of his body a quivering, traversing beam of light. The poet does not so much *impersonate* sunlight's impersonal fall as *extract* from his body its inherent affinity with matter, light, heat, energy. To be able to "see" this long duration, to perceive evolutionary becoming within the apparently discrete objects of experience—that is what it means to be true or faithful to life; in Whitman's words: "As he sees the farthest he has the most faith."

This strangely open-armed, projective, impersonal, elemental judging is surely a difficult skill to master. It requires that one devise or perhaps stumble upon ways to undo, suspend, or confound the default self's restless and persistent urge to rank order (what it currently tends to perceive as) a world of stable subjects and mute objects. The poet must be able, periodically, to skip a beat in the regular pulse of this discriminatory perception, a perceptual style geared toward the instrumental use of things rather than the detection of their singular powers. If it is hard to wrap one's mind around the idea of a nonjudgmental judging, it is perhaps even harder to absorb Whitman's suggestion that objects speak, and in so speaking, they too are participants in solar judgment. They participate in a fairly strong sense: not only as the "context" within which humans make their "judgment calls," not only as the "material constraints" for human action, but as bona fide "actants." The term is Bruno Latour's: an actant is a source of action that can be either human or nonhuman; it is that which has effectivity or sufficient coherence to produce effects that make a difference or alter the course of events. An actant is "any entity that modifies another entity in a trial." The "competence" of an actant can only be deduced from its performance, not posited in advance of the action.[7] Actants contribute in ways that exceed their role as the "objects" of the poet's perception.

"Song of Myself" includes one of Whitman's many lists of these vocal material actants, artifacts and nonhuman animals that possess a "living and buried speech" or vitality elided by the category of object:

> The *blab* of the pave, tires of carts, sluff of boot-soles, . . .
> . . . the *clank* of the shod horses on the granite floor,
> The snow-sleighs, clinking, . . .
> . . . the *fury* of rous'd mobs,
> The *flap* of the curtain'd litter, . . .
> . . . .
> The impassive stones that receive and *return so many echoes,*
> . . . .
> *What living and buried speech is always vibrating here* . . .[8]

On my reading of Whitman, the machines, tools, and artifacts of mid-nineteenth-century urban life, along with the various human types and groups, all have something to say and something worth listening to. The poet "goes solar" in order to linger long enough and to linger with a mind that is open and quiet enough—that has slackened its reflex to categorize and rank, to hear their testimonies.

Vibrant Matter

A few pages after the line about judging as the sun falling appears in the Preface, Whitman makes explicit the broader ethos within which the affects and percepts of solar judgment have a place. This code of conduct is tailored to the heterogeneous, geocultural public of nineteenth-century America as he lived it:

> This is what you shall do: Love the earth and sun and the animals, despise riches, give alms to the every one that asks, stand up for the stupid and crazy, devote your income and labor to others, hate tyrants, argue not concerning God, have patience and indulgence toward the people, take off your hat to nothing known or unknown or to any man or number of men, go freely with powerful uneducated persons and with the young and with the mothers of families, read these leaves in the open air every season of every year of your life, re-examine all you have been told at school or church or in any book, dismiss whatever insults your own soul, and your very flesh shall be a great poem and have the richest fluency not only in its words but in the silent lines of its lips and face and between the lashes of your eyes and in every motion and joint of your body.[9]

What I want to highlight in this famous ethos is its vitalistic cast. One's flesh becomes a great poem; one's moving joints and eyelashes express a liveliness shared with earth and sun and the animals. In "By Blue Ontario's Shore," but also in "Song of the Rolling Earth" and "Song of the Broad-Axe" and many other poems, the exemplary agents of love and impartial regard are not human individuals but natural bodies or forces such as the falling sun or the "glancing" Earth. Indeed, many of the tools, artifacts, and natural bodies that appear in *Leaves of Grass* exhibit a surprising power of action, an ability to make claims upon us. This impersonal power is not dull, flat, or inert, and it is more than merely resistant or recalcitrant in the face of the agency of human intentions: it is a *material vitality*. *Leaves of Grass* arranges words in such a way as to expose the uncanny truth that human action is never exclusively a matter of human agency but an event profoundly dependent upon the participation of a bevy of specimens, from gravity to sunlight to bacteria to plastic to metals to plant matter, which act in concert and in conflict with us:

> The blab of the pave, tires of carts, sluff of boot-soles, talk of the promenaders,
> The heavy omnibus, the driver with his interrogating thumb, the clank of the shod horses on the granite floor,
> The snow-sleighs, clinking, shouted jokes, pelts of snow-balls,
> The hurrahs for popular favorites, the fury of rous'd mobs,
> The flap of the curtain'd litter, a sick man inside borne to the hospital,
> The meeting of enemies, the sudden oath, the blows and fall,

> The excited crowd, the policeman with his star quickly working his passage to the centre of the crowd,
> The impassive stones that receive and return so many echoes,
> What groans of over-fed or half-starv'd who fall sunstruck or in fits,
> What exclamations of women taken suddenly who hurry home and give birth to babes,
> What living and buried speech is always vibrating here . . . [10]

The doggedly *horizontal* lists that frequent *Leaves of Grass* model a world where human beings are positioned not as potential masters of, but as co-participants with, other bodies in a world that vibrates. Persons, places, and things are arranged not in a hierarchy but stand "abreast"—"I am for those who walk abreast with the whole earth," the poet says in "By Blue Ontario's Shore."[11] Randall Fuller suggests that such lists enact a nonanthropocentric mode of poetry: the "prodigious particularity" of *Leaves* conjures up "a surrounding . . . where emotion is subordinate to the presentation of the aggregate relations of all participants, rather than the striking enhancement of singular or single heroes or heroines."[12]

Part of what it may mean, then, to love the earth, despise riches, have patience, dismiss insults, go freely, argue not, and to reexamine school and church teaching is to call forth from the subjectified self a set of naturalistic or elemental capacities, capacities shared with the earth, sun, and the animals. "I find," says the self of "Song of Myself," that "I incorporate gneiss, coal, long-threaded moss, fruits, grains, esculent roots, / And am stucco'd with quadrupeds and birds all over."[13] The voices or frequencies of material objects are emissions that the self, as a materiality, also inhabits. One could say, then, that solar judging involves cultivating the "inorganic" powers resident within; it invokes one's inner coal, bird, and light in order to forge sympathetic links with the minerals in tools, the pigeons in the park, the myriad bodies upon which one's gaze falls. The self most prepared to "arbitrate the diverse" is the self most alert to her *internal* diversity.

A Judgment Adjacent to Moral Agency?

The moral philosopher Martha Nussbaum has also paid attention to Whitman's lines about judgment in "By Blue Ontario's Shore." But she does not really take Whitman at his word when he speaks of a judging devoid of judges, of a discerning perception that does not emerge from the self qua moral agent. The primacy Nussbaum gives to moral agency leads her to focus on just those lines and phrases in "By Blue Ontario's Shore" that I tend to elide or treat as secondary, and to hear them with the stress (my italics below) on the poet's distinctively human powers of decision:

> Of these States, *the poet* is the equable man,
> *Not in him but off from him* things are grotesque, eccentric, fail of
>   their full returns,
> . . . .
> *He bestows* on every object or quality its fit proportion . . . ,
> *He* is the arbiter of the diverse, *he is the key.*
> *He* is the equalizer of his age and land,
> . . . .
> The years straying toward infidelity *he* withholds by his steady faith,
> He is no arguer, *he is* judgment, (Nature accepts him absolutely,)
> He judges not as the judge judges but as the sun falling round a
>   helpless thing,
> . . . .
> He sees eternity *in men and women,* he does not see men and women
>   as dreams or dots.

What, according to Nussbaum, is Whitman saying when he speaks of judging as sunlight falling? He is, she says, following in Aristotle's footsteps and offering "a normative conception of equitable judgment as an alternative to a simple or reductive reliance on abstract principles." Thus Whitman advocates a "flexible, context-specific judging" without making any "concession to the irrational."[14] When Whitman says "judge as the sun falling," he is calling jurists to examine "every curve, every nook," every "qualitative difference," and all "the historical and human complexities of the particular case."[15]

Nussbaum conceives judgment within the frame of law and moral culpability, and, once positioned within this frame, she uses Whitman to defend the view that (juridical) judgment should be more attentive to the biographical, social, and historical *contexts* of the acts of moral agents who practice or who are under judgment. Fair enough: Nussbaum does a fine job of identifying Whitman's possible contribution to a more humane, less coldly rationalistic practice of jurisprudence and courtly decision. But she misses three things.

First, she misses how Whitman uses the sound and sense of poetry (and the memories of vibrant matter it evokes) to induce in himself and his readers a better, more refined capacity to perceive the nonhuman agencies operating *alongside* human actants. Second, she misses how Whitman uses these experiences of a lively outside to induce greater sensitivity toward, a more precise radar for, the nonhuman agencies operating *within* the self. When Nussbaum thinks about the practice of judgment, the image of moral subjectivity swarms to the fore. I read Whitman as instead experimenting with the idea that another kind of judging is possible, one in which the poetic self apprehends its outside with equanimity, and does so long enough to detect the voices of peoples, pavements, and leaves of grass, and then to note how some of these voices have been literally, physically incorporated into one's own body. Here Whitman seems to suggest that human agents capable of moral responsibility are rarely if ever the only actants at work and not always even the most decisive or powerful. To discern this nonhuman agency, one must drop, if only temporarily, the stance of the moral agent and the priority it gives to the activity of ranking in accordance with a single set of criteria.

Finally, Nussbaum's reading misses the connection between Whitman's advocacy of solarity and a certain iconoclasm that he shares with Emerson and Thoreau. To go solar, to accept all with equanimity, is to elide the particular hierarchy of values and the particular regime of perception dominant in the culture; it is to suspend the force of conventional moral criteria. This magnanimity is dangerous—the sun falls on deadly viruses, on torture equipment, and not only on flowers, works of art, and the strong and lovely bodies of workers. But Whitman still seems to think that it is worth the risk, perhaps in part because such solar moments are necessarily fragile and fleeting. While this Whitman would agree that democratic culture requires juridical procedures that attribute to citizens (and enforce the norm of) moral agency, he is wary of the anthropocentrism implied in that image of the self and wary of its tendency toward judgmentalism and its bias in favor of conventional morality. It seems, then, that Whitman invokes a kind of judgment that sits *adjacent* to moral subjectivity, a solar judgment that elides that identity-frame or interrupts attempts to invoke and apply it. It is necessary, and not so hard at all, to judge "as the judge judges," but a democratic ethos also needs bodies able to postpone this identity—and to invent discursive tactics of deferral. Lists that underplay the differences between human and nonhuman specimens are one of the literary techniques Whitman uses to stave off the normal criteria of judgment and to open perception up to more of what Bergson called the "influences of the material world." Whitman's use of the middle voice is, I think, another technique.

The Middle Voice

In "A Song of the Rolling Earth," Whitman describes the kind of "countenance" or orientation toward experience that, I contend, fosters the solar judgment practiced by the poet of "By Blue Ontario's Shore":

> With her ample back towards every beholder,
> ....
> Sits she whom I too love like the rest, sits undisturb'd,
> Holding up in her hand what has the character of a mirror, while her
>   eyes glance back from it,
> Glance as she sits, inviting none, denying none,
> Holding a mirror day and night tirelessly before her own face.
>
> Seen at hand or seen at a distance,
> Duly the twenty-four appear in public every day,
> ....
> Looking from no countenances of their own, but from the
>   countenances of those who are with them,
> From the countenances of children or women or the manly
>   countenance,
> From the open countenances of animals or from inanimate things,
> From the landscape or waters or from the exquisite apparition of
>   the sky,
> From our countenances, mine and yours, faithfully returning them,
> Every day in public appearing without fail, but never twice with the
>   same companions.[16]

The "open countenance" of animals and inanimate things is similar to what in "By Blue Ontario's Shore" is named as an "ever-fresh forbearance and impartiality,"[17] where "impartiality" refers not to a distanced detachment but to the immersion of one's body in many other bodies, as happens when Whitman absorbs "food, air, to appear again in my strength, gait, face."[18] This is also what Whitman may mean when he says: "Are you done with reviews and criticisms of life, *animating now to life itself?*"[19]

To "animate" to life seems to entail a responding to a force outside oneself, but this responsiveness is neither a passive receptivity nor a willful embrace. It is somewhere in the middle. It is akin to what Earth in the poem above does when she glances as she sits, "inviting none, denying none," all the while neither "exhibiting" nor "refusing to exhibit" herself.[20] In other languages, such as Sanskrit, this not-quite-active, not-quite passive mode of being would be expressed in the "middle voice," which is almost absent in English. The middle voice expresses those goings-on in the world that are neither decisive actions nor their mere effects.[21] Such happenings are messily reciprocal coalescences of heterogeneous vibrant forces. One example of this voice in English might be Whitman's "I sing myself." There, the I, the myself, and the sound-event of song mix indeterminately, such that the roles of subject and object are beside the point.

Another example of the middle voice, which of course does not appear in Whitman's oeuvre, is a phrase that emerged in American English sometime in the 1980s: "Shit happens." In the strange grammar of "shit happens," the subject ("shit") is not the agent of the happening: it is not that, by the agency of shit, something separate comes into being; rather, the effect of the action, the happening, is *itself* shit. What is more, regardless of whether one addresses the phrase "shit happens" to oneself or to another person, the human bodies entangled in the shit themselves occupy a space that is neither that of an *agent* nor that of passive *object*. (To say "shit happens" to someone is not the same thing as saying, "How unjust! You were an innocent victim!") To say "shit happens" is to express a sense that life includes processes and identities more ontologically diverse than those recognizable within the binary logic of *either* decisive acts of agents *or* passive objects that express or resist them. It is uttered when the speaker has sensed that agency is *distributive*.[22] This is, I think, the intuition that Whitman tries to express through his lists of lively things.[23]

Angus Fletcher notes that Whitman has, in general, an aversion for verbs that attribute autonomous decision-making power to an individual: "Choosing is always for him a passage through an intermediate state of cohesion, a sense of apprehending a presence, so that only in that rather indirect way is he active, although he gains in intimacy and interest *for* the apprehended object. The grammar for such a poetry has to be mainly written in a middle voice."[24] For example, in "By Blue Ontario's Shore," the poet is said to "inaugurate" the earthy companions with whom he walks abreast: to *inaugurate* is to announce and thus to spur on an already existing lively body; it is not to occupy the position of a living human existing alongside passive things. "Inviting none, denying none," the solar judge respects the fact that I, the myself, and the world together are engaged in what John Dewey named as "conjoint action."[25] The middle voice is thus a grammatical form of expression prompted by the existence *in the world* of multiple modes and types of agency.[26]

Apersonal Regard

Whitman calls us to the difficult practice of judging without becoming the judge, and to the uncanny idea of a human and nonhuman assemblage as the locus of action. This solarity or indifferent magnanimity may seem more like love than judgment. And indeed, in "Song of the Universal" (written nineteen years after the Preface), it is love that is likened to the sun: "Love like the light silently wrapping all." A case could be made, then, that when Whitman calls for a poet who judges as the sun falls, he is echoing Jesus' injunction to judge *not,* to replace judgment with love:

> But I say this to you who are listening: Love your enemies, do good to those who hate you. . . . Be compassionate as your Father is compassionate. Do not judge, and you will not be judged yourselves; do not condemn, and you will not be condemned yourselves; grant pardon, and you will be pardoned. (Luke 6:26)

(It could even be said that Whitman's antijudgmentalism is more radical than that expressed in Luke, for whereas Luke promises a prize for judging-not—divine leniency or pardon—Whitman breaks with the logic of reward and punishment altogether: to judge as falling sunlight is to praise the things themselves, to love them for their own sake.)

But while I think that Whitman probably did draw upon the image of Jesus' voluntary self-sacrifice when he wrote of the sun-poet's donation-dispersal[27] of itself, I do not think that "love" captures all that he wants to say in the phrase "judge not as the judge judges but as the sun falling round a helpless thing." And this is because there is a peculiar kind of *impersonality* attached to solar judgment, a certain psychological distancing, that is not well captured by the idea of love. This point also comes to the fore in "A Song of the Rolling Earth" (1881), where Earth exudes a degree of detachment similar to that of falling sunlight:

> With her ample back towards every beholder,
> With the fascinations of youth and the equal fascinations of age,
> Sits she whom I too love like the rest, sits undisturb'd,
> Holding up in her hand what has the character of a mirror, while her eyes glance back from it,
> Glance as she sits, inviting none, denying none,
> Holding a mirror day and night tirelessly before her own face.[28]

The Earth is "undisturb'd" and has no favorites or preferences. Her attention is not intense enough to interfere or superimpose a rank order, but is merely *glancing*: "Glance as she sits, inviting none, denying none." The solar poet, like the glancing Earth, exudes a distinctly impersonal affect, denoting less the emotional attachments between persons than the gravitational attraction toward and between bodies, bodies in which a psychology and morality may be potentially present but are not at the moment in charge. "Does the earth gravitate? Does not all matter, aching, attract all matter?"[29]

Solar judgment, which calls us to be "done with reviews and criticisms of life,"[30] is not quite love. But the question remains: Can the practice of reviewing and criticizing be excised *entirely* from something called "judging"? Whitman does not address the point directly, but what he seems to be doing is this: he seeks ways to circumvent the urge to reject and condemn for the sake of a wiser, more capacious practice of selection and discrimination. Note that while the poet in "By Blue Ontario's Shore" is no "arguer," Whitman insists that he remain *"the arbiter* of the diverse"—arbiter or negotiator or adjudicator between parties, a chooser of paths who must determine what is the "fit proportion" due to every "object or quality." The self who becomes judgment without becoming the judge suspends for a time the sociomoral categories through which s/he usually differentiates his/her responses to things. To somehow impede their ability to channel and organize perception is to buy time for the things outside to make their mark, to say a little something. To go solar—to "pause, listen, count"[31]—would be to increase the chances of picking up those rarified frequencies. Such information would enrich thinking and may sometimes spur into being new categories of value, which may then serve as new standards for judging in the evaluative sense.

I have attempted to unravel a line of Whitman's that got inside me and would not be still: "Judge not as the judge judges but as the sun falling round a helpless thing." This image, and its resonances in my body, prompted me to recall the unethical tendencies within the practice of moral judgment, and to try to specify the peculiar perceptual antidote that Whitman enacts in his poems and seeks to induce in his readers. My topic, then, has been the family of terms—judgment, perception, attentiveness, materiality—that Whitman recalibrates. Good judgment may require one to periodically inhabit the role of falling sun, for this accepting, nonranking illumination can reveal things as possessing a certain performativity, or what Whitman calls "the pulsation in all matter, all spirit, throbbing forever, eternal systole and diastole of life in all things."[32] The poet is "no arguer; he is judgment": in lieu of I judge/I am judged, there is the middle voice of "I be judgment." Do not judge as the judge judges but be judgment, and this means that I must relax, calm down, step back from my default course of action, and try to discern the "countenances" of things and their hitherto inaudible testimonies.

Notes

1. Henri Bergson, *Matter and Memory*, trans. Nancy Margaret Paul and W. Scott Palmer (London: George Allen and Unwin, 1911), 28–29. Mark Hansen puts the point this way: for Bergson, "the body functions as a kind of filter that selects, from among the universe of images circulating around it and according to its own embodied capacities, precisely those that are relevant to it" (Mark Hansen, *New Philosophy for New Media* [Cambridge: MIT Press, 2004], 2).

2. "Our representation of matter is the measure of our possible action upon bodies" (Bergson, *Matter and Memory*, 31).

3. Ibid.

4. Ibid., 24.

5. Preface to the 1855 edition of *Leaves of Grass*, in *Leaves of Grass and Other Writings*, ed. Michael Moon, Norton Critical Edition (New York: Norton, 2002), 620. I am grateful to Rebecca Brown, Jennifer Culbert, Katrin Pahl, and the members of the "Seminar in Political and Moral Thought" at Johns Hopkins

and the Birkbeck Institute for the Humanities for their comments on and criticisms of this essay.

6. I compile this list from "Salut au Monde," "I Sing the Body Electric," and "Song of Myself."

7. Bruno Latour, *The Politics of Nature* (Cambridge: Harvard University Press, 2004), 237.

8. "Song of Myself," lines 153–63, my emphases.

9. Preface (1855), 622.

10. "Song of Myself," lines 153–63.

11. "By Blue Ontario's Shore," line 291.

12. Randall Fuller, "Ecopoeisis," review of *A New Theory for American Poetry: Democracy, the Environment, and the Future of Imagination,* by Angus Fletcher, *Journal of Modern Literature* 29, no. 4 (2006): 202.

13. "Song of Myself," lines 670–71. Also: "I am large, I contain multitudes" (line 1326).

14. Martha Nussbaum, "Poets as Judges: Judicial Rhetoric and the Literary Imagination," *University of Chicago Law Review* 62, no. 4 (Autumn 1995): 1477, 1519, 1478.

15. Ibid., 1479.

16. "A Song of the Rolling Earth," lines 48, 50–55, 57–62.

17. "By Blue Ontario's Shore," line 192.

18. Ibid., line 204.

19. Ibid., lines 189–90, my italics.

20. "Song of the Rolling Earth," lines 52, 37.

21. "The middle voice intervenes by a preferential or dispositional discourse as opposed to an active, rational deliberative discourse whose sole [perverse] purpose is to solicit passivity. (It says: I prefer not to not!)" (Victor J. Vitanza, *Negation, Subjectivity, and the History of Rhetoric* [Albany: State University of New York Press, 1997], 288). See also Roland Barthes, "To Write: An Intransitive Verb?" in *The Rustle of Language,* trans. Richard Howard (Berkeley and Los Angeles: University of California Press, 1989); and "To Write: An Intransitive Verb? Discussion," in *The Structuralist Controversy,* ed. Richard Macksey and Eugene Donato (Baltimore: Johns Hopkins University Press, 1972), 134–56.

22. Brian Macaskill says that the agency here is "simultaneously configured from inside and outside." (See his "Charting J. M. Coetzee's Middle Voice," *Contemporary Literature* 35, no. 3 (Autumn 1994), 441–75, 459).

23. As middle-voiced, "Shit happens" approximates a linguistic form not formally a part of English, though even English speakers have found (sometimes inelegant) ways to mark the uncanny presence of an agentic power localizable to neither subject nor object. This power of action eludes the grammatical categories

of active and passive voice: not "I made a mistake" (active voice), not "Mistakes were made" (passive voice), but "Shit happens" (middle voice). To cite another example, "The book translates easily" (middle voice) is not "I translated the book into English" (active voice) or "The book was translated in 1986" (passive voice). "Easy translatability," like the "happening" of shit, is neither transitive nor intransitive: the verbs "to translate" and "to happen" don't refer a subject to an object (transitive), but neither do they fail to refer to an object outside of the subject (intransitive). As Macaskill notes, the middle voice is associated with reflexivity, although reflexivity "does not necessarily signal the middle voice, whose characteristics are most compelling defined in relation to notions of semantic *agency* rather than by way of morphology or syntax" (452 n. 13, my italics). Instead, the activity operative here is, as Derrida puts it, "an operation that is not an operation, an operation that cannot be conceived either as passion or as the action of a subject on an object, or on the basis of the categories of agent or patient. . . . For the middle voice, a certain nontransitivity may be what philosophy, at its outset, distributed into an active and a passive voice, thereby constituting itself by means of this repression. (Jacques Derrida, *Margins of Philosophy*, trans. Alan Bass (Chicago: University of Chicago Press, 1982), 9.

24. Angus Fletcher, *A New Theory of American Poetry* (Cambridge: Harvard University Press, 2004), 168.

25. "I am for those who walk abreast with the whole earth, Who inaugurate one to inaugurate all." This is an egalitarian ambulation, not to lead but to "walk abreast" ("By Blue Ontario's Shore," line 291). Donald Pease also points to Whitman's preference for an essentially "*inter*locutive voice. . . . He abandoned the passive and active voice for one in an intransitive mood." The "I" in "I sing myself" refers "to an agent neither totally separated from its activity of singing, as it would be in the active voice, nor wholly acted upon, as it would in the passive." This "I" is (what I would call) an actant in a "verbal performance whose speaker is inside the process of which he presumes to be the agent, who effects something that is simultaneously effected in him." (Donald Pease, "Walt Whitman's Revisionary Democracy," in *The Columbia History of American Poetry*, ed. Jay Parini (New York: Columbia University Press, 1993), 159.

26. For Dewey, there is no action that is *not* conjoint, that does not immediately become enmeshed in a web of connections. This is because an act can only take place in a field already crowded with other endeavors and their consequences, a crowd with which the new entrant immediately interacts, overlaps, interferes (see John Dewey, *The Public and Its Problems* [New York: Henry Holt, 1927], 137). I give an account of how, for Dewey, this field of *political* action is a kind of ecology in *Vibrant Matter: A Political Ecology of Things* (Durham, N.C.: Duke University Press, 2010), chap. 7.

27. Angus Fletcher, drawing upon a letter about Whitman written by Wallace Stevens, notes that though Whitman's poems *collect* "'large numbers of concrete things,' . . . the broader effect of the whole of *Leaves of Grass* is to counterbalance its own aggregation." Whitman's poetry mirrors the simultaneous gathering and dispersal of "any living landscape" (Fletcher, *A Net Theory of American Poetry*, 251).

28. "A Song of the Rolling Earth," lines 48–53.

29. "I Am He That Aches with Love," line 2.

30. "By Blue Ontario's Shore," lines 189–90.

31. "I Sing the Body Electric," line 32.

32. Walt Whitman, *Democratic Vistas* (New York: Liberal Arts Press, 1949), 988. Perhaps this is what Whitman means when he attributes soul to objects. In "Song of the Universal," Whitman names as "soul" the "seed perfection" or that "one ray of perfect light" (line 33) inside every single thing, despite all "the measureless grossness and the slag" (line 5). This seed/ray "justifies" the existence of every thing: "Not the right only justified, what we call evil also justified" (line 20). In the last section of the poem, Whitman shifts attention from the soul of natural bodies to the soul of a historical entity, America. He says that America is the cosmological "scheme's culmination, its thought and its reality"; America has arrived on the scene in order to enact and make visible the soul that is in *every* thing: "All eligible to all" (line 50). To see this is to love: "Love like the light silently wrapping all." Whitman sings this out, sings out the ray, hoping to encourage a new kind of judgment.

PART II

City Life and Bodily Place

CHAPTER 6

"Mass Merger": Whitman and Baudelaire, the Modern Street, and Democratic Culture

Marshall Berman

WALT WHITMAN AND CHARLES Baudelaire didn't know each other's work, and don't much sound like one another. But they share certain deep preoccupations that were shared by very few other writers in their times. Both addressed their readers in intensely personal and sometimes confessional voices. Both saw poetry as an arena for taking existential risks. Both wrote directly about sex—and got in big trouble for it. In the late twentieth century, some of their readers noticed something else. They anointed both men as "poets of the city" who identified deeply with particular great cities—Baudelaire's Paris, Whitman's New York—who called them "my city," and wrote about them with great depth and passion, as if their cities were part of their own flesh. Both poets came of age at a time when their cities, but also hundreds of others around the world, were going through unprecedented, spectacular growth. At first, it seems, Western culture wasn't ready. Today we routinely compare the process of urbanization to a great wave; but in the early nineteenth century, it seems to have hit people more like a ton of bricks. Virtually overnight, a vocabulary of hysterical invective materialized against cities and city life. Cities were demonized even as they became the matrix for more and more human life. People learned to curse their cities as places that were "perjured, murderous, bloody, full of blame, savage, extreme, rude, cruel, not to trust." (This torrent of abuse comes from Shakespeare's Sonnet 129, a poem not about cities at all.) But Western culture gradually adapted to city life, and Whitman and Baudelaire played crucial roles in this collective adaptation. They conceived and dedicated themselves to a new historical task: the task of making people feel at home in the modern city.

We can see this clearly in one of Whitman's classic poems, "Mannahatta," a visionary celebration of New York. The poem, twenty-four lines long, has an arresting pattern of motion. For three-quarters of the poem, Whitman's horizon gradually expands in an ever-wider panorama, as if he were a tourist guide unfolding a vast cityscape from a balloon; then, for the final fourth, the horizon abruptly contracts to street and ground level, and the poem ends. The panorama features "nests of water-bays," "tall and wonderful spires," "numberless crowded streets," "high growths of iron," "the houses of business of the ship-merchants and money-brokers," "vehicles—Broadway—the women—the shops and shows"; a great array of people, "the manly race of drivers of horses," "the brown-skinned sailors," "the mechanics of the city, the masters, well-formed, beautiful faces, looking you straight in the eyes"; human collectives, "immigrants arriving, fifteen or twenty thousand in a week," "parades, processions, bugles playing, flags flying, drums beating." Whitman shows us a sensibility that is large enough and generous enough to embrace them all. Then he offers a political judgment on the people of New York, and on what makes this people lovely: *"The free city! no slaves! no owners of slaves"* (my italics). In the poem's last two lines, he writes from ground level, where real people are, and real human encounters happen. Here he insists that sexual feeling is love's core:

> The city of such women, I am mad to be with them!
>   I will return after death to be with them!
> The city of such young men, I swear I cannot live happy, without I
>   often go talk, walk, eat, drink, sleep, with them!

Whitman's short poem "City of Orgies" has a similar arc: a tourist guide's inventory of Manhattan's great sites, then a jump-cut to everyday life in the street. What makes a city great? the poet asks. "Not these," the formidable official sites, but rather this:

>   your frequent and swift flash of eyes offering me love,
> Offering response to my own . . .

What makes a city great, Whitman believes, is the power to create that *flash,* to generate instants of intimacy between strangers, whether or not the flash leads anywhere beyond itself. Belonging to a city means being awake and responsive to *everybody*—because anyone in the crowd could turn out to be "the one" for you, even if only for an instant. Once we have taken Whitman to heart, we realize that the true meaning of "sexual liberation" is the liberation of sexual *fantasy*. The glory of great cities is the liberation of millions of people's fantasy lives, an environment where everybody in the crowd can imagine themselves naked and intimate with everybody else. From now on, our most powerful aphrodisiac may be an ordinary walk on Broadway—New York's or any other city's Broadway—or on any of the thousands of city streets that feed it. (Even on *"Old* Broadway," a street one block long just off West 125th.) Thanks to Whitman, we will feel the continuity between what we do when we sleep together and what we can do in public as citizens on a democratic street.

If we turn from Whitman's city to Baudelaire's, we will recognize common themes right away. Above all, there is that flash of eyes, which is a social as much as a personal event, springing from the modern city's capacity to generate sparks of life between the millions of strangers in its crowds. In Baudelaire's short poem "A une passante,"[1] the narrator in the midst of a Parisian crowd passes a woman in mourning. Her presence thrills him: "Lovely fugitive whose glance has brought me back to life." They make the very briefest eye contact, then they pass on; the momentum of the crowd that brought them together soon propels them in different directions, away. Yet he is certain she is someone "whom I might have loved," and certain she knows and mourns him, even as he mourns her. Baudelaire sees, with remarkable clarity, how connection between human beings is fraught with emotional complexity. The subject reaches out, but also pulls away, often without knowing what it is doing; the rapturous flash of love can flip into a tragic stab of pain.

Baudelaire's prose poem "Crowds,"[2] written in 1861 as an op-ed piece for a Parisian newspaper, is the greatest one page ever written on people in crowds on streets. He is writing for readers who themselves *are* the crowd; as a writer for a newspaper audience (as he was in his last decade), so is he. This poem, more than most by Baudelaire, has a very clear message: *Do It!* His readers should embrace the crowd they are, should go with the flow. To be a "serious and thoughtful stroller," he says, is to *"take a bath of multitude."* We should imagine other people as a stream of warm water, smooth and comforting; we can take our clothes off and relax with them. A bath isn't meant to last forever; we can end it when we want. But it's possible to go deeper, the poet says: we should try to *"marry the crowd."* This experience of human merging is much more deeply engaging: "being both oneself and someone else," "adopting every profession, every joy, every misery, as one's own." This can bring immense erotic and psychic rewards: "unique intoxication," "universal communion," "feverish delights of which the selfish will be eternally deprived."

> What people call love is awfully small, awfully restricted, and awfully weak, compared with that ineffable orgy, that holy prostitution that gives itself totally, poetry and charity, to the unexpected that appears, to the unknown that passes by.

Marrying the crowd won't dispel the shadows and the sadness of human life—"she whom I might have loved"—but it can sublimate them, absorb them into a wider light that at once enlarges and envelops the whole horizon of being.

Baudelaire and Whitman sing in very different registers. But there is one crucial theme that they share, and that they celebrate: let us call it *mass merger.* Among the prime realities of modern life are rapid urban growth and enormous, noisy crowds of people. Many people are horrified by the sharp contrasts, the density, the dirt, the smells, the noise. For more than two hundred years, this sense of primal horror of the urban crowd—Edmund Burke, in his polemic against the French Revolution, called that crowd "the swinish multitude"—has inspired antidemocratic movements around the world. Ironically, this loathing has been shared by many supporters of democracy. It is expressed, for example, in what Americans could call the Jefferson tradition: they see "the mobs of great cities" as incubators of despotism; they think democracy will thrive only if brakes can be put on urban growth, and citizens can be kept spread out on homesteading family farms. (Of course, in order to keep these free people on the farm, and keep them from moving to the city, we would need a police state; but never mind.) But whether we like it or not, the move to cities has become the prime demographic arc in modern times. And any living democratic culture is going to have to be rooted in that urban crowd. Walt Whitman and Charles Baudelaire see the urban crowd as a source of vitality, of enchantment, of sexual radiance, a vista of possibilities for the expansion of the self. One of the most sophisticated antidemocratic thinkers of the nineteenth century, the philosopher Søren Kierkegaard, often called "the first existentialist," says, "The crowd is always an untruth." I'm sure neither Whitman nor Baudelaire ever heard of Kierkegaard. But if we listen hard, we will hear a way in which their writing is in dialogue with him. Kierkegaard wants everyone to "become what he is—an individual." But in order to protect his individuality, he must "make a stand against the crowd."[3] Our poets believe in "the individual" just as much as Kierkegaard does. But they believe that being on the street, being in the crowd, can enlarge individuals, can deepen them, can make them more profoundly the people they are. This affirmative vision of the individual in the crowd makes them pioneers of a democratic culture that is still urgent and vital today.

Epilogue

When I read Jane Jacobs's beautiful romance of the street, *The Death and Life of Great American Cities*,[4] not quite half a century ago, I felt instantly that she was *right* about city life, but also that she had reduced the horizon of her vision, had censored herself in a way that made her appear less profoundly right than she was. Once a reader is won over by the essential truth of Jacobs's world-picture, it's easy to ask, What's wrong with this picture? What's she leaving out? If we think of Whitman, we can see he was one of her primal sources, and a primary source of her existential depth, whether she knew it or not. Once we put Whitman in the mix, it's easy to see what she leaves out: she leaves out sex. Yet any street life as thick and richly interactive as the one Jacobs celebrates has got to be *sexy*, saturated with sexual fantasy and feeling, lit up with the experience I call "mass merger." Her book evokes the Hollywood movies I grew up on, ruled by "The Code," when studios were forbidden to show couples, even married couples, sleeping together. (That Code was finally coming apart just when her book came out.) If we put the censored footage back on the screen, if we let Sonnet 129 run through those lively streets, we will get a model of the city that will still be profoundly Jacobean, but more delicious, more wild, more disruptive and anarchic in its everyday (and its every-night) life. Can modern streets support this sexy footage, can they sustain this overflowing life, without coming apart? Fifty years after *Death and Life,* I think it's pretty clear, as it was clear to my generation fifty years ago, that this is a silly question:

Yes, my dears, they can. Whitman and Baudelaire could have told us! As a matter of fact, they did tell us. In the words of "Janet, Queen of the Bunny Planet,"[5] *They were there all along.* They urged us to place our faith in the city. They offered us a vision of the city street that can embrace us all, can come through whatever troubles open sexuality may open up, and can make all of us out there feel we are *more alive.*

Notes

1. *Les fleurs du mal* (1857), trans. Richard Howard (Boston: David R. Godine, 1982), #95, 275f; 97f.

2. *Spleen de Paris* (1868), trans. Edward Kaplan as *The Parisian Prowler* (Athens: University of Georgia Press, 1989), #12, 21f.

3. "That Individual," in *Existentialism: From Dostoevsky to Sartre,* ed. Walter Kaufmann (1956; New York: Plume, 1975), 94–100.

4. *The Death and Life of Great American Cities* (New York: Random House, 1961). I discuss Jacobs extensively in *All That Is Solid Melts into Air: The Experience of Modernity* (New York: Viking Penguin, 1988).

5. *Voyage to the Bunny Planet,* by Rosemary Wells, 3 vols. (New York: Dial, 1992). *Voyage* is one of the all-time great children's books, in the vein of Maurice Sendak's *Where the Wild Things Are.* Available at all children's bookstores, it is a remarkable cure for many modes of adult melancholy.

CHAPTER 7

Promiscuous Citizenship

Jason Frank

> The city's eroticism . . . derives from the aesthetics of its natural being.
> —Roland Barthes, "Semiology and the Urban"
>
> Do you know what it is as you pass to be loved by strangers?
> —Walt Whitman, "Song of the Open Road"

SHORTLY AFTER PUBLISHING THE first edition of *Leaves of Grass* in 1855, Whitman wrote several anonymous reviews of his own work. These self-reviews offer important insight into the expressly political motivations or "firstmost purports" animating this most innovative and formally unprecedented of nineteenth-century American literary experiments, particularly when read alongside the preface to the first edition of *Leaves*—a remarkable reflection on aesthetic democracy whose core insights would later be elaborated in "Democratic Vistas" (1871). Whitman's anonymous self-reviews positioned his poetry as a response to the looming crisis of American union. Rather than foreseeing a crisis in formal institutions or law alone, Whitman understood the impending catastrophe as a crisis of lived democratic citizenship, of perception, of the felt experience of relation and attachment on which more formal political relationships are based. "The largeness of . . . the nation is monstrous," Whitman wrote, "without a corresponding largeness and generosity in the spirit of the citizen."[1] In responding to what he alternately characterized as a crisis of political detachment, solipsistic individualism, and sectional discord, *Leaves* worked to transfigure the quality of public attachments and to poetically reshape the way citizens imagined and felt their way into a common democratic people.

This project of political poesis was clearly announced in one of Whitman's self-reviews when he wrote that the poet's "whole work, his life, manners, friendships, writing" have "an evident purpose": that is "to stamp a new type of character . . . and indelibly fix it and publish it, not for a model but an illustration."[2] A crucial aspect of Whitman's "reconstructive poetics" was eliciting a citizenry capacious enough to embrace "the expansive and flowing breadth of American democracy," one that could establish attachments without cramping "the largeness and stir" of democratic politics that he so loudly affirmed and so warmly embraced.[3] A central argument of this essay is that Whitman's image of promiscuous citizenship was his way of responding to a familiar dilemma of democratic theory: how to affectively bind citizens together as a self-authorizing people while mitigating the violence done to the plural constituencies that make up a democratic people; it was his way of navigating the dilemmas of democratic "binding" and "boundary."[4] The role that promiscuous citizenship plays in Whitman's political thought is therefore analogous to that played by "constitutional patriotism" in some contemporary forms of political liberalism, or "civic nationalism" in some communitarian strands of republican political thought.[5]

Whitman's poetry reiterates time and again, on different registers, and with different inflections, the question: "What is then between us?"[6] For him this question was particularly pressing because the usual means of political attachments were of no avail. "Here is not just a nation, but a teeming nation of nations." For Whitman, then, in the United States democratic attachment could not be achieved by Romantic appeal to a common tradition, language, ethnicity, or race, but reasoned allegiance to common principle was also too thinly cognitive, and obligation based in economic interest too narrowly calculating, to achieve the binding preconditions of democratic self-creation.[7] For Whitman, the conditions of democracy, America, and the modern required an aesthetic supplement and a radical re-visioning of inherited images of political belonging.

Gilles Deleuze recognized this dimension of Whitman's poetry when he wrote that, for Whitman, "America is not the fragmentary but the spontaneity of the fragmentary," and that because "there is no innate sense of the organic" in Whitman's America, relations "must be [poetically] instituted or invented" that aim not at "totality" but that emerge from "particular traits, emotional circumstances and the interiority of the relevant fragments" as they are exposed to "an encounter from the Outside."[8] I agree with Deleuze's emphasis on the importance of the poetic establishment of relations in Whitman's work, but, as I elaborate below, I disagree that Whitman believed these relations were simply "instituted or invented" by the poet. Whitman aspired to a poetic translation of the ordinary and commonplace as the vehicle for political attachment. *Leaves* offered an image of citizenship—it was what Whitman would later call a "great image-making work"—that at once drew from and addressed itself to "the tremendous audacity of crowds and groupings" whose "push of perspective spreads with a crampless and flowing breadth."[9]

The felicitous image of promiscuous citizenship I reconstruct here is drawn primarily from Whitman's writing on the city, from what I characterize as his remarkable aesthetics of urban encounter. In one of his anonymous self-reviews, Whitman likened this new image of the democratic citizen to "the very harlot of persons. Right and left he flings his arms, drawing men and women with undeniable love to his close embrace, loving the clasp of their hands, the touch of their necks and breasts, and the sound of their voice. All else seems to burn up under his fierce affection for persons."[10] Whitman is frequently celebrated as the "poet of the American city," one who "virtually alone among his peers . . . chose to extol the city's promise rather than lament its problems."[11] "Whitman felt the human crowd," William James famously wrote, "as rapturously as Wordsworth felt the mountains."[12] Less often noted is how Whitman's poetic translation of everyday urban experience contributed to his project of revising democratic citizenship. In Whitman's poetry, the promiscuity of urban encounter among anonymous strangers provides the experiential and affective basis for his dramatic reimagining of political attachment. For Whitman, the erotic energies among and between nonintimates were the very stuff of democratic spirit. In everyday urban encounters, he found what William Pannapacker has called "the promiscuous attractions of all people towards each other."[13] Whitman embraced the erotics and anonymity of everyday urban encounters as the basis for envisioning—and poetically disseminating—new and less identarian forms of political attachment.

In this, Whitman broke from dominant modes of imaging citizenship in America, which were typically characterized by different versions of democratic anti-urbanism. This is true, for example, of the agrarian pastoral of Jeffersonian republicanism as well as the Transcendentalist embrace of "nature" and the "wild." The contrasting image of citizenship that Whitman offers is promiscuous in several senses of the word. It is promiscuous first in the sense of being *undiscriminating*. "He judges not as the judge judges," Whitman writes in the preface to *Leaves*, "but as the sun falling around a helpless thing."[14] Second, it is promiscuous in the sense that it emerges from mixed and promiscuous public contact and is, as the *Oxford English Dictionary* defines one sense of the term, "mixed and disorderly in composition or character."[15] Finally, it is promiscuous in the sense that it connotes erotic attachment to nonintimates. "Do you know," Whitman asks his reader, "what it is to be loved by strangers?" The essay's first section focuses on the democratic resources of ordinary and everyday attachments; the second section turns to how Whitman develops his normative understanding of this attachment from the aesthetics of anonymous urban encounter.

"The Poet Is the Joiner, He Sees How They Join"

Whitman understood the political crisis of the 1850s as more than a crisis in formal institutions, party politics, policy, or law. The "new frame of democracy," he would later write, cannot be "vivified and held together merely by political means, superficial suffrage, legislation, &c."[16] Like Lincoln, for whom the civil religion of Union was transformed during this period from a reasoned commitment to the rule of law into a spiritual ideal that had "risen to the sublimity of religious mysticism,"[17] Whitman recognized the importance of restoring Americans' corrupted appreciation of the common, but, in doing so, he also dramatically refigured the source and meaning of that commonality. Whitman "abolishes the usual human distinctions," James insightfully wrote, "brings all conventionalisms into solution, and loves and celebrates hardly any human attributes save those elementary ones common to all."[18] "By God!" Whitman exclaims in *Leaves*, "I will accept nothing which all cannot have their counterpart of on the same terms."[19] The "first purposes" and "unconscious, or mostly unconscious" intentions of *Leaves* were "to articulate and faithfully express in literary or poetic form, and uncompromisingly, [Whitman's] own physical, emotional, moral, intellectual, and aesthetic Personality and that of current America," to poetically translate what he called his "[radically democratic] Me," and that of the people themselves.[20] "Into the vacuum created by the dissolution of the nation's political structures," writes David Reynolds, "rushed Whitman's gargantuan I, assimilating images from virtually every aspect of antebellum American culture into a poetic document of togetherness offered to a nation that seemed on the verge of unraveling."[21]

On the basis of this poetic translation of the neglected common, Whitman aspired to refigure the basis of democratic attachment, a goal to which he remained committed throughout his long life. He set about expressing and enacting forms of attachment that did not rely on "edifices or rules or trustees or any argument," but instead on the poetic translation of what is already given, that which tacitly connects and unites: the "subtle currents" that attach human beings below the level of formal contracts, political institutions, and law. "That which really balances and conserves the social and the political world," Whitman wrote, "is not so much legislation, police, treaties, and dread of punishment, as the latent eternal intuitional sense, in humanity, of fairness, manliness, decorum, &c." "This perennial self regulation," he continues, "is the *sine qua non* of democracy and the widest aim of democratic literature may well be to bring forth cultivate and strengthen this sense in individuals and society."[22] This was Whitman's democratic version of what Wordsworth described as "a dark inscrutable workmanship that reconciles discordant elements, makes them cling together in one society."[23] Kerry Larson has called Whitman's bundled practices of immanent self-regulation the "constitution beneath the Constitution."[24] Whitman emphasized the difficulties as well as the vital importance of bringing these practices to poetic articulation and public awareness. He sought a poetry that would at once poetically translate and revivify these unnoticed and unsung ordinary capacities, and that could form the poetic basis of explicitly pronounced democratic attachments. "The profoundest service that poems can do for their reader," Whitman wrote, "is not merely to satisfy the intellect . . . nor even depict great passions, or persons or events, but to fill him with vigorousness and clean manliness, religiousness, and give him *good heart* as a radical possession and habit."[25] This process would work "inside and underneath the elections of Presidents or Congresses," and such poems would infuse "the religious and moral character beneath the political and productive and intellectual basis of the States."[26] Rather than being didactically imposed by some imperious poet-legislator, for Whitman these aesthetic-affective reforms were drawn from latent resources already present in a democratic people that were by him "clarified and transfigured."[27]

As James recognized, the democratic resources of the ordinary and the everyday are one of Whitman's great themes. Whitman was profoundly attuned to what some contemporary political theorists refer to as the politics of the ordinary.[28] Consider the following lines from "A Song for Occupations":

> I bring what you much need yet always have,
> Not money, amours, dress, eating, erudition, but as good,
> I send no agent or medium, offer no representative of value,
>   but offer the value itself.
> There is something that comes to one now and perpetually,
> It is not what is printed, preach'd, discussed, it eludes
>   discussion and print,
> It is not to be put in a book, it is not in this book,
> It is for you whoever you are, it is no farther from you than
>   your hearing and sight are from you
> It is hinted by nearest, commonest, readiest, it is ever
>   provoked by them.[29]

Whitman clearly shares the recurrent theme of turning to the resources of the "nearest, commonest, readiest" for ethical and political orientation with Emerson.[30] Through this theme, Whitman is able to present what is already given in democratic life as a resource for what ails democratic life, which he takes to be the threat of an isolating skepticism, of a kind of world-alienating solipsism. "The great laws take and effuse without argument."[31] "To elaborate is no avail, learn'd and unlearn'd feel that it is so / Sure as the most certain sure, plumb in the uprights, well entretied, braded in the beams."[32] Whitman takes this sense of the world defined by a wordless being with others as "the base of all metaphysics." Somewhat oddly, he uses the cognitive language of "conviction" to describe this sense of the worldly ordinary. Thus he writes that his poetry aims to "convince" beyond "logic and sermons," or to "convince" "like a slumbering woman and child convince."[33] "I and mine do not convince by arguments, similes, rhymes, / We convince by our presence."[34] He warns readers not "to conceive too much of articulation": "Do you know Oh speech how the buds beneath you are folded?"[35] This is a theme brilliantly elaborated in "Crossing Brooklyn Ferry":

> We understand, then, do we not?

> What I promised without mentioning it, have you not accepted?
> What the study could not teach—what the preaching could not accomplish is accomplish'd, is it not?[36]

The democratic valence of bringing what one already has, the preservation and excitation of practices of immanent self-regulation and connection between strangers, is reflected in more than Whitman's aesthetic revaluation of "what is commonest and cheapest and nearest and easiest."[37] Whitman's poetry aims not only to ascribe aesthetic value to the commonest and the low, or to affirm the sublime multiplicity of the self, but to explore the workings of everyday attachments to others. In emphasizing this, I depart from readers who would overemphasize the Emersonian dimensions of Whitman's political thought. George Kateb, to take the best and most persuasive contemporary example, is right to argue that Whitman's "democratic aestheticism" seeks to "receive all things in the world as equal . . . to make the unpromising world worthy of attention; to grant standing to what seems not to merit it; and to hear the often silent or distorted appeal of everyone and everything for perception, interpretation, and contemplation."[38] William James is equally right to insist that Whitman hoped to save the "jaded and unquickened eye" from treating "the recurrent inanities of life" as "all dead and common, pure vulgarism, flatness, and disgust."[39] The emphasis that both Kateb and James place on receptive aesthetic (re)evaluation, however, does not adequately address Whitman's equally pronounced—perhaps even ontologically co-original—emphasis on magnetic, tacit, and subtle connections that bind individuals. These, too, make up the ordinary resources of that which "is commonest and cheapest and nearest and easiest." Whitman does not only aim to illuminate "the significance of alien lives," thereby overcoming "a certain blindness of human beings," but to illuminate the attachments that bind human beings beyond their recognition and consciousness: "The poet is the joiner," he writes, "he sees how they join."[40]

The democratic contributions of Whitman's poet are not limited to a change in individual perception, but include establishing connections or what Whitman called "fusing contributions."[41] This prompts Kerry Larson to describe Whitman's poems as "vehicles—or better yet, the occasion—for social cohesion."[42] "I bequeath poems," Whitman writes, "as nutrient and influences" to Union, to show "themselves distinctly" and to intimate "what they are for."[43] Whitman rejected nonaesthetic bases of political attachment, most notably tradition, race, rationality, or interests. "The genuine union" cannot be based, he writes, "(as is generally supposed) either in self-interest, or common pecuniary or material objects."[44] "Great literature," or what Whitman sometimes simply calls "esthetics," "penetrates all, gives hue to all, shapes aggregates and individuals."[45] The central problem, as Whitman understood it, was that democracy had not yet found its aesthetic expression, and so there was a tragic disconnection between formal democratic institutions and a culture still invested in forms of feudal hierarchy. "Long enough have the People been listening to poems [and singing songs] in which the common humanity, deferential, bends low, humiliated, acknowledging superiors. . . . Literature, strictly consider'd, has never recognized the People."[46] While the aesthetic inheritance of feudalism established affections and attachments—we can think of Burke's aesthetic theory of the "sweetness" of political authority—it did so by establishing relations of domination, deferential subordination, or contemptuous exclusion.[47] Whitman, as Nancy Rosenblum writes, "loved the spectacle of democratic diversity the same way that Burke loved monarchical plumage."[48] Indeed, Whitman could be said to have a profound understanding of Burke's dictum that to make a people love their country, their country must be lovely, but whereas Burke turned in disgust from the "swinish multitude," Whitman sought to make the embodied and unrefined people the source of their own aesthetic attachments.[49]

Whitman asked readers to "re-examine all you have been told at school or church or in any book," and to allow these revaluations of equal human connection to settle into the body, and be manifest in gesture, disposition, manner and gait: "your very flesh shall be a great poem," Whitman wrote, "and have the richest fluency not only in its words but in the silent lines of its lips and face and between the lashes of your eyes and in every motion and joint of your body."[50] For Whitman it was not enough that democratic egalitarianism be conceptualized as a formal principle; it must be further inscribed in flesh. Affection, eros, amativeness, attachment were essential components of this embodiment, of the manner through which the democratic people could become "a great passionate body."[51] While this theme is already clearly present in the first edition of *Leaves* (1855), it becomes more pronounced in each of the subsequent editions, as the crisis of the

1850s slides inexorably into the horror of Civil War. "The subtle fusion of diverse cultural images that he had attempted in 1855," David Reynolds writes, "was replaced by overt insistence on national unity through magnetic, passionate friendship."[52]

Already in the second edition (1856), for example, Whitman included a letter to Ralph Waldo Emerson that makes clear his hope that a dissemination of his poetry will work to stitch the ties of union, "for the union of the parts of the body is not more necessary to this life than the union of These States is to their life."[53] However, the theme of democratic affection and public eros is most pronounced beginning with the third edition (1860), which includes the remarkable "Calamus" cluster, focused on "manly love," "adhesiveness," and the "love of comrades." While some of these themes can already be detected in the first edition—"Urge and urge and urge," Whitman writes there, "Always the procreant urge of the world"[54]—they are nonetheless most pronounced in "Calamus." Whitman would later write that the "special meaning of the Calamus cluster of *Leaves of Grass*. . . . mainly resides in its political significance."[55] At the conceptual center of this cluster of poems is the phrenological understanding of "adhesiveness," which Whitman distinguished from romantic or intimate "amativeness." Whitman believed erotic attachment conceived in terms of intimacy and the private had been the exclusive focus of too much "imaginative literature" and sentimental fiction, greatly inflating the value of the intimate and domestic spheres and neglecting the powerful valences of *public* love. In the "Calamus" poems, by contrast, the focus is on not only the "dear love of man for his comrade, the attraction of friend to friend," but also "of the city for city and land for land."[56]

Consider the poem "For You O Democracy" from the cluster:

> Come, I will make the continent indissoluble,
> I will make the most splendid race the sun ever shone upon,
> I will make divine magnetic lands,
>   With the love of comrades,
>   With the life-long love of comrades.
> I will plant companionship thick as trees along all the rivers
>   of America, and along the shores of the great lakes,
>   and all over the prairies,

> I will make inseparable cities with their arms about each
>   other's necks,
>   By the love of comrades,
>   By the manly love of comrades.
> For you these from me, O Democracy, to serve you ma
>   femme!
> For you, for you I am trilling these songs.⁵⁷

Whitman's focus throughout "Calamus" is on public erotic attachments that destabilize and overcome identarian differences of locality, ethnicity, class and occupation, sex, race, and sexuality. Some critics who have recognized what Samuel Beer describes as the "nation-centered purpose" of Whitman's poetry have insufficiently recognized the real novelty of Whitman's "democratic nationality." Beer, for example, construes Whitman as an advocate of the organic nationalism he believed broadly typical of nineteenth-century Romanticism. This fails to capture the novelty of Whitman's account of democratic nationality, and neglects what I take to be a central dilemma that Whitman hoped to navigate in his poetry, which is how to eroticize political attachments that would bind a democratic people while not succumbing to the erotic lures of demonization. "Of all dangers to a nation, as things exist in our day," Whitman wrote, "there can be no greater one than having certain portions of the people set off from the rest by a line drawn—they not privileged as others, but degraded, humiliated, made of no account."⁵⁸ Or, as he writes in *Leaves*:

> I will not have a single person slighted or left away,
> The keptwoman and sponger and thief are hereby invited
>   . . . . the . . . slave is invited . . . . the
>   venerealee is invited,
> There shall be no difference between them and the rest.⁵⁹

Whitman's relation to the nation and nationality are filled with ambivalence from beginning to end, an ambivalence captured in the title of a late fragment: "Nationality—(and yet)."⁶⁰ It is undeniably true that Whitman claimed his poetry to be "autochthonous song"; that the "ambitious thought of [his] song is to help the forming of a great aggregate nation"; that he cites Herder on the poetic expression of "national spirit." Nonetheless, for

Whitman, nationality was inextricably linked to a horizon of unrealized futurity.[61] Its inclusiveness is based in what he called the "greatest lesson of New World politics," "the lessons of variety and freedom."[62]

Whitman's emphasis on nationality serves primarily to overcome the privation of privatism; through it, he places emphasis on public identity and critiques the limitations of what he called "the prudent citizen." Like other American Romantics, Whitman was appalled by what he called the "toss and pallor of years of moneymaking." He thought the narrow obsession with moneymaking and private life was "the great fraud upon modern civilization and forethought."[63] Whitman is, among other things, America's great poet of public life, not in the sense of public office, but in the sense of investing public identity with meaning and significance. It is not so much national identification that Whitman is calling for, in my view, as an erotic attachment to a common and public world comprised of vital differences.

One of Whitman's great innovations was that he modeled this understanding of public life and citizenship on his experience of urban life: not the urban life of the Athenian agora, or the Italian city-state, but of the bustling commercial metropolis of nineteenth-century New York City. *Leaves of Grass*, Whitman wrote, "arose out of my life in Brooklyn and New York from 1838 to 1853, absorbing a million people, for fifteen years, with an intimacy, an eagerness, and abandon probably never equaled."[64] In everyday promiscuous encounters with a procession of anonymous others, Whitman found the experiential basis for an ethos appropriate to what Deleuze called the "spontaneous fragments" of democracy. It is from "the love of strangers" on the city streets that Whitman's new image of citizenship—of promiscuous citizenship—would arise.

"This Is the City and I Am One of the Citizens"

To get a sense of Whitman's radical revaluation of the promise of urban experience and urban consciousness for democratic politics, it may be useful to sketch the background of the democratic anti-urbanism to which he was responding. Early theorists of American democracy emphasized an inherent tension, if not outright antagonism or contradiction, between democratic politics and the city. Their criticisms still resonate in the sneering invocations of coastal elites and the embrace of "pro-American" towns and counties; even the former mayor of New York City now ridicules out-of-touch cosmopolitans. In *Democracy in America,* Tocqueville wrote, "I look upon the size of certain American cities and above all the nature of their inhabitants as a genuine danger threatening the future of the democratic republics of the New World." He continued: "I do not hesitate to predict that that will be the source of their downfall unless their government succeeds in creating an armed force which will remain under the control of the majority of the nation, but which will be independent of the town population and thus able to repress its excesses."[65] For Tocqueville, the danger posed by American cities was that in them "men cannot be prevented from concerting together and awakening a mutual excitement that prompts sudden and passionate resolutions." Cities should be viewed as "great assemblies," he wrote, that "frequently wield astonishing influence over their magistrates and often carry their desires into execution without the latter's intervention."[66] Tocqueville toured America during a period of mobbish vigilantism, and the passages he dedicates to the subject in *Democracy in America* are haunted by the specter of the revolutionary Parisian underclass. But Tocqueville's concern was not limited to the immediate context of the 1830s, nor was it singularly French in its articulation.

The dangers posed by cities and their endemic corruption to democratic, or more accurately republican, politics was an essential part of the civic republican or "Country" discourse that had such a formative influence on early American political thought.[67] In early America, democratic anti-urbanism was not so much a bias, Thomas Bender writes, as a "political philosophy and a definition of a social ideal."[68] Thomas Jefferson was the preeminent early American theorist of democratic anti-urbanism. In his *Notes on the State of Virginia,* Jefferson wrote that "the mobs of great cities add just so much to the support of pure government, as sores do to the strength of the human body. It is the manners and spirit of a people which preserve a republic in vigor, a degeneracy of these is a canker which soon eats to the heart of the laws and constitution."[69] For Jefferson, the independence of mind and spirit that guarantees the liberties of a free republic was materially grounded in the conditions of independent landholding. As his friend David Ramsay put the point: "with no other dependence than on Almighty God . . . for his daily labor," the yeoman farmer guarantees "the continuance of [American] liberties."[70] As long as the vast majority of citizens were self-sufficient yeoman farmers, the republic would be immune to the corruption and factionalism that had undermined earlier experiments in republican politics. The vast expanse of western territory was, for Jefferson and many of his contemporaries, therefore the key to preserving the liberties of the people, and at the same time preventing the corrupting growth of large urban populations, which Jefferson described as "a cloacina of all of the depravities of human nature."[71] So deep was Jefferson's democratic anti-urbanism that, in a letter to the physician and social reformer Benjamin Rush, he wrote that urban America's ruinous yellow fever epidemics would at least have the advantage of discouraging "the growth of great cities in our nation," which are "pestilential to the morals, the health and the liberties of man."[72]

While Jefferson's anti-urbanism was expressly political and motivated by an overriding commitment to democratic freedoms and independent citizenship, it overlapped in many ways with broader moral reform movements in the first half of the nineteenth century. The understanding of urban populations as "vicious," "abandoned," and "debased" was a commonplace of this discourse. But rather than the Jeffersonian focus on the threats the city posed to virtuous citizenship, these movements, as the historian Paul Boyer has written, responded primarily to the perceived "erosion of an organic sense of community in a period of urban growth."[73] Christian moralists railed against the rootless populations of the city and the shamelessness of their behavior in the absence of communal norms. The association between city populations and shameless depravity was so strong that even Whitman was not above reproving urban populations for their "abnormal libidinousness."[74] The Christian reform efforts that responded to this condition attempted to "devise an urban analogue to the informal but continuous and pervasive scrutiny of behavior upon which the preurban moral order rested. What had been an organic feature of village life would be re-created in the city through voluntary organized effort, systematic surveillance, and journalistic publicity."[75] These antebellum Christian reform movements hoped to engender in city populations the very reformative sense of shame and self-disgust that Whitman's more characteristic "comprehensive program of disgust-extirpation" sought to diminish if not completely overcome.[76]

Closer to Whitman's own time, and much closer to his own political and philosophical orientations, was the anti-urbanism that emerged with American Romanticism in general, and with the Concord Transcendentalists in particular. Transcendentalists abandoned the conceptual rubric of civic and moral corruption in their writings on the city and replaced it with the more distinctly modern conceptual rubric of alienation. If Jefferson worried that cities engendered corrupting economic dependence and decadence, Emerson and Thoreau took the challenge to self-reliance to be a much more encompassing alienation of self and Nature. They sought not only an economic and political independence, but a "greater self-reliance that must work a revolution in all the offices and relations of men; in their religion, in their education, in their pursuits, their modes of living, their association; in their property; in their speculative views."[77] For both Emerson and Thoreau, cities undermined this ideal of self-reliance by proliferating artificial needs—"Cities degrade us," Emerson wrote, "by magnifying trifles"[78]—and entrapped individuals within an intricate choreography of false determinations and corrupted human relationships. "I always seem to suffer some loss of faith in entering cities," Emerson wrote in a letter to Carlyle, "they are great conspiracies; the parties are all maskers, who have taken mutual oaths of silence not to betray each other's secret and each to keep the other's madness in countenance."[79]

For Emerson, the actually existing city—as opposed to regenerative promise of what Thoreau would call "the eternal city of the west . . . [the] Salamanca of the imagination"[80]—was a place of convention, commerce, calculation, instrumentality, and narrow legibility. Emerson sometimes portrays the city as an iron cage of rationality—"it is made up of finites: short, sharp, mathematical lines, all calculable. It is full of varieties, of successions, of contrivances." He contrasts the constricted legibility of this built environment with the stimulating capaciousness of the country: "The country, on the contrary, offers an unbroken horizon, the monotony of an endless road, of vast uniform plains, of distant mountains, the melancholy of uniform and infinite vegetation; the objects on the road are few and worthless, the eye is invited ever to the horizon and the clouds."[81] Both thinkers associate the country and solitude with the regenerative aesthetic experience of the sublime, whereas the city is associated with narrow repetition, "rows upon rows of facts," and the instrumentalization of human relations. Emerson eloquently captured this contrast in an entry from his journal:

> Rest on your humanity, and it will supply you with strength and hope and vision for a day. Solitude and the country, books, and openness will feed you; but go into the city—I am afraid there is no morning on chestnut street, it is

full of rememberers, they shun each other's eyes, they are all wrinkled with memory of the tricks they have played, or mean to play on each other, of petty arts and aims all contracting and lowering their aspect and character.[82]

Emerson's idea that urbanism is associated with a particular form of subjectivity, with a "mode of consciousness," prefigures in interesting ways some of the central insights of later urban sociologists like Georg Simmel or David Riesman.[83] Thoreau, of course, developed the theme of diminished individuality and compromised modes of belonging and of the redemptive power of solitude, nature, and wild in *Walden*. According to Stanley Cavell, *Walden* is best read as "a tract of political education" that "locates authority in the citizens and it identifies citizens . . . as neighbors." It shows that "education for citizenship is education for isolation."[84] Shannon Mariotti has similarly argued for the democratic resources of Thoreau's "politics of withdrawal," as a practice that cultivates the capacities of critical negation necessary for democratic citizenship.[85] And Jane Bennett has explored the politically productive disorientation and unsettlement that comes from contact with "the tonic of wildness."[86] I agree with the broad outlines of these readings. Thoreau's isolation at Walden Pond—his stripping away of all false determinations, conventions, and institutions to return to life—shares much with the decentering provocations of urban encounter we find in Whitman's poetry. There are interesting continuities and discontinuities in their competing aesthetics of citizenship, but here I want to briefly emphasize the discontinuities.

"What do we want most to dwell near to?" Thoreau asks in *Walden*. "Not to many men, surely, the depot, the post-office, the bar room, the meeting house, the school house, the grocery, Beacon Hill or Five Points . . . but to the perennial source of our life."[87] For Thoreau, social encounters were hopelessly mediated by social convention and repetition; they were diminishing of singularity as they enacted over and over again scenes of social subjection and alienation. "The utmost nearness to which men approach each other," he writes, "amounts barely to a mechanical contact."[88] In the "Village" chapter of *Walden*, where this theme is richly developed, Thoreau writes that in our "trivial walks" and in our social behavior, "we are constantly, though unconsciously, steering like pilots by certain well-known beacons and headlands," but it is only when we are completely lost that we appreciate "the vastness and strangeness of nature": "Not till we are lost, not till we have lost the world, do we begin to find ourselves, and realize where we are and the infinite extent of our relations."[89] What Thoreau describes as the disorienting "tonic of wildness" is "the requirement that all things be mysterious and unexplorable, that land and sea be infinitely wild, unsurveyed, unfathomed by us because unfathomable."[90] In witnessing the transgression of "our own limits," we cultivate a heightened awareness of the artificial determinations that bind us and our interconnectedness. It is through a practical attentiveness to daily acts of orienting disorientation that the groundwork is laid for "the re-origination of many of the institutions of society," Thoreau writes.

Unlike Thoreau, Whitman finds a similarly regenerative power in the aesthetics of urban encounter. There is no unsettling psychogeography of the city in Thoreau's work, as there is in Whitman's. Rather than treating withdrawal and isolation as the necessary conditions of a more critically responsive practice of citizenship, it is through the anonymous encounters of urban life that this regenerative sense of the sublime is cultivated and elicited—"a sense of power, fullness, . . . [and] continued exaltation."[91] When Thoreau read *Leaves*, he wrote, "it is as if beasts spoke."[92] When Whitman read *Walden*, he wrote that "the great vice in Thoreau's composition was his disdain of cities, companions, civilization."[93] Whitman has been described as the "poet who introduced the city to American literature," one who waged a "revolution against the poetic resources of his heretofore pastoral culture."[94] This role was in fact an important part of Whitman's self-understanding. "I realize . . . that not Nature alone is great in her fields of freedom and the open air, in her storms, the shows of night and day, the mountains the forests, sea—but in the artificial, the work of man too is equally great—in this profusion of teeming humanity—these hurrying feverish electric crowds of men."[95] Nowhere is this contrast more clearly articulated and developed that in his two-part poem "Give Me the Splendid Silent Sun." In the poem's first part, Whitman marshals with heightened irony the well-worn Romantic tropes of Nature's sublimity—"Give me solitude, give me Nature, give me again O Nature your primal sanities!" But the poem's second part marks an abrupt shift:

> Keep your splendid silent sun,
> Keep your woods O Nature, and the quiet places by the
>   woods,

> . . . .
> Give me faces and streets—give me these phantoms
>   incessant and endless along the trottoirs!
> Give me interminable eyes—give me women—give me
>   comrades and lovers by the thousand!
> Let me see new ones every day—let me hold new ones
>   by the hand every day!
> . . . .
> O such for me! O an intense life, full to repletion and varied!
> . . . .
> People, endless, streaming, with strong voices, passions,
>   pageants
> . . . .
> Manhattan crowds, with their turbulent musical chorus!
> Manhattan faces and eyes forever for me.[96]

In such passages Whitman refigures the city as the locus of a restorative sublimity—"interminable," "incessant," "intense," "endless" pageants and crowds—one that did not spring from solitude and isolation but from promiscuous encounters with numberless strangers—interminable eyes and faces, lovers by the thousands. Whitman refused the conventional Romantic association of the city with alienation and delusive appearances, the treatment of "men and women crowding fast in the street" as nothing more than ghostly "flashes and specks."[97] For while the city posed for Whitman the "terrible doubt of appearances"—and therefore raised the isolating specter of skepticism—it also provided the ordinary resources for overcoming this doubt with a renewed and vital sense of having a place in the world with others, a sense of erotic attachment to others who nonetheless remain strangers.[98] For Whitman, the fact that we remain strangers is not something to be overcome, but rather the very condition of our affective bond; strangeness and urban anonymity are not marks of alienated human relation or the collapse of authentic community, but the basis of erotic attachment. Through the poetic translation of what Michael Warner has provocatively called "the phenomenology of cruising," Whitman envisions a way of relating as citizens that affectively binds without relying on mechanisms of identification.[99]

"When I mix with these interminable swarms of alert, turbulent, good natured, independent citizens, mechanics, clerks, young persons," Whitman wrote, "a singular awe falls upon me."[100] Some readers have associated the "singular awe" Whitman experienced in the spectacle of urban life, what he called the city's "visor'd, vast, unspeakable show and lesson,"[101] with that other great consumer of nineteenth-century urban spectacle, the *flâneur*, whom Baudelaire characterized as a "passionate spectator." "Whitman not only knew the *flâneur*," the critic Dana Brand writes, "he was a *flâneur*."[102] It is true that Whitman's celebrations of the endless processions and pageants of his "Mannahatta," his self-description as a "great loafer," and his aesthetic appreciation for the city's abrupt contrasts of high and low, beautiful and ugly, ignoble and magnificent, sometimes suggest the detached aestheticism of the *flâneur*. This is especially true of some of his early writing in newspapers like the *New York Aurora*, and in his letters to his probable lover Peter Doyle.[103] Before writing *Leaves*, Whitman had spent over a decade writing for newspapers and reviews on "this great, dirty, blustering, glorious, ill-lighted, aristocratic, squalid, rich, wicked, and magnificent metropolis,"[104] and in a letter to Doyle, Whitman described himself as a "great loafer who enjoys so much seeing the busy world move by him, and exhibiting itself for his amusement, while he takes it easy and just looks on and observes."[105]

The *flâneur*, however, does not adequately model the remarkable combination of unsettled wonder and erotic attachment that characterizes Whitman's aesthetics of urban encounter in the poetry of *Leaves of Grass*. The spectatorial experience of the *flâneur*, as Walter Benjamin theorizes it, is essentially one of being "out of place," taking aesthetic pleasure in one's detachment from the enfolding spectacle of urban life. [106] "The *flâneur* does not participate in the spectacles he describes, preferring to look and comment, as if the city and its people were a series of department store windows prepared for his visual, consumerist delight."[107] Whitman's man in the crowd, by contrast, is essentially engaged in and a part of the urban spectacle itself. Whitman writes from within and among the crowd, never in bemused or contemptuous detachment from it. "Both in and out of the game," as he puts it in one of his poems, "and watching and wondering at it."[108] Consistently situating himself "among the multitude," Whitman writes, "I descend to the pavements, merge with the crowd, and gaze with them."[109] "The experience of the street," however, is not only "the epitome of democratic consciousness" for Whitman, as James Dougherty has perceptively written, but also the site of a more embodied subjectivity and relation of contact encompassing dispositions, gestures, touch, and gait.[110]

Whitman writes that he received "curious abrupt questionings" from mingling with urban crowds, but he makes it clear that these were not only intellectual or cognitive events. The city is filled with "askers" that "unsettle what was settled," but their provocations and questionings are sensed and felt more than they are understood. In the innumerable encounters with strangers on the city street, Whitman cultivated a sense of being beyond himself, a processional provocation of subjective dissolution and wonder: I could be you, I could be you, I could be you, I could be you. He at once describes and hopes to poetically elicit "the wonder everyone sees in every one else he sees."[111] Consider the processional encounters Whitman relays in the "interminable," "incessant," "intense," "endless" lists of *Leaves of Grass,* which Wai Chee Dimock has insightfully described as "a poetry of sequence without sedimentation, a poetry that sallies forth, its syntactic possibilities unmarked and undiminished by what it has been through."[112] Such open-ended sequentialism is exemplified in these famous lines from "Song of Myself":

> The blab of the pave, tires of carts, sluff of boot-soles, talk
>   of the promenaders
> The heavy omnibus, the driver with his interrogating thumb,
>   The clank of the shod horses on the granite floor . . .
> The hurrahs for popular favorites, the fury of rous'd mobs . . .
> The impassive stones that receive and return so many echoes,[113]

Whitman works the accumulation of these sensory encounters—these "curious abrupt questionings"—into a series of reflections, thoughts bubbling up from perception:

> What living and buried speech is always vibrating here,
> what howls restrained by decorum,
> Arrests of criminals, slights, adulterous offers made,
> Acceptances, rejections with convex lips,
> I mind them or the show or resonance of them—I come
> and I depart.[114]

Frequently in *Leaves of Grass,* and perhaps especially in the unnamed poems that comprise the first edition, the series of encounters related in the present tense shift to provoked reflections, and then to decentered perspectives on these encounters, to an unsettling decentering of self. Whitman uncannily becomes a series of encountered others:

> I am the free companion, I bivouac by invading watchfires . . .
> I am the hounded slave, I wince at the bite of the dogs . . .
> I am the mash'd fireman with breast-bone broken . . .
> I am the artillerist, I tell of my fort's bombardment . . .[115]

In such passages, Whitman moves from the incessant encounters of urban life to imagined perspectives of others to loosen the grip of "one single naturalized perspective."[116] The cultivation of wonder at both the unbridgeable separation between strangers in the street and at the affective attachment that nonetheless binds them—"What is more subtle," Whitman asks, "than this which ties me to the man or woman that looks in my face?"[117]—is indeed a kind of self-alienation, but one that is best understood as democratically productive rather than defeating. It does not simply engender a sense of reciprocity or mutual recognition—as some admiring political theorists have claimed—but rather a wonder and attachment to what he calls, in "Democratic Vistas," the "lessons of variety and freedom."[118]

The city, then, for Whitman is a figure of excess, and Michel de Certeau's insights about representations of the city having to represent its ultimate unrepresentability certainly applies to Whitman's aesthetics of urban encounter.[119] The "interminable," "incessant," "intense," "endless" encounters of Whitman's poetry always seem to point to a horizon beyond themselves, to encounters that fall outside of the frame of experience. Like Whitman's lists, which seem to arbitrarily begin and end, and to thereby direct the reader's imagination to what lies beyond them, the urban encounters on which these lists are based elicit a sense of exaltation in the face of the city's very unmappability. Whitman's "mettlesome, mad, extravagant city" submits "to no models."[120] The city, then, is not a space of legibility or transparency for Whitman, and he does not nostalgically long for such legibility.[121] He is poorly read as endorsing an "aesthetics of identity" wherein "each person becomes transparent to every other."[122] Nor does he aim to replace "reflective judgment" with "all-encompassing affect" and "physiological affection."[123] To understand how Whitman navigates the tension between reflective unsettlement and passionate connection and investment in the world, we have to return to Whitman's poetry of public attachment.

If urban encounter provoked abrupt questionings that engendered wonder at the contingency of the self, it also offered instructions on the subtle forms of attachment between strangers, not through personal and partial relations of intimacy, but of eroticized impersonality. Urban encounters are the occasion for Whitman's poetic reflections on the democratic "being together of strangers."[124] "Passing stranger!" he writes, "You do not know how longingly I look upon you, / . . . / All is recall'd as we flit by each other, fluid, affectionate, chaste matured."[125] The orchestration of passing glances and longing looks between strangers become one important way that Whitman reenvisions forms of the erotics of citizenship uncorrupted by partial attachments. He isolates a queer proximity between cruising and citizenship.

> Among the men and women the multitude,
> I perceive one picking me out by secret and divine signs,
> Acknowledging none else, not parent, wife, husband,
>   brother, child, any nearer than I am,
> Some are baffled, but that one is not—that one knows me.
> Ah lover and perfect equal,
> I meant that you should discover me so by faint indirections.[126]

In such passages, Whitman is not only dwelling on what James called the "significance of alien lives," or cultivating an admirable receptivity to otherness. He puzzles over the love that can exist between strangers as strangers, a love and attachment that does not try to convert the stranger into an intimate, but retains a distance, perhaps "a pathos of distance."[127] The connection is there, but only by "indirection." In other poems, he even more explicitly connects the erotic attachments to strangers who remain strangers to the pleasures of furtive urban encounters. Consider this poem from the "Calamus" cluster:

> CITY of orgies, walks and joys,
> . . . .

> Not the pageants of you, not your shifting tableaus, your
> spectacles, repay me,
> . . . .
> Not those, but as I pass O Manhattan, your frequent and swift flash
> of eyes offering me love,
> Offering response to my own—these repay me,
> Lovers, continual lovers, only repay me.[128]

Whitman hoped to poetically reenact his aesthetics of urban encounter, with its combined emphasis on unsettling estrangement and promiscuous attachment, and its contributions to a "free and generous spirit in the citizenry," in the physical encounter he staged between readers and his poetic body in—or as—*Leaves of Grass*. This final claim could be elaborated and defended in various ways: by looking at the passages where Whitman describes reading as "a gymnasts struggle," where the "reader is to do something for himself, must be on the alert . . . the text furnishing the hints, the clue, the start,"[129] or in those passages where he describes the contact between his body/text and his reader's hands as a form of promiscuous touching. However, the best evidence of this claim may, appropriately enough, be in the physical design of the first edition of *Leaves of Grass* itself.

In the first edition, Whitman replaced his proper name with an imagistic surrogate. Opposite the book's title, as the book's frontispiece, he placed a suggestive, and—based on the many reviews that mentioned it—highly provocative engraving of himself (see page 340). Whitman stares at the reader, defiant in his open-collared shirt, rumpled pants, and tilted hat. This famous image of Whitman "the rough" has been frequently discussed by scholars for the political self-representation it enacts: Whitman is portrayed as a common man, not a dandy; as a sensuous body, not a composed intellect. One contemporary critic expressed his disgust for "this repulsive, loaferish portrait with its sensual mouth."[130] The image seems to confirm the poet James Russell Lowell's description of Whitman as "a rowdy, a New York tough, a loafer, a frequenter of low places, a friend of cab drivers!"[131] It is my sense that the key to understanding Whitman's provocative use of this image as the frontispiece to *Leaves* lies not only in its modalities of self-representation but in the relation it attempts to enact and establish with its viewer (who is not yet a reader). Whitman's replacement of image for text foregrounds the usually unremarked sensuousness of reading, and both makes visible and attempts to overcome the necessary textual mediation between the body of the poet and the body of the viewer.

> Come closer to me,
> ....
> I was chilled with the cold types and cylinder and wet paper
>   between us
>
> I pass so poorly with paper and types . . . . I must pass
>   with the contact of bodies and souls.[132]

In prefacing the poetry with the image of his body, Whitman attempts to visually enact the anonymous and promiscuous encounters of the democratic street, with their "curious abrupt questionings" and their furtive and indiscrete attachments. This reading is supported by Whitman's own illuminating reference to the image as "the street figure."[133] Whitman refuses to frame or contain the public's encounter with his poems by reference to his proper name. *Leaves* as a whole works to establish a relationship with its audience that duplicates the disorienting and affective scenes of furtive encounter that Whitman celebrated in urban life. He hoped the dissemination of these encounters through the circulation of his body of poems would work to reinvigorate democratic life in the United States and provide a new aesthetic basis for the weakened bonds of Union.

Notes

1. Whitman, Preface to *Leaves of Grass* (1855), in *Poetry and Prose*, ed. Justin Kaplan (New York: Library of America, 1996), 6.

2. Anonymous [Walt Whitman], "Walt Whitman, A Brooklyn Boy," in *Walt Whitman: The Contemporary Reviews*, ed. Kenneth M. Price, 21–22 (New York: Cambridge University Press, 1996), 21.

3. Whitman, Preface (1855), 5. On Whitman's "reconstructive poetics," see Allen Grossman, "The Poetics of Union in Whitman and Lincoln: An Inquiry toward the Relationship of Art and Policy," in *The American Renaissance Reconsidered*, ed. Walter Benn Michaels and Donald E. Pease, 183–208 (Baltimore: Johns Hopkins University Press, 1985), 184.

4. Clarissa Rile Hayward, "Binding Problems, Boundary Problems: The Trouble with 'Democratic Citizenship,'" in *Identities, Affiliations, and Allegiances*,

ed. Seyla Benhabib, Ian Shapiro, and Danilo Petranovi , 181–205 (New York: Cambridge University Press, 2007).

5. See Jan-Werner Müller, *Constitutional Patriotism* (Princeton: Princeton University Press, 2007).

6. Whitman, "Crossing Brooklyn Ferry," in *Poetry and Prose*, 310.

7. Whitman, Preface (1855), 5.

8. Gilles Deleuze, "Whitman," in *Essays: Critical and Clinical*, trans. Daniel W. Smith and Michael Greco, 56–60 (Minneapolis: University of Minnesota Press, 1997), 58, 60.

9. Whitman, Preface (1855), 5.

10. Anonymous [Walt Whitman], "Walt Whitman and His Poems," in *Contemporary Reviews*, ed. Price, 13.

11. Heather Roberts, "The Problem of the City," in *A Companion to American Fiction, 1780–1865*, ed. Shirley Samuels, 287–300 (New York: Blackwell, 2007), 298.

12. William James, "On a Certain Blindness in Human Beings," in *Writings: 1878–1899*, ed. Gerald E. Myers, 841–60 (New York: Library of America, 1992), 851.

13. William Pannapacker, "The City," in *A Companion to Walt Whitman*, ed. Donald D. Kummings, 42–59 (New York: Blackwell, 2006), 59, 54.

14. Whitman, Preface (1855), 9.

15. "Promiscuous," *Oxford English Dictionary*.

16. Whitman, "Democratic Vistas," in *Poetry and Prose*, 959.

17. Edmund Wilson, *Patriotic Gore: Studies in the Literature of the American Civil War* (New York: Norton, 1962), 99.

18. James, "On a Certain Blindness," 851.

19. Whitman, *Leaves of Grass* (1855), in *Poetry and Prose*, 50.

20. Whitman, "A Backward Glance o'er Travel'd Roads," in *Poetry and Prose*, 658. I explore Whitman's aesthetic translation of the vox populi in "Aesthetic Democracy: Walt Whitman and the Poetry of the People," *Review of Politics* 69 (2007): 402–30.

21. David Reynolds, *Walt Whitman's America: A Cultural Biography* (New York: Knopf, 1995), 86.

22. Whitman, "Democratic Vistas," 1013.

23. William Wordsworth, *The Prelude: The Four Texts* (New York: Penguin, 1995), 55.

24. Kerry C. Larson, *Whitman's Drama of Consensus* (Chicago: University of Chicago Press, 1988), 14.

25. Whitman, "Backward Glance," 667.

26. Whitman, "Democratic Vistas," 956.

27. Whitman, *Leaves of Grass* (1855), 50.
28. See Thomas Dumm, *A Politics of the Ordinary* (New York: New York University Press, 1999).
29. Whitman, "A Song for Occupations," in *Poetry and Prose,* 357.
30. Stanley Cavell explores this theme with great depth and insight. See, for example, *This New Yet Unapproachable America: Lectures after Emerson after Wittgenstein* (Albuquerque: Living Batch Press, 1989).
31. Whitman, *Leaves of Grass* (1855), 140.
32. Ibid., 28.
33. Ibid., 98.
34. Whitman, "Song of the Open Road," 303.
35. Whitman, "Song of Myself," in *Poetry and Prose,* 213.
36. Whitman, "Crossing Brooklyn Ferry," 312.
37. Whitman, *Leaves of Grass* (1855), 38.
38. George Kateb, "Aestheticism and Morality: Their Cooperation and Hostility," in *Patriotism and Other Mistakes,* 117–49 (New Haven: Yale University Press, 2006), 143; see also "Whitman and the Culture of Democracy," in *The Inner Ocean: Individualism and Democratic Culture* (Ithaca: Cornell University Press, 1992), 240–66.
39. James, "On a Certain Blindness," 854.
40. Whitman, *Leaves of Grass* (1855), 130.
41. Whitman, "Democratic Vistas," 957.
42. Larson, *Drama of Consensus,* xvi.
43. Whitman, Preface (1876).
44. Whitman, "Democratic Vistas," 960.
45. Ibid., 957.
46. Ibid., 968.
47. On the aesthetic dimensions of Burke's political theory, and in particular his understanding of the aesthetics of political authority, see Stephen K. White, *Edmund Burke: Modernity, Politics, and Aesthetics* (Boston: Rowman and Littlefield, 1994).
48. Nancy L. Rosenblum, "Strange Attractors: How Individualists Connect to Form Democratic Unity," in this volume, 56–57.
49. Edmund Burke, *Reflections on the Revolution in France,* ed. J. G. A. Pocock (Indianapolis: Hackett, 1987), 68.
50. Whitman, Preface (1855), 11.
51. Whitman, "Democratic Vistas," 1013.
52. Reynolds, *Walt Whitman's America,* 401.
53. Whitman, "Letter to Ralph Waldo Emerson," in *Poetry and Prose,* 1351–61.

54. Whitman, *Leaves of Grass* (1855), 28.

55. Whitman, Preface (1876), in *Poetry and Prose*, 129–38. Already in Whitman's own time, however, and certainly in our own, readers emphasized the homoerotic dimensions of the "Calamus" poems. Michael Moon, for example, has argued that the section offers a "critique of the culture's increasingly harsh repression of homoerotic desire as death-dealing." Whitman resisted the homoerotic associations when they were brought to his attention by John Addington Symonds, but later suggested these poems may have had meanings that escaped his conscious intent (Michael Moon, *Disseminating Whitman: Revision and Corporeality in* Leaves of Grass [Cambridge: Harvard University Press, 1991], 170; Reynolds, *Walt Whitman's America*, 396).

56. Whitman, "The Base of All Metaphysics," in *Poetry and Prose*, 275.

57. Whitman, "For You O Democracy," in *Poetry and Prose*, 272.

58. Whitman, "Democratic Vistas," 973.

59. Whitman, *Leaves of Grass* (1855), 44.

60. Whitman, "Nationality—(And Yet)," in *Poetry and Prose*, 1074–76.

61. Frank, "Aesthetic Democracy," 27–29.

62. Whitman, "Democratic Vistas," 953.

63. Whitman, Preface (1855), 20. See Michael T. Gilmore, *American Romanticism and the Marketplace* (Chicago: University of Chicago Press, 1985).

64. Quoted in Reynolds, *Walt Whitman's America*, 83.

65. Alexis de Tocqueville, *Democracy in America*, trans. Gerald E. Bevan (New York: Penguin, 2003), 325.

66. Ibid.

67. See, most obviously, Bernard Bailyn, *The Ideological Origins of the American Revolution* (Cambridge: Harvard University Press, 1967).

68. Thomas Bender, *Toward an Urban Vision: Ideas and Institutions in Nineteenth-Century America* (Baltimore: Johns Hopkins University Press, 1982), 4.

69. Thomas Jefferson, *Notes on the State of Virginia*, ed. William Peden (Chapel Hill: University of North Carolina Press, 1982), 165.

70. David Ramsay, *History of the United States: From Their First Settlement as English Colonies, in 1607, to the Year 1808* (Philadelphia, 1808), 35.

71. Thomas Jefferson, "Letter to William Short, September 8, 1823," in *Writings of Thomas Jefferson* (1905), 15:469.

72. Thomas Jefferson, "Letter to Benjamin Rush, September 23, 1800," in *Writings of Thomas Jefferson* (1903), 10:173.

73. Paul Boyer, *Urban Masses and Moral Order in America: 1820–1920* (Cambridge: Harvard University Press, 1978), 56.

74. Whitman, "Democratic Vistas," 963.

75. Boyer, *Urban Masses and Moral Order*, 19.

76. Martha Nussbaum, *Hiding from Humanity: Disgust, Shame, and the Law* (Princeton: Princeton University Press, 2004), 122.

77. Ralph Waldo Emerson, "Self-Reliance," in *Essays: First and Second Series*, 29–52 (New York: Library of America, 1990), 45.

78. Ralph Waldo Emerson, "Culture," in *The Conduct of Life*, 131–66 (New York: Houghton Mifflin, 1904), 153.

79. Ralph Waldo Emerson, "Letter to Thomas Carlyle, March 18, 1840." While I depart from their interpretations, I was directed to these passages by Morton White and Lucia White's *The Intellectual Versus the City: From Thomas Jefferson to Frank Lloyd Wright* (Cambridge: Harvard University Press, 1962), 21–34.

80. Henry David Thoreau, "Summer," in *Journals of Henry David Thoreau*.

81. Ralph Waldo Emerson, *Journals of Ralph Waldo Emerson*, vol. 5 (New York: Houghton Mifflin, 1911), 311. "In our large cities," Emerson elsewhere writes, "the population is godless, materialized, no bond, no fellow-feeling, no enthusiasm. These are not men, but hungers, thirsts, fevers, and appetites walking."

82. Ralph Waldo Emerson, *The Heart of Emerson's Journals*, ed. Bliss Perry (New York: Houghton Mifflin, 1926), 264.

83. For instance, Simmel writes in his seminal essay "The Metropolis and Mental Life" that the "swift and continuous shift of external and internal stimuli" characteristic of city life leads to the rapid development of the "protective organ of consciousness," and that the resulting calculating and blasé mode of subjectivity leads to the exclusion of "irrational, instinctive, sovereign human traits." Simmel describes the resulting relations between urban strangers in ways that also resonate with Emerson's account: these relations are regulated by "a slight aversion, a mutual strangeness and repulsion, which, in close contact . . . can break out into hatred and violence." The form of subjectivity interpolated by urban life is devoid of all enchantment, infused with calculating consciousness, and soullessly "other directed." According to Simmel, the city has always been the enemy of great individualists like Nietzsche. If we can hear Emerson's words resounding here, Whitman's influence infuses the work of such urbanists as Jane Jacobs, Richard Sennet, and Samuel Delaney (Georg Simmel, "The Metropolis and Mental Life," in *On Individuality and Social Forms*, ed. Donald N. Levine [Chicago: University of Chicago Press, 1971], 224–39, 231).

84. Stanley Cavell, *The Senses of Walden* (Chicago: University of Chicago Press, 1972), 85.

85. Shannon Mariotti, *Thoreau's Democratic Withdrawal: Alienation, Participation, and Modernity* (Madison: University of Wisconsin Press, 2009).

86. Jane Bennett, *Thoreau's Nature: Ethics, Politics, and the Wild* (Beverly Hills: Sage, 1994).

87. Henry David Thoreau, *Walden and Civil Disobedience* (New York: Penguin, 1986), 178.

88. Henry David Thoreau, *The Journals of Henry David Thoreau*, vol. 1 (New York: Dover, 1962), 38.

89. Thoreau, *Walden*, 217.

90. Ibid., 366.

91. Whitman, "Democratic Vistas," 962.

92. Quoted in Reynolds, *Walt Whitman's America*, 364.

93. Quoted in Pannapacker, "The City," 49.

94. James Dougherty, *Walt Whitman and the Citizen's Eye* (Baton Rouge: Louisiana State University Press, 1993), xiii, 30.

95. Whitman, "Democratic Vistas," 962.

96. Whitman, "Give Me the Splendid Silent Sun," in *Poetry and Prose*, 447.

97. Whitman, "There Was a Child Went Forth," in *Poetry and Prose*, 493.

98. Whitman, "Of the Terrible Doubt of Appearances," in *Poetry and Prose*, 274–75.

99. Michael Warner, "Whitman Drunk," in *Publics and Counterpublics*, 269–90 (New York: Zone, 2002), 287.

100. Whitman, "Democratic Vistas," 979.

101. Whitman, "Broadway," in *Poetry and Prose*, 624.

102. Dana Brand, *The Spectator and the City in Nineteenth-Century American Literature* (Cambridge: Cambridge University Press, 1991), 43.

103. See *Walt Whitman of the New York Aurora, Editor at Twenty-two: A Collection of Recently Discovered Writings*, ed. Joseph Jay Rubin and Charles H. Brown (State College, Pa.: Bald Eagle Press, 1950).

104. Cited in Eldwin G. Burrows and Mike Wallace, *Gotham: A History of New York to 1898* (New York: Oxford University Press, 2000), 706.

105. Walt Whitman, "Letter to Peter Doyle October 9, 1869," in *The Collected Writings of Walt Whitman: The Correspondence*, 2:56–58 (New York: New York University Press, 1961), 2:57.

106. On Benjamin's theory of the *flâneur*, see Susan Buck-Morss, "The *Flâneur*, the Sandwichman and the Whore: The Politics of Loitering," *New German Critique* 39 (1986): 99–140.

107. Pannapacker, "The City," 43.

108. Whitman, *Leaves of Grass* (1855), 30.

109. Whitman, "A Broadway Pageant," in *Poetry and Prose*, 384.

110. Dougherty, *Citizen's Eye*, 32.

111. Whitman, *Leaves of Grass* (1855), 92.

112. Wai Chee Dimock, "Whitman, Syntax, and Political Theory," in *Breaking Bounds: Whitman and American Cultural Studies,* ed. Betsy Erkkila and Jay Grossman, 62–79 (New York: Oxford University Press, 1996), 73.

113. Whitman, *Leaves of Grass* (1855), 33.

114. Ibid., 34.

115. Ibid., 65.

116. Alan Trachtenberg, "Whitman's Lesson of the City," in *Breaking Bounds,* ed. Erkkila and Grossman, 171.

117. Whitman, "Crossing Brooklyn Ferry," 312.

118. Whitman, "Democratic Vistas," 953.

119. Michel de Certeau, *The Practice of Everyday Life* (Berkeley and Los Angeles: University of California Press, 1984), 91–110.

120. Whitman, "City of Ships," in *Poetry and Prose,* 430.

121. The ultimate illegibility of city life in Whitman's work, however, clearly does not terminate in paralyzing skepticism or alienation. Here the best contrast text is Poe's "Man in the Crowd." In that story, the illegibility of Poe's eponymous man in the crowd, the inscrutability of his motivations, the "waywardness of his actions," "arouses," "startles," and "fascinates" the narrator. But the narrator's growing captivation by this "phantom" and "ghost" leads not to any enchantment, wonder, or productive disorientation. Rather, the narrator turns away in horror and disgust at the anonymous man in the crowd, who, for Poe, expresses "the type and genius of deep crime." "Es lasst sich nicht lesen" because the man of the crowd has no soul to read (Edgar Allan Poe, *Poetry and Tales* [New York: Library of America, 1984], 388–96).

122. Philip Fisher, "Democratic Social Space: Whitman, Melville, and the Promise of American Transparency," *Representations* 24 (1988): 67.

123. Mary Esteve, *The Aesthetics and Politics of the Crowd in American Literature* (New York: Cambridge University Press, 2003), 27, 28.

124. For an insightful discussion of the "being together of strangers" in contemporary democratic theory, see Iris Marion Young, *Justice and the Politics of Difference* (Princeton: Princeton University Press, 1990), 237.

125. Whitman, "To a Stranger," in *Poetry and Prose,* 280.

126. Whitman, "Among the Multitude," in *Poetry and Prose,* 286.

127. The phrase is Nietzsche's. On the democratic significance of a "pathos of distance," see William E. Connolly, *Identity/Difference: Democratic Negotiations of Political Paradox* (Ithaca: Cornell University Press, 1991), 184–97.

128. Whitman, "City of Orgies," in *Poetry and Prose,* 279.

129. Whitman, "Democratic Vistas," 1016.

130. Quoted in Ed Folsom, "Appearing in Print: Illustrations of the Self in Leaves of Grass," in *The Cambridge Companion to Walt Whitman*, ed. Ezra Greenspan, 135–65 (New York: Cambridge University Press, 1995), 136.
131. Quoted ibid., 137.
132. Whitman, *Leaves of Grass* (1855), 89.
133. Quoted in Folsom, "Appearing in Print," 139.

CHAPTER 8

Walt Whitman and the Ethnopoetics of New York

Michael J. Shapiro

> Holding the pencil like one lonely chopstick
> & grasping the pad like an empty plate
> Waiting to be filled: . . . .
> Nothing decorous but our own clinging minds
> & the piling of her smooth black hair
> —John Yau, *Crossing Canal Street*

Introduction: The Whitman Effect

WALT WHITMAN'S INFLUENCE ON generations of artists, writers, and poets in America and throughout the world is undeniable.[1] The lines, imagery, sentiments, and subjects of attention in his poems continue to emerge in novels, poetry, music, and other art forms. The title and much of the imagery and focus of his poem "I Sing the Body Electric," for example, have migrated into a wide variety of texts, among which are a science fiction story, a Manhattan novel, and an analysis of jazz.[2] Moreover, his song imagery (his most pervasive figuration) has motivated and energized both musical compositions and literary works. In this investigation, my concern is less with the breadth of Whitman's influence than with its ethnopoetical realizations and reinflections as they are articulated in and on the city of New York. Rather than simply demonstrating influence, my aim is to show how applications and alterations of Whitman's musico-poetical subject generate an apprehension of the micropolitics of interethnic New York, while at the same time capturing interpersonal and person-city resonances, as the rhythms of individual and collective "ethnic" becoming encounter the rhythms of the city.

My initial appreciation of ethnic inflections of Whitmanesque urban resonances is owed to a passage in Ralph Ellison's musically inflected description of one of his New York encounters, shortly after he moved there from Alabama. Describing his adjustment to the city, Ellison writes, "I had discovered, much to my chagrin, that while I was physically out of the South, I was restrained . . . by certain internalized thou-shalt-nots that had structured my public conduct in Alabama."[3] Because New York presented a different set of thou-shalt-nots, Ellison found himself to be a "pioneer in what was our most sophisticated and densely populated city."[4] In this guise, he relates a variety of vexing encounters, one of which is especially germane to this analysis. It occurred in a Fifty-ninth Street bookstore, where he was shopping for one of T. S. Elliot's works. After striking up a conversation with a "young City College student" and "recounting an incident of minor embarrassment," he used "the old cliché . . . And was my face red." His interlocutor countered with the remark, "What do you mean by 'red' . . . what you *really* mean is 'ashes of roses'"[5] Ellison continues: "I didn't like it, but there it was—I had been hit in mid flight; and so, brought down to earth, I joined in his laughter. But while he laughed in bright major chords I responded darkly in minor-sevenths and flatted fifths, and I doubted that he was attuned to the deeper source of our inharmonic harmony."[6] While this lyrical, musically figured passage is one among Ellison's abundant Whitman-like moments, there is a significant ethnic inflection of the Whitman effect in his renderings. As he "emerged as a central figure in the process of writing, he . . . engages the poetics of sonic Afro-modernity by returning time and again to questions of sound, technology, and (black) culture."[7]

Thus, although Ellison was clearly influenced by Whitman's poetry, he wrote from a different locus of enunciation and evoked a different sociopolitical imaginary. The way such differences produce an alteration of Whitman's perspectives is evident in Ellison's famous first novel, *Invisible Man*, where, in chapter 5, his narrator tells the story of the founding of a "Negro" college in an unidentified southern state. Dominating the chapter is a eulogy to the Founder that unmistakably mimics Whitman's famous poem "When Lilacs Last in the Dooryard Bloom'd," a eulogy Whitman wrote after the death of President Lincoln. As one commentator summarizes the connection, "All the Whitman symbols are there: the lilac, the star, the thrush—the bells and the funeral train."[8] Yet, as he adds, "Ellison employs them for almost entirely opposite reasons than did the bard of American poetry." While "Whitman was attempting in his poem to measure the potential of the poetic mind within the framework of the death of the great emancipator, Abraham Lincoln," Ellison "uses these same symbols . . . to measure the great irony and bitter disillusion of racial betrayal brought about after the death of another great fighter for emancipation, the beloved Founder—Ellison's picture of a black and mythical Lincoln."[9] Lest there be lingering doubt about Ellison's contrapuntal homology between President Lincoln and the college's Founder, Ellison's eulogist has the Founder confronting a "great struggle" that, rather than South versus North, is between "black folk and white folk . . . each fearful of the other [such that] A whole region is caught up in a terrible tension."[10] And the Founder is variously referred to as "great captain" (echoing one of Whitman's metaphors for Lincoln), and as a "President" whose significance loomed much larger than one would expect of "just a president of a college"; instead, "he was," claims the eulogist, "a leader, a 'statesman' who carried our problems to those above us, even unto the White House."[11]

The style of Ellison's radical reinflection and displacement of Whitman's poetic eulogy on Lincoln accords with Houston A. Baker Jr.'s characterization of those African American writers who evince a "mastery of form," a discursive strategy in which the black writer uses the genres and phrasings of established white writers but effects a displacement in context and tone that will engage effectively with white readers' modes of reception while at the same time addressing "the contours, necessities, and required programs of his own culture."[12] Baker sees Booker T. Washington's *Up from Slavery* as the prime example of this discursive strategy, but he also provides a brief aside in which Ellison's *Invisible Man* qualifies as well.[13] Ellison is but one of many "ethnic" writers who are inspired in part by Whitman while adjusting the tone and context to articulate alternative experiences of the city and address alternative constituencies. However, before analyzing the micropolitical implications of a Whitmanesque ethnopoetics of the city, we need to situate Whitman's poetry, especially the way it is deployed on New York City.

Walt Whitman's "Musico-Literary Poetics" of the City

There are two related dimensions of Whitman's poetic engagement with New York, which like Ellison's is often musically inflected but unlike Ellison's is shaped by the musical trope of the solo—the "I sing"—rather than by a collective (ethnically oriented) soundscape.[14] The first is articulated through the grammar of his poesis, which is in keeping with his musical idiom. Because many of Whitman's poetic subjects undergo a universalizing expansion in city encounters, especially in Whitman's more I-centered poems (or solos), this kind of Whitman subject bears comparison with Immanuel Kant's philosophical subject. Like one version of Whitman's, the Kantian subject is a mentality that achieves what Kant refers to as "enlarged thought" as a result of its engagements with the sensations of experience.[15] To summarize Kant's narrative of the subject's expanding consciousness: Initially, the subject's dynamic of apprehension is activated by an experiential event to which Kant refers as "organic sensation."[16] However, because sensation produces disparate and disorganized perceptions, the cognitive faculty takes over after the events of sensation and orders them to generate "understanding." Kant is clear about this progression: "sense perceptions certainly precede perceptions of the understanding."[17] Thus once a subject is merely affected by the world, the cognitive faculty is engaged; it "joins perceptions and combines them under a rule of thought by introducing order into the manifold."[18] Yet this ordering is merely the penultimate step. The Kantian narrative of productive understanding is not consummated until it universalizes itself by becoming public. However, the public aspect of the Kantian narrative is not a form of social communication; rather it is the consummation of the enlightenment narrative that takes place within the subject's consciousness. The subject becomes absorbed into what Kant calls a "universal communicability" because the judging faculty of taste incorporates a "universal voice."[19]

Often, Whitman's poesis is similarly oriented by a productive perceptual dynamic rather than a social process. The homology between the Whitman and Kantian subject is at times evident in the way Whitman reflects on his experiences of the city as a mobile observer, when for Whitman the city becomes "at once material place and mode of perception."[20] And significantly for a comparison with Kant, that mode of perception has as its primary consequence an enlarged consciousness for Whitman as a poetic subject. For example, in his "To You," he begins by addressing the city's moving crowd as a "you"—"whoever you are"—and then alters the "you" second-person grammar, so that "you gives voice to I";[21] "Whoever you are, now I place my hand upon you, that you be my poem."[22] Here, as in many other poems, Whitman strives for a universalizing consciousness within the I-subject. In such Kantian moments, he presumes that what and how he feels and perceives is owed to a shared humanity that is immanent in the process of judgment. The Whitman "I" fuses with the many. Lines from his most famous New York poem, "Crossing Brooklyn Ferry," exemplify Whitman's universalizing poetic grammar:

> Just as you feel when you look at the river and sky, so I felt,
> Just as any of you is one of the living crowd, I was one of the crowd,
> Just as you are refresh'd by the gladness of the river and the bright flow, I was refreshed,
> . . . .
> These and all else were to me the same as they are to you,[23]

Here for Whitman, as for Kant, the world of experience produces an epistemological lesson. He presumes that his enlarging consciousness is bringing him close to the way humanity as a whole experiences and knows the world. However, while the Kantian geographic imaginary is global, in Whitman's case the condition of possibility for the encounters that render his consciousness enlarged is his city location. His observations on New York venues constitute an "urban instruction"[24] He revels in "Numberless crowded streets, high growths of iron, slender, strong light, splendidly uprising toward clear skies" in what he calls "my city."[25]

However, Whitman's focus on the city's sensorium also suggests a somewhat different Whitman, a post-Kantian version whose poetic subject is at times closer to Walter Benjamin's philosophical subject than to Immanuel Kant's. Like Whitman's, Benjamin's philosophy of experience is evoked in confrontation with the city's variegated sensorium. Reacting to Kant's philosophy of experience, Benjamin affirms the Kantian transcendental emphasis on the conditions of possibility for experience but moves away from a focus on mental structures of apprehension and their intermediation and toward a focus on the "experience of the city," which in Howard Caygill's apt terms, "replaces substance and subject with *transitivity*."[26] Benjamin's philosophy of experience emerges from observations about the way one's experience of the city is inflected by the porousness of its built environment and the ways in which spaces and temporal rhythms constitute the conditions of possibility for interpersonal association, as the city affords varying degrees of cross-space access. In his observations on Naples (written with Asja Lacis), for example, Benjamin suggests that its architecture enacts a porosity that shapes the city's various interpersonal dramas in what he calls "simultaneously animated theaters."[27] Note as well these observations Benjamin wrote in Marseille:

> *"Les bricks"* the red-light district is called, after the barges moored a hundred paces away at the jetty of the old harbor. A vast agglomeration of steps, arches, bridges, turrets, and cellars. It seems to be awaiting its designated use, but it already has it, For this worn out depot is the prostitutes' quarter. Invisible lines divide the area up into sharp, angular territories like African colonies. The whores are strategically placed, ready at a sign to encircle hesitant visitors, and to bounce the reluctant guest like a ball from one side of the street to the other.[28]

Like Benjamin's, Whitman's philosophy of experience—in his case deployed on his interest in a populist mode of democracy—emerges from his city observations. He views a variegated city ethnoscape and classifies the trajectory of identities he sees/imposes as a series of individualities which all belong to an equality-affirming democracy. Thus, although his "Song of Myself" foregrounds himself as an I-subject, it also moves well beyond a preoccupation with mere consciousness. It also observes a variety of those with oppressed or marginal identities who, he suggests, need him to speak for them (even though he also says, "You shall not look through my eyes either, nor take things from me, / You shall listen to all sides and filter them from your self").[29]

> I speak the pass-word primeval, I give the sign of democracy,
> By God! I will accept nothing which all cannot have their
>   counterpart of on the same terms.
>
> Through me many long dumb voices,
> Voices of the interminable generations of prisoners and slaves,

> Voices of the diseas'd and despairing and of thieves and dwarfs,
> ....
> Through me the forbidden voices[30]

Significantly, Whitman's relationship with those whose "forbidden voices" he will ventriloquate is not merely discursive. Whitman brings his entire body to the urban scene he observes. His connection with the city's peoplescape is excursive rather than merely discursive. While he emphasizes voice, he also notes a general in-corporation. Thus in his "Song of Myself," after lending his song to "those long dumb voices," he writes, "And these tend inward to me, and I tend outward to them."[31] And he is at pains to construct himself corporeally: "I believe in the flesh and the appetites, seeing hearing, feeling, are miracles, and each part and tag of me is a miracle . . . If I worship one thing more than an other it shall be the spread of my own body, or any part of it."[32]

Here certainly is the Benjaminian rather than the Kantian Whitman, the Benjamin who insists that a city cannot be apprehended merely as image-space but as an "interpenetration" of "body- and image-space."[33] In his essay on surrealism, Benjamin evokes the disposition of a "collective innervation."[34] According to Benjamin, "the face of the city" becomes palpable not with mere images such as the pictures of Giorgio de Chirico or Max Ernst but only in moments when the "sharp elevations of the city's strongholds" are occupied and overrun by bodies.[35] Rather than mere interpersonal perception, the bodily encounters in/with the city provoke corporeal "innervations," discharges of energy. This model of the body-city relationship comports well with Whitman's imagery of the bodies in the city (his as well as the mass of bodies he observes) as bodies electric. In "I Sing the Body Electric," Whitman begins with imagery of incorporation: "The armies of this I love engirth me and I engirth them"[36] and then proceeds to celebrate bodies, evoking a long list of the bodily attributes of genders and generations. Here as elsewhere, Whitman's mode of perception is not merely optical; it is what Deleuze and Guattari refer to as "haptic," a mode of perception that includes one's bodily experience without hierarchizing the senses.[37] Fulfilling both Deleuze and Guattari's and Benjamin's post-Kantian construction of an embodied subject, Whitman extols the city as an interpenetration of body- and image-space and deploys a haptic mode of perception as his I-subject become an engaged body, and his Kantian fixation on consciousness, so evident in many of his poems, is displaced by a bodily charge he receives from other bodies. I return to "the body electric" trope in the conclusion, where I treat a Whitman-inspired novel that elaborates Whitman's electric imagery and its implications for interethnic encounters. At this point, I want to turn to an "ethnic" poet who, like Whitman, evokes New York's bodies but avoids an I-subject grammar and treats the body's ethnic as well as physical attributes.

Although Whitman refers often to his own body, his whiteness is lent no perceptual effects in his writing. In contrast, a contemporary poet, John Yau, "makes the reader aware of how a Chinese American looks at and transforms New York's Chinatown, how he shapes his world."[38] At the same time, however, Yau expresses distrust of a poesis based on an "I" grammar. Although he frequently focuses on urban Chinese venues and cultural moments, Yau writes, he says, "from an 'I' who doesn't know who that 'I' is."[39] Rather than committing himself to a unified I-subjectivity, Yau asks, "Might it not be possible that the self is made up of many selves, incomplete and fragmented?"[40] Moreover, unlike Whitman's New York, which yields spaces of observation for a human multiethnic diorama with ethnically reified subjects, Yau offers what Priscilla Wald calls a "geo-conceptual space," an ethnically particularized treatment of some of New York's Chinatown venues but with as many subjects who are "divested of cultural identity" as are "reified."[41] Attentive to New York's ethnic geography, Yau notes the way the crossing of Chinatown's boundaries constitutes the enactments that define part of New York's fraught racial-spatial order. While Whitman's famous crossing poem, "Crossing Brooklyn Ferry," meditates on what people across generations will share, Yau's crossing imagery is concerned with an ethnic boundary. Thus in his poems in *Crossing Canal Street* (a Chinatown boundary), in which the I of the poet is repressed, he provides both a glimpse of an ethnic mode of observation and a microcultural geography that is enacted in the movement of persons in their everyday life routines. Note, for example, his "An Old Chinese Gentleman Drops in to See His Cronies in a Coffeeshop (Mott Street)":

> Five faces
> five dried fruit

> pungent & wrinkled
> around a table . . .
> Talking, drinking tea, eating
> Small sweet cakes, almond cookies
> returning to a terrain
> half-imagined. . . . [42]

The second dimension of Whitman's urban poesis also bears comparison with Yau's inasmuch as Whitman also captures the rhythms of city life. But Whitman is less focused on specific venues and moments and more concerned with himself than with the vagaries of other lives. Nevertheless, Whitman's poems achieve harmony between poetic form and reference. His lyrically expressed observations are shaped by the instruction that urban rhythms supply for the rhythms of his poems: for example, "What hurrying human tides, or day or night! / . . . / Thy windows rich, and huge hotels—thy side-walks wide; / Thou of the endless sliding, mincing, shuffling feet! / . . . / Thou visor'd, vast, unspeakable show and lesson."[43] As the flow of humanity he observes resonates within the flow of his poems, he wraps his urban world in song and merges with the crowd of urban humanity. Thus he begins his "One's-Self I Sing," as "a simple separate person," but then continues "Yet utter the word Democratic, the world En-Masse," and the song embraces all: "The Modern Man I sing."[44] In his "Song of Myself," he begins with a musical self-indulgence "I CELEBRATE myself and sing myself";[45] he continues as "Walt Whitman, a kosmos, of Manhattan the son, Turbulent, fleshy, sensual,"[46] and declares, "I dote on myself, there is that lot of me and all so luscious."[47] Although he is deeply involved with shaping what he sees in what he expresses, eventually Whitman begins to take in and incorporate other sounds besides those of his own voice: "Now I do nothing but listen, / To accrue what I hear into this song, to let sounds contribute toward it."[48]

Nevertheless, Whitman remains the spokesperson for those "other sounds." The univocal stance he often adopts makes genre-sense if we accept M. M. Bakhtin's insistence that poetry does not offer polyphony; rather it tends toward monologic discourse:

> The poet is a poet insofar as he accepts the idea of a unitary and singular language and a unitary, monologically sealed-off utterance. These ideas are immanent in the poetic genre with which he works. . . . The poet must as-

sume a complete single-personed hegemony over his own language, he must assume equal responsibility for each one of its aspects and subordinate them to his one, and only his own intentions.[49]

In contrast, Bakhtin states: "a prose writer can distance himself from the language of his own work. . . . He can make use of language without wholly giving himself up to it."[50] Given the dominance of Whitman's musical figuration, Bakhtin's treatment of Dostoevsky's "polyphonic novel," whose composition has a "musical character," provides a telling contrast between Whitman's tendency to a monologic poesis and a dialogic alternative.[51] According to Bakhtin, Dostoevsky's polyphonic poesis is a genre-effect, for in general, novels present a "plurality of voices" that articulate alternative "points of view on the world."[52]

Although as a genre, novels do exhibit more of a dialogic form than other literary genres, Bakhtin's restriction of dialogics to novels is unfair to poetry in general and to Whitman specifically.[53] Certainly poetry tends more toward a monologic style than the novel, but Whitman has nevertheless been justly credited with "breaking the hegemony of the lyric voice."[54] For example, in his "Out of the Cradle Endlessly Rocking," he develops "a complex or shifting discourse situation" as the poem features a fictional interplay of voices among a young boy, a bird, and the sea, along with the narrative voice of the poet.[55] Gilles Deleuze, citing a French critic who attributes polyphony to Whitman's poetry, puts it this way, "Whitman's poetry offers as many meanings as there are relations with its various interlocutors: the masses, the reader, States, the ocean."[56] Moreover, Whitman's *Leaves of Grass* evinces more than one Whitman voice. Or, to put it differently, rather than a fixed poetic being, the changes over four editions of the collection manifest a becoming Whitman.

Over time, faced with a changing civic culture's articulations of a politics of literary aesthetics, Whitman's emended editions testify to his intervention in that dynamic cultural progression. As Michael Moon notes in an analysis of the changing editions of *Leaves of Grass*, Whitman sought to "disseminate affectionate physical presence from one to another."[57] And as Whitman himself insists, his effort is more political than literary. Speaking of the emotional resonances of some of the poems in his 1876 Preface, Whitman states that, "important as they are in my purpose as emotional expressions for humanity, the important meaning of the 'Calamus' cluster of 'Leaves of Grass' . . . mainly resides in its political significance."[58] Moon summarizes the political sensibility arising from Whitman's attentiveness to the changing times through the various editions of *Leaves of Grass:* "The long process of revisionary elaboration that *Leaves of Grass* gradually underwent produced a series of texts that powerfully articulate a politics comprehending ranges of experience as ostensibly disparate as the pleasurable and painful phases of male-homoerotic love ('Calamus') and the national trauma of the sectional division of the country over slavery."[59] Ultimately, however, the political apprehensions that Whitman delivers are inhibited by the grammar of his address.

A More Dialogic New York: "Our Singing"

My turn to a novelist realization of the Whitman effect is encouraged by Bakhtin's recognition of the plurivocal advantages of the novel form. Even though his total denial of dialogics in the lyric genre has been discredited, Bakhtin's recognition of the pervasively dialogic character of the novel remains relevant. My soliciting of the novel is also encouraged by Whitman's sensitivity to changing times in general and specifically to his two political concerns—restrictive ideologies about acceptable modes of human embodiment and the national trauma produced by sectional race conflict. Both encouragements lead me to an analysis of Richard Powers's novel *The Time of Our Singing*, which contains a Whitman-inspired title and race trauma problematic while rendering a polyphonic reinflection of Whitman's song-oriented version of New York.[60] In contrast with the fusion of voices and feelings that characterize Whitman's I-subject-oriented musical view of New York's diverse peoples and classes, Powers offers a contrapuntal interethnic perspective with an alternative grammar of subjectivity. His novel provides at least two (phonically figured) loci of enunciation, one Euro-American and one African American. Moreover, his novel articulates two levels of polyphony. First, as a novel, its voice is not one in which the author expresses himself; it's one in which he *"exhibits* . . . the stratification of language."[61] And second, the languages exhibited in this particular novel are alternative musical genres, belonging to alternative ethnic musical formations.

Powers's *The Time of Our Singing* is not his first novelistic articulation of a Whitman effect. In his earlier *Gain*, Whitman's "Crossing Brooklyn Ferry" makes an appearance within a fraught interaction between a mother and son.[62] The mother, Laura, who is forty-two years old and has just learned that she is dying of cancer, finds her son confounded by a homework assignment for which he must interpret Walt Whitman's poem. Asked what he is supposed to do with it, the son answers that he is "supposed to say what it's fucking about."[63] Feeling diffident about her ability to help with a genre with which she has no experience, Laura gives it a try. As the novel intersperses lines of the poem with Laura's reflections on her situation, it becomes evident to the reader, if not to Laura, that the poem is telling her something relevant:

> "He seems . . . He's trying to talk with everyone who is ever going to be taking this boat," she says. [To which her son replies,] "well what's up with that?" . . . "Why?" Why? She flips back through the poem. Her end-of-term exam. Surely the answer must be in here, somewhere. *I . . . saw how the glistening yellow lit up parts of their bodies and left the rest in shadow . . . Look'd on the haze . . . on the vapor . . . The white wake left by the passage . . . The flags of all nations . . . These and all else were to me the same as they are to you . . . What is it then . . . the count of the scores or hundreds of years between us you?*[64]

Bruce Robbins, noting that Whitman's dominant poetic trope is "care,"[65] effectively captures the significance of Powers's Whitman episode in *Gain*: "The poem confronts [Laura] with the difficult prospect of caring about things she will not be there to see, whether because they come after or because they are far away."[66] What I wish to add to Robbins's insight is that Powers's appreciative gloss on the passages from Whitman's "Crossing Brooklyn Ferry" achieves its effects by adding voices. While Whitman's single-voiced poem is pregnant with potential significance for a variety of profound personal and interpersonal experiences, a realization of that potential is effected through the novel's polyphony, its staging of a dialogic encounter between mother and son, mediated through yet a third voice, Whitman's.

Powers's Whitman-inspired encounters in his later *The Time of Our Singing* are more extended and politically pregnant than what he provides in *Gain's* brief Whitman episode. The contrast between Whitman's and Powers's New York is telling when we consider both the novelistic genre that Powers employs and the way he introduces contrapuntal musical exchanges, in contrast with Whitman's musical poetic solos. Here are some lines from one of Whitman's musically proffered New York poems, focused on its Asian ethnoscape:

> Superb-faced Manhattan!
> Comrade Americanos! To us, then at last the Orient comes.
> ....
> The nest of languages, the bequeather of poems, the race of eld,
> ....
> With sunburnt visage, with intense soul and glittering eyes,
> The race of Brahma comes.
> ....
> From Thibet, from the four winding and far-flowing rivers of
>   China,
> ....
> For I too raising my voice join the ranks of this pageant,
> I am the chanter, I chant aloud over the pageant,
> ....
> I chant the new empire grander than any before, as in a vision it
>   comes to me[67]

It is evident here that Whitman is his own "conceptual persona."[68] Such characters—for example, Plato's Socrates—are not reducible to "*psychosocial types*."[69] Rather, their movements or acts of perception reveal what Gilles Deleuze calls "thought's territories"; they are vehicles for thinking.[70] In contrast with Whitman's thought vehicle, which issues in a single-voiced chant about New York's increasing ethnic diversity, Powers's two main characters articulate alternative voices. They share a harmonious and inharmonious, contrapuntal, musically figured, interethnic marriage. The marriage partners, an African American concert singer, Delia Daley, and a German Jewish emigré scientist, David Strom, meet on Easter 1939 at the famous Marian Anderson concert on the Washington Mall. They have three children, two boys and a girl, and include them in musical evenings that feature Euro-American and African American musical combinations:

> After dinner they came together in tunes, Rossini while washing the dishes,

W. C. Handy while drying.... They'd do workhorse Bach chorales, taking their pitches from Jonah, the boy with the magic ear, or they'd crowd around the spinet, tackling madrigals.⁷¹

The family's musical events are not simply serial, however. Often they involve contrapuntal encounters between Euro-American and African American musical genres. For example, Delia and David play a game they call "Crazed Quotations," in which she would begin with a tune and David would have to counter with a musical countersubject before his wife got to the double bar.⁷² Powers goes on to figure the clash of musical voices thus:

> The game produced the wildest mixed marriages, love matches that even the heaven of half-breeds looked sidelong at. Her Brahms *Alto Rhapsody* bickered with his growled Dixieland. Cherubini crashed into Cole Porter. Debussy, Tallis, and Mendelssohn shacked up in unholy ménages à trois. After a few rounds, the game got out of hand and the clotted chords collapsed under their own weight. Call and response ended in hilarious spinouts, with the one who flew off the carousel accusing the other of unfair harmonic tampering.⁷³

It is evident that Powers's "our" articulates a more complicated and fraught (or contrapuntal) subject than does Whitman's singing I-subject. However, an effective contrast also requires a treatment of the "time" part of Powers's title. Whitman's "Crossing Brooklyn Ferry" reveals a Whitman who celebrates both temporal change and timelessness. In his 1885 Preface, Whitman is explicit about locating the need for the poet to recognize the persistence of the past in the present: "he says to the past, Rise and walk before me that I recognize you" and be sensitive to the future: "he places himself where the future becomes present."⁷⁴ Heeding this and similar passages, Paul Bové suggests that "Whitman's temporal sense is acute" and that "the American poet's success requires that his poems, their forms, be 'informed' by the laws of time which govern nature."⁷⁵ Inasmuch as Whitman rejects both origins and definitive endings, Bové is compelling when he insists that the poems in Whitman's *Leaves of Grass* "assault the traditional ontological assumptions of presence, certainty, and rest as the ground of all being."⁷⁶ As Whitman puts it: "A great poem is no finish . . . but rather a beginning. Has anyone fancied he could sit at last under some due authority and rest satisfied with explanations and realize and be content and full?"⁷⁷

Yet despite his "acute temporal sense," Whitman sees human nature as timeless. As Philip Fisher astutely puts it, "What Whitman implies in

'Crossing Brooklyn Ferry' is that a democratic aesthetics requires that America will have no history of the senses."[78] Further, Whitman, despite his polemics against slavery, presumes a homogeneous social space from which all observers, even unto future generations, will see and feel "as I feel," as he suggests in "Crossing Brooklyn Ferry." For Whitman, "the politics of any aesthetics within a democratic social space requires that there exist experiences across time that not only will happen in identical ways but will be noticed—that is arouse attention—and will even produce the same feelings within people living centuries apart."[79] Certainly the "time" in Powers's title, which references a city (New York) and a nation as a whole that has not lived up to the promise of racial emancipation, departs from Whitman's version of temporality. And that "time" becomes differentiated as some of the novel's characters—specifically the Strom children—react differently to their experiences of the persistence of racial division.

Accordingly, to treat the ways in which Powers both articulates and reinflects the Whitman effect, we have to heed the different modes of becoming racial experienced by the Daley-Strom children. The fraught body-city relation to which much of Whitman's poesis is directed (over the life of his collections) concerns the changing status of the homoerotic body. As Moon puts it: "The revisionary effects which the texts of *Leaves of Grass* are designed to have on his culture's prevailing (or coming-to-be-prevailing) concepts of bodiliness manifest themselves most clearly when one follows them from edition to edition."[80] In Powers's novel, instruction on the body-city relationship concerns the racially hybrid body, which is expressed less by a monologic authorial voice than by the different voices of the Daley-Strom children. Just as the nineteenth century's varying degrees of rejection of homoerotic bodies shaped Whitman's poesis, Powers's novel is shaped by the mid-twentieth century's abjection of interracial bodies. Just as "the city is one of the crucial factors in the social production of (sexed) corporeality,"[81] it is a crucial factor in the social production of race.

Early in the novel, an authorial voice notes that each time the (mixed-race) Strom boys had to venture outside of their house into the city, they got "another dose of torture at the hands of boys . . . who rained down on the two Stroms the full brutality of their collective bafflement."[82] But thereafter, much of the bafflement is expressed by the children themselves, who are hounded by the persistence of the color line. If we visit an episode on Broadway in Powers's novel, the contrast with Whitman's New York ethnic imaginary becomes striking. When the Daley-Stroms try to hail a cab on Broadway, Powers's narrator, the second-oldest son, Joseph, reports, "On Broadway, the first three cabs we flagged wouldn't take us." Once they manage to get one, Mama, who is described as "black, still young, and for five minutes free," is queried by the oldest son, Jonah: "'Mama,' he asked. 'You are a Negro, right? And Da's . . . some kind of Jewish guy. What exactly does that make me, Joey, and Root'?"[83] As this and other conversations throughout the novel indicate, the Daley-Strom children exist on trajectories of becoming. Their world seeks to make them racialized bodies, while they in turn attempt their own self-fashioning.

Powers's rendering of the Daley-Stroms' disruption of the objectifications of ethnicity are echoed in Hortense Spillers's reaction to the famous *Moynihan Report* on the economic problems of the "Negro family." She notes how the report constructs "the 'white' family, by implication, the 'Negro family' by outright assertion, in a constant opposition to binary meanings."[84] Spillers goes on to connect the report's ascription of ethnicity to a temporal strategy that effectively distinguishes Powers's and Whitman's ethnic poesis: "'Ethnicity' in this case freezes in meaning, takes on constancy, assumes the look and affects of the Eternal."[85] In *The Time of Our Singing*, a conversation between Joseph and his father affirms Spillers's point that ethnicity and race achieve their reality through the freezing of time. During a crucial moment in both U.S. and family time (when cities are burning because of "racial unrest") and the family is sundered (Mama is dead, Jonah has emigrated, and Ruth is in hiding), Da says to Joseph: "Race is only real if you freeze time, if you invent a zero point for your tribe. If you make the past an origin, then you fix the future. Race is a dependent variable. A path, a moving process. We all move along a curve that will break down and rebuild us all."[86] In contrast to Powers's "ethnic" New York, which hosts a dynamic of becoming, as struggles take place between those seeking to control, eliminate, or impose meanings on bodies and the bodies themselves, understood as active agents impelled by their own willed and unconscious determinations, Whitman's New York contains ethnic *beings*. For example, dehistorizing the bodies he observes on Broadway, Whitman constructs them as a "Broadway Pageant . . . When a million-footed Manhattan unpent descends to her pavements."[87] And in another glimpse of the same street (in his "Mannahatta"), he discerns none of the tensions that Powers's characters experience:

Trottoirs throng'd, vehicles, Broadway, the women, the shops and shows,
A million people—manners free and superb—open voices—hospitality—the most courageous and friendly young men. . . . [88]

As he celebrates the different kinds of bodies he observes, Whitman's poesis becomes a mythopoesis; his markers of ethnicity are "loaded with mythical presuppositions."[89] As Spillers puts it, in an extended observation that identifies the mythopoesis-ethnicity connection, "'ethnicity' perceived as mythical time enables a writer to perform a variety of conceptual moves all at once."[90] Spillers's concern is with the way that marking ethnicity renders the body a defenseless target. Whitman's markings are more benign. Whitman, as Morton Schoolman effectively shows, is attempting to construct "democratic time."[91] Toward that end, he offers a diorama of ethnic types with the intention of effacing the significance of difference. His version of democratic individuality, articulated within a poetics that embraces difference in order to affirm "the universalism of democratic life,"[92] effectively "allows individuality to distill the transcendental from its finite, transitory experience of diversity and difference," as Schoolman puts it.[93] However, to achieve such a universalism of democratic life, in which ethnic difference possesses no trajectory of historical effect or grievance, Whitman must compress or conjure away finite historical time. Accordingly, in his "Starting from Paumanok," a poem in which he celebrates his place and circumstance of birth on Long Island and figures himself as a "throat . . . joyfully singing" about democracy, he scorns the past (to which he refers as "the antique") and states that he will "make poems, songs, thoughts with reference to an ensemble" and "will not sing with reference to a day, but with reference to all days."[94]

How different is Powers's time! It's not a mythic time in which all moments have the same collective significance. It is finite historical time in which the color line persists and, as one result among many, a family is torn apart. As Joseph says of his father, "he's never once tried to wrap his head around what time is doing to us, to our family."[95] It becomes clear to the children that color cannot be ignored. Ruth, who is "a shade darker" than her mother (unlike Jonah, who can pass), "wants to know if she's a *Schwartze*, a half-*Schwartze*, an anti-*Schwartze*, or what?" She says to Da, who resists color talk, "Only white men have the luxury of ignoring race." The time of schisms that develop in the Daley-Strom family, as the three children take different paths vis-à-vis ethnic choice, is a microcosm of national time. As familial struggles develop over the issue of racial identity, the society as a whole registers the same struggle. For example, Powers evokes February 1965, when "three black men gunned down Malcolm X," the moment when "thousands marched from Selma to Montgomery, and "when Jacksonville burned." These events occur while the family is singing in various cities.[96]

It is not just "time" that takes on different valences within the novel's different voices. At a crucial moment during a family musical practice, "singing" becomes differentiated in a way that also evokes racial difference. In stark contrast with the song imagery with which Whitman references "ensembles" (as he puts it in "Starting from Paumanok") is this event in the Daley-Strom household: While Mama is playing her spinet, Jonah "stopped [her] in midphrase" and remarked, "You could get a smoother tone and have less trouble with the *passaggio* if you kept your head still."[97] Jonah's intervention stuns the family gathering with "the plain of estrangement he'd made." His suggestion reflects the difference between the (white) "conservatory world" and the world of African American music which at that midcentury remained separated. Ralph Ellison's account of his experience as a student of Mrs. Zelia Breaux's music school in the black school system of Oklahoma City addresses the separation. Mrs. Breaux insisted that the students stick to the (white) classics during the day, but at night, "she was the owner/operator of the Ira Aldridge Theater where Duke [Ellington] and Louis [Armstrong] reigned in the footlights, along with Bessie Smith, Ida Cox, Jimmy Rushing and the Blue Devils as creators and perpetrators of the shouts, smear, and muted rhapsodies that characterize blues and jazz."[98] Recognizing the intimate connection between the African American blues/jazz tradition and the moving/dancing body, Ellison expressed discontent with the loss of connection between the music and the body. He valued what he called "the palpable *physical* dimensions of the blues/jazz ritual" (my italics) and attributed the "loss of wholeness" to the growing distance of the music from its most authentic venue, "the Negro public dance."[99] Like Ellison, the jazz composer/musician Duke Ellington valued the relationship of the music to the moving body. He insisted that "rhythm sequences" are more important than "the show part of the band—the melody instruments" because of the bodies the music has addressed ever since its most significant historical space of performance, the dance hall, where reception is experienced in movement rather than mere listening.[100] And also like Ellison, Ellington participated in the Whitman effect. In his case, it occurred in response to the Langston Hughes Whitmanesque poem "I, Too, Sing America." "We Too Sing America," insisted Ellington; "we play more than a minority role in singing 'America.'"[101]

An African American–Inflected Whitman Effect: Langston Hughes's Rhythms of New York

Doubtless Langston Hughes is the best-known Whitman-inspired "black" poet.[102] An admirer of Whitman's politics as well as his poetry, Hughes referred to him as "one of the greatest 'I' poets of all time," where the "I" is a "cosmic 'I' of all the people who seek freedom, decency, and dignity, friendship and equality between individuals and races all over the world."[103] Like Ellison, Hughes was especially attentive to Whitman's poetic eulogy to Abraham Lincoln, "When Lilacs Last in the Dooryard Bloom'd." However, rather than reinflecting the poem's imagery as Ellison does in his riff on the Founder's death in his *Invisible Man,* Hughes first cites the poem, then acknowledges the value of the "Emancipation" Lincoln achieved, and finally goes on to lament the post-Reconstruction reaction in which the freedoms promised by the emancipation have been abrogated. Shortly after citing the lines from Whitman's eulogy, he fashions a poetic recognition that although "the night was dark . . . hope was there":

> Trouble in mind! I'm blue,
> But I wont be always.
> The sun gonna shine
> In my backdoor someday. . . .[104]

Here, as elsewhere, Hughes's poetry, although Whitman-inspired, has a singularity owed to the African American blues aesthetic, which has a different political impetus from Whitman's general celebration of diversity. The blues constitutes both an epistemic and political reaction to the racist oppression of the "plantation bloc," which is to be understood as not only an economic system but also a hegemonic mode of social interpretation. As Clyde Woods puts it, "blues epistemology" is a reaction to "the plantation bloc." It opposes the ontological and epistemological hegemony of the plantation bloc by providing a "constant reestablishment of collective sensibility in the face of constant attacks by the plantation bloc and its allies"; it reaffirms "the historical commitment to social and personal investigation, description, and criticism present in the blues."[105]

As a major participant in the famous Harlem Renaissance, Hughes deployed his blues-inflected poetry on New York's often oppressive racial-spatial order, as it was configured a century after Whitman celebrated the city's growing diversity. And although pursuing a different aesthetic, he, like Whitman, articulated the rhythms of the city with the rhythms of his poesis. These lines from his "Lennox Avenue: Midnight" well express an urban-centered blues/jazz aesthetic:

> The rhythm of life
> Is a jazz rhythm,
> Honey . . .
> The broken heart of love
> The weary heart of love
> The weary heart of pain,—
> Overtones,
> Undertones,
> To the rumble of street cars,
> To the swish of rain . . .[106]

As is the case with Whitman, music imagery is a pervasive part of Hughes's poesis. Whitman portrayed himself as a soloist who expressed the reality of what is common beneath what appears different to the observer. Fisher puts it succinctly: Whitman's "aesthetics . . . imposes the requirement that the common be expanded until it fills out the real."[107] In contrast, Hughes, who lyrically joins Whitman's singing of America (in his "I, Too, Sing America"), eschews the single-voiced solo in favor of the articulation of diverse genres of African American music. In a telling preface to his poem "Boogie Segue to Bop," he expresses the purpose of that articulation:

> In terms of current Afro-American popular music and the sources from which it has progressed—jazz, ragtime, swing, blues, boogie-woogie, and be-bop—this poem on contemporary Harlem, like be-bop, is marked by conflicting changes and sudden nuances, sharp and imprudent interjections, broken rhythms, and passages sometimes in the manner of the jam session, sometimes the popular song, punctuated by the riffs, runs, breaks, and disctortions of the music of a community in transition.[108]

For Hughes, there is no comfortable "in common." His imagery conjures dissonance instead of bland harmony. Moreover, while Whitman's dialogic poesis is not evident in his observations of the city's masses, the (above noted) "breaking of the monologic hegemony of the lyric voice" is richly and pervasively in evidence in Hughes's poetry. Exemplary in this respect is Hughes's "Cultural Exchange," in which he has "the dominant voice of the lyric speaker," along with other African American and Euro-American voices, accompany the different genres of music with which they are affiliated.[109] In passages that bear a similarity to Powers's novelistic (and contrapuntal) articulation of black and white musical genres, Hughes reflects on "the quarter of the Negroes where the doorknob lets in lieder" [a German musical genre] and proceeds with references to the jazz musician Ornette Coleman, and then a mixing of an African American cuisine and singer Leontyne Price, interacting with the lieder:

> In the pot behind the
> Paper doors what's cooking?
> What's smelling Leontyne?
> Lieder, lovely lieder
> And a leaf of collard green.
> Lovely lieder Leontyne.[110]

Another example of Hughes's dialogic lyricism, along with a recognition of the dissonant relations across the color line, is his "Projection," in which he imagines a peaceful black-white interchange, excursions across the boundaries of the city's racialized map and across the city's different genres of expression:

> On the day when the Savoy
> leaps clean over to Seventh Avenue
> And starts jitterbugging
> with the Renaissance,
> on that day when Abyssinia Baptist Church
> throws her enormous arms around
> St. James Presbyterian
> and 409 Edgecombe
> Stoops to kiss 12 West 133rd . . .[111]

Finally, and likely unbeknownst to Hughes, Whitman, the chanter of democracy whom Hughes so admired, held out little hope for black-white coparticipation in that democracy. For example, his celebration of the workingman did not include "the Negro slave mechanic," whom he feared would be treated on a par with "an honest poor [white] mechanic."[112] And his racial attitudes went beyond a fear of leveling. In an 1858 editorial in the *Brooklyn Daily Times*, he imagined excluding blacks entirely from the American republic: "Who believes that the Whites and Blacks can ever amalgamate in America? Or who wishes it to happen? There is no chance for it."[113] In contrast, Hughes, who figures himself as a "darker brother" whom they send "to eat in the kitchen," imagines a "tomorrow" in which "I'll be at the table when the company comes," [and] Nobody'll dare Say to me, 'Eat in the kitchen,' then."[114] Hughes's New York is a place of fear—"We cry among the skyscrapers as our ancestors cried among the palms of Africa because we are alone; it is night and we're afraid"[115]—but it is also a place of hope: "We have tomorrow right before us like a flame."[116]

Another Ethnic Whitman Effect: The Nuyoricans

The Nuyoricans are a group of poets who have adopted and reinflected what was originally "an epithet for those of Puerto Rican heritage born in New York" and have had a gathering place in Manhattan known as the Nuyorican Poets Cafe.[117] Functioning as mediating ethnic poets, their manifesto includes a commitment to "changing the so-called black/white dialogue that has been the breeding ground for social, cultural, and political conflict in the United States."[118] Like Whitman, they celebrate the democratizing impetus of poetic expression, and for them as for Hughes that democratizing inheres in their inclusion as poets who also sing "America." They cite with approval the lines of William Carlos Williams's "Paterson," which they see as contributing to the "democratization of verse."[119] And in keeping with this commitment, their group has not been restricted to poets of Puerto Rican ancestry: "We at the Nuyorican Poets' Cafe ... open our doors to the multi-ethnic, formally poetic world that comes to us to read, to hear, to be heard." For example, the explicit homage to Whitman in their anthology—"Walt Whitman Strides the Llano of New Mexico"—is written by a Mexican American, Rudolfo Anaya. While claiming a Whitman effect throughout the poem, Anaya writes at one point (with a line that recalls the engirthing trope in Whitman's "I Sing the

Body Electric"): "I fell asleep on *Leaves of Grass*, covering myself with your bigote [mustache], dreaming my ancestors, my healers, the cuentos [stories] of their past, dreams and memories."[120]

One of the Cafe's Nuyorican founders, Miguel Pinero is explicit about his ethnic mode of address, about his New York connection, about the inspiration he draws from the African American blues genre, and, finally, about his drug habit:

> ... I'm in New York City
> Crying the junkie blues
> welfare afro hairdos sprout out
> of frye boots
> yeah punk rockers hitting on you
> for subway fare three times. ...
> Sunday morning in New York City
> for the junkie there ain't no pity ...
> hear the people say there goes miky
> miky pinero
> they call him the junkie Christ ...[121]

However, while the dynamic with which the Nuyorican Cafe involves a democratized stream of bodies, arriving from the horizontal plane of the city, New York's identity/difference also involves a verticality, a socioeconomic hierarchy, often architecturally realized, which speaks to a more politically contentious ethnic environment. To appreciate this aspect of the city as it bears on Puerto Ricans as well as other ethnic New Yorkers, I turn to a novel that features a Euro-American/Puerto Rican encounter that explicitly reinflects the Whitman effect. The novel, Colin Harrison's *Bodies Electric*, deploys a profound "reality effect" and challenges Whitman's mythopoetical laundering of ethnic strife. It is a novel that is Whitman-inspired, for it stages the kinds of body-to-body encounters that Whitman often noted, but at the same time, the novel treats the micropolitics of New York's contemporary ethnic-spatial order.

Harrison's *Bodies Electric*

Jason Frank writes that "Whitman addressed the overall condition of the polity as what he called a 'passionate body,' elaborating the 'electric' or 'resonant' interconnections between the utter singularity of the self and the multitudinous and contending voices of democratic politics."[122] In a novel that enacts "electric interconnections" and the figurations that shape Whitman's "passionate body" and "contending voices," Harrison begins his *Bodies Electric* with an epigraph from Walt Whitman's "Specimen Days," a section in which the narrator/Walt Whitman spots a destitute woman begging in the street while holding an infant daughter. The epigraph reads, in part: "He caught a look of her face, and talk'd with her a little. Eyes, voice and manner were those of a corpse, animated by electricity. She was quite young. . . . Poor woman—what story was it out of her fortunes to account for that inexpressible scared way, those glassy eyes, and that hollow voice?" The novel's drama is provoked by a similar public encounter with a seemingly destitute (but much more alive) woman with—in this case—a juvenile daughter whom Harrison's fictional Jack Whitman spots on a New York subway train. Seeing that the woman, a young Puerto Rican, seems to have been beaten and is in need of help, he accosts her briefly, hands her his card, and says that she looks as if she needs help and that he can get her a job. It turns out to be an ill-fated encounter, as the novel's opening lines imply: "My name is Jack Whitman and I should never have had the first thing to do with her. I shouldn't have indulged myself—my loneliness, my attraction to her. . . . if only I hadn't even *seen* her."[123]

Thereafter, Jack Whitman, Harrison's protagonist and narrator, imitates Walt Whitman's lyricism throughout the novel. As the second chapter opens, we are offered his poetic description of waking and then observing, and politically inflecting the early city scene near where he works for a giant media corporation: "Dawn arrives unwanted, snatches you forward. I waited at the corner of Sixth Avenue and Forty-Ninth Street the next morning sun brightening the meager designer trees of Rockefeller Center. Across the street, the Corporation's uniformed maintenance crew had rousted the homeless off the sheltered benches in the building plaza and was steam blasting away the piss and garbage deposited there the night before."[124] As this passage attests, Harrison's novel is *about* New York. In addition to creating such city scenes, it contains a drama surrounding a relationship between Jack Whitman, a fictional descendent of Walt Whitman living in Brooklyn and working in Manhattan, and the young, temporarily homeless Puerto Rican woman, Dolores Salcines, whom he meets on the subway.

However, representational and narrative dimensions of the novel are less significant for appreciating its New York poesis and micropolitics than the way it animates the city's vertical architecture, ethnic boundaries, and the diverse bodies situated in and moving with and against each other and with various degrees of inhibition within that verticality and horizontal ethnic-spatial order.

Certainly Jack Whitman's psychological subjectivity is central to the novel's plot. "Dawn arrives unwanted" for Jack because he has lost his pregnant wife and unborn child to a drive-by shooting in Harlem. Not the intended victim, his wife, Liz, is caught in the crossfire when a young African American teenager shoots at a Korean grocery store from his vehicle. Jack's loneliness and grief is an enabling source of his empathy. Because his own misery renders him alert to the misery of others, when he sees a young Puerto Rican woman, Dolores Salcines, on the subway with her young daughter, he is able to empathize with her distress. However, the novel's micropolitical insights are better appreciated if we view Jack as an aesthetic rather than merely a psychological subject. In a narrative sense, his sensitivity to Dolores's suffering produces an interaction and ultimately a relationship that turns out to be catastrophic. But the novel's narrative trajectory and psychological register pale in comparison with what the psychological state of the characters does to novelistic space and "especially to the range and kinds of movements allowed for in that space."[125]

Although Jack's attempt to have Dolores employed in his corporation leads to frustration and disappointment for both parties when she is fired on the first day, the more politically telling effects of the novel describe the vertical authority structure of the corporation. Jack's initial demand to have Dolores hired is rebuffed until the personnel manager learns that Jack works on a floor above his. But the barriers inherent in the verticality and cellularity of the corporation, where authority is parceled floor by floor and office by office, leads to Dolores being sacked without Jack's learning about it until after the fact. In effect, the city's partitions outside of and within the corporation both control and inhibit exchanges of affect. The initial emotional feelings that Jack experiences are inflected by his deep malaise, which began with the death of his wife and loss of his unborn child. While he finds Dolores attractive and evinces some libidinal energy at first encounter, his more powerful feelings are those of sympathy and the extended emotional generosity they engender toward what turns out to be a spouse-abused Puerto Rican New Yorker. To act out those feelings, he ends up having to cope with the ethnic-spatial frontiers of New York as well as its verticalities.

To connect this story with that part of "ethnic" New York evinced in the more ecumenical sentiments of the Nuyorican Poets, the contrast is in part directional. The poetics associated with the Nuyorican Cafe derive from a series of horizontal flows across the city's racial and ethnic divides, while Jack's micropolitical actions must cope with an entrenched verticality. In the process, Jack gets involved in a contentious series of encounters with the estranged husband, Hector, whose struggles also reveal an implacably hierarchical and racist New York that bears little similarity to the one perceived and chanted by Jack's ancestor Walt Whitman. Hector is abused and battered in front of his family on a subway train by New York policemen, who mistake him for a Puerto Rican rapist, and he loses his flooring business when he refuses to capitulate to a mafia protection scheme.

Harrison's novel thus provides a realism about the micropolitics of the city that is passed over in the mythopoesis of Walt Whitman. For example, while Walt Whitman tends poetically to celebrate the city's working men and women by listing the wide variety of blue-collar occupations (and only rarely registering merely the facts of instances of their destitution),[126] Harrison's novel treats the immiseration of people in a workplace subject to the greed and cynicism of those who run large corporate enterprises. Jack Whitman works for a giant media corporation in a tall downtown Manhattan building. Its verticality and security system inhibit casual entry from the street and control movement within and between floors. As Dolores Salcines puts it when she comes to see Jack in his corporate office, "Are people like me ever allowed up here?"[127] And as Jack Whitman, whose office is up on the thirty-ninth floor, reflects on the atmosphere of the corporation's vertical separations, he notes that "each floor of the Corporation is identified by a certain degree of fear."[128] Effectively, the corporation is a microcosm of what Gilles Deleuze has characterized as modernity's "societies of control."[129] Only sanctioned persons have access and only sanctioned events can transpire within the building, which soars above Manhattan's streets. Meanwhile, below in the chaotic bustle of the streets and on public transportation, chance encounters can occur, hence the drama-precipitating encounter between Jack and Dolores on a subway, a place of contingency where "quotidian humanity" shows up, introducing each other to an "alter-ity" that is sometimes aggressively expressive and sometimes passive in its manifest difference.[130]

Conclusion: Bodies and Cities

In Harrison's *Bodies Electric,* Jack Whitman's involvement with Dolores Salcines takes him out of his usual circuits—for example, to a hotel for transients near Times Square where, seeking to find her after she is fired from the corporation, he walks past "lurking porn palaces . . . past all the squalor, the religious nuts and racial instigators with sound systems harassing crowds of white tourists."[131] Subsequently, seeking out Dolores's estranged and violent husband, Hector, who works weekends at a used-car lot in Brooklyn, he passes the "ubiquitous Brooklyn block: newsstand, barber, toy store, bodega, video store [and then] up on Eighth Avenue some of the Chinese sweatshops, where dozens of women worked under fluorescent lights at a sewing machine next to mountains of pieces of cloth. Slave labor."[132] Earlier in the novel, Jack states, "Walt Whitman was, in my opinion, a better reporter than he was a poet."[133] The observation makes sense because while in his poetry, Walt Whitman simply extols the virtues of different kinds of work, in some of his newspaper articles and other prose writings, he recognizes how the vagrant, poor, and underpaid populations of the city represent a failure-to-come-to-fruition of the ideals of the American Revolution. For example, in one prose piece he refers to "vast crops of poor, desperate, dissatisfied, nomadic, miserably-waged populations."[134]

There is a striking irony in Harrison's novel, which is uttered by the chairman of the corporation: "That a long descended relative of Walt Whitman would come to be an executive of America's largest media company. It's too perfectly ironic."[135] Jack's emotional vulnerability and the way it shapes his actions after a chance encounter allow a city to articulate the kinds of multiplicity of affects and experience that are occasionally touched on in the poesis of Jack Whitman's ancestor Walt. The relationship with Dolores changes Jack from a media executive to what the novel describes as a "body electric": "Forget my hemorrhoids, my taxes, the fat creeping around my torso, my mother and father. There is only the hard pipe that goes from me to her."[136] The relationship ripens from acquaintance to passion, with a promise of future intimacy. But once he leaves their bed to cope with the city that has thrown him and Dolores together, what emerges is a plurality of fraught existences, the coping mechanisms with which diverse ethnic New Yorkers seek to survive (although Jack's relationship with Dolores and with his work does not). In contrast with Walt Whitman's mostly celebratory dioramas is the New York that Harrison's Jack Whitman is able lyrically to describe—in a Whitman-like passage—the interethnic New York that my analysis is aimed at illuminating:

> a young transit cop who superstitiously keeps a laminated picture of his sweetheart taped to the inside of his policeman's cap. . . . the two dozen black men slapping drums and shaking gourds on the Jamaican coast of Prospect Park . . . the hulking box of the nursing home in Fort Greene, where old Chinese women with little remaining hair blink in the sunlight, the wheezing personal injury lawyer painting the horrors of the car accident to the jury in the civil court downtown, and the Salvadoran refugee of dubious legal status, his mind stuffed with the horrors (the dismemberment of his brother, the shallow grave). . . . the refugee alone and wanting the aloneness. . . . the retired bus driver setting up his little canasta table on his nineteenth-floor terrace facing the ocean in Bay Ridge. . . . the Korean shopkeeper showing the new relative how to shrug when the customer claims he's been shortchanged a dime; and the Mexican man trimming cut flowers each day outside the same shop, remembering his mother living in Mexico City above the bakery; and the advertising space saleswoman swimming laps at 5:00 AM in the club pool.

Ultimately, Harrison's Whitman-inspired novel stages difference in a way that maps and mobilizes the ethnically inflected micropolitics of New York. While Walt Whitman himself had observed and lyrically applauded a parade of New York's ethnic diversity, Harrison's poetics goes beyond the side-by-side idioms and monocular and optimistic (often dissensus-denying) point of view that dominates Whitman's riffs on the city. Instead, he offers a cacophony of voices and a realistic model of the contingencies of encounter, which offer both promise and the possibility of catastrophe. As in Whitman's "I Sing the Body Electric," Harrison often focuses on the various dimensions of physicality of the human body. But unlike Whitman, he makes use of the novel form to mobilize encounters. In a gloss on Spinoza, Gilles Deleuze provides an appropriate concluding thought about such encounters: "When a body 'encounters' another body, or an idea another idea, it happens that the two relations sometimes combine to form a more powerful whole. And sometimes one decomposes the other, destroying the coherence of its parts."[137]

Notes

I am grateful to Mort Schoolman and Jason Frank for critical reactions to an earlier version of this essay.

1. In October 2005, at Boston Research Center for the Twenty-first Century symposium entitled "'Talking Back' to Whitman: Poetry Matters," "Whitmanian" scholars from the United States, China, Latin America, and Japan gathered to assess Whitman's intellectual legacy, framed in the ways in which worldwide scholars have explicitly talked back to Whitman (see www.brc21.org/ef_whitman_summary.html).

2. The science fiction story is Ray Bradbury's "I Sing the Body Electric" in a collection of his stories entitled *I Sing the Body Electric* (New York: Knopf, 1972), 150–90; the novel is Colin Harrison's *Bodies Electric* (New York: St. Martins, 1993); the jazz analysis is by Will Friedwald et al. in *Future of Jazz,* ed. Yuvak Taylor (Chicago: A Cappella, 2002).

3. Ralph Ellison, "An Extravagance of Laughter," *Going to the Territory* (New York: Random House, 1986), 148.

4. Ibid.

5. Ibid., 160.

6. Ibid., 161.

7. The quotation is from Alexander G. Weheliye, *Phonographies: Grooves in Sonic Afro-Modernity* (Durham: Duke University Press, 2005), 9.

8. See Marvin E. Mengeling, "Whitman and Ellison: Older Symbols in a Modern Mainstream," in *A Casebook on Ralph Ellison's* Invisible Man, ed. Joseph F. Trimmer (New York: Thomas Crowell, 1972), 269. It is Mengeling's essay that directed my attention to Whitman tropes and framing in Ellison's chapter.

9. Ibid., 270.

10. Ralph Ellison, *Invisible Man* (New York: Vintage, 1980), 119.

11. Ibid., 116.

12. Houston A. Baker Jr., *Modernism and the Harlem Renaissance* (Chicago: University of Chicago Press, 1987), 33–36.

13. Ibid., 27.

14. The expression "musico-literary poetics" is drawn from David Michael Hertz's treatment of the overlap between the poetry and musical compositions of the symbolist movement in nineteenth-century France: *The Tuning of the Word: The Musico-Literary Poetics of the Symbolist Movement* (Carbondale: Southern Illinois University Press, 1987).

15. Immanuel Kant, *The Critique of Judgement,* trans. James Creed Meredith (Oxford: Clarendon Press, 1952), 152.

16. This expression is from Immanuel Kant, *Anthropology from a Pragmatic Point of View,* trans. Victor Lyle Dowdell (Carbondale: Southern Illinois University Press, 1978), 40.

17. Kant, *The Critique of Judgement,* 29.

18. Ibid.

19. Ibid., 154.

20. The observation quoted belongs to Alan Trachtenberg in his insightful essay on Whitman and the city: "Whitman's Lesson of the City," in *Breaking Bounds: Whitman and American Cultural Studies,* ed. Betsy Erkkila and Jay Grossman (New York: Oxford University Press, 1996), 163.

21. The quotation is from Trachtenberg's rendering of Whitman's alteration (ibid., 164).

22. Walt Whitman, "To You," in *The Complete Poetry and Prose of Walt Whitman* (Garden City, N.Y.: Garden City Books, 1948), 227.

23. Ibid., 167–68.

24. Trachtenberg, "Whitman's Lesson of the City," 163.

25. Whitman, "Mannahatta," in *The Complete Poetry and Prose of Walt Whitman,* 409.

26. Howard Caygill, *Walter Benjamin: The Color of Experience* (New York: Routledge, 1998), 120.

27. Walter Benjamin and Asja Lacis, "Naples," in *Reflections,* trans. Edmund Jephcott (New York: Schocken, 1978), 1666–67.

28. Benjamin, "Marseille," ibid., 131.

29. Whitman, *The Complete Poetry and Prose,* 63.

30. Ibid., 82–83.

31. Ibid.

32. Ibid., 83.

33. Walter Benjamin, "Surrealism," in *Walter Benjamin: Selected Writings,* vol. 2, trans. Rodney Livingston et al. (Cambridge: Harvard University Press, 1999), 217. For an extended treatment of body- and image-space in Benjamin, see Sigrid Weigel, *Body- and Image-Space: Re-reading Walter Benjamin,* trans. Georgina Paul (New York: Routledge, 1996).

34. Ibid.

35. Ibid., 211.

36. Ibid., 116.

37. See Gilles Deleuze and Felix Guattari, *A Thousand Plateaus,* trans. Brian Massumi (Minneapolis: University of Minnesota Press, 1987), 492.

38. Priscilla Wald, "'Chaos Goes Uncourted': John Yau's Dis(-)Orienting Poetics," in *Cohesion and Dissent in America,* ed. Carol Colatrella and Joseph Alkana (Albany: State University of New York Press, 1994), 136.

39. Edward Foster, "An Interview with John Yau," *Talisman: A Journal of Contemporary Poetry and Poetics*, no. 5 (Fall 1990): 46.

40. John Yau, quoted in Dorothy J. Wang, "Undercover Asian: John Yau and the Politics of Ethnic Self-Identification," *Asian American Literature in the International Context; Readings on Fiction, Poetry and Performance* (2002): 137.

41. See Wald, "'Chaos Goes Uncourted," 134, 136.

42. John Yau, *Crossing Canal Street* (Binghamton, N.Y.: Bellevue Press, 1976), 8–9.

43. Whitman, "Broadway," in *The Complete Poetry and Prose*, 442.

44. Whitman, "One's-Self I Sing," ibid., 41.

45. Whitman, "Song of Myself," ibid., 62.

46. Ibid., 82.

47. Ibid., 83. As Larzer Ziff points out, in "Song of Myself" as in "Crossing Brooklyn Ferry," "Whitman moves from chanter to universal presence, moves, that is, from a larger-than-life embodiment to a cosmic disembodiment" (see Ziff, "Whitman and the Crowd," *Critical Inquiry* 10, no. 4 [June 1984]: 582).

48. Ibid., 85.

49. M. M. Bakhtin, "Discourse in the Novel," 296–97.

50. Ibid., 299.

51. M. M. Bakhtin, *Problems of Dostoevsky's Poetics*, trans. Caryl Emerson (Minneapolis: University of Minnesota Press, 1984), 41.

52. Ibid., 34.

53. For a critique of Bakhtin's position and examples of changing voices within poems, see Elena Semino, *Language and World Creation in Poems and Other Texts* (New York: Longman, 1997), 43–51.

54. Chanita Goodblatt, "In Other Words: Breaking the Monologue in Whitman, Williams, and Hughes," *Language and Literature* 9, no. 1 (2000): 25.

55. See ibid., 26, in which Goodblatt is quoting Elena Semino, *Language and World Creation in Poems and Other Texts* (London: Longmans, 1997), 145.

56. Gilles Deleuze, "Whitman," in *Gilles Deleuze: Essays Critical and Clinical*, trans. Daniel W. Smith and Michael A. Greco (Minneapolis: University of Minnesota Press, 1997), 58.

57. Michael Moon, *Disseminating Whitman: Revision and Corporeality in Leaves of Grass* (Cambridge: Harvard University Press, 1991), 3.

58. The quotation is from the Library of America edition of Whitman's prose, quoted ibid., 3.

59. Ibid., 3–4.

60. See Richard Powers, *The Time of Our Singing* (New York: Farrar, Straus and Giroux, 2003).

61. The quoted expression belongs to Bakhtin, "Discourse in the Novel," in

The Dialogic Imagination, ed. Michael Holquist (Austin: University of Texas Press, 1981), 299.

62. Whitman's appearance in Powers's *Gain* was initially called to my attention by Bruce Robbins's interpretation of the implications of Whitman's "Crossing Brooklyn Ferry," for the novel's main character, Laura (see Bruce Robbins, "Homework: Richard Powers, Walt Whitman, and the Poetry of the Commodity," *Ariel* 34, no. 1 [January 2005]: 77–91).

63. Richard Powers, *Gain* (New York: Picador, 1998), 86.

64. Ibid., 88–89.

65. For a similar observation about Whitman's concern with care, see Paul Bové, *Destructive Poetics* (New York: Columbia University Press, 1980), 137. Bové suggests Whitman's poetics, with its trope of "care" and its emphasis on "disclosure" share an orientation with Heidegger's philosophy.

66. Robbins, "Homework," 79.

67. Whitman, "A Broadway Pageant," in *The Complete Poetry and Prose of Walt Whitman,* 235–36.

68. "Conceptual personae" are thinking vehicles, according to Gilles Deleuze and Felix Guattari (see their *What Is Philosophy?* trans. Hugh Tomlinson and Graham Burchell [New York: Columbia University Press, 1994], 61–83).

69. Ibid., 67.

70. Ibid., 69.

71. Powers, *The Time of Our Singing,* 13.

72. Ibid.

73. Ibid.

74. See Scully Bradley, Harold W. Blodgett, and William White, eds., *Leaves of Grass: A Textual Valorium of Printed Poems* (New York: New York University Press, 2008), 718–19.

75. Bové, *Destructive Poetics,* 145–46.

76. Ibid., 149.

77. Walt Whitman, *Leaves of Grass* (New York: New York University Press, 1965), 729.

78. Philip Fisher, "Democratic Social Space: Whitman, Melville, and the Promise of American Transparency," *Representations* 24 (Fall 1988): 69.

79. Ibid.

80. Moon, *Disseminating Whitman,* 2.

81. Elizabeth Grosz, "Bodies-Cities," in *Sexuality and Space,* ed. Beatrix Colomina (New York: Princeton Architecture Press, 1992), 242.

82. Powers, *The Time of Our Singing,* 10.

83. Ibid., 29.

84. Hortense Spillers, "Mama's Baby, Papa's Maybe: An American Grammar Book," *diacritics* 17, no. 2 (Summer 1987): 66.
85. Ibid.
86. Powers, *The Time of Our Singing*, 94.
87. Whitman, "Broadway Pageant," in *The Complete Poetry & Prose*, 234.
88. Whitman, "Mannahatta," ibid., 410.
89. Spillers, "Mama's Baby, Papa's Maybe," 65.
90. Ibid., 66.
91. Morton Schoolman, *Reason and Horror: Critical Theory, Democracy, and Aesthetic Individuality* (New York: Routledge, 2001), 240.
92. Ibid., 241.
93. Ibid.
94. Whitman, "Starting from Paumanok," in *The Complete Poetry & Prose*, 58.
95. Powers, *The Time of Our Singing*, 92.
96. Ibid., 306.
97. Ibid., 67.
98. Ralph Ellison in a conversation with Robert O'Meally in *Living with Music: Ralph Ellison's Jazz Writings* (New York: Modern Library, 2002), 17.
99. Ralph Ellison, "Remembering Jimmie [Rushing]," ibid., 47.
100. Duke Ellington, "The Duke Steps Out," *Rhythm* (1931), reprinted in *The Duke Ellington Reader*, ed. Mark Tucker (New York: Oxford University Press, 1993), 46.
101. Duke Ellington, "We Too Sing 'America,'" ibid., 147.
102. After Stephen Henderson's treatment of the genre, I am identifying "black" poetry in terms of "three critical categories: theme, structure, and saturation," where theme refers to the poetry's referents, structure to aspects of its style, and saturation to its "fidelity to the observed or intuited truth of the Black Experience in the United States" (Stephen Henderson, *Understanding the New Black Poetry: Black Speech and Black Music as Poetic References* [New York: Morrow Quill Paperbacks, 1973], 10).
103. Langston Hughes, "Whitman Celebrates All Americans," in *Readings on Walt Whitman*, ed. Gary Wiener (San Diego: Greenhaven Press, 1999), 198.
104. Langston Hughes, "The Glory of Negro History," in *The Langston Hughes Reader* (New York: George Braziller, 1958), 473–74.
105. Clyde Woods, *Development Arrested: Race, Power, and the Blues in the Mississippi Delta* (New York: Verso, 1998), 30.
106. Langston Hughes, "Lennox Avenue: Midnight," in *The Weary Blues* (New York: Knopf, 1926), 39.
107. Fisher, "Democratic Social Space," 67.

108. Langston Hughes, "Note" under "Montage of a Dream Deferred," in *The Langston Hughes Reader*, 89.

109. The quotation is from Goodblatt, "Breaking the Monologue in Whitman, Williams, and Hughes," 33.

110. Hughes, "Cultural Exchange," in *The Collected Poems of Langston Hughes*, 477–79.

111. Hughes, "Projection," ibid., 403–4.

112. Walt Whitman, "American Working Men versus Slavery," quoted in Bryan K. Garman, *A Race of Singers* (Chapel Hill: University of North Carolina Press, 2000), 23.

113. Ibid.

114. Hughes, "I, Too Sing America," in *The Collected Poems of Langston Hughes*, 46.

115. Hughes, "Subway Face," ibid., 41.

116. Hughes, "Youth," ibid., 39.

117. Miguel Algarin and Bob Holman, eds., *Aloud: Voices from the Nuyorican Poets Café* (New York: Henry Holt, 1994), 5.

118. Ibid., 9.

119. Ibid., 14.

120. Ibid., 388.

121. Miguel Pinero, "New York City Hard Times Blues," ibid., 356–57.

122. Jason Frank, "Aesthetic Democracy: Walt Whitman and the Poetry of the People," *Review of Politics* 69, no. 3 (June 2007): 412.

123. Colin Harrison, *Bodies Electric* (New York: St. Martin's Press, 1993), 1.

124. Ibid., 23.

125. The quotation is from Leo Bersani and Ulysse Dutoit's *Forms of Being: Cinema, Aesthetics, Subjectivity* (London: BFI, 2004), 22. I am adapting their observations about what psychic subjectivity does to cinematic space. In reference to Godard's film *Contempt*, they write, "Godard's focus is not on 'the psychic origins of contempt' [but on] its effects on the world, [which in the context of cinema is conveyed by] what contempt does to cinematic space . . . how it affect[s] the visual field within which Godard works, and especially the range and kinds of movement allowed for in that space" (21–22).

126. See "A Song for Occupations," in *The Complete Poetry and Prose of Walt Whitman*, 209–15. Here Whitman does register aspects of immiseration, although without suggesting how oppressive structures are involved in producing them. He emphasized that no matter how destitute, each individual, whether drunk, sickly, involved in crime or prostitution, is equally worthy as a human.

127. Harrison, *Bodies Electric*, 29.

128. Ibid., 32.

129. Gilles Deleuze, "Postscript on Societies of Control," *October* 59 (1993): 1–12.

130. The quotations are from Marc Auge's meditation on his experience of the Paris Metro (*In the Metro*, trans. Tom Conley [Minneapolis: University of Minnesota Press, 2002], 14).

131. Harrison, *Bodies Electric*, 50.

132. Ibid., 165.

133. Ibid., 76.

134. Whitman, "The Tramp and the Strike Questions," Part of a Lecture (*never deliver'd*), in *The Complete Poetry and Prose*), 340.

135. Harrison, *Bodies Electric*, 76.

136. Ibid., 323.

137. Gilles Deleuze, *Spinoza: Practical Philosophy*, trans. Robert Hurley (San Francisco: City Lights Books, 1988), 19.

CHAPTER 9

Democratic Manliness

Terrell Carver

> House-building, measuring, sawing the boards,
> Blacksmithing, glass-blowing, nail-making, coopering, tin-roofing,
> shingle-dressing,
> Ship-joining, dock-building, fish-curing, flagging of sidewalks by flaggers,
> The pump, the pile-driver, the great derrick, the coal-kiln and brickkiln,
> Coal-mines and all that is down there, the lamps in the darkness,
> echoes, songs, what meditations, what vast native thoughts
> looking through smutch'd faces,
> Iron-works, forge-fires in the mountains or by river-banks, men
> around feeling the melt with huge crowbars, lumps of ore, the
> due combining of ore, limestone, coal,
> The blast-furnace and the puddling-furnace, the loup-lump at the
> bottom of the melt at last, the rolling-mill, the stumpy bars
> of pig-iron, the strong clean-shaped Trail for railroads,
> Oil-works, silk-works, white-lead-works, the sugar-house,
> steam-saws, the great mills and factories,
> Stone-cutting, shapely trimmings for facades or window or door-lintels,
> the mallet, the tooth-chisel, the jib to protect the thumb,
> The calking-iron, the kettle of boiling vault-cement, and the fire
> under the kettle,
> The cotton-bale, the stevedore's hook, the saw and buck of the
> sawyer, the mould of the moulder, the working-knife of the
> butcher, the ice-saw, and all the work with ice,
> The work and tools of the rigger, grappler, sail-maker, block-maker,
> Goods of gutta-percha, papier-mache, colors, brushes, brush-making,
> glazier's implements,

> The veneer and glue-pot, the confectioner's ornaments, the decanter and glasses, the shears and flat-iron,
> The awl and knee-strap, the pint measure and quart measure, the counter and stool, the writing-pen of quill or metal, the making of all sorts of edged tools,
> The brewery, brewing, the malt, the vats, every thing that is done by brewers, wine-makers, vinegar-makers,
> Leather-dressing, coach-making, boiler-making, rope-twisting, distilling, sign-painting, lime-burning, cotton-picking, electroplating, electrotyping, stereotyping,
> Stave-machines, planing-machines, reaping-machines, ploughing-machines, thrashing-machines, steam wagons,
> The cart of the carman, the omnibus, the ponderous dray,
> Pyrotechny, letting off color'd fireworks at night, fancy figures and jets;
> Beef on the butcher's stall, the slaughter-house of the butcher, the butcher in his killing-clothes,
> The pens of live pork, the killing-hammer, the hog-hook, the scalder's tub, gutting, the cutter's cleaver, the packer's maul, and the plenteous winterwork of pork-packing,
> Flour-works, grinding of wheat, rye, maize, rice, the barrels and the half and quarter barrels, the loaded barges, the high piles on wharves and levees,
> The men and the work of the men on ferries, railroads, coasters, fish-boats, canals;
> The hourly routine of your own or any man's life, the shop, yard, store, or factory,
> These shows all near you by day and night—workman! whoever you are, your daily life!
> —Walt Whitman, "A Song for Occupations"

BASED ON AN EXTRAORDINARY poetry that celebrates the workaday world with such intensity and at such length, Walt Whitman has enjoyed a considerable reputation as the poet par excellence of democracy. Indeed, he has been celebrated as a political philosopher, and the "teachings" of his poetry analyzed in that vein.[1] Whitman himself was deeply involved in partisan politics and campaigning journalism, and used his poetry self-consciously to be political and to "do" politics. He also wrote essays and political tracts, and he commented vociferously on the issues of the day, attempting to set an agenda at times. While his views and projects necessarily changed over his career, and indeed he rewrote and recast his own works accordingly, there has been little scholarly doubt that there are traceable threads of consistency, and that he qualifies as a political thinker.[2]

However, the scholarly activity of tracing consistency is generally subject to prior issues as to what scholars are interested in finding in an oeuvre and a life, and what their own projects are in the first place. In turn, this is dependent on what scholars think are their terms of communication with their known audiences, and the audiences to which they aspire. The favorites in the themes that constitute the scholarly reception of Whitman as a political poet and writer have unsurprisingly been the stock items in the ongoing fascination that Americans have in fashioning America as a political construction. Undoubtedly Whitman himself embodies that project as much as anybody else in the trade.

I Hear America Singing

I hear America singing, the varied carols I hear,
Those of mechanics, each one singing his as it should be blithe
  and strong,
The carpenter singing his as he measures his plank or beam,
The mason singing his as he makes ready for work, or leaves off work,
The boatman singing what belongs to him in his boat, the deckhand
  singing on the steamboat deck,
The shoemaker singing as he sits on his bench, the hatter singing as
  he stands,
The wood-cutter's song, the ploughboy's on his way in the morning,
  or at noon intermission or at sundown,
The delicious singing of the mother, or of the young wife at work,
  or of the girl sewing or washing,
Each singing what belongs to him or her and to none else,
The day what belongs to the day—at night the party of young
  fellows, robust, friendly,
Singing with open mouths their strong melodious songs.

The United States of America is rightly taken to be the world's first modern democratic nation, having incorporated itself as a republic in 1788, and ever since then there have been notable inquiries into what this democracy might mean, how exactly this relates to America, and how this geographical and cultural specificity applies to a concept that is supposedly universal, or at least universalizable.[3]

My aim in this essay, though, is to step back a bit from the usual framing of Whitman, and indeed his own framing of himself and his work as together a contribution to this project of explaining democracy in America. Too much about democracy is merely taken for granted in the literature, and therefore is not sufficiently contextualized and critically investigated. I am briefly, therefore, going to construct a view of democracy that situates what it *isn't* rather more fully than usual and gets to grips with the pastiche of principles and institutions that pass in practice as "the sort of thing" that counts as democratic. Importantly, I am going to focus on what—at various times—has been reconciled with democracy or explained away. Once that work is done, I argue that we are in a position to see Whitman rather differently—and democracy, too.

Democracy as a Vocation

Whitman is usually viewed as a quintessential democrat in spirit and in practice, but then one with—inevitably and for historical reasons—conservative and indeed undemocratic sides or views. In the literature these are aspects of his thought or character that we can choose to note—keeping to our purest of ideals—but disregard, and if not to erase, at least to forgive and forget. In recent years this kind of attention has been focused on the precise character of his statements concerning slavery—slave states, free states, and new states; women—and what he may or may not have had in mind when he mentioned them; "man" or men—where the same question arises together with the sexual problematic as well;[4] and all manner of issues to do with race, foreignness, and internal and external imperialisms, otherwise known as "manifest destiny." The reception of Whitman has thus been a process of iconization, where saintly attributes are highlighted and frozen in time, and imperfections and "feet of clay" are acknowledged but then backgrounded as aberrations. I am resisting this.

Rather, my view of Whitman as a democrat is that we shouldn't iconize democracy, either. Its history is not only one of violent contestation against an "other" of monarchy, elitism, and exclusion, but also—and importantly—a history of democratic *defenses* of precisely these kinds of principles and "traditional" institutions. While Americans might be familiar with democratic defenses of inequalities of wealth and income against "levelling" or "communism," they are probably less familiar with *democratic* arguments in favor of constitutional monarchy, appointive or even hereditary decision makers, and functional representation for groups or interests in society through the empowerment of "the great and the good." Still less is there much concern—in America—with noting the widespread and predictable popular support that these arguments and institutions enjoy elsewhere, largely free of any suggestion that they represent some kind of pragmatic compromise or regrettable backsliding, or are simply temporary way stations en route to the realization of some American-based but world-historical model of "democracy."

Moreover, actually existing democracies, such as the American one, are by definition founded on exclusions, and not just outside the borders. The United States is a pastiche of liminal spaces where adult "natural born" or "naturalized" citizens jostle with resident aliens, "green card" holders, and "illegals," where racialized identities have played major roles in constructing gradations of civil status (some of them even constitutional still),[5] and where age, sex, criminal convictions, and family relationships create—or work to create—a highly varied set of practices and categories to which the ever-invoked originary phrase "We the people" supposedly refers. In any case, the historic exclusion of women from public life and the concomitant domesticating concepts of femininity and motherhood, combined with the overt and covert masculinization of the human "individual" as "man," have produced a politics of manliness that survives today, feminist campaigns for equalities and notable victories empowering women notwithstanding.

Interestingly, masculinity, unlike femininity, works in two interlinked ways, mapping distinct advantages and "dividends" onto males.[6] Men find themselves congruent with "the individual" as a supposedly sexless abstraction, because—as feminist criticism has shown—that person is never conceived paradigmatically in ways that are specific to females; females enter the narrative when "the nation" needs to reproduce, and men need "family life."[7] But over and above this happy coincidence of the male with the (supposedly) generic, men also benefit from overtly gendered conceptions that are paradigmatic for full citizenship, namely military service as warrior-protectors (of "women and children"), breadwinners as husbands and fathers, and then through projection of both these defining images they appear qualified as if by nature to be rulers.[8]

My claim is that so long as Whitman's democratic manliness is framed by a concept of democracy in America that is itself an icon, rather than encountered through a concept of democracy that is historically contextualized in relation to the diversities of global principle and practice, then he will have little to tell us that Americans don't already know—and love (perhaps rather too much). The point of icons, of course, is precisely to tell us what we already know, and already know we love and revere.

Iconization is the process through which persons, and their interpersonal and historical contexts, are constructed to make sainthood visible. A saint teaches us a truth we already know, and in an icon s/he does this through a highly reductive process. That process strips away aspects of their lives or characters that don't fit—or reinterprets them so that they do fit—the sacred qualities that a saint must embody. The process also adds, in a highly selective and again reductive way, symbols that help us understand the story and get the message. In the case of the iconic Whitman, we are already supposed to know that democracy is the unfolding of certain principles, over and against the forces and failings of quotidian circumstances, and that through him the message will thus become visible in the world for all to realize. A selective reading of his works and tendentious hagiography of his life thus kick in to help him teach us lessons that are comfortingly familiar, and are always and already turning out all right for us as time moves inexorably on.

Whitman's manliness is also put through the same process of selection and reduction, as indeed have the masculinity and femininity of all the saints. While in his day of (nonuniversal) manhood suffrage there may have been a certain obviousness in the connection, these days the whole idea is more of a stretch. However, metaphor comes to the rescue here (as opposed to the near-literalism that defines the principles of democratic practice). Whitman's robust celebration of his "fellow man" is justly famous for its apparent universality, and being poetic, can be read metaphorically as a set of character-qualities that anyone—of whatever sex, race/ethnicity, religion, or nationality—could embody and realize. While this view must struggle hard against contrary discourses of sex and race, for instance, in Whitman, I take an alternative turn and see just how far Whitman's poetic and political fancy goes in constructing varieties and hierarchies of masculinities, all co-constitutive with other well-known markers, such as class and race, but all nonetheless manly enough for his celebrations of men. Here I ask the reader to reread the epigraph quotation from "A Song for Occupations" with manliness (as opposed to womanliness or generic human-ness) specifically in mind. In other words, some characterizations that might register with us as "race" or "class" can also—with our "gender lens" to hand—register as masculinities. Again, my method here is to fight against selection and reduction, and to flesh out diversity and complexity, however anxious and uncertain this might make us, and however disillusioned we might become with comforting truths and inspirational icons. In the end, democracy in my view is not about the selection of principles and reduction of practice but rather the agonistic processes through which this kind of contestation over terms and outcomes can take place at all.

"Of the People, by the People, [but] for the People[?]"

As a political idea, democracy arose out of contestation, not consensus, and until recently it was not a popular form of government, and certainly not widespread. Or at least it wasn't popular with political theorists, who saw grave disadvantages with "rule by the people," or "rule of the many," in the literal ancient Greek. The usual complaints were that the population at large was unfit to rule, that participation by all was incompatible with the efficiencies that ruling requires, and that the whole idea was itself a license for mob rule and disrespect for law and order. Intellectuals, practical men, and even poets, where they addressed—or were seen to address—this issue, have overwhelmingly agreed that ruling is not for the many, even if these various thinkers disagreed on exactly how few the few should be, and how exactly they should proceed with the job. Moreover numerous regimes, including numerous twentieth-century "Western" ones in Europe (not just in South America), slipped in and out of democracy, often more than once. The argument that in and of itself democracy produces stability is suspect, to say the least.

And overwhelmingly, where we have recorded opinions that are *not* in praise of democracy, those who are on the record in that way are those whose education, aspirations, and connections mark them out from the common man, so eloquently celebrated in Whitman's poetry. Of course, even within the very limited experience we have of democracy before the modern era, many common men were ruled out from belonging to "the people" in the first place through gradations of inferiority involving slave or caste status, rural or other devalued occupations, lack of wealth or family connections of "birth," and innumerable kinds of "otherness" dividing insiders from outsiders. Chief among these outsiders were women, whose position as a sex—however rationalized and whatever the rare individual exceptions—constituted a major exclusion with respect to manly rule, democratic or otherwise. But as I have been at pains to note, manly rule rarely if ever included all men who might in some way be seen to be, or might claim to be, part of "the people."[9]

Thus the history of modern democracy is not that of a progressive development proceeding of its own accord, a germination, growth, and flowering of the human spirit, say, but rather one that involved lengthy intellectual contestation and—on numerous occasions—widespread popular revolts, uprisings, civil wars, invasions, reprisals, massacres, political murder, and the like. Within these developments—taking just the later European Middle Ages as a point of illustration here—numerous men and women of "the many" were quite *un*convinced that anything other than monarchy, particularly because monarchy was already religiously sanctified, was at all desirable. In the battles and struggles, the "cannon fodder" was overwhelmingly common folk on both sides, and, of course, there were often more than two sides. By definition, there aren't enough kings and aristocrats or even gentry or "bourgeoisie" to go round, even to make up one side in defense of the ancien régime.

In any case, being antimonarchical isn't enough to make anyone very democratic, though, logically speaking, it's a start. Again, working from the political history of the later European Middle Ages, it's clear that the antimonarchical camp was overwhelmingly republican, rather than strictly democratic on a model that maximizes citizen participation in decision-making processes. The "mixed" or Roman constitution was a common exemplar, involving the representation of "the many," through the choice—in some fashion—of spokes*men* to present views to a senate or council. Again these conciliar bodies were representative, but of a different, wealthier, and better-educated community of families, and again, chosen through any number of procedures, often hereditary selection.[10] And even in conciliar rather than monarchical systems, there were, of necessity, an even smaller number of executives, charged with everything from day-to-day business to strategic, visionary roles and oftentimes ultimate command of military forces for internal and external purposes. These constitutions are thus "mixed" in that the institutions involved have a basis in communal distinctions *dividing* "the people" and then assigning various functional powers to a mix of representatives and persons, rather than to one person as monarch. Somewhere in this rather general excursus on republican constitutional forms most readers should be able to recognize the outlines of the U.S. Constitution as variously amended.

This is especially so if we scrutinize the Constitution carefully for its fine distinctions among humans: "Indians not taxed," "free persons," "all other persons," and (in the Nineteenth Amendment) "sex" (otherwise known as women). The historically inclined will know that the Senate was originally indirectly elected (by state legislatures), and that the broader franchise for congressional and presidential elections was left to the states to implement as they saw fit. This "reservation" of powers necessitated further bitter and highly destructive contestations involving race, wealth, literacy, sex, and other factors relating to the electoral rolls, including the operative freedom to vote and otherwise participate in the civil and political processes that—one way or another—are presumed in sum to constitute democracy as an American achievement.

This is to say that Alexis de Tocqueville's great work *De la démocratie en Amerique* (2 vols., 1835, 1840) was an inquiry into what this form of government and concomitant social organization might be, rather than a descriptive account of how something already well known and understood had been instituted in practice. And, famously, it was more an account of what the author took to be distinctive national sentiments and character, rather than an institutional discussion of the sort that most political theorists would recognize. Its audience was—obviously—French, and the author spoke to the political situation there, where—even in the reign of the constitutional citizen-king Louis Philippe—the weight of the aristocratic order and the institutions of Catholic monarchism pressed very hard against the popular revolutionary success of 1830.

Democracy in America looked an easy ride by contrast, and from Tocqueville's perspective the title is apt. From an American perspective, though, the institutions of 1788 were republican ones, the common men were barely franchised, and—for a radical few, such as Tom Paine—the situation looked hardly democratic at all. While monarchy was out of the question, a de facto aristocracy of wealth and land held the high ground of major offices. While new money vied with old for positions of power, and the (narrowly and locally defined) electorate was part of the mix, the common man's role in politics was hardly central, even in terms of representation, whether practical or iconic. New England town meetings might seem an exception, but then they prove the rule—they were not a defining feature of American republicanism outside New England.

As new states entered the Union, the bloody battle was over the institutionalization of racialized chattel slavery, not over the further democratization of republican forms, and the end of postbellum Reconstruction was exactly that: the democratization of political institutions was put into reverse, with striking effects on the North, not just the South, because "Jim Crow" had appallingly undemocratic effects on black and other minority peoples everywhere in the country. Whitman's major efforts as a democratic poet date from the antebellum crisis years, when the further democratization of republican institutions was in play, and for capital stakes, as it turned out. While some of Whitman's language is apparently celebratory, it is at heart aspirational and contestatory—it was written to convince, not to confirm. Indeed, that is arguably what democracy and democratic language are really about—promoting an ideal through which realities are constructed in struggle, where consensus is temporary and strategic, and where institutions and practices never entirely measure up. If ever there was an agonistic democrat, it was Whitman.[11]

> How the great cities appear—how the Democratic masses, turbulent, willful, as I love them,
> How the whirl, the contest, the wrestle of evil with good, the sounding and resounding, keep on and on,
> How society waits unform'd, and is for a while between things ended and things begun,

It should now be apparent that one of the things that is crucially contested here is not just government, but manliness, and that this is central to democracy, insofar as it has ever been practised in the inchoate ways I have described above. The entire exercise of politics has been—and still is—not just male-dominated but masculine-inscribed. Where there is contestation over rulers, the argument turns—heavily—on what sort of *man* this is, and isn't. Whitman is quite an authority on this point, particularly on the kind of men who completely fail—in his view—to qualify: "swarms of cringers, suckers, dough-faces, lice of politics, planners of sly involutions for their own perferment to city offices or state legislatures or the judiciary or congress or the presidency . . . a bound booby and rogue in office at a high salary."[12]

While in his character studies Whitman mentions women, and indeed repeatedly celebrates their equality with men, his references are feminist only in a mainstream nineteenth-century sense of women's bodily, vocational, and moral difference in relation to men as the obvious point of reference. This played out both as economic dependency by right (the "family wage" and men's responsibility for it) and as moral and sometimes domestic superiority (women's mission to ameliorate and control men's violence, sexual promiscuity, and drunkenness).[13] Note that in the enormously long list of occupations quoted in the epigraph above, through which Whitman constructs his poetry of the American "common man," he is clearly invoking masculinized and masculinizing activities.[14] He says very little in sum about women's work of any comparable character in relation to politics generally, American civilization or democracy as such: "serpentine poison of those [men] that seduce women . . . the foolish yielding of women . . . prostitution . . . harshness of officers to men or judges to prisoners or rather to sons or sons to fathers or husbands to wives or bosses to their boys . . . [in contrast to] . . . all that a male or female does that is vigorous and benevolent and clean."[15] Whitman's celebration of women is rather generically directed to birth and motherhood, sexual qualities of seductive softness and faithful surrender in relation to men, and occupational domesticity and occasional frillery. Of course, this is not surprising, on two levels. As he looked around, that is very largely what he was seeing, and indeed, those women concerned with women as a political project didn't usually differ all that much from this view anyway. However, as feminist historians have shown, a closer look reveals considerable numbers of women doing all kinds of things that were "unwomanly" and thus somewhat unrepresentable, unsayable, and often hidden or at least not highlighted.[16]

Today in America after considerable struggle, well against the odds, and with very little male help, women can be representatives and rulers, so one sort of man may—exceptionally—be a woman.[17] Where gender—that is, masculinity and femininity—is understood to relate to surface appearances and evident behavior, the terms themselves inevitably draw us back to the "oppositely" sexed bodies that are presumed to lie beneath the surface—in most cases.[18] In or out of political office, masculine women are a focus of cognitive dissonance, provoking violence and exclusion in some cases, "live and let live" forms of tolerance in others, and very little male admiration. As prime minister, Margaret Thatcher became an icon, but it is unclear of exactly what, and the contestations surrounding Hillary Clinton in various guises are very well known. Sir Winston Churchill—and the American "founding fathers"—all became icons, posing no major hermeneutic difficulties. They were visibly male, and evinced masculinity in rulership mode, evoking the urbane patricians and landed gentry of the Greek and Roman classics. Patriarchy is hardly some private realm of family rule: it's public, readily intelligible, and widely approved of by men and women, democratic institutions and values notwithstanding.

Whitman's democratic manliness is perceived now to pose two major problems: it excludes women, and it pushes manly sentiments toward a supposed equality in homoeroticism. No one today is really concerned to rescue him on the former point, but the latter line might be generalizable as a metaphor. Or rather equality in homoeroticism might be a metaphor—whether Whitman understood it this way or not—for sentiments that could and would promote what are widely understood today to be democratic forms of communication and practice.[19]

"I Sing of Arms and the Man"

My purpose here is not to resolve either of these problems separately, or to propose some resolution that would transcend both difficulties at once. Rather, I am concerned to explore, as best one can, how varied masculinities are constructed within Whitman's verse, and how these are mapped onto power relations, which is where politics necessarily lies. Some of this work will involve guessing the "other" against which Whitman's verse contests, but then that is merely exposing the tension that arises when political theorists get to work on texts that aren't treatises on the principles and institutions of ruling and being ruled—though Whitman comes surprisingly close on occasion:

> The American compact is altogether with individuals,
> The only government is that which makes minute of individuals,
> The whole theory of the universe is directed unerringly to one
>   single individual—namely to You.

Of course, most of the standard treatises in political theory were not academic exercises anyway but rather political contestations in their time, a point sometimes missed in decontextualizing forms of analysis and appropriation. However, the texts to which political theorists find themselves turning in recent years are increasingly varied in terms of genre, and rightly so. Any genre can be a vehicle for contestation, and can thus become political. In the context of the 1850s, Whitman self-consciously made himself a political poet and addressed the national situation in that way, proposing a resolution of a certain character. This was notably nonviolent, as opposed to the enduring popularity of violence as a way of settling political differences; it was radical, in that it appealed to the common man in various ways, rather than to his "betters" and rulers; it was strategic, in that it proceeded through a redefinition of manliness or masculinity; and it was calculating, in that it was expected to work through the stimulation of feelings in the reading public.

My project is thus to pluralize Whitman's notion of manliness into masculinities, and to pluralize the feelings he was trying to evoke as ecstatically varied, rather than predominantly those of male same-sex desire. In the first case, I am importing a contemporary notion—pluralizing masculinities—into a reading of Whitman, as a way of making his text address an area of current intellectual curiosity where readers might be "feeling their way";[20] in the second case, I am retreating somewhat from an area in sexuality and gay studies that has become rather too formulaic and easily absorbed, since Whitman has for many years been appropriated as a gay voice *avant la lettre*. There are, after all, areas of mixed and overlapping feelings and rather undercharacterized relationships in Whitman's work that might bear some scrutiny, and so I propose—not a desexed reading—but rather a nonreductionist one.

The real difficulty with the iconic Whitman as a democratic poet is America. Anyone expecting an American evocation of democracy along the lines of "America the Beautiful"

> For amber waves of grain,
> For purple mountains majesties
> Above the fruited plain!
> . . . .

And crown thy good with brotherhood,
From sea to shining sea.

or "Columbia the Gem of the Ocean" (which dates from Whitman's time)

> The home of the brave and the free,
> The shrine of each patriot's devotion,
> . . . .
> Thy mandates make heroes assemble,
> When Liberty's form stands in view;
> Thy banners make tyranny tremble

is going to be at least somewhat disappointed.[21] Whitman announces himself as the poet of democracy:

> I speak the pass-word primeval, I give the sign of democracy;
> By God! I will accept nothing which all cannot have their
>   counterpart of on the same terms.[22]

And he addresses himself from America "To Foreign Lands":

> I heard that you ask'd for something to prove this puzzle the New
>   World,
> And to define America, her athletic Democracy,
> Therefore I send you my poems that you behold in them what you
>   wanted.

And he has a theory about the solution to this puzzle of nationhood:

> "For You, O Democracy"
> Come, I will make the continent indissoluble,
> I will make the most splendid race the sun ever shone upon,
> I will make divine magnetic lands,
>   With the love of comrades,
>   With the life-long love of comrades.
> I will plant companionship thick as trees along all the rivers of America,

> and along the shores of the great lakes, and all over the prairies,
> I will make inseparable cities with their arms about each other's necks,
>> By the love of comrades,
>> By the manly love of comrades.
> For you these from me, O Democracy, to serve you ma femme!
> For you, for you I am trilling these songs.

However, Whitman's poetry is most famously observant of—and transcendentally celebratory of—life as it is lived out in practical activities (the dirtier the better, as in the epigraph to this essay). Most of the practical activities and human interest that mark this could have been anywhere that was urban and industrialized, and the American identities that are invoked are largely regional and state-based (southwesterner, slave owner, Louisianan, Kentuckian, etc.). The most distinctively American identities are "negro" (slave or free) and "red squaw" (whose male counterpart is invoked in tribal names). Distinctively American political institutions are mentioned—president, Congress, governors—but they are hardly celebrated as democratic forms of *rule:* such persons occupying high office are told not to think too much of themselves, and not to imagine that as *men* they are any better than any other man. In terms of other men, Whitman's vast catalog of ordinariness extends to Canada, Mexico, China, Ireland, Denmark, and a huge number of other nations, all existing in a hu*man* equality, which is where his democratic message lies. His lines on the Alamo certainly reflect a white and masculinized politics that he celebrated—the "defense" of an American white-settler and slave republic carved out of the declining and racially mixed Spanish empire—but the poetry itself is a meditation on the wartime massacre of defenseless prisoners. The poet's voice is really arguing a manly democracy that could be anywhere.

> I was looking a long while for Intentions,
> For a clew to the history of the past for myself, and for these
>> chants—and now I have found it,
> . . . .
> It is in Democracy—(the purport and aim of all the past,)
> It is the life of one man or one woman to-day—the average man of
>> to-day,

> It is in languages, social customs, literatures, arts,
> It is in the broad show of artificial things, ships, machinery,
> > politics, creeds, modern improvements, and the interchange of nations,
> All for the modern—all for the average man of to-day.

Or could it really be just anywhere?

> Who are you indeed who would talk or sing to America?
> Have you studied out the land, its idioms and men?
> Have you learn'd the physiology, phrenology, politics, geography,
> > pride, freedom, friendship of the land? its substratums and objects?
> Have you consider'd the organic compact of the first day of the
> > first year of Independence, sign'd by the Commissioners, ratified by the States, and read by Washington at the head of the army?
> Have you possess'd yourself of the Federal Constitution?
> Do you see who have left all feudal processes and poems behind them,
> > and assumed the poems and processes of Democracy?

Whitman's manly democracy is laden with unmarked whiteness, and precisely where his vision of American nationhood demarcates itself in relation to a universalizable concept of democracy is very unclear. While the poetry contains evocative accounts of the poet's care for a runaway (male) slave, and a moving invocation of common hu*man*ity, that "negro" is clearly on the way to something other than full citizenship and nonracialized equality, inside America at least. In that way, and outside the slave states, the freed (black) slave resembles the vivid but furtive indigenous aboriginals who also feature in Whitman's sweeping canvas.

The democratic nationalisms of Whitman's time were generally construed as consistent with a harmony of nations based on equal respect, founded on a recognition of difference. This was combined with a resolve to map that respect onto political geographies where different "races" could fulfill their cultural potentials peacefully within borders (supposedly guaranteed by local uniformities) and between borders (supposedly guaranteed by nonviolent settlement of international differences). The idea that manly democracy and equal respect for men and women (in different racialized identities) could resolve political issues peacefully specifically in America (or indeed anywhere else) isn't really in the vision.

Notably Whitman's highest scorn is reserved for the dead King George of Britain, whose spirit of imperial intolerance—so the poet says in "A Boston Ballad"—was reinvoked by arrogant federal marshals who acted with force to return a slave to "its" owner in the South. However, as research has shown, Whitman was not an all-out abolitionist in the run-up to the Civil War but rather a defender of the preceding compromises that had preserved the Union to date.[23] Slavery was legal only in the original southern states, and escaped slaves who made it to the North were freed, but—as noted above—that didn't make them manly democrats on the white model, since they weren't white.

Thus the manly qualities that Whitman celebrates can be parsed as differing masculinities, racially, culturally, and morally inflected. The added value of this view—rather than seeing just race, or culture or morals in his characterizations—is that it emphasizes the exclusion of women from the democratic virtues the poet celebrates, and so highlights the blurred vision that results when the supposedly generic "human" view of democratic life and values that seems to apply to women actually cashes out in specific terms. These terms presuppose female difference as domesticity, child care, and sexual availability to men. However, given the invocations of almost innumerable different masculinized and masculinizing activities, crosscut with race, culture, and nationhood, it is entirely fair to ask whether we are seeing different masculinities or simply different ways of being masculine, and therefore whether being masculine is really all that important. The affirmative answer lies in fine-grained observation of men's hierarchies over each other, and the extent to which gender-strategies *among men* tell us something about how racialized hierarchies, say, actually operate.

Whitman's generalized manly democracy works against this, seemingly, since his message is one of equality of respect, rather than the construction of power differentials among men. This, of course, has its "other," namely those grasping, venal, dishonorable men whose corrupt activities the poet deplores. Whitman is clearly using his poetry politically to construct a power difference among men that will put the inferior sort in their place—though it's unclear where this is, presumably prison or some other form of correction or exclusion. True, the poet says he understands all that is human (including some aspects of women's experience) and that he thus transcends race and nation, good and evil. However, the poetry tells us quite a lot about what's wrong with some men, their attitudes and activities, and gradations of masculinity are part of the moral and political vocabulary invoked to make this clear.

While Whitman's verse is extraordinary in terms of sexual explicitness, and male-male relations in particular (another masculinizing exclusion), his manly democracy has more to do with the sweat of manly occupations. These were both low- and high-tech in mid-nineteenth-century terms—there are trappers and sailors as well as all kinds of crafts and trades in his vision. The physicality of it all is a masculinizing exclusion—the Brooklyn of Whitman's day had plenty of male workers in offices and retail premises, but they get little celebration. Middle-class and wealthy forms of masculine *politesse* are perhaps backgrounded and aligned with femininity and financial corruption, but we get little overt sense of that. It's important to consider what kinds of masculinities are *not* in the vision, as well as to revel in the ones that are, as in the epigraph to this essay. Whitman's manly democracy seems to draw a sharp line between the virtues of worker-masculinity and the violence that comes with soldiering, where tragedy absorbs the lads, rather than the industrial vigor that the poet celebrates at huge length.

The wide range of ecstatic feelings evoked in Whitman's poetry might themselves be a metaphor for the sexual feelings he portrays, rather than the other way round. This is a way of cashing out equality of respect that has some promise, in that the poet encourages us to find some sensual and intellectual pleasures in other people in innumerable ways, and indeed that is possibly the central point of his vision. While the close observation of life in the natural world appears—in any case a standard poetic trope—what is strikingly original in Whitman is the celebration of the industrial, the occupational, the everyday, the unfiltered variety of human beings, their ways of life, bodies, and minds that he surveys locally, regionally, overseas, and globally. America is a good place to do this, to be sure, but there's no suggestion that it's the only place in the world like this or that everyone there is a part of just one "imagined community."[24] Such inclusion as there is comes through the assertion of common feelings and the poet's projection of just how this feels to him, but it's a long way from that to any overarching commitment to the equalities of race and sex that we strain for today.

Conclusions

Nations are constructed through processes of iconization that produce exemplary rulers, soldiers, writers, poets, musicians, artists, actors . . . even criminals, cowards, traitors, and monsters. Men and women are distributed rather unequally through these processes, though alternative and overlapping pantheons and infernos are currently and widely under construction. America is interesting in that it iconizes a political system—democracy—more than most, and turns particularly to poets to illustrate and argue this point. This kind of political project is clearly one that is used to bring forth unity from difference (*e pluribus unum*), and in that it works well on its own terms. However, these terms are constantly redefined with respect to changing political projects, lately involving race/ethnicity and sex (but rather less involved with social class and inequalities of wealth, though that might be changing).

Whitman's poetry presents—it seems—some congruence with his known political projects, and these are of course derived from the issues of the time as he contested them. Peeling the politics off the poetry is about as worthwhile as peeling the poetry off the politics—they go together in his vision. Thus iconizing Whitman—or even some of his metaphors—in order to pursue current contestations of democracy is, on the one hand, fair enough, and, on the other hand, rather dangerous. The pursuit of politics through icons is inaccurate and unfair to everybody—and in the case of democracy, everything—but then that is possibly the only way politics works and anything ever gets done.

> —This seething hemisphere's humanity, as now, I'd name—the still
> small voice vibrating—America's choosing day,
> (The heart of it not in the chosen—the act itself the main, the
> quadriennial choosing,)
> The stretch of North and South arous'd—sea-board and inland—
> Texas to Maine—the Prairie States—Vermont, Virginia,
> California,
> The final ballot-shower from East to West—the paradox and conflict,
> The countless snow-flakes falling—(a swordless conflict,
> Yet more than all Rome's wars of old, or modern Napoleon's:) the
> peaceful choice of all,
> Or good or ill humanity—welcoming the darker odds, the dross:

> —Foams and ferments the wine? it serves to purify—while the heart pants, life glows:
> These stormy gusts and winds waft precious ships,
> Swell'd Washington's, Jefferson's, Lincoln's sails.

Democratic manliness is in the reception-literature, not in Whitman, because reception-literature *reads;* it doesn't merely reproduce. In his reception, Whitman is iconized, despite the obvious exclusions in his views that current democratic thought cannot countenance. These exclusions are typically American, but hardly unique; the country would not have been founded at all without them. These exclusions were also nearly fatal to the Union, as dramatically witnessed by Whitman's passionate turn in poetry and prose to preventing this very outcome.

Manliness is extracted in Whitman to iconize democracy (yet again), but closer reading reveals that this concept generates its hierarchies—industry over office, sweat over society, macho-butch over whatever else. And it generates its exclusions—notably over race and alleged foreignness—balancing order and unity over racial diversity and individual mobility. Whitman's manliness, as a rather narrow range and questionable hierarchy of masculinities, can't be all that democratic in the end, if we are looking for a consistent celebration of equality in diversity. Political theorists are inclined to see this vision—at least as much as possible—in the American experience, and to identify it as an American project. But that view erases—or at least romanticizes—the struggles, some quite recent and indeed ongoing—that it took and still takes to realize this project as far as it has got. It also does little justice to the fragility and contingency of the exercise.

Whitman's agonism is on surer ground here: struggle and contest over what counts as democratic principles and practices offer the best testament to democracy in America. Whitman the political communicator, not the icon of democracy, played a notable part in this. Even his free verse struggles agonistically against the idea that poetry is a given set of principles and practices, and in that way as a poet he limns democracy, however we read him.

Notes

1. See, for example, George Kateb, "Walt Whitman and the Culture of Democracy," in this volume.

2. For a useful overview, see David S. Reynolds, "Politics and Poetry: Leaves of Grass and the Social Crisis of the 1850s," in *The Cambridge Companion to Walt Whitman,* ed. Ezra Greenspan (Cambridge: Cambridge University Press, 1995), 66–91.

3. "We did not charge hundreds of miles into the heart of Iraq and pay a bitter cost of casualties and liberate 25 million people only to retreat before a band of thugs and assassins, [U.S. President George W.] Bush said. We will help the Iraqi people establish a peaceful and democratic country in the heart of the Middle East" ("Bush: 'Democracy Will Succeed' in Iraq," CNN, November 19, 2003. http://edition.cnn.com/2003/WORLD/europe/11/19/bush.speech/index.html).

4. For an exploration of this particular use of the gender "lens," see Terrell Carver, *Men in Political Theory* (Manchester: Manchester University Press, 2009).

5. The current variety of arrangements concerning Native Americans and "reservations" or special status areas of various sorts descends from constitutional provisions.

6. Terrell Carver, "'Public Man' and the Critique of Masculinities," *Political Theory* 24, no. 4 (1996): 673–86; R. W. Connell, *Gender* (Cambridge: Polity Press, 2002).

7. Carole Pateman, *The Sexual Contract* (Cambridge: Polity Press, 1988); Diana Coole, *Women and Political Theory: From Ancient Misogyny to Contemporary Feminism,* 2nd ed. (New York: Prentice Hall, 1993); Jacqueline Stevens, *Reproducing the State* (Princeton: Princeton University Press, 1999).

8. Jean Bethke Elshtain, *Women and War,* 2nd ed. (Chicago: University of Chicago Press, 1995); R. Claire Snyder, *Citizen Soldiers and Manly Warriors: Military Service and Gender in the Civic Republican Tradition* (Lanham, Md.: Rowman and Littlefield, 1999); Charlotte Hooper, *Manly States: Masculinities, International Relations and Gender Politics* (New York: Columbia University Press, 2001).

9. There are rather more controversies about democratic exclusions, and the precise terms of what anyone is being excluded from, than is generally realized. Age qualifications for voting and age restrictions on officeholding vary considerably; there are numerous hybrid and diasporic forms of voter-inclusion operative in the European Union and numerous other countries, for instance.

10. This survives at the time of writing in the U.K. House of Lords, where the remaining ninety-two "hereditaries" are still choosing replacements—by election!—for the deceased.

11. For current theorizing in this vein, see Chantal Mouffe, *The Return of the Political* (London: Verso, 2005).

12. Walt Whitman, *Leaves of Grass: The First (1855) Edition,* ed. Malcolm Cowley (New York: Viking Press, 1960), [original preface], 17.

13. Mary E. Hawkesworth, *Globalization and Feminist Activism* (Lanham, Md.: Rowman and Littlefield, 2006).

14. It is also quite clear that he is envisioning "white workingmen," not "Negroes" (see the discussion in Reynolds, "Politics and Poetry," 71–72).

15. Whitman, *Leaves of Grass: First Edition*, 19–20.

16. Hawkesworth, *Globalization and Feminist Activism*, esp. chap. 1.

17. For a definitive overview of this area, see Judith Halberstam, *Female Masculinity* (Durham, N.C.: Duke University Press, 1998).

18. For an extended analysis and political meditation on the terms of sex, gender, and sexuality, and their various performative instantiations, see Judith Butler, *Undoing Gender* (New York: Routledge, 2004), esp. chap. 9.

19. For a recent overview, see Mark Maslan, *Whitman Possessed: Poetry, Sexuality, and Popular Authority* (Baltimore: Johns Hopkins University Press, 2001); for a more generic use of homosexuality as a political and ethical model, see Mark Blasius, *Gay and Lesbian Politics: Sexuality and the Emergence of a New Ethic* (Philadelphia: Temple University Press, 1994).

20. R. W. Connell, *Masculinities*, 2nd ed. (Cambridge: Polity Press, 2005).

21. For a discussion of "the nation" as kitsch and how national anthems and patriotic songs construct this performatively, see Klaus Sondermann, "Reading Politically: National Anthems as Textual Icons," in *Interpreting the Political: New Methodologies*, ed. Terrell Carver and Matti Hyvärinen (London: Routledge, 1997), 128–42.

22. Whitman, *Leaves of Grass: First Edition*, 48.

23. Reynolds, "Politics and Poetry."

24. Benedict Anderson, *Imagined Communities: Reflections on the Origin and Spread of Nationalism*, 2nd ed. (London: Verso, 2006).

PART III

Death and Citizenship

CHAPTER 10

Whitman as a Political Thinker

Peter Augustine Lawler

MY TASK IS TO present and assess Whitman as a political thinker. To make my task simpler, I've pretty much limited myself to the prose he wrote after the Civil War. That may or may not be his best writing, but it is certainly his most mature thought. I've compared him to what Alexis de Tocqueville says in his great *Democracy in America*, but mainly in search of points of agreement and not with the intention of finding Whitman wanting. Whitman shared the concerns of the best of the political thinkers, and he even seems, in many ways, more alike than different from the ambivalent aristocrat Tocqueville in thinking about the need for greatness to justify democracy—even in light of its undeniable superiority when it comes to justice and prosperity (II.4.8).[1] True greatness is that of individuality or the person—the being who has the moral character to live well, be animated by a dutiful love that's much more and even other than physical satisfaction, and die well. Whitman even agreed with Tocqueville that democracy languishes without a religion, and that religion must support the person's longing for immortality, even personal immortality, if personal greatness—the only real form of greatness—is to flourish in America's future.

Where Tocqueville and Whitman disagree, it seems to me, is on the question of whether the democratic poet can find the resources in democracy itself to generate a wholly new religion. Certainly Richard Rorty was wrong not to regard Whitman as a deeply religious thinker, many have been wrong to regard him primarily as celebrating an "expressive individualism" that found its culmination in the cultural libertarianism of our 1960s, and just as many have been wrong to dismiss him as succumbing to a democratic pantheism incompatible with the truth about irreducible personal identity. I've presented Whitman's political thought as he did, as a series of moments or facets. I've done what I could both to connect them and to show their contradictions. As Whitman himself says, displaying their inner unity is the project for the democratic poet to come.

The Democratic Political Principle

Whitman asserted the complete political victory of the "democratic principle" in America (915).[2] It is established "for good," "never to be overturn'd" in our political institutions (1000). This "American programme" of rights and republican government "not for classes, but for universal man" is put forward in the American compact of the Constitution—as illuminated by the Declaration of Independence and fleshed out by the amendments (1000–1001). The political history of our country is the working out in detail of the principle of general suffrage—pointing to its extension, for example, to women and eventually to every person everywhere in the world. For Whitman, "America and democracy" are "convertible terms," and the whole world is destined to become democratized under American leadership (954). There's nothing specifically American—that is, tied to a people living in a specific place—in the idea of an American, and so the idea of America is unlimited by time, place, or other particular circumstances. Because America is "for universal man," no human being or class of human beings can be excluded from being American. "Manifest Destiny" was probably more imaginatively manifest to Whitman than to any other American. America, in his eyes, has an "imperial destiny as dazzling as the sun" (1014).

Europe's statesmen know that the only thing left to do is to choose "*how* . . . most prudently to democratize*" (974). By becoming democratic, the European becomes American, because America is, most deeply, an idea. Politically speaking, there's no conceivable progress beyond the foundation laid by our Constitution and Declaration. As a Hegelian would say, the American Constitution established a universal and homogeneous state, one free from all contradictions and through the recognition of the equal human dignity of every person. Whitman wrote positively of Hegel's system as the final stage in the development of human thought—more profound than the mere empiricism of modern (especially Darwinian) science. But what he affirmed about Hegel he had already seen—at least imaginatively—in

America. The spread of the principles of the universal and homogeneous state through all of American society would resolve America's remaining contradictions, making every nook and cranny of our country democratic.

Whitman's understanding of the American "ardent belief in and substantial practice of, radical human rights" seems to be indebted, above all, to Thomas Paine. Paine described what government must become upon its "severance . . . from all ecclesiastical and superstitious dominion." Whitman and Paine thought that, prior to the emergence of the democratic principle, all government was "feudal"—or some mixture of monkish ignorance and aristocratic pride. And Whitman also thought, following Paine, that all ecclesiastical or organized religion was about despotic superstitions that have been discredited by the light of science (822). A nation radically devoted to rights should, in fact, inspire religious devotion, but its churches should wither away or be wholly without influence. Whitman embraced Paine's boldness; what they said in print and to everyone, Jefferson said in private letters.

The American or democratic principle was, initially, a clear victory of philosophy or science over Eastern (mainly biblical) superstition. Against various rumors about the disease that killed him having put him out of his mind, Paine, Whitman claims, "died calmly and philosophically, as became him," a fitting culmination to his "good life, after its kind" (822). The ancient materialistic philosophies of Epicurus and Lucretius—negative poems that deprive death of its sting—are what freed the minds of American democratic Revolutionaries from superstitious terrors (1013). Maybe it was the Bible, as Whitman suggests, that taught them that "common morality and death" are "men's great equalizers" (1164), and that philosophers and such had no right to think of themselves as above the fundamental experiences of every human life. All persons are stuck with the responsibility of being virtuous, of living, loving, and dying well. And it's a testimony to the realization of the democratic faith that nobody—as none of the soldiers, Whitman claims, did during the "Secession War"—any longer approaches death "with cowardly qualms or terror" (970).

Hobbes thought fear of death could be a reliable foundation for modern government; Whitman thought fear of death was slavish and had to be overcome for democracy to flourish. The liberation from the terror of death of the philosophers has to be shared by us all. Even or especially the perfected democratic culture of the future will depend on "manly and courageous instincts" and on self-respect, not to mention a kind of fraternal love that could easily be compromised by fearful self-obsession (986–87). The future of any people "depends on how it faces death, and how it stands personal anguish and sickness." It also depends on whether it remains courageous and resolute or unterrified and unparalyzed in the face of emergencies (802). So democratic America will stand or fall on the manly courage—as much as the manly love—of most people. No amount of progress will eradicate the need to live well with death to live well at all, and no people will ever be free of the possibility of war. The difference between the feudal, aristocratic world described by Shakespeare is that ordinary Americans will face death well, like the philosophers of old, without having to be superstitiously manipulated.

Whitman observes that "Paine's practical demeanor and much of his theoretic belief, was a mixture of the French and English schools of a century ago, and the best of both" (822). Whether or not that's exactly true of Paine, it's surely the way Whitman thought of himself. The French—or the French revolutionaries at least—thought that democracy couldn't be secured only through the English methods of contract and consent. More conscious attention had to be given to formation of citizens, including even a civil religion.

Whitman usually seemed indifferent to political institutions because he took their existence as a given. But the "Secession War" was evidence enough that a government instituted through Lockean calculation, by itself, leads to secession or the reduction of human attachments to alliances from which it's possible to withdraw at will. So he agreed with the French that a nation needed to be held together through "manly friendship" or camaraderie. Without such "loving comradeship," he asserted, democracy "will be incomplete, and incapable of perpetuating itself" (1006).

Manly friendship, for Whitman, was a sort of idealization or sublimation of physical eros. It does have a Jacobin element, and it is arguably at the expense of friendship as it's actually experienced by beings with bodies. It's opposed to what we might call the English celebration of personal intimacy—including the affirmation and physical satisfaction of homoerotic and heteroerotic impulses. "Manly" certainly means for Whitman, at least after the experience of the Secession War, "Platonic" in the sense of not oriented around physical enjoyment or any other merely private and material pursuit. But it's not the completely de-eroticized depersonalization characteristic of the revolutionary French "citizen" or the Soviet "comrade." It's not a feature of the abstract homogenization of all of life, of the general will of some totalitarian democracy. The emotional unity of the nation and eventually the world depends on an unprecedented, imaginary transcendence of the limitations of human knowing and loving so far. But it's not to be at the expense of real personal identity, and neither is it to depend on coercion.

Moral Character and Political Life

Whitman explains that "the democratic republican principle" is "the theory of development and perfection by voluntary standards" (953). So that principle is less about perfecting the institutions of government than of being "the only effectual method of surely, however slowly, training people on a large scale to voluntarily ruling and managing themselves." And that kind of perfection is "the ultimate aim of political and all other development." Democratic progress is "to gradually reduce the fact of *governing* to its minimum," because people will be trained or habituated to ruling themselves (915). "What is independence," Whitman writes, but "freedom from all yokes and bonds except those of one's own being," which are limited only "by the universal ones," those that flow from recognition of the independence all persons share (1002).

Whitman doesn't join the libertarian or the Marxist in holding that the ultimate aim of modern freedom is the withering away of the state for each person's free, unobsessive pursuit of private goals or whims. Political life and political devotion are indispensable features in the development of self-discipline or character. "Political democracy," he explains, "supplies a training-school for making first-class men." Political contests are "life's gymnasium" for "freedom's athletes," and they satisfy their desire for action, "irrespective of success" (976). There's nothing "grander," after all, "than a well-contested American national election" (978). Whitman often claims that there has to be lots for the democratic person to do to satisfy his athletic desire for action and display his greatness or have an outlet for his pride.

The withering away of the state would be the withering away of political greatness, of part of what's intrinsic to personal identity. It's the contest—or not just heart-enlarging affection—that each of us can't help but crave, and political democracy's distinctiveness is training us all to be actors on the political stage. The constant political danger, Whitman cautions, is that "savage, wolfish parties," obeying "no law but their own will," become so combative that they lose contact with "overarching American ideas" and "equal brotherhood" (990). But who can deny that contests among brothers are an indispensable feature of character development? Brotherhood surely is consistent enough with strong personal identity and considerable self-assertiveness.

Whitman doesn't address the issue of the necessarily aristocratic character of elections. Only a few ever run and fewer still ever win, and obvious distinctions can't help but emerge between first- and second-class politicians. Universal suffrage can't produce, in a representative democracy, the universal sharing of offices. It's hard to deny that the perfection of political democracy would require either a return to the participatory polis of the Greeks or the Puritans, as Tocqueville reminded us, or a withering away of all the distinctions present in the very existence of the state, as Marx predicted. But Whitman follows the lead of the dominant American founders by pointing in the direction of a universal empire oriented around the rights all human beings share and toward the conclusion that political life in some sense is part of the activity characteristic of great personalities. Every human person, his democratic faith was, is capable of greatness, and that democratic greatness, he claims, "flourishes best under imperial republican forms" (983).

Still, it's hard to see how political life—especially modern, technoimperial political life—can exist without gradations of greatness. Lincoln, in Whitman's eyes, emerged from a common background to be a singularly great man, and the very future of American democracy depended on him. It was "his idiosyncrasy, in its sudden appearance and disappearance," that shaped the American republic more than anyone else (1069). As long as political democracy continues, we'll need "captains," and Whitman was especially interested in reforming the American military system so the officers would be promoted from the ranks based on pure merit (767–68). Whitman was never so egalitarian in the sense of being leveling as to obliterate all vision of a natural aristocracy based on virtue.

War and Greatness

Whitman actually found in the Secession War the most convincing evidence—"immortal proofs"—of democracy's unequalled greatness. "Two great spectacles" are of special note—"one at the beginning, the other at its close." The first was "the general voluntary arm'd upheaval" (731). The least regimented people of all time voluntarily submitted to regimentation, showing how compatible the voluntary principle can be with the perpetuation of the national Union. "The people," Whitman claimed to see, "of their own choice, fighting, dying, not for gain or even glory, but "for their own idea" represented by the American, democratic flag (968). They provided ample evidence that "the genuine union, when we come to a mortal crisis," turns out not to be "written law" or "(as is generally supposed,) either self-interest, or common pecuniary or material objects"—but "a fervid and tremendous IDEA" (960). Devotion to an idea so strong that it can be the basis for the voluntary, personal risk of life—the authentic display of the virtue of courage—is the only thing that can prevent the death of a nation and the progressive, democratic idea it embodies.

The "unconquerable resolution" of the ordinary American soldier, Whitman claims, surpassed by far all the "vaunted examples" of heroes found in all the books of the past, "in all the records of the world" (968). The war may and should turn out to be the fit subject for the poet of the future who writes the American, democratic equivalent of the *Iliad*, who finds in the war "an inexhaustible mine for the histories, drama, romance, and even philosophy, of people to come" (1084). Whitman found in the *Iliad* and the *Odyssey* "courage, craft, full-grown heroism in the face of danger, the sense and command and leadership" (1181) that the Americans displayed more fully in their great war than the Greeks ever did in their great wars (1048). In imagining the American *Iliad*, Whitman, almost despite himself, joined the Greeks in thinking in terms of extraordinary characters. The example of a "heroic eminent life" and "especially of a heroic eminent death" is to "unerringly, age after age," give "color and fibre to the personalism . . . of that age." And, in thinking especially of the death of the great Lincoln, Whitman said that nothing cements a "whole people better" than "death identified thoroughly with that people, at its head, and for its sake." It was less America's many, many ordinary martyrs than our "first Great Martyr in Chief" that "condense[d]" America as a nation (1070–71).

To live well, people must die well and find meaning in death, and a noble death unites us more than separates us. That means that more important than the fact of the great man's life and death is what the poet gives us—"the portrait of the hero" (1162). Heroes can't be people in general, but only particular persons with names. The immortality achieved in a people's poetry is "the immortality of identity," and that means, from the political view at least, that all men are far from destined to be equally immortal (1272). The heroic death at the nation's head—for people's sake, to be sure—is more remembered, more unifying, and more Christ-like than the war's many, many others. And Whitman rightly predicts, in one place, that Americans, when remembering the war, will be elevated mainly by Lincoln, Grant, Lee, and Sherman (1222).

Whitman is at least inconsistent in his musings about how much the war will move the Americans of the future. The second great American wartime spectacle was "the peaceful and harmonious disbanding of the armies in 1865" (731). The war, Whitman claims, ended in "victory over the only foes we need fear" (960), and the common idea turned out to be stronger than the spirit of secession. The memories of "hatred, conflict, death" generated by the war were quickly obliterated. By 1872, Whitman claimed all that was unspeakably horrible about the war seems "now like a dream." The "oceanic currents" pulling the young toward economic progress and self-development wash away the "scars" of the past (1028).

The example of the democratic greatness of the war can't be definitive when it comes to American moral character; war won't, in fact, be an ordinary fact in American, democratic life. And Americans won't be all that inspired by even their own past wars. Still, Whitman's concern with character caused him to remind us often that men are tested and ennobled by war, and it pointed him away from the fashionable opinion that the horrible suffering and death of millions of ordinary men (which he observed firsthand in the hospital wards) just wasn't worth it. Whitman's appreciation of character was, of course, mixed with his faith in progress; out of the war came "our at last really free Republic, born again, henceforth to commerce its career of genuine homogeneous Union, compact, consistent with itself" (1069). The war, from a Hegelian view, perfected many of the details—or eliminated many of the remaining contradictions—of our ever more consistent universal and homogeneous state. The most important or revolutionary step of that war—the most important in our history since the founding, was "the absolute extirpation and erasure of slavery" (1071).

Average Identity

Given the necessarily inegalitarian manifestations of human greatness of war and politics, they can't, Whitman concludes in his deepest reflections, be the source of the American poem of "average identity" (the poem for *you*, "whoever you are," that he claimed is his *Leaves of Grass*). "A man," Whitman contends, "is not greatest as victor in war, nor inventor or explorer, nor even in science, or his intellectual or artistic capacity, or exemplar in some vast benevolence" (1034). All of those forms of greatness Whitman regards as *real*, or not dependent on feudal or aristocratic illusion and of real benefit to democratic personal and historical progress. They are certainly not characteristic of average men and women. War separates men into winners and losers, based on skill, strength, and courage. Few have the intelligence to be a Franklin or Lewis and Clark or Darwin, but their inventions and discoveries improve almost immeasurably both how and so who we are and what we know. The bards of past and future who, Whitman says, preserve, create, and give meaning to whole worlds have talent and imagination given to very few. And the benevolent exemplar Lincoln, of course, had for Whitman an altogether singular greatness. "What Shakespeare did in poetic expression," he explained, "Abraham Lincoln did in his personal and official life" (1222).

Whitman doesn't claim that these natural inequalities of talent, virtue, and accomplishment wither away with the end of feudalism and the perfection of democracy. The general, the poet, the scientist, and the "Martyr in Chief" never become dispensable, and it would, in fact, be human regression if Marx's predictions about unalienated, unobsessive, depoliticized "communism" ever made them superfluous. Whitman's relatively modest claim (by the standards of nineteenth-century progressivism or indefinite utopianism) is that, from "the highest democratic" view, there is a form of greatness both more average and somehow more singular than all of theirs.

This claim is nothing more or less, it seems to me, than a poet thinking through what's implied in the modern individualism originated by Descartes, Hobbes, and Locke and radicalized in the sense of openly celebrated in America by Paine: There is, in truth, nothing more singular and wonderful than ME. And that must, in some sense, be true of every ME, every personal identity. Even "the significant wonders of heaven and earth," Whitman mused in his "devout hours," are "significant only because of the Me in the center" (984). Every human person, to some extent, identifies being with his own being, and nothing in nature is as wonderful as the particular human person.

Whitman presents, "in the midst of immense tendencies toward aggregation" characteristic of modern democracy, "the image of completeness in separatism, of individual personal dignity, of a single person." The idea of "perfect individualism . . . gives character," he explains, "to the idea of the aggregate." The aggregate is composed of real characters who display personal dignity; their moral virtue must be real or voluntary (966). "Even for the treatment of the universal, in politics, metaphysics or anything," Whitman adds, "sooner or later we come down to the one single, solitary soul." The solitary soul, the being with "precious idiosyncrasy" and "special nativity," is, in fact, unique and irreplaceable (984–85). He knows his birth and death and life in between are singular events, and it's up to him to display his significance or greatness.

Notice how restrained and edifying Whitman's language is in describing the dignity of the average identity: "man is most acceptable in living well in practical life" (1034). That human life is essentially practical is the modern view. Theory is for practice—or not for its own sake. We know only what we make for ourselves, and we make only on the basis of the undeniable knowledge each of us has about the existence of the self or the person or the "I." In practice, as Machiavelli and Marx say, we find the possibility of eradicating both all the cruelties and all the mysteries that have plagued the thinkers and societies of the past. And given the primacy of the individual or personal consent, practice can't really be grounded in what the species in general does. That is one reason—maybe the key reason—that Whitman insists that Darwin doesn't explain it all, even from the point of view of science or what we can see with our own eyes. The undeniable human fact is that "I do"—each of us does. So who I am—including my greatness—must be discovered in what I do. Nothing else could be an acceptable account of who each of us is and who we are as a people.

We aren't most characteristically—I'm tempted to say essentially—warriors or thinkers or poets. The average person, Whitman claims, has the capacity to perform nobly in war and to be moved deeply by poetry. But those qualities aren't what he or she most needs to live well most of the time, and so they can't be the source of the virtue that's most his or her own. The virtue that is most *his* own (and I'm now privileging being masculine because Whitman did distinguish between the characteristic virtues of men and women—because they are given different responsibilities by nature [982]) is living well with the "lot which happens to him as ordinary farmer, seafarer, mechanic, clerk, laborer, or driver." The task of the democratic poet and virtue is to identify and celebrate the virtue—I am tempted to say the freedom and responsibility—that comes with living well with the ordinary duties most of us have been given most of the time. It's in the duties of the "citizen, son, husband, father"—as well as those of the ordinary "employ'd person"—that the highest human greatness, from a democratic view, is found (1934). (Whitman also celebrates "splendid mothers, daughters, sisters, wives" [1025].)

For Whitman's dignified man of moral character, "solitary" does not mean isolated or purely idiosyncratic or endlessly expressive; it also doesn't mean average in the sense of mediocre or undistinguished. It means doing the duties you—the particular being—have been given without falsely coming to understand yourself merely as part of a greater whole. So it means the person experiencing justified pride in himself acting voluntarily and virtuously (982). The democratic whole is an "aggregate"—or not really a whole at all—because it's composed of particular human beings with "individuality" or "personalism," who are, in themselves, wholes (982). Whitman celebrates the average identity as embedded in but not reducible to the relationships and duties that constitute real human lives. Pure "idiosyncrasy" is not a description of who any of us is. If it were, any poetic sharing of human greatness would become impossible.

According to Whitman, "the great poems, Shakespeare included, are poisonous to the idea of the pride and dignity of the common people," and the antidote to that poison must be poetic portrayals finding pride and dignity and the moral lives of average persons (979). Who can deny that Whitman is right that the poets and thinkers of the past unrealistically disparaged ordinary virtue—and so could not even see the pride and dignity that average men display? Certainly, Tocqueville agreed that aristocrats saw only themselves and their kind as worthy of dignity and love (II.3.1).

The reason that the virtuous person Whitman lives "a flight loftier than any of Homer's or Shakespeare's" and "broader than all poems and bibles" is that his life is most "Nature's own," meaning the one most in accord with a true account of "Yourself, your own identity, body and soul" (1034). The life of democratic virtue, as Tocqueville argues, is the one freest of illusions, or the one that comports best with who we really are (II.1.17). Whether or not that is really true, we can see that Whitman has taken with dead seriousness the poetic project Tocqueville laid out of reconciling the greatness of aristocratic individuality (which always depended to some extent on vain illusions that justified injustice) and democratic justice.

The average man—with average identity—is, Whitman goes on, "greatest of all, and nobler than the proudest mere genius or magnate in any field," when "he fully realizes the conscience, the spiritual, the divine faculty, cultivated well, exemplified in his all deeds and words, through life, uncompromising to the end" (1034). The morally cultivated man displays his godlike virtue in what he says and does; his is a whole life of living and dying well. This description reminds me at least of the portraits of the morally virtuous man in Aristotle's *Nicomachean Ethics,* but without the haughty and unrealistic self-denials of the magnanimous man or the general contempt for practical life on behalf of the life of leisure. It is a portrait of the pride that the human being—the person—can take in himself as a particular being, or not merely as part of some "aggregate" or larger unity (983). It is a portrait of the "moral character" Whitman says must be the real foundation of even political democracy; if it is lacking, "the main things . . . are entirely lacking" (956). Compared to such personal moral identity, political attachments are superficial (959).

Not every such life, surely, could ever be fully realized conscientiously or spiritually. But America could be fully justified only if there's something real about the nobility or greatness of seemingly ordinary lives of workers of ordinary means. The "last-needed proof of democracy," Whitman acknowledges, must be "in its personalities" (970). The goodness of the idea of democracy depends on the possibility that most people can display the capacity of living and dying well with who they really are. Who can deny that such ordinary display of virtue is greater than "mere genius"? And so even genius is justified only by its service to the flourishing of ordinary identity. Statesmen, scientists, and poets display their true greatness by the political, technological, and inspirational service they provide to democracy. Whitman equates "serving art at its highest" with "serving God," which he equates to "serving humanity" (999).

Material Prosperity and the Ordinary Practice of Virtue

The importance Whitman places on the practice of personal, practical, relatively self-sufficient virtue explains why he's so insistent that political democracy is only the first stage of democratic development. The "second stage," he says, relates to what's required for the production of "material prosperity," "cheap appliances for comfort," "trade with all lands," "numberless technical skills," as well as "books, newspapers" and, as we say today, various other media of mass communication (976). Aristotle says the practice of moral virtue requires the wherewithal or equipment, and it is free economic and technological progress that supplies those means to the average man and woman.

Living at the level of miserable mere subsistence or as slavish or feudal dependents on others makes the voluntary display of moral character between tough and impossible. Whitman contends that as "ungracious as it may be" and even "a paradox after what we've been saying, democracy looks with a suspicious, ill-satisfied eye on the very poor, the ignorant, and those out of business." Democracy can't be justified by pitying those who can't help themselves, but only through justifiable pride in personal, practical accomplishments. So democracy "asks for men and women with occupations, well off, owners of houses and acres, and with cash in the bank—and some cravings for literature too" (974–75). Middle-class self-sufficiency requires money, property, and a job, and one result would be a life not so full of drudgery that it wouldn't be open to poetic inspiration. Whitman consistently favored policies that maximized economic freedom and opposed those with any hint of the paternalism we now routinely associate with the welfare state. He was rather extreme, in a democratic fashion, in associating any form of practical dependence with being dominated, and the virtues of the man of moral character did seem to include the unmanliness of gratitude.

Democracy doesn't point to the reduction of the great mass of human beings to nothing, or to some homogeneous community based upon the abolition of private property—toward the abolition of what Whitman regarded as the indispensable precondition of the flourishing of a variety of admirable moral identities. "The true gravitational hold of liberalism in the United States," he proclaimed confidently, "will be a more universal ownership of property," and so toward "general comfort" and widespread wealth. The "firmest" principle of unity in our in many ways "great and varied" nation is the "safety and endurance of the aggregate of its middling property owners." The economic condition, as thinkers from Aristotle onward have thought, most appropriate to social stability and a relatively voluntary or self-determined practical life is bound to be shared by more and more Americans. The greatness of average identity can be widely displayed only in a middle-class nation—one without the extremes of any form of feudalism or a significant proletariat (974–75). Genuine moral diversity depends on an unprecedented more fundamental economic homogeneity. The economic and technological means—in addition to democratic political institutions—are necessary, but not sufficient, for the display of such virtue, as they are a necessary but not sufficient cause of national and eventually global union.

Our Present Hollowness of Heart

Whitman makes it all too clear that his poetic presentation of the dutiful nobility of the average identity doesn't correspond particularly well to the average Americans he sees with his own eyes. What those Americans needed, he thought, is "the perfect character, the heroic" version of themselves presented to them as an ideal that "although never attain'd, is never lost sight of." And that image of perfection is to inspire them through their failures and sorrows (896). The Americans he actually sees, he seems to say, are unworthy of the poet because they lack such idealistic poetic inspiration. The poet must make them, through his poetry, worthy of his poetry.

When viewing Americans in ordinary times—before and especially after the Secession War—Whitman often saw little yet to admire. He looked at his time and his nation "searching like a physician diagnosing some deep disease." "Never was there, perhaps," he even claimed, "more hollowness of heart at a present." He saw "no genuine belief," doubted "there are any personalities worthy of their name," proclaimed America "almost a complete failure in all its social aspects." Particularly among "the business classes," he saw the very great "depravity" of excessive materialism and selfishness. And among the fashionable, there was nothing more than "flippancy, tepid amours, weak infidelism, small aims, or no aims at all." Fashionable life seemed to exist, in fact, "only to kill time" (961). The evidence so far, for Whitman, was that democracy had emptied life of its moral contents, and our economic prosperity had produced lives that were either selfish—or that confused the means of wealth for ends of life—or pointless. So far, he sees, "New World Democracy" has been "an almost complete failure in all social aspects" (962).

Whitman's "yet unshaken faith" in both "the American masses" and Americans "consider'd as individuals" (964) had yet to be confirmed by works. The truth is, Whitman proclaimed, that "a great moral and religious civilization" is "the only justification of a great material one" (963), because merely material greatness is not worthy of the persons we are. His America of the greatness of average identity existed in his imagination as a faith—a prophecy—about America's future. Whitman observed that it is universally "acknowledged that we of the States are the most materialistic and money-making people ever known." While "fully accepting" the truth of this observation, his "theory"—one not widely acknowledged at all—"is that we are the most emotional, spiritualistic, and poetry-loving people also" (1042). Whitman's "theory" or prophecy contradicts the critical observations of aristocrats such as Tocqueville and Carlyle, but not so much what he sees with his own eyes.

Whitman's "Democratic Vistas" was written in response to Carlyle's moody, European aristocratic pessimism. According to Carlyle, the individual liberty produced by democratization comes at the expense of social, moral responsibility. The new order doesn't replace the old with something equally or more worthy. Instead, moral life itself is emptied out; the only values left are capitalism's loss and gain. Whitman, after feeling some appropriately democratic anger (967), actually embraced Carlyle's "taunting" sort of criticism as the kind "most wanted amid the supple, polish'd, money-worshipping, Jesus and Judah-equalizing, suffrage sovereignty echoes of contemporary America" (922). Carlyle is right that the Americans so far see nothing higher than money and the raw will. Whitman adds that Longfellow, that "poet of the mellow twilight of the past," also provides the sort of counteraction "most needed for our materialistic, self-assertive, money-worshipping Anglo-Saxon races, and especially for the present age in America," a world "tyrannical regulated" by those with unregulated economic and political ambition and short on the courtesy and sympathy of the gentleman (941). Whitman joins Carlyle and Longfellow in doubting that there are any "*men* here worthy of the name"—men with "beautiful manners" and artistic accomplishments worthy of a free and wealthy people (963).

That reconciliation of the contradiction between democratic political idealism and the reality of its banal, unregulated materialism—a world without real *men,* he thought, was less a poetic presentation of American life than its poetic transformation. Humanity, "in its faith, love, heroism, poetry, and even morals," is, deep down, "emotion." And the poet appeals to the emotions that are "the unseen impetus and moving-power of all" to make an imaginary world reveal (947). Just like Aristotle's *Ethics* didn't really merely or even mainly reflect the moral understandings of Athenian life, but aimed, instead, at a transformational clarification of who we are as moral beings. Aristotle aimed to make men more moral, and so their thoughts and deeds more genuinely voluntary or free and responsible. The indispensable "third stage" of democratic development would be such a poetic transformation.

Whitman's poetic aim was to reconcile the moral greatness that animated "antique" and feudal poetry and lives with the democratic achievement of universal justice or rights and universal prosperity. A difference between Aristotle and Whitman, of course, is that Aristotle thought of himself as stuck with natural limits to human knowing and loving. As even Tocqueville says, the Greek aristocrats certainly underestimated the possibilities of the life of moral dignity, including some reconciliation, at least, of magnanimity and justice (II.4.8; II.2.8). But Whitman surely was too confident about how indefinitely malleable—or unconstrained by natural limitations—the emotions of human love and human pride could be. Because he expected much more of democracy than did Tocqueville, he reacted far more assertively and imaginatively against its perceived shortcomings than did the ambivalent aristocrat.

Whitman had basically two criticisms of the poet of his time. The first was of those who, in a way, faithfully reflected the hollowness of actual democratic life. They were animated by a "scornful superciliousness"; they were inspired only to make fun of the world around them (961). Meanwhile, those poets in the broadest sense—including the theologians and everyone who sets "social standards"—who really are concerned with elevating the moral character of Americans "are entirely held possession of by foreign lands." Their heroes—their portrayals of pride, dignity, and love—have "shreds" of the Hebrews, Romans, Greeks, London, Paris, and Italy, but they don't express anything faithful to what's highest and most deserving of pride about "America herself." What's been written by the best poets in other places and times is "original, superb . . . where they belong," but they're "secondhand here, where they do not belong" (1002). That means, of course, that

American poets remain in the thrall of "feudalism, caste, and ecclesiastical traditions" and their undemocratic premises and standards (955).

The thought underlying all American poetry in Whitman's time is that there's nothing really poetic or ennobling about democratic life as actually experienced. So democracy is either to be mocked by the disengaged or seriously criticized from an aristocratic view. Our serious poets point us away from American, democratic reality to the greatness that was Greece and Rome or medieval Christendom. Arguably, Whitman viewed the democratic poet as fulfilling the responsibility. Tocqueville gave to those responsible for elevating democratic language (II.1.14–16). Learn what you can about human greatness from the poetry of the past, but employ what you learn to elevate democracy according to its own genius. Whitman thought his task was not to ignore or disparage, but to "recast the types of highest personality from what the oriental, feudal, ecclesiastical world bequeath us" (992).

Democratic Poetry

That absence of democratic poetry, in Whitman's view, is the reason for American hollowness, for the lack of deep attachments and ennobling idealism that are indispensable for the cultivation of moral character. Poetry in the broadest sense is "of greater importance than their political institutions." Calculation, contract, and consent are not enough either to ennoble and/or unite Americans emotionally—or around love and pride (941). Every people needs a poetry that "fraternizes" them through "appeals to emotions, pride, love, spirituality common to humankind." Although human emotions are universal, they "perhaps only actually touch" someone "through autochthonic lights and shades, flavors, fondnesses, specific incidents, illustrations," and so forth. The effectiveness of poetry depends "far more on association, identity, and place," on "the materiality and personality" of a particular land "than is supposed." All poetry that actually touches a people has such "invisible roots" (1002–3). That's why Whitman did what he could to describe greatness in ordinary American lives found in particular American places.

But Whitman's effort to find and give proud moral character in the dutiful lives of average identities could be only part of his American poetry.

One reason he needed to write more is that he certainly shared Tocqueville's political criticism of democratic individualism, which is a tendency for the individual to become locked up emotionally in the narrow circle of families and friends. Democracy, according to Tocqueville, "constantly leads him back toward himself alone and threatens finally to confine him wholly in the solitude of his own heart" (II.2.3). Americans need further inspiration in the direction of Union—to devotion to their nation and its democratic idea. Given the interchangeability of America and the universal democratic idea, its poetry must be different from that of other peoples in being far less tied to a particular place and time. American poetry can be only ambiguously autochthonous.

America or democracy, Whitman sometimes says, is extreme in its power both to isolate the individual and to point in the direction of the universal union of all persons (973). So America, it seems, is pretty tough on poetry that celebrates a socially embedded person with a particular, relational identity. The highest place given to the identity of the solitary individual—in our Declaration and Paine and so forth—can't help but erode particular attachments. Whitman's poetry, in fact, doesn't have much about celebrating the love of family members for one another or that of members of some local community for one another. Everything in between the isolated person and the homogeneous "aggregate," Whitman sometimes says, is not really part of the identity of the American. That's why Tocqueville, for example, highlighted the threat democracy poses to the intermediary associations—including local government, the family (both extended and nuclear), and organized religion—that have been our nation's ways of combating the heart disease of individualism (II.1–2. passim). Certainly both the idea of the isolated individual and the homogeneous aggregate seem, at first glance, fatal to proud personal significance and personal love.

Whitman countered apolitical or isolated individualism with his poetry of "mainly . . . political significance." This part of his poetry is an emotional—or not at all "intellectual or scholastic"—appeal to a "terrible, irrepressible yearning" found somewhere "in most human souls," a "never-satisfied appetite for sympathy." Sympathy, he contends, can be the foundation of a "universal democratic comradeship"—a "boundless offering of sympathy" could make all persons friends and so fellow citizens (1035). Sympathy, of course, is not erotic love or the sublimated manly love of men engaged together in war or some other noble endeavor. It is, in fact, a kind of emotional response to suffering—particularly to the pain of loneliness or isolation. Today, in this context, we would surely say empathy. The universality of the response depends on the feeling being common to at least almost all men.

Sympathy or pity or compassion, Tocqueville says, really does have the capacity to level the boundaries of family, sect, class, and nation that have separated men. It is, more precisely, a cause and effect of the democratic leveling that seems to make us all more and more alike (II.3.1–2). Sympathy is felt for our common vulnerability and the other miseries of our mortality that we all share. It becomes easier and easier to feel for more and more and more people as the world becomes homogenized or democratized. We feel each other's pain as we become more identical in our suffering. Universal sympathy suggests that diversity and idiosyncrasy are increasingly superficial. What's most basic is what's most common to all—the same insatiable yearning.

The contradictions between the proud moral character of average identity and the comradeship of whiny sufferers created by a boundless need for sympathy are obvious. The average man self-sufficiently finds dignity in performing the social duties given him by his "lot." He has what it takes not to deserve pity, and he never experiences his singular identity in asocial isolation. He's moved by a sort of infinitely inexpressive, miserable loneliness that's the source of a neediness that can't even be exhausted by the fellow-feeling of hundreds of millions. That yearning by an isolated identity is in reaction against—a desire to be freed emotionally from—his "lot." The poetic appeal to that kind of yearning is surely undignified. And universalized sympathy, surely, erodes the duties experienced out of love for the small number of people one knows well. Universal comradeship couldn't possibly have anything to do with the idiosyncrasies of a particular person or shared duties or accomplishments or even interests. It must be at the expense of fraternity as it actually exists.

We have no reason to believe—certainly there's no evidence from the modern, Darwinian science Whitman accepts—that our capacity to feel emotion is boundless in the sense of being indefinitely expansive. Our powers of knowing and loving, Tocqueville says, are limited. Intense love is necessarily localized and particular. It is capable of sublimation or idealization in the direction of manly nobility, but even then only with the assistance of pride (II.3.18–19). The modern diffusion of love in the name of egalitarian justice weakens personal love into an indiscriminate sympathy for those whom you don't know or love as unique and irreplaceable beings (II.3.1). Sympathy, of course, is a much less reliable source of duty than personal love. Whitman, in fact, writes of needing—not giving—sympathy. So he really doesn't attempt to defend sympathy as a source of virtue, even of the virtue of gratitude. In that sense, Whitman's mainly political poetry is actually deeply depoliticizing. The sympathetic cosmopolis that America intends to be, in this respect, doesn't seem to have room for the personal greatness and political contests that Whitman celebrates elsewhere.

Pantheism?

According to Tocqueville, democracy, in the name of truth and justice, unmasks all the illusions that make possible the poetic portrayals of heroic greatness. What remains, finally, as the material for poetry is the strange and wonderful being who experiences himself as existing mysteriously or somewhat incomprehensibly "wandering, lost, between the limits of two abysses." Whitman never explicitly celebrates the greatness that might flow from that truthful experience of anxiety. But Tocqueville shows the "pity" and "terror" that accompany the experience of true or democratic greatness, and it's both the singular greatness and singular misery of man that makes possible Whitman's appeal to boundless universal sympathy (II.1.17). Tocqueville himself fears that experience of isolation and contingency might be the source of a regressive impulse to self-surrender (II.4.6). It might be the main reason why the concept of unity becomes an obsession in democracy; the isolated individual has a boundless yearning to be relieved of the contingency of his isolated being (II.1.8).

The way, Tocqueville explains, that the poetic pursuit of pure homogeneity or universality can become consistent with human pride is through pantheism. We are all gods, and so free from the burden of having to have moral character. Pantheism, Tocqueville observes, is both seductive and lazy. All that it requires is the imaginary surrender of all the idiosyncrasy characteristic of our unique and irreplaceable personal identity. Pantheism, Tocqueville contends, is the chief threat to "the genuine greatness of man in democratic times. And so every true friend of the future of human individuality should "do combat against it" (II.1.8). Whitman, for his part, seems to be caught between embracing and struggling against pantheism, between yearning for "cosmic brotherhood" and preserving personal identity. And he even thought the conflict in his soul was a sign of his greatness: the "individual becomes truly great," he thinks, "who understands well that, while complete in himself in a certain sense, he is part of the divine eternal scheme" (1052). He comes very close to agreeing with Tocqueville that God must be an "eternal Being . . . who sees distinctly, though at once, the whole human race and each man" (II.4.8).

Whitman finally thought that the only way to counter Carlyle's seemingly empirically justified "pessimism and world-decadence" was through "recounting Hegel a little freely." Whitman's Hegelianism is a way of "floating high . . . above technical metaphysics," and a *both* "essential and crowning justification of New World Democracy in time and space." There is no such essential democratic justification, it appears, without the unifying theology that "Hegel translates into science," a promise of theological/scientific resolution of "all the apparent contradictions of the Deific nature" by showing them all to "factional and imperfect expressions of the one essential unity." Without that perfect faith in "the perfect moral unity" of "all of life in time present and future," Whitman writes, he readily experiences "darkness and despair" under "the spell of himself and his circumstance" (921–22).

Whitman echoes the faith of St. Paul when he writes that while he has faith that "there is a moral purpose, a visible or invisible intention, certainly underlying all," "its results and proof" still have "to be patiently waited for" (1011). Whitman can't present his faith as an argument or support it with what he can see with his own eyes. "America," so far, "is a prophecy" (1035). "Time, space, in the will of God," the prophecy is, will "solve all discrepancies, fears and doubts, and eventually fulfill happiness," allowing even "the explanation of the physical universe through the spiritual."

It's sometimes hard to see why that faith or prophecy is anything more than a pantheistic reverie. Physical homogeneity, as described by modern science, will be incorporated into a more perfect spiritual unity. The result will be the unhappiness that comes when the alienation of the isolated person from the cosmos will disappear both physically and spiritually. This projection of "cosmic brotherhood," Whitman even claims, is "the dream of all hope" (1166). Whitman's projection of even happiness into the future—or our hopes for it—shows us that he's as alienated as the Augustinian Christian from his miserable present. He believes as much as the Christian that all men yearn to be freed from the misery of their mortal isolation.

One obvious objection to any Hegelian or historical projection of truth, unity, and happiness into the future is that it deprives the personal lives of today of any real meaning. They might be understood only to have significance by what they do to contribute to future historical perfection. The noncontradictory or unalienated, fearless, happy lives won't be theirs. So the real Hegel had the effect of turning most people across time and space into history fodder, just as Darwin turns them into species fodder, and the Greeks turned them into city fodder. That's the reason why so many millions of people in the twentieth century were so ruthlessly sacrificed for a historical future they were never meant to enjoy.

The Great Positive, Democratic Poem about Death

Whitman, the defender of the greatness of individuality, was alive to such objections to understanding persons as merely historical beings, as he was to objections to a merely physical Darwinism, a completely politicized theology, and a wholly impersonal pantheism. Any poetic account of time and space, for him, needed to be completed by one concerning immortality or eternity. He usually didn't mean that the person should lose himself completely in some pantheistic reverie about being one with the eternal cosmos, or, as the Platonists say, that the person becomes most who he is through contemplation of what's eternal (so not personal). He seems, instead, to have in some loose way agreed with Tocqueville that, even or especially in democratic times, personal identity depends in some sense on the person's perception of his immortality, that human greatness could be extinguished by the belief that personality—or everything that a particular person thinks and does—is ephemeral (II.2.15) The deepest truth can't be, for the great democratic poem, that each of us exists for a moment between two abysses.

Tocqueville thought that modern democracy, because of its materialism and skepticism, is incapable of generating such poetry, and so that all those who want to reconcile democracy with great individuality should preserve religion as "the most precious inheritance from aristocratic centuries." What the democratic person needs most of all, Tocqueville claimed, is support for his proud resistance to being absorbed into some materialistic or pantheistic whole, for resisting "degrad[ing] himself" by surrendering "the use of his most sublime faculties." And the advantage of aristocracy over democracy is that the aristocrat always thought highly enough of himself not to doubt that he had a soul with its own needs (II.2.15). Whitman claimed that "the radical foundation of the new religion" has to be "the divine pride of man in himself," and he always meant, in part, the divine pride that the person or moral character takes in himself (1004). It's easy to see why Tocqueville and Whitman agree that every person, in a democracy, has to think and feel himself sharing the divine immortality of God himself, without losing his personal identity in a pantheistic revelry. Nothing less that the "idea of immortality, above all other ideas," Whitman proclaims, is what's required to "vivify . . . democracy in the New World" (1030). Whitman and Tocqueville agreed that religion's main purpose is as a "general, simple, and practical means of teaching men the immortality of the soul," and that "democratic people"—really, democratic individuals—have a particular need for that belief (II.2.15). Democratic greatness, for Tocqueville, in America depends on what amounts to the aristocratic or soul-preserving poetry of Plato and Aristotle as embodied in Christianity as a sort of Platonism for the people (II.2.15).

Whitman thought the credibility of democracy's claim to greatness depended on the democratic poet's ability to write "the great poem of death." That poem has to combine the "religious fire and abandon of Isaiah," Homer's "epic talent," the "proud character" portrayed by Shakespeare, while being consistent with both Hegel and "modern science" (1013). It somehow has to say more about who we are than what Hegel and Darwin say, but without negating or contradicting anything Hegel or Darwin say. The part of the democratic poem that shapes what America "thinks of death"—what Whitman calls at least once the most important part of the democratic poem (1030)—can't be some Greek myth or Eastern civilization given by the few to comfort the many. It can't be some lie most people need to die well, because the democratic faith is that the average identity can live and die well in light of what we really know.

Whitman does write in one place of a happily "fit born and bred race" that, filled with "wholesome ecstasy," "would find it enough merely *to live*" (1007–8). They would be emotionally free from the miseries of self-conscious mortality. But such beings, arguably, would have gotten beyond the proud concern for one's own moral character, and they would need neither to give nor receive boundless sympathy. They wouldn't need a democratic, spiritual poem about immortality, but it's hard to see how they would really display personal greatness. Whitman certainly wouldn't have usually agreed with Richard Rorty that it's either possible or in accord with great democratic individuality to work to put death to "death" by refusing to talk about or be moved by it.

The negative poem of Lucretius—the one that allows a few to live beyond common hopes and fears about death—that was enough for the philosophers of old is not enough to sustain democracy's "best personalism." That poem depended upon privileging the theoretical life over the practical and justified the exemption of few from the duties of the many. And that poem can't be enough in a world where the anxious terror of the solitary person has become common enough to inspire universal sympathy, and, as Whitman says, sympathy itself can never be enough. The negative poem of the ancient sages can't be the impetus for reconfiguring pride and dignity to ennoble the ordinary, practical life or for securing the average identity against the temptation to unitary or pantheistic self-surrender. Nor can democratic poetry merely be about resolutely facing up to death in the manner of the ancient warrior/hero or even the calm dying common soldier who so graced our Secession War. The immortality won through noble deaths can never be available to the average man, and dying as a warrior will not ordinarily be a common democratic experience.

Whitman doesn't criticize Lucretius or the old philosophic approach to death only because of its undemocratic implications. He says he "feels and knows that death is not the end," as the philosophers and poets used to believe. He believes it's true that death is "the real beginning" for each of us, and that "nothing" is ever lost or really dies. This insight, which he presents as consistent with and vaguely dependent on modern science, allows reasonable hope that "what was long wanted will be supplied" by the democratic poet in his "great poem of death" (1012–13).

The great, positive poem about death has to show—and move our thoughts and emotions fundamentally by showing—that death is "not at all the cessation of personal identity," but instead personal "entrance" into what will be "by far the greatest part of existence" (1030). What's most important is not this mortal life, but what's "permanently real" (994), and what's permanently real includes "the immortal continuation of our identity" (1008–9). The poet has to show that this life is little compared to the life to come, and that each of us doesn't really have to secure his personal identity through his character and accomplishments in this life. To sustain my identity and display my greatness, I have to believe that the ME in the center of my cosmos will always BE, and that MY identity is somehow immortally sustained by the cosmos as a whole that's not me. There is no other way, Whitman thought, to sustain the "permanent and unitary meaning" common to all persons, "even the meanest" (1013).

Whitman said often and in various ways that what we *see* in this life is not enough, and he admits, in his way, that to be inspired by some prophecy about the historical future of democracy is not enough either. For we spiritual beings, there has really to be more to us than what we can see or even imagine. The democratic positive poem surely saves the meanest life from being degraded by pity and saves us all from the temptation of degrading, illusory, pantheistic self-surrender. It's no wonder that Whitman once remarked that it's the Bible that "taught men how best to endure illness and death," and that democratic philosophy should be some fusion of Greek or Platonic philosophy and Christianity (1321). The democratic poet can't avoid the philosophical task of showing how the biblical insight about the immortal reality of the person in no way disagrees with what Hegel shows about our historical being and what Darwin shows about our natural being.

Whitman's Noble Failure

Whitman finally feels more than thinks that it must be true that death is not the cessation of personal life. He says he's done what he can to "end my books with thoughts, or radiations from thoughts, on death, immortality, and a free entrance into the spiritual world." But he adds that the "full construction of such a work is beyond my powers, and must remain for some bard in the future" (1030). That means, of course, that Whitman was incapable of writing the most important part of the democratic poem, of being the founder of the true democratic religion, of providing what's required both to justify and to bring into being democracy as a great moral and religious civilization.

Because Whitman didn't write the political/philosophical poem about death, we really don't know how the idea that the person is so free that he can freely enter into a spiritual world could possible square with the skepticism about the soul and spiritual distinctions that Tocqueville says fuels modern thought. When Hegel says that we're historical beings, he means that we're not more than that. Human identity is formed and displayed in history, and so not in eternity. There is no human reality beyond space and time. When Darwin says that we're natural beings, he means that there's nothing to us beyond our biological being, and that nature is, to say the least, no respecter of persons. What Tocqueville would say to Whitman is that the deepest moral and religious longings of human beings can't be incorporated into the democratic idea, and that the reductionism of modern science opposes itself to the true greatness of each of us (II.2.15; II.1.1–2).

Whitman, it turns out, was too critical of the democracy he could actually see, because his idea of its perfectibility was too vague and contradictory to be credible. There's no point in revisiting all those contradictions, because each moment in Whitman's effort to ennoble our country and its idea can still teach us something. Tocqueville would close by saying that Whitman was right to feel that political justice and personal prosperity aren't enough. Democracy stands or falls on the man of average identity displaying some greatness or deserved dignity. And that the perpetuation of the greatness of human individuality or identity may well depend on believing that we're more than biological beings. It may even be true that the best account of the love and pride of the person can be given only in light of a personal God. But there's no denying that modern science dogmatically denies the existence of such a God and so may, in fact, be at war with what we really know about personal identity.

Whitman's most debilitating dogma was surely his extreme anti-ecclesiasticism; he believed, without any real inquiry, that the churches taught nothing democratic or nothing fundamentally true about who we are. And so he couldn't see the indispensable contribution they make to personal self-understanding, even or especially in a democracy. He couldn't see why Tocqueville was right to say that freedom of religion is for protecting the spiritual or soulful truth about who we are from completely incorporating into the dogmatic skepticism or pop Cartesianism of mainstream democratic thought (II.1.1–7). Whitman knew all too well that his own personal longings pointed way beyond the democratic world of politics and business he could actually see, but he just wasn't at all clear where. That's why Tocqueville wouldn't have been surprised to find his deepest musings about who we are to be characterized by both obscurity and the vagueness that has "a secret charm" among democratic writers (II.1.16).

Notes

1. References to Tocqueville's *Democracy in America* are given parenthetically in the text by volume, part, and chapter number. I've relied on the translation by Harvey Mansfield and Delba Winthrop (Chicago: University of Chicago Press, 2002).

2. References to Whitman's writing are given parenthetically in the text by page number. I've used *Walt Whitman: Poetry and Prose* (New York: Library of America, 1996).

CHAPTER 11

Whitman, Death, and Democracy

Jack Turner

ONE OF THE MOST striking moments in Plato's *Apology* is when Socrates declares, "To fear death, gentlemen, is no other than to think oneself wise when one is not, to think one knows what one does not know."[1] Fear of death is intellectually presumptuous; it implies that one knows for certain that death is bad. Yet as limited mortals, we cannot know the nature of death in its entirety, or what—if anything—comes afterward.

The corollary of Socrates' startling suggestion is that—by embodying intellectual humility—indifference toward death is wise. But this stance seems astonishingly bloodless. One of humanity's defining features is consciousness of mortality. Given the human animal's self-reflective nature, curiosity about death is understandable. Our penchant for wonder defies indifference toward death. Perhaps this is why, later in the *Apology*, Socrates ventures guesses as to what death is; death, he speculates, is either (1) reunion with "all who have died" or (2) "dreamless sleep."[2] In the end, however, Socrates recommits himself to agnosticism about death: "I go to die, you go to live. Which of us goes to the better lot is known to no one, except the god."[3]

Socrates' coolness in the face of death has a nineteenth-century American heir in the antebellum Walt Whitman.[4] Given that Socrates' serenity about mortality left a long legacy in the Western philosophical tradition—helped along by Epicurus, Lucretius, Cicero, Seneca, and Marcus Aurelius—that fact itself is unremarkable.[5] What is remarkable, however, is the way Whitman revealed affinities between coolness in the face of death and the character dispositions and sensibilities most conducive to democracy. Whitman articulated three visions of death in his antebellum work: the first and second sought to allay readers' mortal anxiety by intimating the self's material immortality; the third sought to encourage affirmation of death, even in the absence of spiritual or material immortality. All three were intended to promote affirmation of the self and the world as they are, and therefore rejection of the idea that the self and the world are fallen and need supernatural redemption. Affirmation of the self and the world as they are both signals and compounds the generosity of perception and spirit necessary for democratic culture, a culture wherein every individual regards every other individual as beautiful and sublime. While George Kateb, Morton Schoolman, and Jason Frank have helpfully elaborated this idea of democratic culture in Whitman,[6] none has analyzed Whitman's tripartite poetics of death and explained their crucial role in Whitman's quest to inspire democratic culture. This essay takes up this task, in the hope it can enhance our appreciation of the radicalism of Whitman's democratic theory, a theory that not only acknowledges but also celebrates human finitude.

The First Vision: Organic Transformation

Whitman's best-known view of death is that of organic transformation. The axial imagery of "Song of Myself" (1855) is of corpses sinking into the ground and returning as grass:

> The smallest sprout shows there is really no death,
> And if ever there was it led forward life, and does not wait at the end
>   to arrest it,
> And ceased the moment life appeared.
>
> All goes onward and outward . . . . nothing collapses,
> And to die is different from what any one supposed, and luckier.[7]

Characterizing the grass as both "the beautiful uncut hair of graves" and "the produced babe of the vegetation,"[8] Whitman illustrates how the bodies of the dead nourish new life. Human decomposition enriches the soil and gives rise to flora that then cycles through nature. The imagery on its own is neat, suggestive, and designed to console those anxious about death. But strictly speaking, that consolation is small, for the endurance of atoms dispersed by our decomposed bodies hardly implies the endurance of the self.

Yet the endurance of the self through the endurance of our dispersed atoms is precisely the claim Whitman wants to make. He implies the self's immortality when he writes:

> And as to you life, I reckon you are the leavings of many deaths,
> No doubt I have died myself ten thousand times before.[9]

The possibility of a single "I" dying "ten thousand times before" suggests not just the continuity of the body's atoms, but also the self's—the I's—immortality, its persistence and integrity across ten thousand deaths and ten thousand lives. The self retains identity, notwithstanding the body's decomposition and resurgence in diffuse new forms. But this idea on its face is implausible—especially in light of Whitman's insistence that the body gives the self identity. "I too had received identity by my body," he writes in "Crossing Brooklyn Ferry" (1856).[10] "It is not to diffuse you that you were born of your mother and father—it is to identify you," he says in "To Think of Time" (1856).[11] If the body gives the self identity, then the self must lose identity when the body decomposes. Though the body's atoms may be immortal, neither the body nor the self can be as unified wholes.

At the same time, Whitman's idea that the self is materially immortal becomes intelligible if we account for his belief in Lamarckian evolution. The French evolutionist Jean Lamarck held that changes experienced by the body over its lifetime become hereditary. If a physically weak body gets strong through exercise, that body's progeny will inherit that strength, notwithstanding the body's original weakness. Whitman subscribed to Lamarck's theory, and if we may assume he understood the body's changes to imprint themselves on every atom, we can see why he thought the self immortal.[12] Though the self receives identity from the decomposed body matter of previous generations, its distinctive life experience leaves a mark on every atom, transforming the matter then passed on to future generations. The self is immortal not as a single entity, but as dispersed atoms taken up by other bodies. Though the self materially disintegrates, it leaves an organic signature on the world.

This exceptional view of the self's immortality unlocks some of the mysteries of Whitman's "Crossing Brooklyn Ferry." The "I" of the poem stands on the ferryboat's edge as it crosses from Manhattan to Brooklyn one evening at sunset. In observing the ferry's quotidian scene—the "Crowds of men and women attired in the usual costumes . . . / . . . the hundreds and hundreds that cross, returning home"[13]—the "I" feels gratitude for life, which activates in him a serene and exhilarating rapture. The "I" contemplates the relation of present to past and future:

> The impalpable sustenance of me from all things at all hours of the day,
> The simple, compact, well-joined scheme—myself disintegrated,
>   everyone disintegrated, yet part of the scheme,
> The similitudes of the past and those of the future,
> . . . .
> The others that are to follow me, the ties between me and them,
> The certainty of others—the life, love, sight, hearing of others.[14]

When the "I" mentions the "impalpable sustenance of me from all things at all hours of the day," he evokes how we and the living things around us exchange breath at every moment. In this way, we contain others' atoms and others contain ours. When the poem's "I" mentions "The simple, compact, well-joined scheme—myself disintegrated, everyone disintegrated, yet part of the scheme," he asks us to consider our place within the full expanse of time and space. Kateb interprets "myself disintegrated, everyone disintegrated" as suggesting the inward plurality and agonism of democratic individuals;[15] this interpretation makes sense if the line refers to present selves. Yet if the line refers also to past and future selves, new meanings emerge.

As we look backward in time, we contemplate "myself disintegrated, everyone disintegrated": the atoms that today compose us once belonged to people of previous generations. Remarkably, these atoms have cycled through multitudes of people stretching back to time and space's inception. The idea that we contain the atoms of multitudes gives new meaning to Whitman's famous line "I am large . . . . I contain multitudes."[16] The idea that we contain atoms stretching back to time and space's inception also gives new meaning to the line "There was never any more inception than there is now."[17]

As we look forward in time, we contemplate "myself disintegrated, everyone disintegrated" in an even stronger sense. The future is composed of current selves disintegrated, and if Lamarck is right, this endurance is both material and characterological. The lives we fashioned, according to Lamarck's theory, left distinctive marks on the body's atoms: material endurance is thus characterological endurance. Integrated characters live on in disintegrated atoms, which death throws into the future.

"Crossing" specifically notes the way our atoms unite past, present, and future: "The similitudes of the past and those of the future, / . . . / The others that are to follow me, the ties between me and them." These lines then converge in an important message of solace to those anxious about mortality. Even as we face death, there is the consoling "certainty of others—the life, love, sight, hearing of others." Others' future existence guarantees our future existence. Just as past selves live in us, through atoms bearing their mark, we live on in future selves, through atoms bearing our mark.

Whitman's poetics of organic transformation suggest that there is no death, only change of form.[18] Yet this vision does not overcome the problem of death, but rather evades it. The vision problematically suggests that, in death, there is no loss. This not only delegitimizes feelings of bereavement, but also defies some of the terms of the organic vision itself. Whitman's evocative poem "Full of Life Now" from the 1860 "Calamus" series sets out these terms in sharp relief:

> Full of life, sweet-blooded, compact, visible,
> I, forty years old the Eighty-third Year of The States,
> To one a century hence, or any number of centuries hence,
> To you, yet unborn, these, seeking you.
>
> When you read these, I that was visible, am become invisible;
> Now it is you, compact, visible, realizing my poems, seeking me,
> Fancying how happy you were, if I could be with you, and become
>   your lover;
> Be it as if I were with you. Be not too certain but I am now with you.[19]

On its plainest register of meaning, the first stanza records Whitman in 1859 writing a poem for posterity, while the second line envisions a reader "a century hence, or any number of centuries hence" reading the poem, and in so doing, "realizing" it. Whitman combines two key words—"compact" and "visible"—to designate the poem's living subjects at their respective points in time, the writer writing in 1859 and the reader reading "a century hence, or any number of centuries hence." "Compact" and "visible" are Whitman's words for living, corporeally unified selves. The words, however, imply that death entails loss—specifically, the loss of compact (versus dispersed) corporeality, as well as visibility as a self. Adherents of Whitman's first vision of death might respond that this is not death but only change. But such a view attaches too little importance to our existence as corporeally unified individuals. Only through corporeal unity do we achieve self-consciousness and social visibility, and only through self-consciousness and social visibility do we experience subjectivity and recognition. The loss of corporeal unity entailed by death is therefore weighty, and cannot be consoled by the thought that our dispersed atoms live on in flora, fauna, and future selves.

Whitman's vision of death as organic transformation fails as consolation, and cannot by itself allay mortal anxiety. Yet Whitman's second vision of death—as inspiration to creative immortality—gives us a more satisfying vision of both material and subjective endurance: we live on not in the atoms we are, but in the work that we do.

The Second Vision: Inspiration to Creative Immortality

Even as it exposes the limitations of Whitman's first vision of death as organic transformation, "Full of Life Now" powerfully reveals Whitman's second vision of death: as inspiration to creative immortality. Recall the poem's first stanza:

> Full of life, sweet-blooded, compact, visible,
> I, forty years old the Eighty-third Year of The States,
> To one a century hence, or any number of centuries hence,
> To you, yet unborn, these, seeking you.

Earlier I argued that the words "compact, visible" in the stanza's first line refer to the poem's author as a corporeally unified self. When viewed in conjunction with the second stanza's second line—"Now it is you, compact, visible, realizing my poems, seeking me"—this meaning makes sense. But the first stanza's first line also reflexively refers to the poem itself: the "I" of the stanza is not just the voice of the *poet* in the past, but the voice of the *poem* in the present. As a material artifact, the poem embodies the dead and disintegrated poet, and in so doing, revives and reintegrates him. Making the poet "compact" and visible," it also makes him immortal.

The poem acts as a vessel of immortality both in its material existence—embodying a corporeally disintegrated self in integrated form—and in its capacity to give voice to the poet each time the poem is read. The poem's first words—"Full of life, sweet-blooded, compact, visible"—suggest that whenever the reader starts reading the poem, she meets the poet in the fullness of his life. In the act of interpreting the poem, she engages in a transgenerational conversation that defies both time and death. The act of reading illustrates time's, space's, and therefore death's relativity; it shows, in the words of "Crossing Brooklyn Ferry," how "It avails not, neither time or place—distance avails not."[20]

Whitman draws close analogies between bodies and written words elsewhere. In "A Song of the Rolling Earth" (1856), he writes:

> Human bodies are words, myriads of words,
> In the best poems re-appears the body, man's or woman's,
>   well-shaped, natural, gay
> Every part able, active, receptive, without shame or the need of
>   shame.[21]

In written words, the self is literally present, whether or not the body that wrote the words is literally living and breathing. We are wherever we leave words behind, and through those words we figuratively live and breathe. Through written words, the self can defy the commonsensical notion that an individual can occupy only one point in space and time; through written words, the self can inhabit multiple points in space and outlast its bodily time. Furthermore, when those words are poetic—evocative and capacious in meaning—the self's revival is dynamic, "able, active, receptive," every time they are seriously read. The more "able, active, receptive" the reader, the more alive the writing, and hence the writer.[22]

One place where Whitman takes the body/poem analogy quite far is the 1860 "Calamus" poem "Scented Herbage of My Breast":

> Scented herbage of my breast,
> Leaves from you I yield, I write, to be perused best afterwards,

> Tomb-leaves, body-leaves, growing up above me, above death,
> Perennial roots, tall leaves—O the winter shall not freeze you, delicate leaves,
> Every year shall you bloom again—Out from where you retired, you shall emerge again[23]

The axis of the poem is a threefold analogy between chest hair, leaves of grass, and pages of poetry. The poem's first line wonderfully evokes human body odor, especially given that all three editions of *Leaves of Grass* published up to this date (1855, 1856, and 1860) contained frontispieces with vivid portraits of the bearded Whitman. The famous 1855 and 1856 frontispiece even gives the reader a faint glimpse of Whitman's chest hair. The lesser known 1860 frontispiece does not provide this glimpse, but Whitman's beard and hair are fuller, making it easy for consumers of this edition to envision the "scented herbage" of the poet's breast (see pages 340–41).

"Scented Herbage of My Breast" also evokes the death-laden vegetative imagery of *Leaves of Grass*. Whitman makes this reference explicit when he refers to the "scented herbage" as "Tomb-leaves, body-leaves, growing up above me, above death." As in "Song of Myself," the I's decomposed body gives rise to grass, to "beautiful uncut hair of graves."[24] At the same time, by so strongly overlapping the imagery of grass with the imagery of chest hair, "Scented Herbage" sharpens the suggestion from "Song of Myself" that the grass grows from "the breasts of young men."[25]

"Scented Herbage of My Breast" refers, finally, to pages of poetry. The earliest edition of *Leaves of Grass* of course drew strong parallels between the bodies of women, men, and land, on the one hand, and bodies of poetry, on the other. But "Scented Herbage" deepens these parallels and makes them even more vivid. Aside from his insistence that "Leaves from you I yield, I write, to be perused best afterwards," Whitman's metaphor of scented herbage emphasizes the materiality of written words and printed poetry and their capacity for material endurance long after the body dies. The metaphor of *scented* herbage also provokes the thought that the pages of books have their own scent; old letters and manuscripts by deceased persons sometimes bear those persons' odor. Whitman reaffirms the idea that handwriting and printed pages have their own smell when he writes, "O I do not know whether many, passing by, will discover you, or inhale your faint odor—but I believe a few will."[26] This vibrant materiality[27] of written words and pages, whose potential to activate the senses of not only sight and touch, but also smell, makes the corporeally absent physically present. In so doing, it brings the dead back to life. No wonder then that "Scented Herbage of My Breast" converges in a tribute to death, and to the strange way death enables new forms of presence:[28]

> Death is beautiful from you—(what indeed is beautiful, except Death and Love?)
> O I think it is not for life I am chanting here my chant of lovers—I think it must be for Death,
> . . . .
> Through me shall the words be said to make death exhilarating[29]

The central claim is that death is beautiful when poeticized: "Death is beautiful from you," from, that is, the "scented herbage of my breast." While in one sense Whitman is saying that death is always beautiful—for insofar as we find the grass beautiful, we find death beautiful—in another sense Whitman is saying that death is beautiful only insofar as we poeticize it. The idea that grass represents death, after all, is essentially poetic: though an argument can be made that the idea is also naturalistic, it is crucial to remember that the idea of nature is also poetic, for it represents an infinitely variegated phenomenon as an elegant and simple whole. This type of representation is better described as poetic than as scientific or philosophical. Insofar as science and philosophy reduce infinitely complex phenomena to simple and elegant units of representation, they are also forms of poetry.

Whitman's line "O I think it is not for life I am chanting here my chant of lovers, I think it must be for death" brings us back to the essence of Whitman's second vision of death. Death is not, in the first instance, immortal poetry; rather, death is *inspiration* for immortal poetry. Consciousness of our mortality inspires us to make memorable words out of our experience, so that we may live and converse with future generations. Poetry, in this sense, exists for those who come after us. Poetry lets future generations know the depth of our experience, and by informing them of our existence, gives them perspective on time's breadth. Poetry helps future generations realize that others before them experienced feelings of sublimity; this then helps them appreciate their own chance to experience sublimity.

But poetry exists also for us. Poetry—and all creative work which takes enduring material form—allays mortal anxiety by giving us hope that we may still be present in the world even after we are absent. Whitman's own work illustrates the striking results that can flow from frank acknowledgment of mortality combined with desire for immortality:

> Give me your tone therefore, O Death, that I may accord with it,
> Give me yourself—for I see that you belong to me now above all, and
>   are folded together above all—you Love and Death are,
> Nor will I allow you to balk me any more with what I was calling life,
> For now it is conveyed to me that you are the purports essential,
> . . . .
> That may be you are what it is all for—but it does not last so very long,
> But you will last very long.[30]

Whitman allays his mortal anxiety by creating a poetics of death, by subduing death to his form, so that death "belongs" to him before he "belongs" to it. Yet Whitman poetically masters death, paradoxically, by surrendering to it, by conceding its finality, that it lasts "very long." At the same time, Whitman enigmatically suggests that death may be "what it is all for." This claim that death is the aim of life is in one sense obvious: our bodies decay; every moment of our living is also a moment of our dying. The claim that death is "what it is all for," however, also hearkens back to the more complex view of the ancients that life is preparation for death, and that the task of philosophy is learning how to die.[31] The irony of saying that philosophy's task is learning how to die points to the dictum's true meaning—that philosophy's task is learning how to live, specifically how to live in the knowledge of mortality. Whitman intimates an answer to this task when he declares that love and death "are folded together."

Death intensifies our love for both people and the world around us by making us conscious of the fleetingness of our experience. Death compounds love by making lovers realize that time for love is limited. Death thus serves life. Viewed from one angle, death could inspire resentment of our condition by making us view it as one essentially of loss. Yet viewed from Whitman's angle, death should inspire infinite love, for it reveals our condition as one of infinite gain. Death reveals that we have something instead of nothing, though it easily could be otherwise; death helps us see that existence is a happy accident, for which we should be infinitely grateful.[32] Whitman answers the riddle of death by ordering us to give ourselves over to a love coextensive with wonder at and gratitude for existence.[33] Yet this lesson ventures beyond Whitman's second vision of death, as inspiration to creative immortality, into the third, as a condition that makes us human.

Whitman's second vision of death commands us to create so that we may be immortal. Transform the world with your minds and hands, the second vision orders, while you still have time. Leave your mark on the visible world, so that future others may know that you were here, and that the world as it appears to them could not exist without you. We leave our immortal signature, Whitman's second vision says, not on our invisible atoms, but on our visible environment. The transcendence of death lies in world-building.

Whitman's second vision of death is more satisfying than his first vision, for it offers a path to immortality more worldly than organic endurance. But the second vision is far more heroic than democratic. This is not to say that democracy and heroism are incompatible. Democracy inspires its own distinctive forms of heroism, realized through "self-trust."[34] Yet truthfully speaking, only a few of any given generation will achieve creative immortality. No matter how creative democracy makes its citizens, some will always shine more brightly, and thus be more likely to live on in human memory. Furthermore, some works of genius will go unrecognized; creative virtuosity does not guarantee creative immortality. Creative immortality is a result of not just skill, but luck. Which great works don't get destroyed? Which great works find sympathetic readers and powerful interpreters? Because human memory is not completely meritocratic, Whitman's second vision of death as inspiration to creative immortality is not completely consoling. In extremely hopeful moments, the second vision may allay mortal anxiety, but when sobriety returns, it is for most people inadequate. So how should democrats console themselves in the face of mortality?

Whitman's third vision of death suggests that the promise of immortality is unnecessary for consolation. Even if death is a full stop, it still deserves our affirmation. Affirming death in the confidence that it is a full stop is essential to affirming ourselves and our world as they are and to transcending Puritan superstition, and thus to achieving the ecstatic gratitude for being born of democratic perspective.[35]

The Third Vision: A Human Condition

The third way Whitman views death is as a human condition. It is a human condition, first, in a weak sense: death is an inescapable and undeniable part of human life; no human life—no plant or animal life, for that matter—evades it. Death is a human condition, second, in a strong sense: it is a *precondition* of humanity. Death is the outer limit of humanity: if we were deathless, we would be superhuman. Some may find super-humanity desirable. Whitman, however, counsels against this desire. He encourages us to see our humanity—a humanity we too often see as deficient and imperfect—as sufficient and perfect. By choosing to see our mortal condition as sufficient and perfect, we free ourselves from mortal anxiety and from what Emerson calls the "false prayers" of regret.[36]

Whitman intimates this view of death most evocatively in "Who Learns My Lesson Complete?" (1855):

> Who learns my lesson complete?
> . . . .
> It is no lesson . . . . it lets down the bars to a good lesson,
> And that to another . . . . and every one to another still.[37]

Whitman's insistence that his "lesson complete" is "no lesson," but "lets down the bars to a good lesson, / And that to another . . . . and every one to another still," indicates that the "lesson complete" lacks positivity but still unlocks positive lessons. What might such a lesson be?

> The great laws take and effuse without argument,
> I am of the same style, for I am their friend,
> I love them quits and quits . . . . I do not halt and make salaams.[38]

When Whitman writes that "The great laws take and effuse without argument," he suggests that the laws of the universe—including its cycle of birth and death—do not explain themselves completely. Our expectation that we should be able to understand these laws completely is therefore misplaced. Because one of the defining features of the universe is its mystery, quests for a complete metaphysics are futile.[39]

Whitman then encourages his reader to befriend the universe in its lack of complete intelligibility. When he says, "I am of the same style, for I am their friend / I love them quits and quits . . . . I do not halt and make salaams," he implies that it is possible to love the universe without grasping its metaphysics. He urges us, furthermore, to love the universe as an equal. Not even the universe merits our *abject* worship, for the self is itself a universe.

Yet even as it registers the sometimes frustrating mystery of the universe, "Who Learns My Lesson Complete" portrays it as astonishingly wonderful, notwithstanding its resistance to intellectual mastery:

> It is no little matter, this round and delicious globe, moving so exactly in its orbit forever and ever, without one jolt or the untruth of a single second;
> I do not think it was made in six days, nor in ten thousand years, nor ten decillions of years,
> Nor planned and built one thing after another, as an architect plans and builds a house.[40]

Feeling an acute sense of awe in the face of the universe's physics, Whitman becomes more and more atheistic about the universe's metaphysics. He rejects not only the orthodox Judeo-Christian belief that the earth was made in six days, but the idea that it was made at all.

Yet Whitman's "lesson complete" is not atheism, but rather a sober and responsible agnosticism—an agnosticism that acknowledges that the universe exceeds even our most expansive reflective capacities. Our response to the universe's sublimity should not be the ascription to it of a supremely intelligent design. Our response, rather, should be respect for its sublimity through refusal to enclose it in an all-subsuming metaphysics or theology—a metaphysics or theology that breeds intellectual and spiritual self-satisfaction and smothers openness and wonder. "Song of Myself" anticipates Whitman's "lesson complete":

> And I call to mankind, Be not curious about God,
> For I, who am curious about each, am not curious about God,
> No array of terms can say how much I am at peace about God and about death.

> I hear and behold God in every object, yet I understand God not in
> the least,
> Nor do I understand who there can be more wonderful than myself.[41]

It seems strange for a poet of openness and wonder to urge us to "Be not curious about God." It also seems strange for a poet who claims he is "not curious about God" to then say that he hears and beholds "God in every object." Whitman's rhetorical strategy here is not to deny the possibility of God, but to democratize our awe and wonder by redirecting them away from a divine author who may or may not exist to the self and the world that—if our senses are to be believed—certainly do exist:

> Why should I wish to see God better than this day?
> I see something of God each hour of the twenty-four, and each
> moment then,
> In the faces of men and women I see God, and in my own face in the
> glass[42]

"Beholding God in every object," Whitman appears to preach pantheism. But since pantheism constitutes an understanding of God, and Whitman insists that he understands "God not in the least," agnosticism remains Whitman's overriding commitment.[43] With or without God, the self and the world are worthy of reverence; Whitman finds their sheer existence miraculous. Whitman wants us to linger with our wonder, awe, and gratitude over "the sheer fact of existence,"[44] and not rush from the experience of sublimity to the dubious, parochial, and anthropomorphic project of ascribing to existence a reason and author.[45] The universe may be uncaused and self-existent in the same way we imagine God as uncaused and self-existent. Why hastily insist that the universe must have a maker, and narcissistically envision that maker in our own image?

Whitman's serene agnosticism about God produces serene agnosticism about death. "Who Learns My Lesson Complete?" promotes agnosticism about death not by preaching it didactically, but by (1) promising immortality in order to allay mortal anxiety and relax the reader enough to open him or her to alternative possibilities,[46] and (2) working to adjust downwardly the reader's sense of immortality's importance, so as to loosen the hold of the desire for immortality and emancipate energy for a more intense and loving engagement of life. First is the promise of immortality.

> I do not think seventy years is the time of a man or woman,
> Nor that seventy millions of years is the time of a man or woman,
> Nor that years will ever stop the existence of me or any one else.[47]

On its plainest register of meaning, the stanza assures the reader that the self is not ultimately hostage to the body's decay over time. The stanza even hints that the self lives above and beyond time: years will not stop the existence of any given self. Several ambiguities, however, point to a second register of meaning that does not so much promise immortality as note the ways the human condition compensates us infinitely for our mortality. To say that one does not think that "seventy years" or "seventy millions of years" is "the time of a man or a woman" or that "years will ever stop the existence" of any given self is in one sense to say that the self is either immortal or eternal: either the self ends when time ends or the self lives beyond time. But in another sense, it is to say that measurable expanses of time are not where life is lived. Life, rather, is lived in moments—when the sense of time dissipates and a minute might as well be an hour or an hour a minute. The measure of life is not time but exhilaration. So when Whitman says, "I do not think seventy years is the time of a man or woman, / Nor that seventy millions of years is the time of a man or woman," he is in a sense saying that the time of a man or a woman is not any measurable quantity of time, but is rather the moment of lived intensity. The time of a man or woman is always now. In light of this reading, a new meaning emerges for Whitman's insistence that years will never "stop the existence of me": Whitman will not allow consciousness of time or mortality to detract from the sublimity he feels in moments of intense awareness or experience. Time and mortality will not stop him from giving himself completely to life.

Whitman then turns to the project of putting the value of immortality in perspective.

> Is it wonderful that I should be immortal, as every one is immortal;
> I know it is wonderful . . . . but my eyesight is equally wonderful /
>   . . . . and how I was conceived in my mother's womb is equally wonderful,

> And how I was not palpable once but am now . . . . and was born on the last day of May 1819 . . . . and passed from a babe in the creeping trance of three summers and three winters to articulate and walk . . . . are all equally wonderful.
> And that I grew six feet high . . . . and that I have become a man thirty-six years old in 1855 . . . . and that I am here anyhow—are all equally wonderful;
> And that my soul embraces you this hour, and we affect each other without ever seeing each other, and never perhaps to see each other, is every bit as wonderful:
> And that I can think such thoughts as these is just as wonderful,
> And that I can remind you, and you think them and know them to be true is just as wonderful.[48]

Whitman here concedes the fact of immortality without promulgating any particular vision of immortality. Though elsewhere he offers naturalistic and poetic visions of immortality as substitutes for the Christian idea of immortality, here he lets his reader hold on to whatever vision of immortality he or she prefers. After having assured the reader of immortality and thus relaxed the reader into a state of intellectual and spiritual openness, he gently but systematically devalues immortality by placing it on an equal evaluative footing with eyesight, conception, birth, growth, speech, movement, literature, materiality, thought, reading, and intuition. All of these are miracles and objects worthy of wonder, Whitman implies, just as we conventionally regard immortality as a miracle and object worthy of wonder. The cumulative effect of this poetic reevaluation is to allow the reader to affirm mortal life in the absence of immortality—for if eyesight, conception, birth, growth, speech, movement, literature, materiality, thought, reading, and intuition are just as wonderful as immortality, then the subtraction of immortality from the human condition is no great loss, for these other miraculous features of mortal existence remain, and more than compensate for our lack of immortality.

Against the background of this devaluation of immortality, the radicalism of Whitman's explicit affirmations of mortal life register more strongly:

> I exist as I am—that is enough,
> If no other in the world be aware, I sit content,
> And if each and all be aware, I sit content.[49]

Notice how this passage on the self-sufficiency of mortal existence repudiates key elements of Whitman's first and second visions of death. If it is "enough" to exist as one is, then consolation in the face of mortality is unnecessary. If it is "enough" to exist anonymously, then desire for immortality is superfluous. Mortal existence is worthy of affirmation on its own, without the promise of immortality.

Whitman's poetic effort to affirm mortality is part of a larger poetic effort to encourage his fellow citizens to surmount their Puritan heritage and say with him, "The earth—that is sufficient."[50] If Whitman can convince them of the adequacy of the earth even in the absence of heaven, he can open them up to a more loving and intense engagement with life, which in turn can open them up to unforeseeable and unsuspected forms of creation, beauty, and sublimity. In "A Song of the Rolling Earth" (1856), Whitman ties earth-affirmation and self-affirmation together inextricably:

> I swear the earth shall surely be complete to him or her who shall be complete!
> I swear the earth remains broken and jagged only to him or her who remains broken and jagged![51]

Affirming the earth is vital to realizing oneself. Seeing the earth as perfect instead of fallen emancipates energy from misplaced regret and disappointment. The here and the now become sites of abundance and infinite possibility rather than of incorrigibility and lack. Viewing the present as a site of abundance and infinite possibility in turn allows the imagination to soar to unforeseeable heights and conceive forms of world-building unimaginable in the cramped mental landscape of Puritan self-abasement. Whitman affirms mortality to emancipate life from mortal anxiety. Conceding that life will someday end encourages individuals to value mortal life appropriately: as an abundant site of potential beginning.[52]

Marking the achievement of intellectual maturity and optimizing the freedom of its adherents, Whitman's third vision of death is his best. Of the three visions, it most powerfully embodies the Socratic virtue of respecting the limits of knowledge, and of preferring to live in ambiguity and admitted ignorance than in the deluded sureness of false knowledge.[53] Of the three visions, it also does the most to reconcile its adherents to the world's lack of metaphysical certainties. By helping readers see that metaphysics and theology distract us from the things we can best know and know best—the things of everyday life—the third vision redirects its adherents toward proper appreciation of ordinary experience.[54] Reimmersed in ordinary life and fully attentive to it, Whitman's readers can then see how the earth is more wondrous than history's most magnificent visions of heaven. The wondrousness of the ordinary seduces them into a fuller participation in the present, and reveals why the present should command our greatest reverence. The present is the time of freedom, the only time we can exercise freedom. "Give me insight into to-day, and you may have the antique and future worlds," Emerson said in "The American Scholar" (1837). "This time, like all times, is a very good one, if we but know what to do with it," he also declared.[55] Spotlighting the present as freedom's time, Whitman's third vision of death moves us to reflect on how best to use that time; it also urges us to live some of it spontaneously, while we still have the chance for adventure. Agnosticism about death energizes wonder, freedom, and life in Whitman. The question remains, however, how it enhances democratic citizenship.

Death and Democratic Life

If we conceive of democracy as a form of common life based on respect for the equal dignity of every individual, and that aims to promote the equal freedom and flourishing of every individual, then democracy demands that citizens regard each other as ends, as embodiments of infinite potential.[56] So conceived, democracy requires that citizens show maximal openness to one another, so that they may find the beauty in one another, even when antidemocratic historical legacies and social forces condition them to see themselves or others as fundamentally lacking. Maximal openness to others in turn requires intellectual humility, vigilance against prejudice, and a disposition to resist ways of seeing and interpreting that mark some people as unimportant or irredeemably inferior.

Instantiating both intellectual humility and critical distance from inherited orthodoxy, agnosticism about death comports with the personal openness democracy requires. Citizens capable of overcoming fear of the unknown—death being the ultimate unknown—are more likely to respond constructively to difference than those so terrified by death that they would rather subscribe to a predetermined view of it than let its unknown quality be. Citizens agnostic about death, in other words, are more likely to confront difference with equanimity, to let it speak, and to revise their worldviews in light of it, than to prematurely categorize difference within a rigidly held, totalizing worldview. James Baldwin highlighted the danger mortal anxiety posed to democracy when he wrote, in *The Fire Next Time* (1963), "Perhaps the whole root of our trouble, the human trouble, is that we will sacrifice all the beauty of our lives, will imprison ourselves in totems, taboos, crosses, blood sacrifices, steeples, mosques, races, armies, flags, nations, in order to deny the fact of death, which is the only fact we have."[57] In the quest for immortality, Baldwin suggests, we imprison ourselves in identities forged through condemnation of difference. Through religion, race, and nation, in other words, we abandon the self "to a larger self from which one regains oneself magnified"[58] to attain heavenly salvation or immortal membership in a death-defying, world-historical, national, or racial project. Mortal anxiety thus destroys the affirmation of both self and other that democracy requires.

In staving off the desire for metaphysical certainty, however, agnosticism about death enhances democratic citizenship. Citizens who can live with uncertainty about death are better prepared to live with the diversity and turbulence democracy sets free. Democracy's uncertainty consists not just in the unpredictable results of elections and legislative decisions, but also in the uncertainty that inevitably results from the proliferation of freedom.[59] The proliferation of freedom entails the upending of traditional boundaries and the unsettling of comforting conventions.[60] She who can bear both mortality and freedom's turbulence lightly is more likely to assume the posture of welcoming curiosity that Whitman associates with the democratic self:

> Aside from the pulling and hauling stands what I am,
> Stands amused, complacent, compassionating, idle, unitary,
> Looks down, is erect, bends an arm on an impalpable certain rest,
> Looks with its side-curved head curious what will come next,
> Both in and out of the game, and watching and wondering at it.[61]

Agnosticism about death is a form of looking with "side-curved head curious what will come next." Instantiating the courage and openness needed to respond constructively to democracy's "diversity of differences,"[62] it marks the maturation of the democratic self.

Notes

Thanks to Thomas Dumm, Kennan Ferguson, George Kateb, and John Seery for constructive comments on an earlier draft of this essay. Thanks especially to Melvin Rogers and Morton Schoolman, whose challenging criticisms have proven enormously helpful.

1. Plato, *Apology*, trans. G. M. A. Grube and John M. Cooper, in *The Trial and Death of Socrates*, 3rd ed. (Indianapolis: Hackett, 2000), 29a.

2. Ibid., 40c–d.

3. Ibid., 42. For two important commentaries on Socrates' orientation toward death in the *Apology*, see John E. Seery, *Political Theory for Mortals: Shades of Justice, Images of Death* (Ithaca: Cornell University Press, 1996), 48–52; and Jeffrey E. Green, "The Morality of Wonder: A Positive Interpretation of Socratic Ignorance," *Polis* 21, nos. 1 and 2 (2004): 65–66.

4. For the purposes of this essay, I confine myself to Whitman's antebellum work, specifically the first, second, and third editions of *Leaves of Grass* (1855, 1856, 1860). Whitman's encounter with the mass death of the Civil War complicates his views on mortality in important ways, which I hope to address in future work.

5. Simon Critchley, *The Book of Dead Philosophers* (New York: Vintage Books, 2008), xx–xxiv, 37–42, 55–59, 63–64.

6. George Kateb, *Hannah Arendt: Politics, Conscience, Evil* (Totowa, N.J.: Rowman and Allanheld, 1983), 178–83; George Kateb, "Democratic Individuality and the Meaning of Rights," in *Liberalism and the Moral Life*, ed. Nancy L. Rosenblum (Cambridge: Harvard University Press, 1989), 183–206; George Kateb, *The Inner Ocean: Individualism and Democratic Culture* (Ithaca: Cornell University Press, 1992); George Kateb, *Patriotism and Other Mistakes* (New Haven: Yale University Press, 2006), 142–47; Morton Schoolman, *Reason and Horror: Critical Theory, Democracy, and Aesthetic Individuality* (New York: Routledge, 2001), 164–250; Jason Frank, "Aesthetic Democracy: Walt Whitman and the Poetry of the People," *Review of Politics* 69, no. 3 (2007): 402–30; Jason Frank, "Promiscuous Citizenship," this volume.

7. Walt Whitman, "Song of Myself" in *Leaves of Grass*, 1st ed. (1855), in *Leaves of Grass: A Textual Variorum of the of the Printed Poems*, ed. Sculley Bradley, Harold W. Blodgett, Arthur Golden, and William White, vol. 1, *Poems, 1855–1856* (New York: New York University Press, 1980), 8. I have used the variorum to reproduce Whitman's text as it originally appeared in the 1855, 1856, or 1860 editions. For ease of cross-referencing, however, I refer to poems by their titles in the 1891–92 *Leaves of Grass*.

8. Ibid., 7.

9. Ibid., 80.

10. Walt Whitman, "Crossing Brooklyn Ferry" in *Leaves of Grass*, 2nd ed. (1856), in *Leaves of Grass: A Textual Variorum*, 1:221.

11. Walt Whitman, "To Think of Time," in *Leaves of Grass*, 2nd ed., in *Leaves of Grass: A Textual Variorum*, 1:105.

12. See Harry Gershenowitz, "Whitman and Lamarck Revisited," *Walt Whitman Review* 25 (September 1979): 121–23; Gershenowitz, "Two Lamarckians: Walt Whitman and Edward Carpenter," *Walt Whitman Quarterly Review* 2 (Summer 1984): 35–39; and David S. Reynolds, *Walt Whitman's America: A Cultural Biography* (New York: Random House, 1995), 246.

13. Whitman, "Crossing Brooklyn Ferry," 217.

14. Ibid., 217–18.

15. Kateb, *Inner Ocean*, 248.

16. Whitman, "Song of Myself," 82.

17. Ibid., 3.

18. The formulation that "there is no death, only change of form" is Morton Schoolman's, which expresses his interpretation of Whitman on death. Commentary on the panel "Walt Whitman and Democratic Vistas Today" (at the annual meeting of the American Political Science Association, Boston, Massachusetts, August 28–31, 2008). Schoolman intimates this view—but does not state it this forcefully—in *Reason and Horror*, 172.

19. Walt Whitman, "Full of Life Now," in *Leaves of Grass*, 3rd ed. (1860), in *Leaves of Grass: A Textual Variorum of the of the Printed Poems*, ed. Sculley Bradley, Harold W. Blodgett, Arthur Golden, and William White, vol. 2, *Poems, 1860–1867* (New York: New York University Press, 1980), 407–8.

20. Whitman, "Crossing Brooklyn Ferry," 218. For an account of how Whitman relativizes time and space and gives birth to new conceptions of "democratic time" and "democratic space," see Schoolman, *Reason and Horror*, 240–47.

21. Walt Whitman, "A Song of the Rolling Earth," in *Leaves of Grass*, 2nd ed., in *Leaves of Grass: A Textual Variorum*, 1:266.

22. For a fine consideration of the way written words enable the transcendence of time and space, see Susan McWilliams, "Thoreau on Body and Soul," in *A Political Companion to Henry David Thoreau*, ed. Jack Turner (Lexington: University Press of Kentucky, 2009), 247.

23. Whitman, "Scented Herbage of My Breast," in *Leaves of Grass*, 3rd ed., in *Leaves of Grass: A Textual Variorum*, 2:365–66.

24. Whitman, "Song of Myself," 7.

25. Ibid.

26. Whitman, "Scented Herbage," 366.

27. I owe the matchless concept of "vibrant materiality" to Jane Bennett. See her *Vibrant Matter: A Political Ecology of Things* (Durham, N.C.: Duke University Press, 2010).

28. On the idea of the presence of the present, see Stanley Cavell, *The Senses of Walden,* expanded ed. (1981; Chicago: University of Chicago Press, 1992), 9–10, 61; Thomas Dumm, *A Politics of the Ordinary* (New York: New York University Press, 1999), 21, 67; and Thomas Dumm, *Loneliness as a Way of Life* (Cambridge: Harvard University Press, 2008), 154–55.

29. Whitman, "Scented Herbage," 366–67.

30. Ibid., 367.

31. Critchley, *Book of Dead Philosophers,* xv–xix.

32. Cf. Kateb, *Inner Ocean,* 146–47; and Kateb, *Patriotism and Other Mistakes,* 145.

33. Cf. Kateb, *Hannah Arendt,* 180–81; and Kateb, *Patriotism and Other Mistakes,* 145.

34. Ralph Waldo Emerson, "The American Scholar" (1837), in *Emerson: Essays and Lectures,* ed. Joel Porte (New York: Library of America, 1983), 63–67.

35. This ecstatic gratitude for being is similar to the "nontheistic gratitude for the earth and the abundance of life" professed by William Connolly ("Confessing Identity/Belonging to Difference," in *Identity/Difference: Democratic Negotiations of Political Paradox,* expanded ed. [Minneapolis: University of Minnesota Press, 2002], xxvii).

36. Emerson, "Self-Reliance" in *Essays: First Series* (1841), in *Emerson: Essays and Lectures,* 276.

37. Whitman, "Who Learns My Lesson Complete?" in *Leaves of Grass,* 1st ed., in *Leaves of Grass: A Textual Variorum,* 1:152–3.

38. Ibid.

39. As Schoolman observes, "Whitman is adamant in his refusal to decipher or interpret the unknown" (*Reason and Horror,* 167).

40. Whitman, "Who Learns My Lesson Complete?" 153.

41. Whitman, "Song of Myself," 79.

42. Ibid.

43. Contrary to Martha C. Nussbaum's claim that Whitman understands God as "immanent in the world" (*Upheavals of Thought: The Intelligence of Emotions* [Cambridge: Cambridge University Press, 2001], 657).

44. Kateb, *Inner Ocean,* 266.

45. Cf. Schoolman, *Reason and Horror,* 185, 200: "Whitman is convinced and makes plain his conviction that nothing before us is without wonder and that

no wonder, on that account, should be left out of account or can be given a complete account, and that every account only returns us reflexively to the mystery and wonder that provoked it. . . . Mystery and wonder . . . appear as the definitive *gestalt*, the definitive value of the being of the world." Cf. 176.

46. For discussion of popular attitudes toward death in Whitman's time, see Gary Laderman, *The Sacred Remains: American Attitudes toward Death, 1799–1883* (New Haven: Yale University Press, 1996); and Drew Gilpin Faust, *This Republic of Suffering: Death and the American Civil War* (New York: Knopf, 2008), chap. 1.

47. Whitman, "Who Learns My Lesson Complete?" 153.

48. Ibid., 153–54.

49. Whitman, "Song of Myself," 26.

50. Whitman, "Song of the Open Road," in *Leaves of Grass*, 2nd ed., in *Leaves of Grass: A Textual Variorum*, 1:226.

51. Whitman, "A Song of the Rolling Earth," 270.

52. In this way, Whitman anticipates Hannah Arendt's effort to emancipate modern men from obsession over physical self-preservation and to reorient them toward freedom: "though they must die, men are not born in order to die but in order to begin" (*The Human Condition*, 2nd ed. [1958; Chicago: The University of Chicago Press, 1998], 246).

53. Whitman's third vision of death is also arguably his best claim to what Stephen K. White calls "the only sort of dignity that belongs uniquely to humans": "bearing witness truthfully to my condition of subjection to mortality" (*The Ethos of a Late-Modern Citizen* [Cambridge: Harvard University Press, 2009], 73).

54. On the extraordinariness of the ordinary in democracy, see Dumm, *Politics of the Ordinary*; Frank, "Aesthetic Democracy"; and Frank, "Promiscuous Citizenship."

55. Emerson, "American Scholar," 69, 68.

56. Nussbaum credits Whitman with teaching readers "what it is to see men and women as ends, and to see the boundless and equal worth of each and every one of them" (*Upheavals of Thought*, 645). See also Martha C. Nussbaum, *Poetic Justice: The Literary Imagination and Public Life* (Boston: Beacon Press, 1995).

57. James Baldwin, *The Fire Next Time* (1963), in *Baldwin: Collected Essays*, ed. Toni Morrison (New York: Library of America, 1998), 339. On Baldwin as a theorist of democracy, see Lawrie Balfour, *The Evidence of Things Not Said: James Baldwin and the Promise of American Democracy* (Ithaca: Cornell University Press, 2001). For a beautiful consideration of Baldwin's effort to reconcile his fellow citizens to mortality, see George Shulman, *American Prophecy: Race and Redemption in American Political Culture* (Minneapolis: University of Minnesota Press, 2008), chap. 5.

58. Kateb, *Patriotism and Other Mistakes*, 324.

59. Eric H. Fromm, *Escape from Freedom* (1941; New York: Owl Books, 1994).

60. William E. Connolly, *Politics and Ambiguity* (Madison: University of Wisconsin Press, 1987).

61. Whitman, "Song of Myself," 5.

62. Schoolman, *Reason and Horror*, 219–20. Cf. Connolly, *Politics and Ambiguity*, 9–16.

CHAPTER 12

Morbid Democracies: The Bodies Politic of Walt Whitman and Richard Rorty

Kennan Ferguson

ON JANUARY 30, 2007, Microsoft released its newest computer operating system, dramatically christened "Vista." The multinational corporation thus simultaneously evoked the grandiosity of Walt Whitman's expansive embrace of American democratic aspirations, redefined the visual-aesthetic domain where many of the world's workers spend their greatest amounts of time and attention, and produced new destabilizations in our data, encouraging our computers to crash in new and speedier ways. Microsoft's near-monopoly on the programs that bring computer hardware to life guaranteed the subsequent spread of Vista over (and within) the vast network of information and knowledge that makes up the machinery of the capitalist world, while not coincidently resulting in no small profit for themselves.

On June 8, 2007, the American philosopher Richard Rorty, broadly known for his pragmatism, his critique of reason, and his calls to political action, died. Like Microsoft, Rorty evoked Whitman, grouping him with Dewey and Baldwin as one of the great thinkers of American democracy.

Now, noting the temporal proximity of these two events may gently imply a causal relation between them. Nothing could be further from my intent; I certainly do not mean to intimate softly that Microsoft had anything to do with Rorty's death. No, I have little patience for such implications. I will state it, instead, quite openly: Microsoft killed Richard Rorty.

This was not murder, admittedly. The multifaceted transnational profit-motivity machine that is Microsoft probably never was concerned one way or the other about American philosophy, either ontological or epistemological in focus. So the question here is not, How should we punish Microsoft?

(though I do invite you to envision your own poetic justice), but instead, By what means did Microsoft dispossess Richard Rorty of life? And the answer to this latter question, I fear, is an easy one: It (and others like it) deprived him of his conditions of his future.

To fully understand the causes and implications of this deprivation requires further explanation. Central to this process are the poetry and prose of Walt Whitman, whose democratic imaginary and commitments undergirded many of Rorty's. Thus, it is vital to understand precisely what Rorty meant when he hearkened back to Whitman. Rorty's Whitman was a sort of superhero of the American imaginary, a visionary of a greater, celebratory ideation of the United States. For Rorty, this sort of idealized, transcendent universalism allows for (even encourages) a creative, egalitarian, patriotism. And yet turning to Whitman himself, especially his poetry, reveals a more complex though equally idealistic model. For Whitman, the American ideal was not "yet-to-come": the individuals and ideas and regions he celebrated were already all around him, fully in existence. They needed to be properly celebrated, true, but they did not exist strictly in an abstract future. At the end of this essay, I turn to the aspect of life where the contrast between their two embodied democracies becomes the clearest: the relationship each has toward death. In the end of life, Rorty's model can see only a failure to achieve, the destruction of the life for which the struggle has been waged. Whitman, on the other hand, not only did not fear death, he was happy to celebrate it as an intrinsic and central aspect of life.

The Unvaried Carols of Rorty's Whitman

Rorty's version of Whitmanesque patriotism proves appealing to many people, especially those whose political commitments coincide with the national projects affiliated in the United States with early twentieth-century movements generally associated with "leftism," stretching from certain strains within progressivism up to the eclipsing of the labor movement. For Rorty the critical leftism that emerged from the Frankfurt school, underpinned the "New Left," and defined what he terms "postmodernism" all took away from what he considered the ultimate goal and applicable tool of leftism: the dream of a more perfect union.

The purpose of politics, in Rorty's mind, was first to provide an exhortative vision of what could be, and then provide the organizational capabilities to work toward that goal. Whitman, for Rorty, provided the necessary first half, while Dewey (the pragmatist par excellence for Rorty) helped conceptualize the second. In other words, Whitman inspired; Dewey organized.

Overall, Rorty's vision of Dewey is both neat and accurate. By holding to a pragmatic version of truth, Dewey conceptualized a progressivism that relied on people and the state to reform one another, using the tools at hand. Dewey, like Rorty, was rarely shy about prescribing solutions to the problems of the day, many of which (such as income inequality, education, and imperial warfare) either remain with us today or have reemerged in recent years.[1] Dewey, like Rorty, saw in philosophical thought both the ability to analyze problems and, closely conjoined, the anti-ideological resources needed to address them.

It is, instead, Rorty's Whitman that needs attention. In Rorty's telling, Whitman was merely a sort of proto-Dewey, a precursor with "little difference in doctrine."[2] Whitman celebrated the United States as a country that—through its founding—had discovered the secrets to transcending the bonds of history, or at least had achieved the potential to do so. In Rorty's eyes, this makes Whitman not only the poet of American destiny, but the perfect model of a leftist-oriented patriotism, an exemplar for how to have pride in the United States by focusing on and lionizing what the country can be.[3]

Rorty has culled from Whitman's writings a fairly representative list of celebratory sayings and maxims. "The United States themselves are essentially the greatest poem."[4] Whitman, Rorty held, wrote, at least in some of his works, "the words America and democracy as convertible terms."[5] "How long it takes," he wrote, "to make this American world see that it is, in itself, the final authority and reliance!"[6]

Rorty bypasses a number of equally laudatory statements, each of which helps him make the point that Whitman's overall goal is a patriotic celebration of the simultaneous diversity and unity of the United States. "Democracy," Whitman stated in "Democratic Vistas," "is law, and of the strictest, amplest kind."[7] "I count with absolute certainty on the great future of America," Whitman proclaims in his centennial preface: "America, too, is a prophecy."[8] "What most needs fostering through the hundred years to come," he argues, is a "fused and fervent identity of the individual, whoever he or she may be, with the idea and fact of AMERICAN TOTALITY, and with what is meant by the Flag, the stars and stripes."[9]

Unsurprisingly, Whitman's writing sounds to Rorty as a call to a future America. If the potential of democracy can be fulfilled in the unity of the people with their national pride, then an America of great power and true justice can arise. Such a dream, Rorty hopes, can provide a form of leftism that provides an alternative to the negative, critical, and censorious Left that focuses primarily on the failures and betrayals of U.S. history.

This outlook could ideally lead to a programmatic list of governmental reforms that could be debated, discussed, and defended. "Nothing would do more to resurrect the American Left," he argues, "than agreement on a concrete political platform, a list of specific reforms."[10] Once those reforms are developed, the Left could stand for something positive rather than merely criticizing U.S. foreign policy or its treatment of minorities or women. "If the intellectuals and the unions could ever get back together again," he wished, the United States could "conceivably" create "a Second Progressive Era."[11] And the only way to create this unity is for intellectuals to give up critical philosophizing and learn to embrace optimism.

Rorty here built on a long tradition of reading Whitman as proposing, or even enacting the conditions of, a future democratic condition.[12] Many critics, especially those committed to progressive and socialist democracy, saw (and continue to see) Whitman as building a template for a democratic future, often using his poetic self as the embodiment of the kind of democracy for which we should strive. In these readings, as well as Rorty's, Whitman points us to a better future through what Leadie Clark called the "divine literatus," the ideal that could be fought for and (possibly, depending on the idealism of the critic) achieved.[13] Whitman, Clark argued, "transferred the flowering of democracy to the distant future. He saw in this democracy to come the sum of all education, literature and religion." This is a Rortian Whitman, who by inspiring the ideals and possibilities in the American imaginary, can transform the future.

"The World's Portents"

So what, after all, separates these two all-American thinkers? In one reading (Rorty's), nothing at all. For Rorty, Whitman's American imagination is both necessary and complete. Even if never fully redeemable, the Whitmanesque dreams of a great nation, fully committed to the equality of each citizen (that is, every "rational uncriminal person, twenty-one years old"), each of whom in turn will both embody and work toward his or her country's continued achievements.[14] This Whitman is what Rorty calls a "romantic utopian," a thinker like Marx or Dewey.[15]

This is certainly a defensible Whitman, and one that much of Whitman's prose undergirds. But another Whitman beckons, one that has a temporal dynamic as well as a physical one, one of transformation and currency. This other Whitman is more closely attached to poetry and to the present. This is a Whitman of death as much as of life, a Whitman who begins within the boundaries of the individual only to escape the body into realms beyond.

Let us call this the poetic Whitman, one who attends to the present more than does Rorty's prosaic Whitman. *Leaves of Grass* does have a degree of futurity, as well as a number of reminiscences. But the vast majority of his poems take place in the moment. Whitman's poems live in the present tense; they are paeans to the people and places of the United States as they are, not as they have been or will be.

Even further, these are poems of doing, of current action. Usually these actions are physicalized: walking, rowing, dancing, working. Whitman takes to the open road, hears America singing, unscrews the doors from their jambs. At other times they are exultations, perhaps most famously in "Song of Myself" (where the verbs "celebrate," "flaunt," and "exult" appear and reappear throughout the poems).

Larzer Ziff describes this poetry in terms of transmutation of the self: "Whitman moves from chanter to universal presence, moves, that is, from a larger-than-life embodiment to a cosmic disembodiment." Yet, Ziff continues, he does not do so by belittling the limitations of the individual but by identifying with them. Whitman passes "through the crucial stage of revealing himself as commonest or cheapest because most possessed of all the petty passions and mean thoughts which afflict us in what we hope are only our weak moments. In this middle stage he is life-size, if not, at times, a bit smaller than life."[16]

The temporality of these various personae, however, remains constant: they are committed to the present. The narrative of "Starting from Paumanok," for example, seems at first to be a straightforward history, starting from birth and retelling the progress of a life. But by the end Whitman has expanded his subject to be the commingled "greatnesses" of love, democracy, and religion, all celebrated through the stipulation that one need only "See!" the aspects of American life that are taking place right now across the continent.[17] And to whom is this panegyric addressed? To all Americans, past and future, for whom the celebration continues:

> See, projected through time
> For me an audience interminable
> With firm and regular step they wend, they never stop,
> Successions of men, Americanos, a hundred millions.[18]

This projection through time, what could be called a dramatic *presentism*, occurs even when speaking to the future and of the past. And this attention appears notably often in Whitman's poetry.

In his "Song of the Rolling Earth," Whitman notes that the earth itself is already its own potentiality: "It has all attributes, growths, effects, latent in itself from the jump."[19] This conception of the present, in which both past and future are contained, precludes the strictly future-oriented attitude of Rorty's outlook. Whitman does not call the future into being so much as he addresses the present as already containing futurity. "Whoever you are," he addresses, "For none more than you are the present and the past, / For none more than you are immortality."[20] Singing takes place in the present, he reminds us, and is for the singer. Teaching, likewise, is for the teacher, as love is for the lover. These are not gifts to the future, at least not primarily; if they are, it is only as evidence of for whom life is lived in the present.

"Crossing Brooklyn Ferry" is perhaps the poem most commented upon by those emphasizing Whitman's political commitments, for this is where he most explicitly explores his myriad connections to his fellow citizens. It is also where he most overtly emphasizes the role that the present plays in his connection with a greater polis. As Gay Wilson Allen and Charles Davis note, the temporality of experience that Whitman here develops works both to commingle identity and history in such a way that all flow together as the poem continues.[21] "What is it then between us?" Whitman asks, where "distance avails not, and place avails not."[22] In describing his experience as identical to those who will follow, Whitman develops a sort of eternal present, whereby the experience of the crossing encompasses time.

Rorty would no doubt argue that such experience shows Whitman's ever-future-facing idealism. One follower of Rorty, Stephen John Mack, interprets the temporality of "Crossing Brooklyn Ferry" as an overcoming of what he calls "aesthetic time," the Bergsonian *presentism* that I have been arguing appears throughout Whitman's poetry.[23] For Mack, the latter sections of the poem attempt to make the earlier *presentism* serve the ideals of a future political sphere, most notably as experience "serves to generate identity."[24] Mack's interpretation must mitigate, however, the repeating tropes of current, flow, and frolic that conclude the poem, where Whitman accepts even the "dumb, beautiful ministers" into our selves: "We use you, and do not cast you aside—we plant you permanently within us."[25]

That which was created in the past does not belong to the past, Whitman reminds, but to those of us who see, live, and experience it. "All architecture is what you do to it when you look upon it. / . . . /All music is what awakes from you when you are reminded by the instruments."[26] This pragmatic interpretation sounds similar to a Rortian or Deweyan epistemology, but not to their political theories. For the creations of the past, however intended, can be (will be!) reused and repurposed in the present; the institutions created by our forefathers and foremothers are important in the here, in the now.

One more crucial point about the poetic Whitman, which is often glossed over by interpretations of him as a futurist: Whitman wrote most of *Leaves of Grass* in the first person. The poetic voice of the later poems, the "I" who loves, appreciates, lives, and grieves over America—who in fact often is America—is a voice in the now. This "I" does not aim at future redemption, but cries out that redemption is always already here, walking among the democratic peoples who make up the country.

The lack of futurity in Whitman's poetry most dramatically differentiates him from the Deweyan progressive that Rorty wants him to be. Whitman's poetry calls not for us to change America, certainly not to agree upon a "concrete political platform, a list of specific reforms" (to repeat Rorty's call). What leaders does Whitman wish for? "Let the reformers descend from the stands where they are forever bawling—let an idiot or insane person appear on each of the stands."[27] Instead, the "I" of his poetry calls upon the rest of us to understand, appreciate, and embrace the joyful multiplicity and universality of the country that exists in its present, in the right-now of time that his poetry consistently reiterates.

One particularly powerful trope in *Leaves of Grass*—death—shows this most powerfully. For the death of an individual is generally understood to be an end, the extinguishing of potential and future. In an incremental, reformist mode, the death of a project (for example, of a nation) would seem to be the failure of that ideal—in a Rortian model, death and ends are to be avoided at all costs. But the poetic Whitman voice, the "I" of the poems, does not shrink from death; it is not even a fearful state. It is, Whitman says, not a cessation but instead "the entrance upon by far the greatest part of existence."[28]

"Wonderful to depart; wonderful to be here!"

Whitman is often quoted saying that he considered *"Leaves of Grass* and its theory experimental—as, in the deepest sense, I consider our American republic itself to be, with its theory." What is less often quoted is the parenthetical continuation: "(I think I have at least enough philosophy not to be too absolutely certain of any thing, or any results)."[29] One might think that Rorty would have reduplicated this sentiment—after all, Rorty, too, was a supporter of contingency and democracy, one who bracingly argued that the latter could never survive without the former.

But what Whitman preached, and what Rorty at times remembered but more often forgot, was the unimportance of consequence in the face of truth and love. For as Rorty's critique of recent "leftist" thought shows, Rorty as pragmatist is more interested in the results and political effects of formulations of political identity than he is interested in the truth or experience of those identities themselves. Put simply, the idea of a dead American is one that Rorty could not stomach, for such a death signified only limitation to him. Whitman, on the other hand, implied what Wallace Stevens would later declare: that death is the mother of beauty. Without ends, life stagnates and loses meaning.

Let us take Whitman at his word, or at least at his poetical word. The "I" of *Leaves of Grass* is no simple individual, as his commentators point out, but instead a grandly pluralized American identity. (Other political theorists in this volume have examined further implications and difficulties of Whitman's conflation.) As the poems progress, the multitudes present in the earlier poems become imbricated in an embodied voice, simultaneously that of America and of Whitman himself. It is this constellation of identity and encompassing that makes Whitman the poet of the uniting of the United States.

So what to make of this identity? One focus of the poems, difficult to ignore, shows the importance of death to all individuals, even (or perhaps especially) this amalgamated "I." But before exploring the role of death within the specifics of this American "I," it is important to note that even when poems refer specifically to Whitman himself, the attitude toward the end of life remains strangely ebullient.

Results need not be the meaning of lives. One may die and die well without leaving behind inventions or bequests:

> No labor-saving machine
> Nor discovery have I made. . . .
> Nor literary success nor intellect, nor book for the bookshelf,
> But a few carols vibrating through the air I leave,
> For comrades and lovers.[30]

Whitman may have been wrong about "literary success" (though most came posthumously), but his point remains that human vitality is not reducible to consequence. The mere existence of his poetry, however widely it is to be read or remembered, is enough.

In *Leaves of Grass,* Whitman reminds the reader of the surprisingly equivalent impetuses emergent from different parts of life. "Youth, large, lusty, loving—youth full of grace, force, fascination / Do you know that Old Age may come after you with equal grace, force, fascination?"[31] Whitman himself here embraced the old as well as the fresh, even when it applied to his own aging. These themes are especially evident in the section entitled "Songs of Parting." These poems speak to the absolute connections between emergence and life, aging and death. "I sing to the last the equalities modern and old / I sing the endless finalés of things,"[32] Whitman wrote.

Whitman set the Civil War alongside other democratic deaths. The blood of the men of the war continued to stain the land, serving both as a reminder of the stakes involved and bringing their lives into the being of the land. "Absorb them well, Oh my earth," the Mother of All sings,

> I charge you lose not my sons, lose not an atom
> And you streams absorb them well, taking their dear blood,
> And you local spots, and you airs that swim above lightly impalpable,
> And all you essences of soil and growth, and you my rivers' depths,

> And you mountain sides, and the woods where my dear children's
>   blood trickling redden'd,
> And you trees down in your roots to bequeath to all future trees,
> My dead absorb or South or North—my young men's bodies absorb,
>   and their precious precious blood,
> Which holding in trust for me faithfully back again give me many a
>   year hence.
> . . . .
> O years and graves! O air and soil! Oh my dead, an aroma sweet!
> Exhale them perennial sweet death, years, centuries hence.³³

Whitman's mourner here sees these deaths neither as a tragic mistake nor as a frozen memory. Instead, they live as emanations of life lost, through the continued life of the land. Their bodies—gone from us—are memorials to their own deaths, but their bodies—present among us—are continuations of the lives they lived. She grasps their memories firmly, but allows them to continue along a path of death.

Contra Rorty, the lives and deaths of these young soldiers do not need to be interpellated into a national narrative to make political sense. They do not need to be lionized as martyrs nor heroized as warriors. They do not need to take sides after death, and to fit them into the Procrustean bed of nation building would do a disservice to their lives. Whitman's mourner feels their loss acutely, but as part of a simultaneous embrace of the continuation of life.

"What underlies the precedent songs," he explains, is "the seed I have sought to plant in them, / of joy, sweet joy, through many a year, in them, / (For them, for them have I lived, in them my work is done)."³⁴ Joy may seem a strange emotion to emerge from a prolonged analysis of death, but for Whitman the combination of life and death means that to celebrate one is to celebrate the other.

This is no mistake; Whitman's repetition of the theme throughout the final third of *Leaves of Grass* clearly spells out his attitude toward the end of life:

> Joy, shipmate, joy!
> (Pleas'd to my soul at death I cry,)
> Our life is closed, our life begins.³⁵

A reason underlies this joy. For with death come change, rebirth, and re-creation. One Song of Parting, "The Years of the Modern," begins with a description close to the idealistic futurism of Rorty, describing (among other wonders) "not America only, not only Liberty's nation but other nations preparing;" an embodied Freedom, "completely arm'd and victorious," arm in arm with "Law on one side and Peace on the other;" aristocracies and "the landmarks of European kings removed."[36] At such a time, Whitman sees "the People beginning their landmarks (all others give way)," and a profound individualism emergent. "Never was average man, his soul, more energetic, more like a God."[37]

Nor is this approach ignored by Whitman's prose, though it remains most in evidence when he discusses his own poetry. "And e'en for flush and proof of our America," he writes in a preface to *Leaves of Grass,* "for reminder, just as much, or more, in modes of towering pride and joy, I keep my special chants of death and immortality to stamp the coloring-finish of all, present and past."[38] In a footnote, Whitman describes his original plan for a volume of poetry subsequent and equal to *Leaves of Grass,* focused on death. Instead, he says, his corpus of poetry ends on such a note, which as well as emphasizing "death, immortality, and a free entrance into the spiritual world," also seeks "to set the key-stone to my democracy's enduring arch."

This, above all, is the goal Whitman has set for himself. "In the future of these States," Whitman famously intones, "must arise poets immenser far, and make great poems of death."[39] His prosaic hope, properly achieved, would lead to a nation and a series of individuals well prepared for life, in that they have properly understood death as harmonious with life. And yet, who can doubt that the final third of *Leaves of Grass* is an attempt to write the great poems of death?[40] To understand Whitman's achievement, an achievement he both denies and embraces in "Democratic Vistas," one must attend to what these poems of death can achieve.

Concluding

Rorty's hopes for the future, while important, are not enough. What must also be recognized is that a focus on the future often elides the present. Where Whitman speaks of what a future poetry can do—call into being a new kind of democratic nation, for example—is too easily misread as a call to the future. Whitman speaks of his now; his "I" is both the "I" of the individual man Whitman and the "I" of the nation. He, not some future poet, creates "Comradeship, uniting closer and closer not only the American States, but all nations and all humanity."[41]

Which is what ultimately made Rorty's life, energetic and vital as it was, come to an end. His future-oriented model for the achievement of "our" country must end in failure. The continued political and economic dominance of corporations in the United States, and the continuous emergence of other forms of powerful capitalistic mechanisms, make impossible his dream of a new old Left. For Microsoft and its ilk will not be defeated by a new coalition of labor and intellectuals. When it disappears in its turn, its corporate death will come from causes not yet apparent.

But Whitman lives on, just as dead. For Whitman's poetry reminds us that human lives, nations, and ideas exist within the present (whenever that present may be). Their value is not reducible to their permanence or their upkeep. A moment of exultation may outweigh an instauration or an institutionalization, no matter the earnest intent of any creator. List close, scholars dear: if "histories and statistics" are "not breathing and walking here, where would they all be?"[42]

Notes

1. See, for example, John Dewey, *Characters and Events: Popular Essays in Social and Political Philosophy*, ed. Joseph Ratner (New York: Henry Holt, 1929); James T. Kloppenberg, *Uncertain Victory: Social Democracy and Progressivism in European and American Thought, 1870–1920* (Oxford: Oxford University Press, 1986); Kevin Mattson, *Creating a Democratic Public: The Struggle for Urban Participatory Democracy during the Progressive Era* (University Park: Pennsylvania State University Press, 1998); and the essays in John Dewey: *Critical Assessments*, ed. John Tiles (New York: Routledge, 1992).

2. Richard Rorty, *Achieving our Country: Leftist Thought in Twentieth Century America* (Cambridge: Harvard University Press, 1998), 25.

3. For a telling analysis of how Rorty depends upon and reinforces a version of patriotism that is intrinsically exculpatory, no matter what history or event is considered, see Steven Johnston, *The Truth about Patriotism* (Durham: Duke University Press, 2007).

4. This (and the next two quotations) are chosen by Rorty, and thus I point the reader to his work rather than Whitman's (quoted in Rorty, *Achieving our Country*, 22).

5. Quoted ibid., 17.

6. Quoted ibid., 29.

7. Walt Whitman, "Democratic Vistas," in *Complete Poetry and Collected Prose* (New York: Library of America, 1982), 948. All subsequent Whitman citations are to this volume.

8. "Preface, 1876," 1011.

9. "Nationality (And Yet)," 1050.

10. Rorty, *Achieving our Country*, 99.

11. Ibid., 56.

12. See Gay W. Allen, "Walt Whitman—Nationalist or Proletariat?" *English Journal*, no. 26 (1937): 4852; Ralph Henry Gabriel, *The Course of American Democratic Thought* (New York: Roland Press, 1940); Cleveland Rogers, "Walt Whitman the Poet of Democracy," *Mentor* 6 (1923): 3–14; and Roland Sawyer, *Walt Whitman, The Prophet-Poet* (Boston: Gorham Press, 1913).

13. Leadie M. Clark, *Walt Whitman's Concept of the American Common Man* (New York: Philosophical Library, 1955), 111–51.

14. Whitman, "The Eighteenth Presidency: Voice of Walt Whitman to Each Young Man in the Nation, North, South, East, and West" (1856), 1319.

15. Rorty, *Achieving our Country*, 138.

16. Larzer Ziff, "Whitman and the Crowd," *Critical Inquiry* 10, no. 4 (1984): 582.

17. "Starting from Paumanok," 181.

18. Ibid., 177.

19. "A Song of the Rolling Earth," 363.

20. Ibid., 366.

21. Gay Wilson Allen and Charles T. Davis, "Introduction to Whitman's Poems," *A Century of Whitman Criticism*, ed. Edwin Haviland Miller (Bloomington: Indiana University Press, 1969), 330.

22. "Crossing Brooklyn Ferry," 319.

23. Stephen John Mack, *The Pragmatic Whitman: Reimagining American Democracy* (Iowa City: University of Iowa Press, 2002), 38–59. Mack overtly aligns his project with Rorty's call in his introduction, where he explains Rorty's exhortations and follows with "I intend to make just such an examination of the civic religion behind Whitman's patriotism" (xvii).

24. Ibid., 56.

25. "Crossing Brooklyn Ferry," 313.

26. "A Song for Occupations," 359.

27. "Transpositions," 551.

28. Preface, 1976, 1006n.

29. "A Backward Glance O'er Travel'd Roads," 657.

30. "No Labor-Saving Machine," 283.
31. "Youth, Day, Old Age, and Night," 688.
32. "Song at Sunset," 604.
33. "Pensive on Her Dead Gazing," 605–6.
34. "As They Draw to a Close," 607.
35. "Joy, Shipmate, Joy!" 608.
36. "Years of the Modern," 597–98.
37. Ibid., 598.
38. "Preface, 1876," 1005–6.
39. "Democratic Vistas," 988.
40. For more argument as to the segmentarity of *Leaves of Grass*, see Kerry C. Larson, *Whitman's Drama of Consensus* (Chicago: University of Chicago Press, 1988).
41. "Democratic Vistas," 1024.
42. "A Song for Occupations," 359.

CHAPTER 13

Democratic Enlightenment: Whitman and Aesthetic Education

Morton Schoolman

> One part does not counteract another part,
> he is the joiner, he
> sees how they join.
> —Walt Whitman, "Song of the Answerer," from *Leaves of Grass*

Democratic Vistas: The Map to Whitman's Poetry

ROUGHLY TWELVE TOPICS CAN be distinguished in Whitman's essay *Democratic Vistas*, all of which he brings to bear on the three questions he struggles with most.[1] What constitutes the uniqueness of democracy in America? What is required for American democracy to develop its unique potential and break with all past societies, their cultures, and the principles on which they are based? How would global history be altered if America's unique democratic potential were to reach fruition? To appreciate how Whitman's discussion of these twelve topics answers these questions, special attention should be paid to a structural feature belonging to *Democratic Vistas*. As each is introduced, none of the topics is discussed fully before he moves on to the next. Each is examined only in part before yielding to another introduced for the first time or being taken up again. By the time his essay concludes, all topics have been returned to often, while certain have been treated more often and more completely. Reading Whitman with the structural logic of *Democratic Vistas* in mind highlights the topics around which it revolves, underscores any among them that play a more pivotal role in his argument, and focuses our analysis of his essay on its three central questions.

Individual—Mass—Equality

Whitman writes more than four thousand of his nearly twenty-six-thousand-word essay before signaling his intention to "proceed with my speculations, Vistas" (964). In this prologue, as I want to describe it, to *Democratic Vistas*, the structure of his argument unfolds as he foregrounds all but two of the topics he will engage in the essay.

Whitman begins with brief observations on America's democratic ambitions with which he celebrates its "democratic republican principle" and "theory of development and perfection by voluntary standards, and self-reliance" (953). By the democratic republican principle, Whitman understands "political liberty [and] equality" (966), or equal rights recognizing individuals universally to be the *same*, whereas "development and perfection by voluntary standards, and self-reliance" refer to the individual's right to self-determination, the right to be and to become *different*. Equal rights as sameness and individual rights as difference are suggested by the plurality of meanings Whitman associates with equality and personal development in his essay as a whole. On the side of equality, he speaks of the "People" (or the "people"), the "mass, or lump character," the "leveler, the unyielding principle of the average," while on the side of personal development he refers to "lessons of variety and freedom," a "large variety of character," "individualism" or "individuality," "personalism" or "varied personalism."

Wherever Whitman discusses these and analogous terms, he is returning to his first and second topics, the individual and the mass, which he maintains stand in contradiction and must be reconciled. Whitman has in mind this problem of contradiction and reconciliation when in short order he joins his opening observations to the promise not to "gloss over the appalling dangers of universal suffrage," specifically the "people's crudeness, vice, caprices," about which, he reports, "I mainly write this essay" (954). Untutored popular suffrage threatens a range of democratic convictions, individuality in his estimation the most important.

To balance the undemocratic sensibility expressed by such a blunt circumspection about the mass, Whitman turns to attack remnants of feudalism he insists America has to "surmount . . . or else prove the most tremendous failure of time" (954). Feudalism, the caste-based enemy of equality, is "grown not for America" (998). Whitman's concern with lingering feudal institutions extends to the influence of ecclesiastic practices on democracy's private sphere, where mores insinuated by religious teachings contribute to the perpetuation of inequality, religious inequality surely, though he may well have had gender inequality in mind as well. He objects to the church's sustained impact on "education . . . social standards and literature" *despite* "feudalism . . . palpably retreating from political institutions" in America (955). Whitman's anxiety about feudal influences on moral education and manners not only illustrates his allegiance to equality. It reveals that for him the achievement of equality anticipates the question of what form the civic education of the people in a democratic society ought to take. Whitman eventually will allow all "democratic vistas," America's future prospects, that is, to rest on the answer to this question.

Artwork of the Future—Nativity—Cultural Revolution—Hegemony

Once his prologue begins to wind its way through the individual, the mass, and the affirmation of equality represented by the American imperative to surmount feudalism, Whitman has positioned himself to introduce the topic around which will revolve further considerations of the former three as well as all subsequent topics. Realizing America's democratic vistas depends, without exception, on the unique, native development of its art, specifically literature, the highest form of art for Whitman (997). From the opening to the closing paragraphs of *Democratic Vistas,* Whitman is insistent. Democracy in America needs "Literatures . . . expressing democracy and the modern," a "New World literature" and "democratic literature of the future," and it "can never prove itself beyond cavil, until it founds and luxuriantly grows its own" "native literary and artistic" forms (955, 995, 996, 955, 1018). A new class of literati must emerge univocally committed to "displacing all that exists, or that has been produced anywhere in the past, under opposite influences" of inequality and the absence of rights. To begin anew so comprehensively requires America to refuse the examples of "All the best experience of humanity" (996). Remarkably, Whitman proposes that although the "Old and New Testament, Homer, Eschylus, Plato, Juvenal, &c," and "the likes" of these and "what belongs to" and "has grown of" these all have arrived at America's shores as "little ships," which by "miracles . . . have [been] buoy'd [and] convey'd . . . over long wastes, darkness, lethargy, ignorance" (997, 996, 996), America nevertheless must choose,

> appalling as that would be, to lose all, actual ships,
> this day fasten'd by wharf, or floating on wave, and see them,
> with all their cargoes, scuttled and sent to the bottom. (997)

With one of the most startling recommendations in the history of Western literature, Whitman proposes that, by means of the work of art, America must break with all past cultures as the prerequisite for forging a new beginning. Indeed, although *Democratic Vistas* (1871) was published nearly a century after America's founding, Whitman believes democracy in America to be as yet in its "embryo condition" (983). Despite its epic political revolution and economic achievements, which he designates the first and second stages of democracy for having ushered in the "American programme" of "universal man" and the "material prosperity" (1001) on which universal well-being rests, Whitman's claim is that America either is not quite born or yet remains in the circumstances of its birth. Whitman's thought is to join the fourth of his topics, the American artwork of the future, to the fifth of his topics, the nativity of American democracy, which lies in the "present . . . the legitimate birth of the past" (953). American democracy will be born through the birth of an archetypal American art, a literature on which everything American will be patterned and that stands not in the least on the shoulders of the Western and non-Western cultural past. Through the work to be performed by such a "great original literature," America will have an art that is "the justification and reliance (in some respects the sole reliance,) of American democracy" (957). An art of justification and reliance, Whitman means, is one from which democracy truly would develop. For Whitman the nativity of democracy in America is a "long-continued nebular state" (995), a founding continuous with the evolution of an American literary culture that will sponsor the future formation of a fully developed democracy. Why democratic development depends on art is Whitman's sixth topic.

Literature, the American artwork of the future and bridge to the democratic future of America, is assigned this weighty historical burden, ultimately a world-historical burden, as shall become evident—to remedy the considerable deficiencies of the first two stages of American development. Each stage appears to have made as much progress on its own terms as to Whitman seemed necessary to have proven the nature and extent of its real contribution to American democratic life. If Whitman estimates the accomplishment of the American Revolution, in his words the "planning and putting on record the political foundation rights of immense masses of people" (1000), to be of an "amplitude rivaling the operations of the physical cosmos" (953), he adjusts the value of its political stage of development by reminding us "that the people of our land may all read and write, and may all possess the right to vote—and yet the main things may be entirely lacking" (956). And the requisites for democracy neglected by America's political revolution are multiplied by its second, economic stage of development. Notwithstanding the benefits of economic prosperity, to Whitman "uplifting the masses out of their sloughs," in its "materialistic developments" democracy "is, so far, an almost complete failure in its social aspects, and in really grand religious, moral, literary, and esthetic results" (962).

Whitman imagines what I will call "democratic enlightenment," a cultural revolution in its effects exceeding those of America's political and economic revolutions. His insight is greatly advanced—the enlightenment of modern times was not a womb from which democracy in America could be born, as it was limited to moral-ethical (political) and instrumental (economic) rationalities retarding or arresting its development after engendering its first two stages. Without a cultural revolution revolving around aesthetics, "our modern civilization," Whitman decides gravely, "with all its improvements, is in vain, and we are on the road to a destiny, a status, equivalent, in its real world, to that of the fabled damned" (1016). In his own time, Whitman concedes, America may "dominate the world" economically (954). Far more important will be America's world-cultural hegemony, Whitman's seventh topic, "a nationality superior to any hither known" (955) able "to dominate," to the point of being able to "even destroy"—as in *Democratic Vistas* it is evident Whitman himself is bent on destroying—what institutions earlier cultures had bequeathed, those "little ships" bearing cultural traditions then continuing to prevail within America (998). Whitman foresees America setting the democratic example to be replicated globally, for only "Soul has ever really, gloriously led, or ever can lead. (This Soul—its other name, in these Vistas, is LITERATURE)" (1005). Democratic enlightenment is to proceed by way of aesthetic education.

Whitman's conception of democratic enlightenment by means of aesthetic education will not elaborate normative ideals comparable to democratic visions before, during, and after him. Although his work exhibits an abiding concern for the poor and suffering, and he finds extreme material inequalities to be obscene, he proposes no theories of classless society or of government maximizing the welfare of its citizens or of justice. His vision is designed to realize the principle of *all-inclusiveness* on which democratic societies, their political and legal systems and political economies, and their theories together all falter. Democratic enlightenment, proceeding by way of art, will teach us to leave no one out by overcoming the evil at the root of exclusion.

Poetry—Reconciliation—Identity

Whitman's readers will go afield if they interpret his bold analogy between literature and the soul to imply an overly generous conception of what counts as literature. While Whitman does not overlook or explicitly omit literary genres, throughout *Democratic Vistas* he accords only a few the revolutionary merit he reserves for literature. A new metaphysics, "perhaps," though "certainly a new Poetry," Whitman reports, will be "the only sure and worthy supports and expressions of the American democracy" (1008). Whitman is never equivocal about the privileged role poetry is to play, his eighth topic. Democracy can "prove itself" only by originating poems (955). He admits to his specialized interest in the bearing on democratic vistas of "imaginative literature," and in this category to his still narrower interest in "poetry, the stock of all" (958). And he holds that "some two or three really original American poets . . . mounting the horizon like planets, stars of the first magnitude . . . would give more . . . than all [America's] Constitutions, legislative and judicial ties, and all its hitherto political, warlike, or materialistic experiences" (959).

Improving on the pedagogical work of political institutions, poetry is charged with teaching all-important *political* lessons about democracy and the modern. Whitman's enlightenment project of aesthetic education is a democratic politics, not a general education in the arts and sciences. If it were the latter, he would conscript the great books and authors, the miraculous "little ships" we saw he discarded. Surely equality is one political lesson, as Whitman appears to convey by inviting the poet to replace the priest—the "priest departs . . . the poet of the modern is wanted" (956)—alluding to his demand to displace the remnants of feudalism in America yet supporting systems of fixed caste and class relations. Equality is paired with another broad political objective to be accomplished by aesthetic education, with regard to which he calculates the effect of poetry on politics to be greater than "popular superficial suffrage" (956). By "comprehending and effusing for the men and women of the States what is universal, native, common to all," which is to compose works that absorb and express the "central spirit and the idiosyncrasies" of the people, poetry addresses the "whole mass of American mentality, taste, belief" (959, 979, 956). With generalities of this sort abounding in *Democratic Vistas,* Whitman is arguing that a democratic ethos already lying inchoate in Americans waits for its fullest expression and further development upon poets, "races of orbic bards . . . sweet democratic despots of the west" (998), who can articulate a cultural image for the People—a "single image-making work for them" (979)—able to seep more deeply into hearts and minds to form democratic personalities and characters. Painted for the most part with such broad brushstrokes, Whitman's own image of the political goals of a democratic education through poetry nevertheless eventually focuses on a more definite pedagogical mission to be carried out by imaginative literature, namely, reconciling the contradiction between the individual and the mass, his ninth topic.

Reconciliation, which he makes a particular point of explaining is "our task" (965), is implicit throughout Whitman's exhortations on the individual and the mass. If there are times he seems to favor the individual over the mass, or vice versa, his reflections on balance neutralize the apparent prejudice to restore the image of reconciliation he is intent on maintaining. Nearing the halfway mark of *Democratic Vistas,* for example, Whitman asks what it is that civilization, in the sense of a whole or society as a whole, both rests upon and has as its object, an object, he emphasizes, to which "*all bends*"? (982, my italics). While seeming to privilege the individual, his reply, that civilization rests on "rich, luxuriant, varied personalism [individualism, individuality]" (982), in fact circles back to the sentiment expressed in the first line of his essay—"Nature through the universe" and "New World politics" together illustrate the "greatest lessons," those of "variety and freedom." Civilization, nature coextensive with the universe, and New World democratic politics, Whitman is arguing, all seamlessly incorporate parts moving independently, contingently, *and synchronously* in relation to their wholes. All are models of reconciliation, analogies to reconciled parts and wholes Whitman supports with a comment on John Stuart Mill. Mill's "profound essay on Liberty in the future" proved to Whitman's satisfaction that in modernity what ennobles the relations of peoples to their nations, what produces a "truly grand nationality," as he refers to this model of a reconciled whole, is individualism, that is, "a large variety of character" and the "full play for human nature to expand itself in numberless and even conflicting directions" (953). Yet, whereas variety is given in nature and human nature, individualism in democratic society still must be perfected—an individual's particular variety of excellence must be developed. To the extent what is unique to individuals does achieve such perfection, which it is for "literature, songs [poetry], esthetics" to ensure (982), it is then that the "aggregate," the mass, will receive its "deepest tinges" and "character" (966). In all these and similar ways, Whitman consistently reconciles the advancements he values for the one with the progress he secures for the many.

Of course, as much as an end in itself that also doubles as a means to the end of collective progress, individualism and its perfection are pursued by Whitman to internally differentiate and break up the mass, to weaken normalizing pressures constraining individual development or the proliferation of "variety." Precisely because he believes communities will "rule themselves" if political education, "beginning with individuals and ending there again," trains each in practice to be the "separate and complete subject for freedom" each is in principle (971), he worries about the individual's loss of self in "countless masses of adjustments" (986). Perhaps from such arguments it would be fair to conclude that Whitman does not equally weight the democratic salience of the mass with that of the individual, and that his valorization of variety, personalism, individuality, and so on unevenly weights "difference," our late modern term of art favoring one of two values only apparently being reconciled for the future benefit of American democratic development.

For all the importance Whitman attaches to the individual, however, difference finally is neither more nor less important than the mass. He chastises literature for its past neglect of "the People," which he surmises issued from some basic hostility of the literati toward "the rude rank spirit of the democracies" (968). To the contrary, Whitman imagines a "rare . . . artist-mind" able to dissolve this antipathy. An aesthetic sensibility of a "cosmical" breadth "lit with the Infinite" would discover its counterparts in the "manifold and oceanic qualities" (967) spanned by the people and in "their vast, artistic contrasts of lights and shades" (968). All such aesthetic qualities and contrasts illuminate a variegated, individuated, capacious mass ignored by a contemporaneous literature packaged for the "mean flat average" (998). Focusing on the aesthetic differentiation of the mass, Whitman ingeniously revises our concept of the people. Rather than uniform throughout, the People are internally differentiated, as internally differentiated as the individuals of which it is composed, albeit individual differences are suppressed or as yet remain undeveloped, the situation to be corrected by poetry. For this reason, it makes sense when Whitman argues that the individual and the mass "are contradictory" and "our task is to reconcile them," and at the same time—and in the same breath—that *"Only [from the mass]* . . . comes the other, comes the chance of individualism" (964–65, my italics). Whether aesthetic education perfects individuality or the mass, in other words, it has the same object of enlightenment. For in Whitman's aesthetic view, individuals as "variety" and the mass as "contrasts of lights and shades" are one and the same. Either art develops individual differences, "variety," or it perfects differences within the mass, "contrasts." Actually two names for difference, variety and contrasts, indicate that the contradiction between the individual and the mass is only historical, not essential. At bottom, *essentially*, the two already are reconciled, a virtual reconciliation—a "democratic vista" in Whitman's terms—that waits upon the poet and poetry to forge it into a reality justifying—developing or perfecting—democracy in the future.

Since reconciliation between the individual and the mass is a virtual reality, does Whitman at some point not also tell us what specific form reconciliation takes? At first the answer to this question seems beyond our interpretive reach because he conceptualizes reconciliation at a high level of generalization where he speaks directly either of an aesthetically enlightened people or individual. We hear of the people's "perfect beauty, tenderness and pluck" (970), their "moral conscience" (961) and "moral conscientiousness" (1006), and the strengthening of their belief in democracy and humanity and of the faith of men and women in each other. Regarding the individual, he refers to the perfection of character, "a main requirement" (1005), a "true personality, develop'd, exercised proportionately in body, mind, and spirit" (993), and the fruition of "freely branching and blossoming" individuality, "bearing golden fruit" (992), and the like. Whitman regularly treats us to such vague normative aspirations for democracy (whose poignancy is not diminished by their dreamlike quality). Perhaps to be impatient with Whitman is unfair. After all, can he say more than this since democratic vistas, including reconciliation, all are future achievements? At one point, Whitman pauses frankly to confess this handicap—"Thus we presume to write, as it were, upon things that exist not, and travel by maps yet unmade and a blank" (981). Yet at another moment, Whitman more confidently ventures to "formulate beyond this present vagueness" and succeeds in visualizing the future shape of certain democratic vistas. One such instance is his model of native personality, a vivid and detailed picture of a healthy, athletic, "well-begotten selfhood" belonging to future Americans (987). Similarly, our inquiry into how Whitman understands reconciliation is not disappointed. To the extent it must if the meaning of his concept is to be fleshed out, Whitman's image of reconciliation comes into focus sharply in the context of his discussion of identity, the tenth topic he introduces in *Democratic Vistas*.

Whitman admits to being haunted continually by "the fear of conflicting and irreconcilable interiors and the lack of a common skeleton, knitting all close." Over the "long period to come," he worries, "nothing is plainer than the need . . . of a fusion of the States into the only reliable identity, the moral and artistic one" (959). To be sure, at one level Whitman's concern with a shared identity is in reference to the Civil War and its divisive aftermath; America's problem was to secure a national identity that had remained tenuous. At another level, for Whitman the conflict represents the latest, most egregious example of social differences in contradiction and need of reconciliation. For as *Democratic Vistas* progresses, Whitman evinces a broader sociological interest in society's exclusion of minorities.

> Of all dangers to a nation, as things exist in our day, there can be no greater one than having certain portions of the people set off from the rest by a line drawn—they not privileged as others, but degraded, humiliated, made of no account. (973)

Approaching the conclusion of his essay, Whitman further broadens his sociological interest by thinking of the predicament of difference as a historical problem America could overcome. "Long enough," he writes,

> have the People been listening to poems in which common humanity, deferential, bends low, humiliated, acknowledging superiors. But America listens to no such poems. Erect, inflated, and fully self-esteeming be the chant; and then America will listen with pleased ears. (1004)

From our contemporary perspective, it is not possible to read such thoughts as mere concerns with legal rights and formal equality. Certain of Whitman's terms have an even larger resonance—degradation, humiliation, bending low, and inferiority are symptomatic of the marginalization of difference. Healing these injuries and ending the exclusions they entail require more than the formal equality legal rights bestow. What is required is that identity incorporate the difference it excludes, in the way Whitman's "fusion of the States" would constitute a national identity incorporating the Northern and Southern differences excluded by the way each side self-identified before and after the Civil War. Or in the way the "People," a term Whitman most often capitalizes to indicate it sets itself apart as a distinct identity, would be inclusive of the individual differences he associates with the contrasts internally differentiating the mass of the common people.

Whitman's many examples of an all-inclusive American identity actually are parallel descriptions of reconciliation whereby identity becomes different by creating itself through its *inclusion* of difference. Inclusive of rather than repelling difference, identity no longer forces difference down or outside as the "contradiction," to recall Whitman's term, it required to affirm its own integrity whenever it believed difference threatening to that integrity. For Whitman, the reconciliation of contradictions between social differences through an aesthetic education assumes the form of an aesthetic constitution of identity. Superintended by poetry, identity would include difference to become different, an act of creation that abolishes the marginalization and exclusion of difference, abolishes, in a word, Otherness. Moving identity and difference beyond contradiction, Whitman achieves reconciliation—between North and South, the People and the people, the individual and the mass. Reconciliation between identity and difference is the democratic vista looming largest in Whitman's imagination. It is the answer to the three questions I proposed Whitman struggles with most. First, it is the real possibility of reconciliation that for Whitman makes democracy in America unique; second, not just equality and rights or wealth—the first two, inadequate stages of democratic evolution—but poetry is what is required for American democracy to develop its unique potential for reconciliation through which it will break with all past societies, their cultures, and the principles on which they are based; and, third, global history will be altered through America's record of reconciliation, a recorded history of proving democracy "alone can bind, and ever seeks to bind, all nations, all men, of however various and distant lands, into a brotherhood, a family . . . making the races comrades, and fraternizing all" (972–73).

The Unknown—Death

If Whitman's democratic ideal of reconciliation is to leave no one out of the ensemble of individualities composing the mass, how is such all-inclusive openness to difference to be created and then sustained? Haunted by the specter of divided identity, we saw, Whitman appears not entirely confidant that America can reconcile its social contradictions. To thus ensure that America creates itself as an open society, Whitman builds two metaphysical safeguards into democratic culture, the ideas of the "unknown" and "death," the eleventh and twelfth topics he introduces relatively late in *Democratic Vistas,* although both fall within the province of poetry.

Democracy's openness to difference appears tightly connected to the idea of the unknown, as is suggested when Whitman says:

> As we have shown the New World including in itself the all-leveling aggregate of democracy, we show it also including the all-varied, all-permitting, all-free theorem of individuality, and erecting therefor a lofty and hitherto unoccupied framework or platform, broad enough for *all* . . . realizing, above the rest, that known humanity, in deepest sense, is fair adhesion to itself, for purposes beyond—and that, finally, the personality of mortal life is most important with reference to the immortal, the unknown, the spiritual, the only permanently real, which as the ocean waits for and receives the rivers, waits for each and all (994, my italics).

To decipher the relation between democracy and the unknown, we should notice Whitman's contention that those on the American platform—which includes *all*—realize the unknown confers highest importance on mortal life. Although Whitman's claim is somewhat obscure, it is clarified where he appears troubled such a realization becomes precarious the more democracy is influenced one-sidedly by modernity through scientism and the alliance of scientific progress and material prosperity, or "realism." To "confront the growing excess and arrogance of realism," Whitman advises, the idea of the unknown "must be brought forward with authority" (1009). Whitman's argument is that the idea of the unknown marks the limits of scientific understanding, and by extension the limits of the civilized life scientific progress makes possible. Establishing limits to what can be known, the unknown shields the plausibility of metaphysical, spiritual, and religious ideas (he does not distinguish one from the other) important to mortal life if it is to graduate to a stage of existence higher than the second, materialistic stage it has reached. With this argument, Whitman advances his project for a democratic enlightenment. By circumscribing the limits of science, the unknown protects poetry, for the metaphysical, spiritual, and religious ideas shielded by the unknown are sources of Whitman's poetic inspiration and sources he finds for great poetry generally. Just as Whitman had argued democracy depends on poetry, he argues now that the possibility of poetry depends on poeticizing the unknown so that it retains a prominent stature in the popular imagination. Hence he so tightly weds democracy to the unknown.

How does poetry's work of aesthetic education, its pedagogy of democratic reconciliation through the all-inclusiveness of difference, rest on poeticizing the unknown? I will turn to work this out shortly, and at the moment I can offer only a clue to the relation between poetry and the unknown since Whitman says little about it in *Democratic Vistas*. What little he does say nevertheless reflects profoundly on the enlightenment of a democratic society. Poets, he announces, must emerge who "make great poems of death" (1012). Such poems will not eulogize death or offer frightening or consoling images of the afterlife. Death, which Whitman understands philosophically in materialist terms, is not the end of life, rather its continuation in other and unknowable forms. "Nothing," Whitman declares, "ever is or can be lost, nor ever die, nor soul, nor matter." If it were to incorporate this view of death as the metamorphoses of life into unknown, unfathomable forms, poetry would be consistent with the "rational physical being of man, with the ensembles of time and space, and with this vast and multiform show" (1012). Speaking of death as change of form and not life's end, poetry, Whitman is saying, would imitate nature, would include, as nature includes, all things in their endlessly changing forms, and thus all time and all space through which all things in nature pass as they assume eternally, infinitely changing forms. To certify nature as the standard for poetry, in fact, Whitman makes nature and poetry into interchangeable terms. Just as poetry, after nature's example, must include all, nature, containing all things in all their forms throughout all time and space in which their evolution continues interminably, is *"the only complete, actual poem"* (1012, my italics). Here, then, we find the explanation for what is perhaps Whitman's most decisive theoretical move, his claim that the American democracy of the future could have no finer teacher than poetry. Modeled on poetry as poetry is modeled on nature, democracy in America would not be less than all-inclusive of the infinite variations found in both.

To summarize my first arguments—in *Democratic Vistas*, Whitman's opening observations on American democracy distinguish the principles of the individual and the mass, and by problematizing popular suffrage, he alludes to a contradiction between them betraying a fundamental conflict within America's democratic convictions. Whitman also indicts America's feudal remnants for their anti-equalitarian influence on American mores, there implying the need for civic education as an overture to his proposal for an original American literature that breaks definitively, not only with feudalism, but also with all past cultural history.

Democracy's very nativity, America's authentic democratic birth and development, he contends, depends on a cultural revolution, the genesis of an underived, original American democratic aesthetic, the artwork of the future democratic America. Whitman endorses aesthetic education as the means of reconciling the contradiction between the individual and the mass, and as a prelude to these proposals he offers two predictions. He envisions that only through aesthetic education will democracy exceed its fledgling political and economic stages and, once fully fledged, America's democratic enlightenment will dominate the world stage and hegemonically propel global democratic development.

From all forms of literature, Whitman elects poetry to carry out the work of aesthetic education, and the reconciliation of the individual and the mass are foremost among the tasks he commissions the poet and poetry to perform. Within the context of Whitman's discussion of identity, it becomes possible to flesh out the form he believes reconciliation would take—it assumes the form of a relation in which identity becomes different by incorporating difference. Ideally, an aesthetically constructed identity would include all, leaving outside no one who is different. *Reconciliation appears as the abolition of the Other.* Reconciliation would be the realization of Whitman's vision of a future democratic America from which would be engendered nothing less "long ages hence" than "a new earth and a new man" (981). It is the best-articulated vista of an otherwise general collection of democratic vistas to be realized through aesthetic education.

The privilege Whitman accords reconciliation among all democratic vistas suggests he believes it is the purpose for which democracy is constructed. And it suggests reconciliation is the purpose for which he constructs his argument for an original American art and the democratic enlightenment for which it holds the promise. Accordingly, Whitman proposes cultural ideas—a poetry of the unknown and its great poems of death—to create and maintain the all-inclusiveness and openness to difference defining democracy in America, to secure the reconciliation of the individual and the mass.

In these first arguments, I have pursued an interpretation of *Democratic Vistas* informed by what I find to be the structural logic of Whitman's composition. Throughout my discussion, I have tacked back and forth between Whitman's prologue, as I have called it, and the text following to trace the topics he gradually distinguishes and weaves together into a whole as he returns often to each to elaborate its meaning and significance and connections to others. So densely packed with ideas is Whitman's essay, however, it could be argued to the contrary that his interest is in topics other than those whose centrality I underscore. Hypothetically, it might be objected, in particular, that if Whitman's interest is in the twelve topics I contend he selected on the basis of his commitment to a project of aesthetic education, how are we to account for his glaring omission of both poets and poetry exemplifying, even to some small extent, the future aesthetic on which he argues the future of democratic enlightenment depends? Should Whitman the destroyer of the cultural past not also have shown examples that the literature of the future should resemble as it takes form with respect to the topics, the constellation of ideas, from which democracy is to be born?

To explain Whitman's alleged omissions, of course, we could recall his self-conscious explanation of the necessary vagueness with which any future projections of democratic vistas must be surrounded. My preferred explanation, however, and my response to our hypothetical objection, is that Whitman omits no such exemplar and that it is with us through all his formulations of the standards a future poetry and its poets must meet if they are to sponsor democratic growth. The poetry of the "future" Whitman describes in *Democratic Vistas* is his own. After all, why would he recommend standards for an art he has not himself met? I defend the topics I have found Whitman to be preoccupied with in *Democratic Vistas* by proposing they are the map of Whitman's own work, the key to unlocking the deepest purpose and meaning of *Leaves of Grass*. That purpose is to offer an aesthetic solution to the problem of reconciliation. Democratic enlightenment would be spread through a poetry equipped to "perfect" democracy by educating its people to realize the principle of all-inclusiveness by overcoming their practice of treating difference as Otherness. Through aesthetic education, democratic enlightenment becomes democracy's barrier to evil, the evil of constructing, marginalizing, excluding, punishing, and exterminating an Other.

Ideally, from here I should follow with an analysis of Whitman's poetry that locates within it the twelve topics I have found to be central to *Democratic Vistas* and show how they circulate through his poetry to form the defining project of *Leaves of Grass*—a poetry that teaches reconciliation as the realization of the all-inclusiveness of social differences by overcoming the construction of Otherness, a project of democratic enlightenment through aesthetic education, democratic enlightenment as democracy's barrier to evil. Through that analysis we would discover that in *Leaves of Grass* Whitman elaborates his idea of reconciliation to consist of three interrelated dimensions. The first of these, realizing all-inclusiveness by overcoming the practice of converting difference to Otherness, appears in *Democratic Vistas* as the essential meaning of reconciliation itself. If reconciliation is to deeply root democratic life, however, it must be more than accepting social differences just as they appear, more than a mere all-inclusive tolerance of differences. Whitman thus also designs poetry in *Leaves of Grass* to teach reconciliation as an *aesthetic receptivity* to difference. A democratic people must be drawn to the inclusion of difference in their own lives, sensuously attracted to difference as an image of how their own lives potentially could become different. Thus, finally, reconciliation would entail a social relation among individuals where they actually become different by *imitating* each other's differences, where they create themselves differently through an aesthetic, mimetic relation to the social differences surrounding them to which they have become receptive.

Reconciliation's three dimensions of all-inclusiveness, aesthetic receptivity, and imitation are wonderfully illustrated by Whitman's verses 15 and 16 of "Song of Myself."[2] With the famous concluding lines of verse 15,

> And such as it is to be of these more or less I am,
> And of these one and all I weave the song of myself. (328–29)

Whitman imagines that through imitation he creates himself from the images of the nearly one hundred social differences surrounding him he includes in that verse (264–326) and the verse following (330–48). Imitating differences "more or less," as he importantly qualifies his mimetic praxis, Whitman explains he does not intend to become their exact copy. Rather, he means that without exception everyone around him offers him something different of value—some belief or insight or understanding, an idea or ideal, a sense or sensibility, a bodily gesture or facial expression, in a phrase, another way of being—from which he can enlarge himself to a greater or lesser extent by adopting it, *more or less,* as his own. And by reporting that this expansive plurality of different social identities "tend inward to me, and I tend outward to them" (327), Whitman expresses his receptivity to all differences he has included in his poetry, the receptivity that is prelude to his self-weaving. By means of receptivity and mimesis, Whitman creates his own all-inclusive, democratically constructed identity. Genders ("The spinning girl," 271; "the marksman," 284; "The paving-man," 296; "The bride," 303), occupations ("The machinist," 280; "The President," 308), vocations ("The connoisseur," 291; "The conductor," 298), classes ("The farmer," 272; "The groups of newly-come immigrants," 285; "the great Secretaries," 308), cultural ("A Southerner soon as a Northerner," 335), racial ("The quadroon girl," 279; "The half-breed," 282; "The squaw," 290), and religious ("The deacons," 270; the "priest," 348) personas, most belonging to the norm, many Others ("The lunatic," 273; "The prostitute," 305; the "Prisoner," 348) on the outside of the norm and looking in, all of whom in verse 16 he describes as forming *his own* irresistible diversity ("I resist anything better than my own diversity," 349), are included in Whitman's democratic model of identity so often represented throughout *Leaves of Grass* as his model of democracy in America. With the words "I am large, I contain multitudes" (1326) in "Song of Myself," Whitman effects a reconciliation within his identity of the plurality of different voices he imitates that compel him to "contradict" himself ("Do I contradict myself? Very well then I contradict myself," 1324–25). In "Our Old Feuillage," Whitman's self-same model of reconciliation is again encountered as "my lands"—the great differences among America's states—"inevitably united and made ONE IDENTITY" (77).[3]

What might be the significance of Whitman's tripartite concept of reconciliation if it were fully assembled from *Leaves of Grass*? And what might be the significance of the project of democratic enlightenment—of an aesthetic education where reconciliation would be taught by poetry?

Inseparably tying together an *all-inclusive acceptance* of differences just as they appear, a *receptivity* to differences as images of how lives could become different, and the *imitation* of differences as images through which lives actually would become different, Whitman's proposal for aesthetic education and his image of reconciliation would be among the most radical notions in the history of political thought, perhaps the most radical in modern democratic theory. As Whitman imagines it, reconciliation would establish democracy as the one form of life where differences can exist together free of the conflicts and contradictions and violence attached to the construction of Otherness, where, no longer encumbered by the stigma of Otherness, each form of difference would present a future image of how each of us can envision actually becoming different through the mimetic relation to difference democratic enlightenment teaches. In a democracy every image of difference would be an image of a future that mimesis makes available to all who would imitate the differences surrounding them, a future lost to every life separated from differences excluded as the Other.

Here I only can begin this much longer discussion of Whitman's tripartite concept of reconciliation that I develop fully elsewhere.[4] For my present purposes, I will limit myself to explicating just the first of the three dimensions I have proposed reconciliation takes in Whitman's poetry by demonstrating how it crystallizes in *Leaves of Grass* out of the philosophical work performed by one of his twelve key topics, that of the "unknown." Although my discussion will be confined to the first of Whitman's three dimensions of reconciliation, democracy's all-inclusiveness of differences just as they appear, it will clarify the way in which Whitman develops his project of democratic enlightenment from a poetry designed to perform the work of aesthetic education.

Reconciliation through an Aesthetic Orientation to Appearances

If Whitman believed his own art discharged the cultural-political tasks of enlightenment that he assigned poets and that it had met the standards to which he held poetry, he surely would have had confidence in his ability to use language and in the powers of language itself. Yet when he regards language, it seems a less than potent site for poetry to achieve his aesthetic ends. In "A Song of the Rolling Earth," Whitman sings:

> A song of the rolling earth, and of words according,
> Were you thinking that those were the words, those upright lines?
>   those curves, angles, dots?
> No, those are not the words, the substantial words are in the
>   ground and sea,
> They are in the air, they are in you. (1–4)
> The workmanship of souls is by those inaudible words of the earth,
> The masters know the earth's words and use them more than
>   audible words. (15–16)
> I swear I begin to see little or nothing in audible words. (98)[5]

Language is inadequate, a problematic aesthetic resource for poetry if that were the sum of Whitman's argument. It is not. Poetry reflexively highlights the brute insufficiencies of language to illuminate a line dividing language from a world of meaning inaccessible to it. Language is not so much impoverished as there are *worlds*—the ground or sea, the air, the earth, nature, each of us—whose essential meaning is remote, "inaudible." Unless Whitman is specific, such as when he speaks of "the ground and sea . . . the air," I will use the term "world" to stand in generically for whatever he believes possesses meaning inaccessible to poetry (nature, being, and human being in their every form and aspect), meaning he will blanket as the "unknown." Poets, "masters," do not employ language to express the inexpressible, a Romantic view of art with which Whitman here parts company. Poetry confirms, does not dissolve, boundaries dividing us from the underlying, unknowable reality of the world. Using "inaudible words," words paradoxically unable to be spoken or written, poets express the *silence* of worlds having no voice. It is a silence the poet makes us hear. "I speak not," Whitman explains, "yet if you hear me not of what avail am I to you?" (26). Where speech is inarticulate appear the "words of the *eloquent dumb* great mother" earth (41, my italics), as appear all words that cannot be spoken, and thus are heard through poetry.

Language does not fail Whitman. To the contrary, his great confidence in poetic language springs precisely from its aesthetic capacity to create an awareness of the *absolute limits* to which language can make an extralinguistic reality known. Whitman composes "A Song of the Rolling Earth" to teach that poetry creates such an aesthetic awareness through an *angle of reflection,* as I will call it, that only poetry affords us. Poetry's reflection on linguistic representation discovers something excluded from representation on which it then focuses our attention. Whitman's line "I swear I begin to see little or nothing in audible words" and his allusion to a world "untransmissible by print" (23) are this reflective awareness forced upon him by the aesthetics of poetry, perhaps forced on all poets since this instruction originally is the privilege of "masters." Poetic language reflectively draws Whitman's eyes to "words" that catapult him beyond language to the mute reality outside.

By Whitman's design, poetry's reflection on its aesthetic practices is to place us in an aesthetic relation to the world identical to his own. Poetry's angle of reflection, which enables Whitman to view language from the mute reality lying beyond it, is precisely the vantage point of the "unknown" to which he assigned such importance in *Democratic Vistas*. Worlds we might seek to represent, poetry argues, are unknown to us; their meaning is fathomless. Poetry is not representational, it is reflexive, and refuses representation by refusing to speak with audible words what with *inaudible* words it makes heard. Poetry teaches that to be oriented *aesthetically* to the world is to treat the reality of the world as unspoken, unknown, its intrinsic meaning unknowable. By arguing that meaning is wordless at the level of reality, essence, or truth, that we are denied meaning of the depth of a world, poetry teaches that meaning resides on surfaces, moves to the level of appearances. Making us aesthetically aware of the unknown, poetry focuses our perception on appearances. And in the absence of a reality, essence, or truth that upon comparison appearances can be said to have in common, absent a common denominator rendering appearances the same, all appearances appear to be different. Everything that appears is a difference, different from every other appearance. Poetry's aesthetic orientation to the world is a relation to appearances in all their diversity of differences. Poetry models an aesthetic orientation as a relation to difference just as it appears.

Here we begin to get ethical soundings of Whitman's contribution to formulating an aesthetic orientation to appearances that resists converting their differences to forms of Otherness. Poetry teaches an aesthetic relation that shields worlds from injuries meted out to the Other. For if the essential meaning of a world cannot be known, neither can its identity be assigned a truth converting it to some form of Otherness. Nothing that appears can be alleged to be untrue or unfaithful to an unknown and unknowable truth. An aesthetic relation to the world may not protect it from injury, however, if the meaning Whitman argues is unknown is believed to the contrary to be absent. If meaning is absent, the world can be assigned any meaning, making it vulnerable to every human project regardless of its appearance. If an aesthetic orientation to the world is to immunize it against injurious treatment, it must be based on the dual understandings that the world is both unknown *and* meaningful. Whitman's worlds are fathomless though meaningful. Establishing the meaning of an otherwise unknown world in "A Song of the Rolling Earth," Whitman describes our earth as "latent in itself from the jump," wherein its "truths . . . continually wait" (19, 22). Meaning lies "Underneath the ostensible sounds," in "possessing words that never fail" (38, 40). No less declarative in "Song of Myself," Whitman reports, "All truths wait in all things" (648).[6] Similarly in *Democratic Vistas*, Whitman refers to the "purport of objective Nature . . . doubtless folded, hidden somewhere here" (1010). Nature, the world, the world that is each of us, has meaning. This is the motif constant throughout his poetry, permitting him, as we find in "Song of the Redwood Tree," to attribute an identity to worlds-in-themselves that in any more specifiable way remains opaque with an "untold life" (24).[7] Warding off our interest in the secrets we hope poetry to reveal, Whitman admonishes in "A Song of the Rolling Earth":

> I swear I see what is better than to tell the best,
> It is always to leave the best untold. (102–3)
> The best of the earth cannot be told anyhow . . . (108)

Adamant in his refusal to decipher the unknown, Whitman implicitly invokes the intrinsic meaningfulness of diverse worlds while leaving their depth meanings anonymous. This is an aesthetic strategy deliberately confining perception to worlds' surfaces so that the perceiver, focusing solely on their appearances, attributes meanings just as they appear.

Is each of us, however, not a world at least knowable to ourselves? Surely one's own world, one's self, is knowable to its owner—this is Whitman's single exception to his discourse on the unknown—a conviction he expresses in "A Song of the Rolling Earth":

> The song is to the singer, and comes back most to him . . . (82)
> The love is to the lover, and comes back most to him . . . (86)

> The oration is to the orator, the acting is to the actor and the actress
>   not to the audience,
> And no man understands any greatness or goodness but his own,
>   or the indication of his own. (88–89)

Self-knowing is not Whitman's Cartesian point of departure from which certainty can be reclaimed and generalized to worlds outside ourselves. He intends it to impose further restrictions on the possibility of our knowing any other world. Whitman sometimes suggests, for instance, that knowing oneself or about oneself limits whatever else I can know, as though the self gets in its own way to obstruct its own view, which he intimates in "Song of Myself" when he observes, "One world is aware and by far the largest to me, and that is myself" (416). Narrowing what can be known to what is contained within the boundaries of the self carefully distinguishes the unknown to be everything else surrounding the self. By tracing this sharp ontological divide between the known and the unknown, poetry exemplifies an acute aesthetic sensibility to difference—every "I" ought to recognize every appearance that is "not-I" as a uniquely different world by virtue of its indelible opacity. Accordingly, in "Are You the New Person Drawn toward Me?" Whitman cautions us not to trust that we can know another.[8] "To begin with take warning, I am surely far different from what you suppose," he assures us, as only one could who can distinguish himself knowingly as different from our image of him, an appearance that even "may be all maya, illusion" (2, 9).

Whitman refuses to abridge the distance his poetry inserts between differences even where he allows there may be one "Among the Multitude," as he entitles his wish for a "lover," who from Whitman's "faint indirections" (6) becomes that special one who "knows" him.[9] Lovers do not penetrate beyond their different appearances to discern the depth meaning of those whom they know and love, because for Whitman a lover actually is not attracted to another owing to how different he or she appears. Lovers are "perfect equal[s]" (5)—Whitman means lovers are *the same, not different.* As he explains, "And I when I meet you mean to discover you by the *like* in you" (7, my italics). A lover's knowledge of another is not knowledge of difference; in other words, it proceeds from self-knowledge, that the one loved resembles the lover known only to him or her self. Love, at least in part, is a projection of the lover's own self on the one loved.

So appearances resist disclosure universally. No matter who the interested party, difference is impenetrable. "The skies of day and night, colors, densities, forms," Whitman speculates in "Of the Terrible Doubt of Appearances,"[10] "may-be these"

> are (as doubtless they are) only apparitions, and the real something has yet to be known,
> ....
> (How often I think neither I know, nor any man knows, aught of them). (6, 8)

Whitman, it should be stressed, does not mean poetry should encourage a distrust of appearances and a search for the real something yet to be known. Quite the opposite—poetry is to teach that from appearances we can know nothing real of the diversity of worlds that appearances identify. And since "identity"—appearance—is the "*only* entrance to all facts," as he puts it in *Democratic Vistas* (984, my italics), if we can know nothing real from appearances, we can know nothing real at all. Appearances act like language. It is their peculiarity to intimate a presence that eludes our grasp. How often Whitman tells us that no sooner does something catch his eye than, paradoxically, it brings into view what cannot be seen. "Oxen that rattle the yoke and chain or halt in the leafy shade, what is that you express in your eyes?" Whitman asks in "Song of Myself." "It seems to be more than all the print I have read in my life" (235–36).

What is true of oxen is true of all worlds as they appear. Each different world exceeds its apparent meaning. Each exceeds its identity and perhaps infinitely, we can never be certain, which is one of the consequences belonging to the unknown. What certainty we do possess is the paradoxical certainty Whitman installs deeply into our lives, the presence of some truth to appearances established through the absence of truth belonging to an unknowable reality. Whatever appears, appears different because it cannot be known at a deeper level of commonality to be the same as anything else that appears. Poetry leaves us with the interpretive darkness we find thematized famously in "Song of Myself."

> A child said *What is the grass?* fetching it to me with full hands;

> How could I answer the child? I do not know what it is any more than he.
> I guess it must be the flag of my disposition, out of hopeful green stuff woven.
> Or I guess it is the handkerchief of the Lord,
> A scented gift and remembrancer designedly dropped,
> Bearing the owner's name someway in the corners, that we may see and remark, and say *Whose?*
> Or I guess the grass is itself a child, the produced babe of the vegetation.
> Or I guess it is a uniform hieroglyphic. (99–106)

Uniform hieroglyphics, leaves of grass stand, if they stand for anything, for what *resists* interpretation, for an unanswerable "*Whose?*" Whitman concludes this inquiry with lines completing a journey from puzzlement to interpretive indeterminacy to an interpretive darkness that is heard at the moment it is unspoken.

> This grass is very dark to be from the white heads of old mothers,
> Darker than the colorless beards of old men,
> Dark to come from under the faint red roofs of mouths. (116–18)

Too dark to be white, too dark to be colorless, too dark to be colored—the grass, its meaning, that is, is opaque. Resisting representations made by means of comparisons in relation to some common underlying reality presumed to be knowable, the grass becomes an unspoken darkness at the moment it is a spoken dark. Whitman abandons commonality, sameness, essence as the means to fathom some truth belonging to an appearance in its depth. Difference simply appears—dark. He immerses himself in a web of comparisons not as an interpretive means to fathom a truth to what appears different but to clarify his choice between knowing a world in relation to others comparatively known and accepting the darkness of the unknown. Whitman accepts the darkness, as he assures us again in his "Song of the Open Road."[11]

> You road I enter upon and look around, I believe you are not all that is here,

> I believe that much unseen is also here. (16–17)
> I believe you are latent with unseen existences. (29)

Now Whitman's unknown is but one of *two* angles of aesthetic reflection through which his poetry conceptualizes an aesthetic orientation to appearances. Once it has taught us to recognize the world to be unknown and unknowable and we have discarded the authoritative standpoint of truth guaranteed by knowledge of reality, poetry urges we become perspectival. Objects perceived, Whitman teaches in "Of the Terrible Doubt of Appearances,"

> May-be seeming to me what they are (as doubtless they indeed
> but seem) as from my present point of view, and might
> prove (as of course they would) nought of what they
> appear, or nought anyhow, from entirely changed points
> of view. (9)

Not one "seeming" corresponding to reality more than another "seeming," Whitman describes perception as a perspectivism that confines us to appearances by not privileging perceptions thought to more closely represent what is real. His perspectivism goes further still. As does his first angle of reflection on the unknown, Whitman's perspectivism also undermines the very idea of representation by implying that what is perceived is disconnected from what it identifies and consequently is no representation at all. This seems to be Whitman's more radical intention, especially as it is implied by his figurative "or nought anyhow"—*the perceived is nothing anyhow*—"from entirely changed points of view."

Disconnecting appearances from what is real of worlds, poetry does not deny that there is an objectively meaningful reality underlying them. It is that there ceases to be a meaningful interpretive sense in which appearances are representational. We cannot know or even infer anything "true" of the real based on our perception of appearances. Poetry forbids searching for knowledge of reality for moral or ethical guidance not only because what is real is unknown—rather also because our perceptions only are perspectival forms we impose on the world. Appearances are our perceptual impositions. Whitman speaks directly to the extent to which our perception imposes form on the world in "A Song for Occupations."

> All architecture is what you do to it when you look upon it,
> (Did you think it was in the white or gray stone? or the lines of
>   the arches and cornices?)
> All music is what awakes from you when you are reminded by the
>   instruments,
> It is not the violins and cornets, it is not the oboe . . .
> It is nearer and farther than they. (93–97)[12]

The world appears meaningful to us when we first "look upon it"—as that which we make of it or as what we "do to it." Appearances are projections behind which the reality of the world, its objectivity, vanishes into the unknown. Like the architecture we see and the music we hear, perceptions in the first and also final analysis are preconceptions. Worlds are "nearer" than our perceptions suggest because perceptions are based on our preconceptions, though also "farther" than we realize because whatever is "perceived" finally is more outside perception than the preconceptions that shape it.

God, Death, the Afterlife, and the Unknown

To sustain our orientation to appearances taught by poetry, Whitman would have to revise the relationship between appearance and reality even more fundamentally than has poetry already with its two angles of aesthetic reflection, its angle of reflection on the unknown and its perspectival angle of reflection. Poetry cannot keep open an unbridgeable ontological divide between appearance and reality without revising the relationship between God and the world as well. For when appearances are granted an authority no longer indebted to what is real, God must cease to infuse appearance with the spiritual power to represent reality. Appearances are retired as a source of light illuminating the worldly immanence of the transcendental. Even if God were yet believed to define and to be embodied by what is real, poetry would have to relinquish all connection between God and a world of appearances thought to reveal something of a transcendent meaning or purpose. Without this most fundamental revision, the division between appearance and reality and the orientation to appearances and their differences this division supports would dissolve. Once Whitman severs the connection between appearance and reality, then, what does he allow poetry to teach democratic society of its relationship to God?

Whitman revokes all possibility of learning God's identity. "O Thou transcendent, *Nameless*," Whitman cries in "Passage to India"[13] (194–95, my italics), and he says this after honoring all gods and confessing to a certain devotion to beliefs with which they are associated, as he does in "Song of Myself" (verse 43). Since we are unable to identify God, in "Passage to India" Whitman holds that God becomes a "mystery" with which "we dare not dally," although he also professes a belief in God even greater "than any priest" (185, 186). Whitman's decisive move is where he brings his unknowable God squarely into alignment with the division he inserts between appearance and reality. As he counsels in "Song of Myself," in what surely are among the most moving, beautiful, and provocative lines in all of Whitman's poetry:

> And I say to mankind, Be not curious about God,
> For I who am curious about each am not curious about God . . .
>   (1278–79)
> Why should I wish to see God better than this day? (1283)

Leaving God remote powerfully affirms life—God must not lure away our interest in life to what transcends life, and if *God* cannot, surely nothing can lure away our interest in life. Whitman's affirmation of life springs from the opacity he attributes to God. To observe a nameless, mysterious, unknowable God would be to fail to observe life. Whitman does not mean to interfere with our need to feel close to an unknown God, as his frequent uncensored professions of faith prove. Rather, our need to feel close to God should not interfere with our absorption in the world. God, a mystery of insoluble proportions, must distract our attention neither from living nor from what lives.

Opacity is the measure, his critical test of God's distance from the world. Though Whitman is able to "hear and behold God in every object," he confesses he "understand[s] God not in the least" and cannot "understand who there can be more wonderful than myself" ("Song of Myself," 1281–82). Nothing around us or about us serves as a sign of God meant to orient us to appearances as though they contain clues to the unfathomable mystery of God. Keeping our eyes fixed on appearances for their own sake, Whitman emphatically removes God from our lives so that life can be lived.

For all intents and purposes belonging to the world, nature, and to life in all its different forms, God does not exist, nor does God's domain, death and the afterlife, which must make no difference to life. Like God, the afterlife is that "unknown region," "all a blank before us," an "inaccessible land," even "undream'd of" by the soul, Whitman insists in "Darest Thou Now O Soul" (2, 8, 9).[14] And death, the "unknown shores," as he calls it in "Passage to India" (180), "I cannot define," he admits in "To Think of Time" (106).[15]

God, death, and the afterlife, the "supernatural" (as Whitman summarily describes the unknown in "Song of Myself") being of "no account" (1050), should we conclude Whitman goes further than even creating an unbridgeable divide between appearance and reality? If appearance can serve so weakly as an exemplar of faith, perhaps he means appearances to become reality. What we can be certain of is that what we believe to be real, Whitman so far removes from appearances, makes so inaccessible and protected, that appearances and the differences among them, though not reality, he intends to become *our* reality.

Democracy's Barrier to Evil

By writing poetry to teach two angles of aesthetic reflection and by revising our relationship to God, Whitman intends for poetry to introduce the idea of the unknown into the culture of democratic life. By doing so, his poetry conforms to his own recommendations in *Democratic Vistas* for an artwork of the future able to nurture a culture of reconciliation. Poetry's first angle of reflection, its reflection on the unknown, teaches a number of lessons—what is real, essential, or true is hidden from us; the world to which we relate is all appearance, the level at which meaning resides; the authority of appearance cannot be derived from a prior or fundamental truth but is intrinsic to it; appearances are diverse and different because their differences are not effaced by anything essential they could be said to have in common. A democratic culture enlightened by poetry's teachings could not but understand that in the absence of truth nothing that appears can be thought of as lower or inferior to anything else that appears or less perfect or imperfect or less than equal to others; that in the absence of truth no one may be excluded; that in the absence of truth nothing different in the diversity of different appearances can be converted into a form of

Otherness. Poetry's second angle of reflection secures the lessons of the first by teaching a perspectivism that unwaveringly confines perception to the realm of appearances to further shield the unknown from its invasions. Poetry's two angles of aesthetic reflection together alter the ethical value of appearances by reshaping our orientations to nature, the world, and to one another. And by removing God's presence from the world, poetry assures that appearances can regain no philosophical claim to the certainty of truth on which depends the construction and destruction of the Other. Under the tutelage of poetry, all social relations become aesthetic relations, an orientation to differences just as they appear. As Whitman expresses it poignantly, unequivocally, and powerfully in his 1855 Preface to *Leaves of Grass*, "Men and women and the earth and all upon it are simply to be taken as they are."[16]

Aesthetically valorizing appearances to oppose the evil of converting difference to Otherness, poetry teaches reconciliation by opposing the marginalization and exclusion of difference and the more extreme forms of violence victimizing difference, genocide the most horrifying. Only having entered into Whitman's poetry, we already have located the principle of all-inclusiveness at the core of reconciliation and of the project for which he designs his art, an enlightenment that democracy can achieve under the instruction of an aesthetic education provided by a poetry pedagogically erecting a cultural barrier to evil.

Notes

With gratitude for introducing me to the work of the Poet, the "Answerer," I dedicate this essay to George Kateb, whose belief that Whitman may be our greatest democratic philosopher I have come to share. "[O]nly the Poet begets."

1. *Democratic Vistas*, in *Whitman: Poetry and Prose* (New York: Library of America, 1996), 953–1018; hereafter cited as *WPP*. Citations from *Democratic Vistas* are given parenthetically in my text. Whitman refers to "topics" he addresses in *Democratic Vistas* (994), a practice I have followed, although in political theory "concepts" would be the appropriate term.

2. "Song of Myself," in *Leaves of Grass* (New York: Norton, 1973), 28–89; hereafter cited as *LG*. Line numbers for all poetry are given parenthetically in my text.

3. "Our Old Feuillage," in *LG*, 171–76.

4. In "Democratic Enlightenment I: Whitman and Aesthetic Education," part 1 of a book in progress tentatively titled "Democratic Enlightenment: Aesthetic Education through the Visual Image."

5. "A Song of the Rolling Earth," in *LG*, 219–25.

6. "Song of Myself," ibid., 28–89.

7. "Song of the Redwood Tree," ibid., 206–10.

8. "Are You the New Person Drawn toward Me?" ibid., 123.

9. "Among the Multitude," ibid., 135.

10. "Of the Terrible Doubt of Appearances," ibid., 120.

11. "Song of the Open Road," ibid., 149–58.

12. "A Song for Occupations," ibid., 211–19.

13. "Passage to India," ibid., 411–21.

14. "Darest Thou Now O Soul," ibid., 441–42.

15. "To Think of Time," ibid., 434–40.

16. "Preface 1855—*Leaves of Grass*, First Edition," ibid., 721.

Frontispieces from *Leaves of Grass*

The frontispiece of the first edition of *Leaves of Grass* (1855). The image replaced the author's name and was critically discussed by several reviewers. Whitman later referred to the image as "the street figure." (Courtesy of Special Collections and University Archives, Rutgers University Libraries)

Title page and frontispiece of the 1860 edition of *Leaves of Grass* (Courtesy of Rare Books Division, Library of Congress)

Selected Bibliography

Edited Collections

Allen, Gay Wilson, ed. *Walt Whitman Abroad.* Syracuse, N.Y.: Syracuse University Press, 1955.

Bergman, Herbert, Douglas A. Noverr, Edward J. Recchia, Gay Wilson Allen, Sculley Bradley, eds. *The Journalism: Volume I: 1834–1846.* New York: Peter Lang, 1998.

Berman, Richard, ed. *Whitman's Men: Walt Whitman's Calamus Poems Celebrated by Contemporary Photographers.* New York: Universe, 1996.

Bloom, Harold, ed. *Walt Whitman.* Broomall, Pa.: Chelsea House, 1999.

Cady, Edwin H., and Louis J. Budd, eds. *On Whitman.* Durham: Duke University Press, 1987.

Christman, Henry M., ed. *Walt Whitman's New York: From Manhattan to Montauk.* New York: New Amsterdam, 1989.

Clarke, Graham, ed. *Walt Whitman: Critical Assessments.* Robertsbridge, East Sussex: Helm Information, 1995.

Erkkila, Betsy, and Jay Grossman, eds. *Breaking Bounds: Whitman and American Cultural Studies.* New York: Oxford University Press, 1996.

Folsom, Ed, ed. *Walt Whitman: The Centennial Essays* Iowa City: University of Iowa Press, 1994.

———. *Whitman East and West: New Contexts for Reading Walt Whitman.* Iowa City: University of Iowa Press, 2002.

Folsom, Ed, and Gay Wilson Allen, eds. *Walt Whitman and the World.* Iowa City: University of Iowa Press, 1995.

Greenspan, Ezra, ed. *The Cambridge Companion to Walt Whitman.* Cambridge and New York: Cambridge University Press, 1995.

———, ed. *Walt Whitman's "Song of Myself": A Sourcebook and Critical Edition.* New York and London: Routledge, 2005.

Hindus, Milton, ed. *Leaves of Grass: One Hundred Years After.* Stanford: Stanford University Press, 1955.

Kramer, Lawrence, ed. *Walt Whitman and Modern Music: War, Desire, and the Trials of Nationhood.* New York: Garland, 2000.

Krieg, Joann P., ed. *Walt Whitman.* Westport, Conn.: Greenwood Press, 1985.

Kummings, Donald D., ed. *Approaches to Teaching Whitman's Leaves of Grass.* New York: Modern Language Association of America, 1990.

———, ed. *A Companion to Walt Whitman.* Malden, Mass., and Oxford: Blackwell, 2006.

LeMaster, J. R., and Donald D. Kummings, eds. *Walt Whitman: An Encyclopedia.* New York: Garland, 1998.

Levin, Jonathan, ed. *Walt Whitman 1819–1892.* New York: Sterling, 1997.

Martin, Robert K., ed. *The Continuing Presence of Walt Whitman: The Life after the Life.* Iowa City: University of Iowa Press, 1992.

Marx, Leo, ed. *The Americanness of Walt Whitman.* Boston: D. C. Heath, 1960.

McElroy, John Harmon, ed. *The Sacrificial Years: A Chronicle of Walt Whitman's Experiences in the Civil War.* Boston: David R. Godine, 1999.

Miller, Edwin Haviland, ed. *A Century of Whitman Criticism.* Bloomington: Indiana University Press, 1969.

Myerson, Joel, ed. *Walt Whitman: A Documentary Volume.* Detroit: Gale Group, 2000.

———, ed. *Whitman in His Own Time: A Biographical Chronicle of His Life, Drawn from Recollections, Memoirs, and Interviews by Friends and Associates.* Iowa City: University of Iowa Press, 2000.

Padgett, Ron, ed. *The Teachers and Writers Guide to Walt Whitman.* New York: Teachers and Writers Collaborative, 1991.

Perlman, Jim, Ed Folsom, and Dan Campion, eds. *Walt Whitman: The Measure of His Song.* Duluth, Minn.: Holy Cow! Press, 1998.

Price, Kenneth M., ed. *Walt Whitman: The Contemporary Reviews.* Cambridge: Cambridge University Press, 1996.

Reynolds, David S., ed. *A Historical Guide to Walt Whitman.* New York: Oxford University Press, 2000.

Schmidgall, Gary, ed. *Conserving Walt Whitman's Fame: Selections from Horace Traubel's Conservator, 1890–1919.* Iowa City: University of Iowa Press, 2006.

Shively, Charley, ed. *Calamus Lovers: Walt Whitman's Working-Class Camerados.* San Francisco: Gay Sunshine Press, 1987.

Sill, Geoffrey M., ed. *Walt Whitman of Mickle Street: A Centennial Collection.* Knoxville: University of Tennessee Press, 1994.

Sill, Geoffrey M., and Roberta K. Tarbell, eds. *Walt Whitman and the Visual Arts.* New Brunswick, N.J.: Rutgers University Press, 1992.

Woodress, James, ed. *Critical Essays on Walt Whitman.* Boston: G. K. Hall, 1983.

Books

Allen, Gay Wilson. *The New Walt Whitman Handbook.* New York: New York University Press, 1986.

———. *A Reader's Guide to Walt Whitman.* Syracuse: Syracuse University Press, 1997.

Aspiz, Harold. *So Long! Walt Whitman's Poetry of Death.* Tuscaloosa: University of Alabama Press, 2004.

Asselineau, Roger. *The Evolution of Walt Whitman.* Iowa City: University of Iowa Press, 1999.

Austin, Kelly. "A Poet of the Americas: Neruda's Translations of Whitman and North American Translations of Neruda." Ph.D. diss., University of California, Los Angeles, 2005.

Bauerlein, Mark. *Whitman and the American Idiom.* Baton Rouge: Louisiana State University Press, 1991.

Beach, Christopher. *The Politics of Distinction: Whitman and the Discourses of Nineteenth-Century America.* Athens: University of Georgia Press, 1996.

Bellis, Peter J. *Writing Revolution: Aesthetics and Politics in Hawthorne, Whitman, and Thoreau.* Athens: University of Georgia Press, 2003.

Bohan, Ruth L. *Looking into Walt Whitman: American Art, 1850–1920.* University Park: Pennsylvania State University Press, 2006.

Bollobas, Eniko. *Tradition and Innovation in American Free Verse: Whitman to Duncan.* Budapest: Akademiai Kiado, 1986.

Callow, Philip. *From Noon to Starry Night: A Life of Walt Whitman.* Chicago: I. R. Dee, 1992.

Ceniza, Sherry. *Walt Whitman and Nineteenth-Century Women Reformers.* Tuscaloosa and London: University of Alabama Press, 1998.

Clarke, Graham. *Walt Whitman: The Poem as Private History.* London: Vision Press, 1991.

Davis, Robert Leigh. *Whitman and the Romance of Medicine.* Berkeley and Los Angeles: University of California Press, 1997.

Dougherty, James. *Walt Whitman and the Citizen's Eye.* Baton Rouge: Louisiana State University Press, 1993.

Dutta-Roy, Sonjoy. *(Re)constructing the Poetic Self: Tagore, Whitman, Yeats, Eliot.* Delhi: Pencraft International, 2001.
Epstein, Daniel Mark. *Lincoln and Whitman: Parallel Lives in Civil War Washington.* New York: Ballantine Books, 2004.
Erkkila, Betsy. *Whitman the Political Poet.* New York and Oxford: Oxford University Press, 1989.
Fletcher, Angus. *A New Theory for American Poetry: Democracy, the Environment, and the Future of Imagination.* Cambridge: Harvard University Press, 2004.
Folsom, Ed. *Walt Whitman's Native Representations.* Cambridge and New York: Cambridge University Press, 1997.
Folsom, Ed, and Kenneth M. Price. *Re-Scripting Walt Whitman: An Introduction to His Life and Work.* Malden, Mass.: Blackwell, 2005.
Fone, Byrne R. S., *Masculine Landscapes: Walt Whitman and the Homoerotic Text.* Carbondale: Southern Illinois University Press, 1992.
Gardner, John Fentress. *American Heralds of the Spirit.* Hudson, N.Y.: Lindisfarne Press, 1991.
Gardner, Thomas. *Discovering Ourselves in Whitman: The Contemporary American Long Poem.* Urbana: University of Illinois Press, 1989.
Greenberg, Robert M. *Splintered Worlds: Fragmentation and the Ideal of Diversity in the Work of Emerson, Melville, Whitman, and Dickinson.* Boston: Northeastern University Press, 1993.
Greenspan, Ezra. *Walt Whitman and the American Reader.* Cambridge and New York: Cambridge University Press, 1990.
Grossman, Jay. *Reconstituting the American Renaissance: Emerson, Whitman, and the Politics of Representation.* Durham: Duke University Press, 2003.
Grunzweig, Walter. *Constructing the German Walt Whitman.* Iowa City: University of Iowa Press, 1995.
Haigney, Jessica. *Walt Whitman and the French Impressionists: A Study of Analogies.* Lewiston, N.Y.: Edwin Mellen Press, 1990.
Hartnett, Stephen. "Cultural Fictions: The Critical Theory of Historiography, the Political-Economy of Modernity, and the Paradoxes of Whitman's America." Ph.D. diss., University of California, San Diego.
Huang, Guiyou. *Whitmanism, Imagism, and Modernism in China and America.* Cranbury, N.J.: Associated University Press, 1997.
Hutchinson, George. *The Ecstatic Whitman: Literary Shamanism and the Crisis of the Union.* Columbus: Ohio State University Press, 1986.
Ignatow, David. *Walt Whitman in the Civil War Hospitals.* West Hills, Long Island [New York]: Walt Whitman Birthplace Association, 1988.

Jang, Cheol-U. "Becoming: Toward a Deleuzian Reading of Walt Whitman and Emily Dickinson." Ph.D. diss., University of California, San Diego, 2005.

Jensen, Beth. *Leaving the M/other: Whitman, Kristeva, and Leaves of Grass*. Madison, N.J.: Fairleigh Dickinson University Press; London and Cranbury, N.J.: Associated University Presses, 2002.

Kantrowitz, Arnie. *Walt Whitman*. Philadelphia: Chelsea House, 2005.

Kerley, Barbara. *Walt Whitman: Words for America*. New York: Scholastic Press, 2004.

Killingsworth, M. Jimmie. *Walt Whitman and the Earth: A Study in Ecopoetics*. Iowa City: University of Iowa Press, 2004.

Klammer, Martin. *Whitman, Slavery, and the Emergence of Leaves of Grass*. University Park: Pennsylvania State University Press, 1995.

Knapp, Bettina Liebowitz. *Walt Whitman*. New York: Continuum, 1993.

Krieg, Joann P. *Whitman and the Irish*. Iowa City: University of Iowa Press, 2000.

———. *A Whitman Chronology*. Iowa City: University of Iowa Press, 1998.

Kuebrich, David. *Minor Prophecy: Walt Whitman's New American Religion*. Bloomington: Indiana University Press, 1989.

Kushner, William. *In the Hairy Arms of Whitman*. Hoboken, N.J.: Melville House, 2003.

Larson, Kerry C. *Whitman's Drama of Consensus*. Chicago: University of Chicago Press, 1988.

Lawson, Andrew. *Walt Whitman and the Class Struggle*. Iowa City: University of Iowa Press, 2006.

Lenhart, Gary. *The Stamp of Class: Reflections on Poetry and Social Class*. Ann Arbor: University of Michigan Press, 2006.

Li, Xilao. "The Song of Ethnic Self: An Affinity Study of Walt Whitman and Ethnic American Writers." Ph.D. diss., State University of New York, Stony Brook, 1993.

Lin, Jian-Zhong. "Walt Whitman and His Readers: A Problem in Communication." Ph.d. diss., University of California, Riverside, 1991.

Loving, Jerome. *Walt Whitman: The Song of Himself*. Berkeley and Los Angeles: University of California Press, 1999.

Mack, Stephen John. *The Pragmatic Whitman: Reimagining American Democracy*. Iowa City: University of Iowa Press, 2002.

Mancuso, Luke. *The Strange Sad War Revolving: Walt Whitman, Reconstruction, and the Emergence of Black Citizenship, 1865–1876*. Columbia, S.C.: Camden House, 1997.

Martin, Douglas Darren. *A Study of Walt Whitman's Mimetic Prosody: Free-bound and Full Circle*. Lewiston, N.Y.: Edwin Mellen Press, 2004.

Maslan, Mark. *Whitman Possessed: Poetry, Sexuality, and Popular Authority*. Baltimore and London: Johns Hopkins University Press, 2001.

Mazur, Krystyna. *Poetry and Repetition: Walt Whitman, Wallace Stevens, John Ashbery*. New York: Routledge, 2005.

Miller, Edwin Haviland. *Walt Whitman's "Song of Myself": A Mosaic of Interpretations*. Iowa City: University of Iowa Press, 1989.

Miller, Emily Anne. "Puritan Thought in Walt Whitman: The Word as Word." Ph.D. diss., 1986.

Miller, James E., Jr. *Leaves of Grass: America's Lyric-Epic of Self and Democracy*. Boston: Twayne, 1992.

———. *Walt Whitman*. Boston: Twayne, 1990.

Moon, Michael. *Disseminating Whitman: Revision and Corporeality in Leaves of Grass*. Cambridge: Harvard University Press, 1991.

Morris, Roy, Jr. *The Better Angel: Walt Whitman in the Civil War*. Oxford and New York: Oxford University Press, 2000.

Myerson, Joel. *Walt Whitman: A Descriptive Bibliography*. Pittsburgh: University of Pittsburgh Press, 1993.

Nathanson, Tenney. *Whitman's Presence: Body, Voice, and Writing in Leaves of Grass*. New York: New York University Press, 1992.

Nolan, James. *Poet-Chief: The Native American Poetics of Walt Whitman and Pablo Neruda*. Albuquerque: University of New Mexico Press, 1994.

Oliver, Charles M. *Critical Companion to Walt Whitman: A Literary Reference to His Life and Work*. New York: Facts on File, 2006.

Olney, James. *The Language(s) of Poetry: Walt Whitman, Emily Dickinson, Gerard Manley Hopkins*. Athens: University of Georgia Press, 1993.

Pannapacker, William. *Revised Lives: Walt Whitman and Nineteenth-Century Authorship*. New York: Routledge, 2004.

Perkovich, Mike. *Nature Boys: Camp Discourse in American Literature from Whitman to Wharton*. New York: P. Lang, 2003.

Pollak, Vivian R. *The Erotic Whitman*. Berkeley and Los Angeles: University of California Press, 2000.

Price, Kenneth M. *To Walt Whitman, America*. Chapel Hill: University of North Carolina Press, 2004.

———. *Whitman and Tradition: The Poet in His Century*. New Haven: Yale University Press, 1990.

Pucciani, Oreste F. *The Literary Reputation of Walt Whitman in France*. New York: Garland, 1987.

Reef, Catherine. *Walt Whitman*. New York: Clarion Books, 1995.

Reynolds, David S. *Walt Whitman*. Oxford and New York: Oxford University Press, 2005.

———. *Walt Whitman's America: A Cultural Biography*. New York: Knopf, 1995.
Sánchez-Eppler, Karen. *Touching Liberty: Abolition, Feminism, and the Politics of the Body*. Berkeley and Los Angeles: University of California Press, 1993.
Schmidgall, Gary. *Walt Whitman: A Gay Life*. New York: Dutton, 1997.
Schwiebert, John E. *The Frailest Leaves: Whitman's Poetic Technique and Style in the Short Poem*. New York: P. Lang, 1992.
Shenk, Genie, and Jim Machacek. *An Interpretation of Walt Whitman's "A Font of Type."* San Diego: Mesa Arts Press, 1996.
Shucard, Alan. *American Poetry: The Puritans through Walt Whitman*. Boston: Twayne, 1988.
Sill, Geoffrey M. *Walt Whitman of Mickle Street: A Centennial Collection*. Knoxville: University of Tennessee Press, 1994.
Sowder, Michael. *Whitman's Ecstatic Union: Conversion and Ideology in Leaves of Grass*. New York: Routledge, 2005.
Srivastava, Santosh Kumari. *Symbolism in the Poetry of Poe and Whitman*. New Delhi: National Book Organisation, 1988.
Thomas, M. Wynn. *The Lunar Light of Whitman's Poetry*. Cambridge: Harvard University Press, 1987.
———. *Transatlantic Connections: Whitman U.S., Whitman U.K.* Iowa City: University of Iowa Press, 2005.
Thurin, Erik Ingvar. *Whitman between Impressionism and Expressionism: Language of the Body, Language of the Soul*. Lewisburg, Pa.: Bucknell University Press, 1995.
Vendler, Helen Hennessy. *Invisible Listeners: Lyric Intimacy in Herbert, Whitman, and Ashbery*. Princeton: Princeton University Press, 2005.
———. *Poets Thinking: Pope, Whitman, Dickinson, Yeats*. Cambridge: Harvard University Press, 2004.
Wardrop, Daneen. *Word, Birth, and Culture: The Poetry of Poe, Whitman, and Dickinson*. Westport, Conn.: Greenwood Press, 2002.
Warren, James Perrin. *Walt Whitman's Language Experiment*. University Park: Pennsylvania State University Press, 1990.
Wartofsky, Steven Andrew. "The Crisis of the Whole: National and Personal Identity in Walt Whitman's Poetry, 1855–1865." Ph.D. diss., University of California, Berkeley, 1988.

Journal Articles

Auclair, Tracy. "The Language of Drug Use in Whitman's 'Calamus' Poems." *Papers on Language and Literature* 40, no. 3 (Summer 2004).

Beer, Samuel H. "Liberty and Union: Walt Whitman's Idea of the Nation." *Political Theory* 12, no. 3 (August 1984).

Blake, David Haven. "Reading Whitman, Growing up Rock 'N' Roll." *Virginia Quarterly Review* 81, no. 2 (Spring 2005).

Bluestein, Gene. "Sex as a Literary Theme: Is Whitman the Good, Gay Poet?" *Journal of Popular Culture* 31, no. 3 (Winter 1997).

Bromwich, David. "Whitman and Memory: A Response to Kateb." *Political Theory* 18, no. 4 (November 1990).

Buinicki, Martin T. "Walt Whitman and the Question of Copyright." *American Literary History* 15, no. 2 (Summer 2003).

Campo, Rafael. "Whitman Now." *Virginia Quarterly Review* 81, no. 2 (Spring 2005).

Coviello, Peter. "Intimate Nationality: Anonymity and Attachment in Whitman." *American Literature* 73, no. 1 (March 2001).

Creeley, Robert. "Reflections on Whitman in Age." *Virginia Quarterly Review* 81, no. 2 (Spring 2005).

Cushman, Stephen. "Whitman and Patriotism." *Virginia Quarterly Review* 81, no. 2 (Spring 2005).

Dawidoff, Robert. "The Jeffersonian Option." *Political Theory* 21, no. 3 (August 1993).

Donoghue, Denis. "*Leaves of Grass* and American Culture." *Sewanee Review* 111, no. 3 (Summer 2003).

Elfenbein, Andrew. "Whitman, Democracy, and the English Clerisy." *Nineteenth-Century Literature* 56, no. 1 (2001).

Folsom, Ed. "'What a Filthy Presidentiad!' Clinton's Whitman, Bush's Whitman, and Whitman's America." *Virginia Quarterly Review* 81, no. 2 (Spring 2005).

Francis, Sean, "'Outbidding at the Start the Old Cautious Hucksters': Promotional Discourse and Whitman's Free Verse." *Nineteenth-Century Literature* 57, no. 3 (December 2002).

Garman, Bryan K. "'Heroic Spiritual Grandfather': Whitman, Sexuality, and the American Left, 1890–1940." *American Quarterly* 52, no. 1 (March 2000).

Handley, George B. "On Reading South in the New World: Whitman, Marti Glissant, and the Hegelian Dialectic." *Mississippi Quarterly* 56, no. 4 (Fall 2003).

Kateb, George. "Democratic Individuality and the Claims of Politics." *Political Theory* 12, no. 3 (August 1984).

———. "Walt Whitman and the Culture of Democracy." *Political Theory* 18, no. 4 (November 1990).

Kauffman, Bill. "Walt Whitman, Free Trader." *American Enterprise* 16, no. 7 (October/December 2005).

Klier, Ron. "Walt Whitman, Woody Guthrie, Bob Dylan, and the Anxiety of Influence." *Midwest Quarterly* 40, no. 3 (Spring 1999).

Lawson, Andrew. "'Spending for Vast Returns': Sex, Class, and Commerce in the First *Leaves of Grass*." *American Literature* 75, no. 2 (June 2003).

Levinson, Julian. "Walt Whitman among the Yiddish Poets." *Tikkun* 18, no. 5 (September/October 2003).

MacPhail, Scott. "Lyric Nationalism: Whitman, American Studies, and the New Criticism." *Texas Studies in Literature and Language* 44, no. 2 (Summer 2002).

Maslan, Mark. "Whitman, Sexuality, and Poetic Authority." *Raritan* 17, no. 4 (Spring 1998).

Morton, Heather. "Democracy, Self-Reviews and the 1855 *Leaves of Grass*." *Virginia Quarterly Review* 81, no. 2 (Spring 2005).

Mosher, Michael. "Walt Whitman: Jacobin Poet of American Democracy." *Political Theory* 18 no. 4 (November 1990).

Neely, Mark E., Jr. "Whitman and the Civil War: A Response to Helen Vendler." *Michigan Quarterly Review* 39, no. 1 (Winter 2000).

Outka, Paul H. "Whitman and Race ('He's Queer, He's Unclear, Get Used to It')." *Journal of American Studies* 36, no. 2 (August 2002).

Pinsker, Sanford. "Walt Whitman and Our Multicultural America." *Virginia Quarterly Review* 75, no. 4 (Autumn 1999).

Price, Kenneth M. "Whitman in Selected Anthologies: The Politics of His Afterlife." *Virginia Quarterly Review* 81, no. 2 (Spring 2005).

Reece, Erik Anderson. "Instead of the Ten Commandments: Walt Whitman's Laws for Creations." *Dissent* 47, no. 3 (Summer 2000).

Roche, John F. "The Culture of Pre-Modernism: Whitman, Morris, and the American Arts and Crafts Movement." *ATQ* 9, no. 2 (1995).

Rosenblum, Nancy L. "Strange Attractors: How Individualists Connect to Form Democratic Unity." *Political Theory* 18, no. 4 (November 1990).

Smith, Greg. "Whitman, Springsteen, and the American Working Class." *Midwest Quarterly* 41, no. 3 (Spring 2000).

Snodgrass, W. D. "Whitman's Selfsong." *Southern Review* 32 (Summer 1996).

Trachtenberg, Alan. "Democracy and the Poet: Walt Whitman and E. A. Robinson." *Massachusetts Review* 39, no. 2 (Summer 1998).

White, Stephen K. "Weak Ontology and Liberal Political Reflection." *Political Theory* 25, no. 4 (August 1997).

Zancu, Liliana. "Burns, Eminescu, and Whitman: Romantic Nationalism or Xenophobia?" *History of European Ideas* 16, nos. 1–3 (1993).

Other

Kateb, George. *The Inner Ocean: Individualism and Democratic Culture*. Ithaca and London: Cornell University Press, 1992.

Nussbaum, Martha C. *Poetic Justice: The Literary Imagination and Public Life.* Boston: Beacon Press, 1995.

———. *Upheavals of Thought: The Intelligence of Emotions.* Cambridge: Cambridge University Press, 2001.

Rorty, Richard. *Achieving Our Country: Leftist Thought in Twentieth-Century America.* Cambridge and London: Harvard University Press, 1998.

Rosenblum, Nancy L. *Another Liberalism: Romanticism and the Reconstruction of Liberal Thought.* Cambridge and London: Harvard University Press, 1987.

White, Stephen K. *Sustaining Affirmation: The Strengths of Weak Ontology in Political Theory.* Princeton: Princeton University Press, 2000.

Contributors

Cristina Beltrán is an associate professor in political science at Haverford College. She is author of *The Trouble with Unity: Latino Politics and the Creation of Identity*. Her work has appeared in *Political Theory, Political Research Quarterly*, and various edited volumes.

Marshall Berman is Distinguished Professor of Political Science at the City College and at the Graduate Center of the City University of New York. He is author of *On the Town: One Hundred Years of Spectacle in Times Square; Adventures in Marxism; All That Is Solid Melts into Air: The Experience of Modernity;* and *The Politics of Authenticity: Radical Individualism and the Emergence of Modern Society*.

Jane Bennett teaches political theory at Johns Hopkins University, where she is a professor of political science. She is a founding member of the journal *theory & event*, and her most recent book is *Vibrant Matter: A Political Ecology of Things*.

Terrell Carver is a professor of political theory at the University of Bristol, U.K. He is the author or editor of numerous books, articles, and other contributions on sex, gender, and sexuality, including, most recently, "The Machine in the Man"; "Sex, Gender and Heteronormativity: Seeing 'Some Like It Hot' as a Heterosexual Dystopia"; and, with Samuel A. Chambers, *Judith Butler and Political Theory: Troubling Politics*.

Kennan Ferguson teaches political theory at the University of Wisconsin at Milwaukee. He is the author of *William James: Politics in the Pluriverse; The Politics of Judgment;* and *All in the Family: On Community and Incommensurability* (forthcoming).

Jason Frank is the Gary S. Davis Assistant Professor in the History of Political Thought in the government department at Cornell University. He is author of *Constituent Moments: Enacting the People in Postrevolutionary America* and coeditor of *Vocations of Political Theory*.

George Kateb is the William Nelson Cromwell Professor of Politics Emeritus at Princeton University. He is author of *Patriotism and Other Mistakes; Emerson and Self-Reliance; The Inner Ocean: Individualism and Democratic Culture; Hannah Arendt: Politics, Conscience, Evil; Political Theory; Its Nature and Uses;* and *Utopia and Its Enemies*.

Peter Augustine Lawler is the Dana Professor of Government at Berry College. He is the author or editor of numerous books, including: *Homeless and at Home in America; Stuck with Virtue; Postmodernism Rightly Understood; Aliens in America;* and *The Restless Mind: Alexis de Tocqueville on the Origin and Perpetuation of Human Liberty*. He is also editor of *Perspectives on Political Science* and served on President Bush's Council on Bioethics.

Martha C. Nussbaum is the Ernst Freund Distinguished Service Professor of Law and Ethics at the University of Chicago. She is author or editor of numerous books, including: *From Disgust to Humanity: Sexual Orientation and Constitutional Law; Liberty of Conscience: In Defense of America's Tradition of Religious Equality; The Clash Within: Democracy, Religious Violence, and India's Future;* and *Frontiers of Justice: Disability, Nationality, Species Membership*.

Nancy L. Rosenblum is the Senator Joseph S. Clark Professor of Ethics in Politics and Government at Harvard University. She is the author of *Another Liberalism: Romanticism and the Reconstruction of Liberal Thought; Membership and Morals: The Personal Uses of Pluralism in America;* and

On the Side of the Angels: An Appreciation of Parties and Partisanship. She is also the editor of *Thoreau: Political Writings*.

Morton Schoolman is a professor of political science at the State University of New York at Albany. He is the author of *Reason and Horror: Critical Theory, Democracy, and Aesthetic Individuality* and *The Imaginary Witness: The Critical Theory of Herbert Marcuse*; and he is coeditor of *The New Pluralism: William Connolly and the Contemporary Global Condition*; and of Modernity and Political Thought, a series in modern political theory. He currently is completing a book tentatively entitled *Democratic Enlightenment: Aesthetic Education through the Visual Image*.

John E. Seery is the George Irving Thompson Memorial Professor of Government and Professor of Politics at Pomona College. He is the author of *Too Young to Run? A Proposal for an Age Amendment to the U.S. Constitution* (forthcoming); *America Goes to College: Political Theory for the Liberal Arts*; and *Political Theory for Mortals: Shades of Justice, Images of Death*.

Michael J. Shapiro is a professor of political science at the University of Hawaii. Among his recent publications are *Deforming American Political Thought: Ethnicity, Facticity, and Genre*; *Cinematic Geopolitics*; and *The Time of the City: Politics, Philosophy and Genre*.

Jack Turner is an assistant professor of political science at the University of Washington. His essays on Tocqueville, Emerson, Thoreau, and Ellison have appeared in such journals as *Political Theory, Raritan*, and *Polity*. He is currently completing a book exploring the relationship among American individualism, racial injustice, and democratic citizenship. He is also the editor of *A Political Companion to Henry David Thoreau*.

Index

abolitionists, 68
acceptance, 325, 327
"accumulative identity," 28
"actants," 134
Adam, 108–9
adhesiveness, 21, 38, 163
aesthetic awareness, 328–29
aesthetic education, 314–15, 323, 324–25, 327
aesthetic expression, 162
aestheticism
  democratic, 161
  of Whitman, 40
aesthetic orientation, 327–35
aesthetic receptivity, 325
aesthetic reflection, poetry's angles of, 337–38
aesthetic relations, 338
aesthetics of urban encounter, 170–76
"aesthetic time," 302
African Americans
  black identity, 81–82
  erotic gazing and, 117–18
  exclusion from sexual desire, 116, 118
  Whitman's rehabilitation of sexual desire and, 114–18
  writers, 187
agnosticism
  about death, 285–89
  about God, 284–85

Alamo, 234
alienation, 265–66
Allen, Gay Wilson, 301
"amativeness," 163
American identity
  in *Democratic Vistas*, 319–21
  in *Leaves of Grass*, 303–4
  Whitman's criticism of, 258–61
American Revolution, 314
"American Scholar, The" (Emerson), 289
"American spirit," 87–88
"America the Beautiful," 232–33
"Among the Multitude" (Whitman), 331
Anaya, Rudolfo, 206–7
"animate" to life, 140
anti-ecclesiasticism, 270, 311–12
anti-urbanism
  democratic, 165–67
  transcendentalist, 167–70
anxiety, 283, 290
Anzaldúa, Gloria, 11, 62, 63, 81, 82–84, 85
apersonal regard, 141–43
Apology (Plato), 272
appearances
  poetry's angles of aesthetic reflection and, 337–38
  reconciliation through an aesthetic orientation to, 327–35
  revising the relationship to reality through poetry, 335–36, 337

357

Arendt, Hannah, 8
"Are You the New Person Drawn toward Me?" (Whitman), 331
aristocracy, 255, 260, 266–67
Aristotle, 114, 256, 257, 260, 267
art
    cultural revolution and, 314–15
    native development of, 312–14
atoms, 23, 64, 274, 275, 276
Audacity of Hope, The (Obama), 77–78
Autobiography, An (Collingwood), 43
average identity
    importance to democracy, 270
    in a middle-class nation, 258
    universalized sympathy and, 263
    Whitman's notion of, 252–56

Baker, Houston A., Jr., 187
Bakhtin, M. M., 193–94, 195
Baldwin, James, 290
Balfour, Lawrie, 85
"Base of All Metaphysics, The" (Whitman), 106
Baudelaire, Charles, 149, 151–53, 154, 172
beauty, 31
Beer, Samuel, 47, 164
Beltrán, Cristina, 11
Bender, Thomas, 166
Benjamin, Walter, 172, 189–90, 191
Bennett, Jane, 11–12, 169
Bergson, Henri, 131
Bergsonian presentism, 302
Berman, Marshall, 12
Bible, 247, 269
Black, Stephen, 63
black identity, 81–82
"black" poets, 203–6
blues, 202, 203–4
"blues epistemology," 203–4
Bodies Electric (Harrison), 207–12
body
    body-city relationship, 191, 199
    body/poem analogy, 277–79
    as a concept in "Song of Myself," 24, 25, 26–27
    "encounters" between, 212
    Whitman's reclamation of, 108–12
    Whitman's rehabilitation of sexual desire and, 112–20
"Boogie Segue to Bop" (Hughes), 204
Borderlands/La Frontera (Anzaldúa), 82
"Boston Ballad, A" (Whitman), 236
Bové, Paul, 198
Boyer, Paul, 167
Brand, Dana, 172
Breaux, Zelia, 202
Broadway, 151, 200
Brooklyn, 165
Brooklyn Daily Times, 206
Burke, Edmund, 39, 152, 162
"By Blue Ontario's Shore" (Whitman)
    democratic connectedness in, 63–64
    horizontal lists in, 136
    on the influence of good poetry, 37
    material vitality in, 135
    middle voice in, 141
    "open countenance" in, 139–40
    "solar" judging in, 132, 136–37, 142–43

"Calamus" (Whitman)
    aesthetics of urban encounter in, 175–76
    expression of homoerotic desire in, 102–4, 117
    theme of democratic affection and public eros in, 163–64
    Whitman on the political significance of, 194–95
camaraderie, 248–49
captains, 250
"care," 196
Carlyle, Thomas, 259, 265
Carver, Terrell, 12, 13
catalogs
    effect of in "Song of Myself," 71–72
    poetics of inclusiveness and, 71–72, 73, 74
    Whitman's use of, 61
    See also lists
Cavell, Stanley, 3, 169
Caygill, Howard, 189
Certeau, Michel de, 174
Chauncey, George, 101

Index

Children of Adam (Whitman), 108–9
Chinatown (New York City), 192
Christian reform movements, 167
Churchill, Winston, 231
cities
    aesthetics of urban encounter and, 170–76
    American anti-urbanism, 165–70
    Baudelaire and, 149, 151–54
    Walter Benjamin's notion of, 190, 191
    body-city relationship, 191, 199
    democratic citizenship and, 157
    Jane Jacobs on, 153
    mass merger and, 152–53
    sexual desire and, 150–53, 154
    Whitman's fascination with, 12–13, 149–51, 152–54, 165
    Whitman's "musico-literary poetics" of, 188–95
citizenship
    in Thoreau's *Walden*, 169
    See also democratic citizenship; promiscuous citizenship
"City of Orgies" (Whitman), 150
civic nationalism, 155
Civil War
    democracy's greatness and, 250–52
    Whitman's views of death and, 304–5
Clark, Leadie, 299
Clinton, Hillary, 231
Coffman, Stanley, 73
Coleman, Ornette, 205
Coles, Romand, 83–84
Collingwood, R. G., 43
"Columbia the Gem of the Ocean," 233
communitarian ethos, 77
"competence," of an actant, 134
composite self, 26–27, 48–49
comradeship, 38
"conceptual persona," 197
"conjoint action," 141
connectedness
    democratic individuality and, 20–21, 63–67
    democratic potentialities and, 63–67
    poetics of inclusiveness and, 68–74

    in "Song of Myself," 31, 32–33
    See also democratic connectedness
consciousness, in Whitman's poesis, 188–89
constitutional patriotism, 155
constitutions, 227–28
continuity, Whitman's views of death and, 122–23
corporations, 210
corporeal unity, 277
"cosmic brotherhood," 264, 265
cosmology, 106–7
    of the body, 109–10
country, in Transcendentalist thought, 168–70
courage, manly, 248
creative immortality, 277–82
Critchley, Simon, 85
"Crossing Brooklyn Ferry" (Whitman)
    on the aim of poetry, 160–61
    in Richard Powers's *Gain*, 196
    the self as composite in, 26–27
    temporal sense in, 198, 199, 301–2
    universalizing poetic grammar in, 189
    use of catalogs in, 73
    visions of death in, 274–76
Crossing Canal Street (Yau), 192
"Crowds" (Baudelaire), 151–52
crowds. *See* urban crowds
cubism, 48–49
"Cultural Exchange" (Hughes), 205
cultural revolution, 314–15
Cushman, Stephen, 64

Dante Alighieri, 107
"Darest Thou Now O Soul" (Whitman), 337
Darwin, Charles, 254, 267, 270
Davis, Charles, 301
death
    democratic life and, 289–90
    fear of, 247, 272
    the great, positive democratic poem about, 266–69
    heroic immortality and, 251–52
    as a human condition, 283–89

death (*continued*)
  as an inspiration to creative immortality, 277–82
  as an opportunity for social progress, 124
  as organic transformation, 273–77
  Socrates on, 272
  Whitman's elegy on Lincoln, 123–24
  Whitman's vision of, 13–14, 122–23, 272–73, 302–3, 304–6, 322
Death and Life of Great American Cities, The (Jacobs), 153
decomposition, 273–77
"deep ecologists," 53
Deleuze, Gilles, 155–56, 165, 191, 194, 197, 210, 212
democracy
  aesthetic expression and, 162
  association with grossness, 39
  average identity and, 252–56, 270
  danger of mortal anxiety to, 290
  in early America, 228–29
  fear of death and, 247
  heroism and, 282
  historical criticisms of, 226
  iconization of, 238–39
  individualism and, 47
  issues of representation in, 226–28
  manliness and, 229–31 (*see also* democratic manliness)
  poetry and, 315–16, 322–23
  religion and, 245
  significance of reconciliation to, 323–24, 327
  Tocqueville on aristocracy's advantage over, 266–67
  Tocqueville's criticism of, 262
  as vocation, 223–26
  war and greatness, 250–52
  Whitman on democratic life in America, 258–61
  Whitman's recommendations for, 10
Democracy in America (Tocqueville), 166, 228, 245
democratic aestheticism, 161
democratic affection, 163–64
democratic anti-urbanism, 165–67
democratic attachment, 155, 159
democratic body, 105–8
democratic citizenship
  agnosticism about death and, 289–90
  Whitman's image of, 157
democratic connectedness
  Obama and, 82
  risks of, 89
  Whitman's notion of, 20–21, 32–33, 63–67
  See also connectedness
democratic culture
  characteristics of, 19
  transcendence and, 44–45
  Whitman as a philosopher of, 19
democratic development, 256–57, 260
democratic diversity, 61, 162
democratic education, 315–16
democratic egalitarianism, 162–63
democratic enlightenment, 314–15, 322, 324–25
democratic equality, 115
democratic grace, 39–40
democratic greatness, 250, 267
democratic individuality
  connectedness and, 20–21, 32–33, 63–67
  democratic culture and, 19
  Emersonian notion of, 20
  ethnic differences and, 201
  Obama and, 82
  religion and, 267
  rights of the individual and, 19–20
  in "Song of Myself," 21–45
  Tocqueville's criticism of, 262
democratic life, agnosticism about death and, 289–90
democratic love
  American optimism for social progress, 124–26
  democratic body and, 105–8
  flaws in Whitman's poetic execution, 121–22
  homosexual, 101–5
  issues of national forgiveness and reconciliation, 99–100
  personal spirituality and, 120–21

Index

problem of racial hatred and, 97–99
Whitman's elegy on Lincoln's death, 123–24
Whitman's mystical views of death and, 122–23
Whitman's notion of, 96–105, 120–21
Whitman's reclamation of the body, 108–12
women's equality and, 100–101
democratic manliness
  generation of exclusions and, 230, 235–36, 239
  iconization of democracy and, 225
  masculinization of the individual and, 224
  problems of, 231
  in reception-literature, 239
  Whitman's notion of, 225–26, 229–30, 231–37
  women and, 230–31, 236
democratic nationality, 21, 164–65
democratic philosophy, 269
democratic poetics, of Obama, 76–77
democratic poetry
  the great, positive democratic poem about death, 266–69
  significance of, 261–64
  Whitman's noble failure, 269–70
democratic poets, 8–10, 261
democratic political principle, 246–49
democratic potentialities, 63–67, 82
democratic progress, 249
democratic receptivity
  of Obama, 77
  poetics of inclusiveness and, 68–74
  Whitman's catalogs and, 65
democratic republican principle, 249, 311
democratic self, 290
democratic spectacle, 56–57
"democratic time," 201
democratic union, 86
democratic unity, 47–57
democratic virtue, 255–56
Democratic Vistas (Whitman), 259, 298
  democratic culture and, 19
  on democratic education through poetry, 315–16

democratic self in, 174
identity in, 35, 36, 319–21, 332
the individual, the mass, and equality in, 311–12
on the native development of literature, 312–14
Nature and meaning in, 330
political themes in, 2
reconciliation of the individual and the mass in, 316–18
soul in, 35, 36
structural logic of, 310
topics Whitman discusses in, 310
transcendence and solitude in, 45
"unknown" in, 321–22
Whitman's aestheticism in, 40
democratic writers, 9
detachment, 141
Dewey, John, 141, 298
dialogic lyricism, 205
dialogics, 194
Dimock, Wai Chee, 173
discernment, 131–32
discourse, monologic, 193–94
diversity
  democratic, 61, 162
  moral, 258
  racial, 62
"divine literatus," 299
Dostoevsky, Fyodor, 194
Dougherty, James, 172–73
Doyle, Peter, 172
dramatic presentism, 301
Dreams from My Father (Obama), 81–82, 84–85
Drum-Taps (Whitman), 21, 70–71
Duberman, Martin, 101

earth, Whitman's affirmation of, 288
egalitarianism, democratic, 162–63
elections, 250
Ellington, Duke, 202–3
Ellis, Havelock, 117
Ellison, Ralph, 186–87, 188, 202
Emerson, Ralph Waldo
  anti-urbanism and, 168–69
  on being free of mortal anxiety, 283

Emerson, Ralph Waldo (*continued*)
    differences between Emerson and Whitman, 33–34
    on the present, 289
    reaction to *Leaves of Grass*, 97
    resurgence of interest in, 3
Emersonians, 3, 20
Émile (Rousseau), 109
empathy, 31–32, 41–44, 263
encounters, 212
enlightenment, democratic, 322, 324–25
"ensembles," 202
Epicurus, 247
equality, 315
equal rights, 31–32, 311
Erkkila, Betsy, 2, 61
erotic gazing, 117–19
eroticism
    homoerotic poems, 101, 102–5
    mystery of death and, 115
    in Whitman's aesthetic of urban encounter, 172
    See also sexual desire
ethnicity, 200–202
"ethnic" poets, 192–93
ethnopoetics
    Colin Harrison's *Bodies Electric* and, 207–12
    of Langston Hughes, 203–6
    Nuyoricans, 206–7
    overview, 12–13
    Richard Powers's *The Time of Our Singing* and, 195–98, 199–200, 201–2
    Whitman's "musico-literary" poetics of the city, 185–86, 188–95
Everybody's Autobiography (Stein), 28
evolution, Lamarckian, 274, 276

"Faces" (Whitman), 31
Fairey, Shepard, 78
faith, 265
fantasy, 151
fear of death, 247, 272
Ferguson, Kennan, 13
Fern, Fanny, 112

feudalism, 162, 311–12
Fire Next Time, The (Baldwin), 290
"First O Songs" (Whitman), 70–71
Fisher, Paul, 198–99, 204
flâneur, 172
Fletcher, Angus, 140–41
"flipbooks," 73
Folsom, Ed, 65, 69, 78
"For You, O Democracy" (Whitman), 163–64, 233–34
Frank, Jason, 12, 207–8, 273
freedom
    agnosticism about death and, 290
    of religion, 270
"free love," 119
French revolutionaries, 248
"Full of Life Now" (Whitman), 276, 277–78
"fusing contributions," 161

Gain (Powers), 196
gays. *See* homosexuals
gazing, 117–19
gender equality, 68
genres, in "Song of Myself," 29
George (king of Britain), 236
Gettysburg Address, 59
Ginsberg, Allen, 10
Girl with Mandolin, 49
"Give Me the Splendid Silent Sun" (Whitman), 170–71
God, 265, 270, 335–37
grace, democratic, 39–40
"Grand Is the Seen" (Whitman), 33
"Great Are the Myths" (Whitman), 30–31
greatness
    average identity and, 253
    democratic, 250
    of the individual, 245
    Lincoln and, 250, 253
    material, 259
    war and, 250–52
    Whitman's notion of, 253
grief, in Whitman's elegy on Lincoln's death, 123–24
Grossman, Allen, 61, 75

Index

grossness, democracy and, 39
Guattari, Felix, 191

Hale, Edward Everett, 112
happiness, 265–66
"haptic" perception, 191–92
Harrison, Colin, 207–12
Hegel, Georg Wilhelm Friedrich, 34, 50, 246, 265, 266, 267, 269–70
"Here the Frailest Leaves of Me" (Whitman), 102–3
heroism
   democracy and, 282
   heroic death, 251–52
   Whitman's notion of heroic life, 32–33
historical beings, 269–70
Hobbes, Thomas, 247
homoerotic poems, 101, 102–5
homosexual love, 101–5
homosexuals
   desiring gaze and, 118–19
   Romer v. Evans and, 125–26
   Whitman's rehabilitation of sexual desire and, 116–17
horizontal lists, 136
Hughes, Langston, 203–6
human decomposition, 273–77
human identity, 270
humanity, death as a precondition of, 283
human rights, 247
humility, intellectual, 289

"I, Too, Sing America" (Hughes), 203, 204
iconization
   the construction of nations and, 238
   defined, 225
   of democracy, 225, 238–39
   of Whitman, 223, 225
Idealism, 50
identity
   "accumulative," 28
   in *Democratic Vistas,* 35, 36, 319–21
   reconciliation with difference, 319–21
   Whitman's democratic model of, 326
"I have a dream" speech (King), 80
"I Hear America Singing" (Whitman), 222

Iliad, 251
imitation, 325–26, 327
immortality
   agnosticism about death and, 285–88
   death as organic transformation, 273–77
   heroic death and, 251–52
   Tocqueville on, 266, 267
   Whitman's devaluation of, 286–87
   Whitman's views of death and, 122–23
   See also creative immortality
"impartiality," 140
"inaugurate," as defined by Whitman, 141
inclusiveness, Whitman's poetics of, 68–74
independence, 249
individual
   in *Democratic Vistas,* 311, 316–17
   masculinization of, 224
   reconciliation with the mass, 318–19, 323
individualism
   countering with democratic poetry, 262
   creation of democratic unity and, 47–57
   democracy and, 47
   sympathy and, 262–63
individuality, being in the crowd and, 153
individual rights, 19–20, 311
Ingraham, Mark, 117
intellectual humility, 289
interpretation, 7
interpretive darkness, 332–34
Invisible Man (Ellison), 186–87
Ira Aldridge Theater, 202
"I Sing the Body Electric" (Whitman)
   body-city relationship in, 191
   counter-cosmology of the body in, 109–12
   democratic union in, 86
   influence of, 185
"I Sit and Look Out" (Whitman), 37

Jacobs, Jane, 153
James, William, 25, 52, 158, 159, 161, 175
jazz, 202
Jefferson, Thomas, 118, 166, 167
Jesus Christ, 141
judgment
   moral, 131–32, 143

judgment (*continued*)
    nonjudgmental, 132–34
    See also "solar" judging

Kant, Immanuel, 188, 189
Kantian subject, 188–89
Kaplan, Justin, 54
Kateb, George, 273
    criticism of Kateb's account of Whitman, 11
    on individualists and democratic unity, 47–56
    on "myself disintegrated," 275
    Obama and, 82
    on potentialities and democratic connectedness, 62, 63–67
    on Whitman as a philosopher of democracy, 2–3, 10
    on Whitman's democratic aestheticism, 161
Kennedy, Anthony, 125–26
Kierkegaard, Søren, 153
King, Martin Luther, Jr., 80
"kosmos," 64

Lacis, Asja, 190
Lamarck, Jean, 274, 276
Lamarckian evolution, 274, 276
language, 328–29
Larson, Kerry, 159, 161
Latour, Bruno, 134
Lawler, Peter, 13
Lawrence, D. H., 28, 50, 119, 122
Leaves of Grass (Whitman)
    aesthetics of urban encounter in, 176
    body-city relation in, 199
    democratic egalitarianism in, 162–63
    democratic individuality in, 20–21, 326
    democratic nationality in, 164–65
    frontispiece portrait of Whitman in, 78, 176–77, 279
    homosexual love in "Calamus" sequence, 102–4
    horizontal lists in, 136
    importance of Whitman's urban life to, 165
    material vitality in, 135–36
    Michael Moon on the political significance of, 195
    the place of women's issues in, 100–101
    pluralized American identity in, 303–4
    poem of sexual shame in, 104–5
    poetic aim of, 155–56, 158–59
    poetic voice in, 302
    polyphony in, 194
    promiscuous citizenship in, 157, 158
    public responses to, 97, 112–13
    sequentialism of lists in, 173–74
    "solar" judging in, 132
    special meaning of the "Calamus" sequence, 163–64
    temporal sense in, 198, 300
    three dimensions of reconciliation in, 325–27
    vision of life and death in, 302–3, 305–6
    Whitman's orientation to differences just as they appear, 338
    Whitman's self-reviews of, 155, 156, 157
    youth and aging in, 304
Left, 299
"leftism," 297, 299
"Lennox Avenue: Midnight" (Hughes), 204
lesbians, 125–26
Library of Congress, 1
Lincoln, Abraham
    Ralph Ellison's eulogy in *Invisible Man*, 187
    greatness and, 250, 253
    Allen Grossman on the policy of union in, 75
    Obama and, 59, 60
    political crisis of the 1850s and, 158
    Second Inaugural Address, 99
    slavery and, 99
    Whitman on the martyrdom of, 251
    Whitman's 1871 epitaph for, 97–99
    Whitman's elegy on the death of, 123–24
lists
    horizontal, 136
    sequentialism in *Leaves of Grass*, 173–74
    Whitman's mention of women in, 230
    See also catalogs

Index

literature
  performative dimension of, 6–8
  Whitman on native development of, 312–14
Longfellow, Henry Wadsworth, 259
love
  judgment and, 141
  "public," 12
  Tocqueville on modern diffusion of, 263–64
  Whitman's view of, 11–12
  See also democratic love
lovers, 331
Lowell, James Russell, 176
Lucretius, 247, 268
Luke, 141

Mack, Stephen John, 301–2
Mahler, Gustav, 106, 120–21
"Manifest Destiny," 246
manliness, 239
  See also democratic manliness
manly courage, 248
manly friendship, 248–49
"Mannahatta" (Whitman), 150, 200–201
Mariotti, Shannon, 169
marriage, 100
Marseille, 190
Marshall, Thurgood, 117
masculine women, 230–31
masculinity, 224, 232, 237
Mason, John, 73
mass
  in *Democratic Vistas*, 317–18
  reconciliation with the individual, 318–19, 323
mass merger, 152–53
mass rallies, 85–88
material greatness, 259
materialism, 259
material prosperity, 256–58
material vitality, 135–36
meaning, 330
menstrual cycle, 117
"mestiza consciousness," 11, 62, 81, 82–84, 85

"mestiza poetics," 62
Microsoft, 296–97
middle voice, 139–41
Mill, John Stuart, 32, 36, 100, 316–17
minorities, 319–20
miscegenation, 78
"mixed" constitutions, 227–28
mobs, 152–53
moneymaking, 165, 259
monologic discourse, 193–94
Montaigne, 30
Moon, Michael, 194–95, 199
moral agency, 136–39
moral character, 249–50, 256, 261
moral diversity, 258
morality, democratic body and, 105–8
moral judgment, 131–32, 143
moral life, 259
moral responsibility, 259
moral virtue, 257
mortal anxiety, 283, 290
mortality, 287–88
Moynihan Report (Spillers), 200
music, 202–3
musicality, 12–13
musical voice
  in Richard Powers's *The Time of Our Singing*, 195, 197–98
  in Whitman's New York poems, 197
music imagery, 204–5
"musico-literary poetics," 188–95
"Myself and Mine" (Whitman), 22

Naples, 190
narrative, Kantian, 188
national identity, 319–21
nationalism, 50–51
nationality, democratic, 164–65
nation-building, 238
natural beings, 270
Nature (Emerson), 34
nature
  as conceived by Emerson and Whitman, 34–35
  poetry and, 322
  in Transcendentalist thought, 168–70

negative poems, 268
"negative receptivity," 55
"Negro family," 200
Nehamas, Alexander, 54
"New Left," 297
New York Aurora, 172
New York City
  Chinatown, 192
  Ralph Ellison on, 186
  ethnopoetics of (*see* ethnopoetics)
  influence on Whitman, 149, 150, 151, 165
  Nuyoricans, 206–7
  Richard Powers's interethnic novelistic articulation of, 195–98, 199–200, 201–2
  Whitman's ethnopoetics of, 185–86
Nicomachean Ethics (Aristotle), 256, 260
Nietzsche, Friedrich, 27, 43–44, 54, 132
nonjudgmental judging, 132–34
  See also "solar" judging
Notes on the State of Virginia (Jefferson), 166
novels, "polyphonic," 194
"Now Lucifer Was Not Dead" (Whitman), 98–99
Nussbaum, Martha, 3, 11, 12, 136–39
Nuyorican Poets Cafe, 206–7, 210
Nuyoricans, 206–7, 210

Obama, Barack
  campaign speeches of 2008, 78–80
  Cristina Beltrán on, 11
  challenges of the poetics of inclusion and, 89
  keynote address at the 2004 Democratic National Convention, 75–77
  Lincoln's notion of union and, 59–60
  mass rallies and, 85–88
  mestiza poetics and the crisis of race, 80–85
  notion of "American spirit" and, 87–88
  Philadelphia speech on race (2008), 80–81, 84, 85
  poetics of equivalence and, 61–62
  poetics of union and, 74–80
  political future of, 89–90
  political opacity of, 88
  politics of racialization and, 78–80
  racial ambivalence of, 77–78
  racialized subjectivity and, 62
  significance of election of, 60, 88–89
  strategies in speeches of, 79
  Whitman's poetics and, 60–62, 89
Odyssey, 251
"Of the Terrible Doubt of Appearances" (Whitman), 332, 334
"O Hot-Cheek'd and Blushing" (Whitman), 104–5, 109
"Old Chinese Gentleman Drops in to See His Cronies in a Coffeeshop (Mott Street), An" (Yau), 192–93
"One's-Self I Sing" (Whitman), 26, 77, 193
On Liberty (Mill), 36
"open countenance," 139–40
optimism, social progress and, 124–25
"organic" sensation, 188
organic transformation, 273–77
Otherness, 14, 325, 329
"Our Old Feuillage" (Whitman), 69–70
"Out of the Cradle Endlessly Rocking" (Whitman), 194
"Over the Carnage Rose Prophetic a Voice" (Whitman), 38
ownership of property, 257

Paine, Thomas, 48, 247, 248, 253
Pannapacker, William, 157
pantheism, 264–65, 285
Paris, 149, 151–52
"Passage to India" (Whitman), 336, 337
"Paterson" (Williams), 206
patriarchy, 231
patriotism, Whitmanesque, 297, 298–99
Paul, Saint, 265
"People," the, 319
  See also mass
perception
  of appearances, 334–35
  Henri Bergson on, 131
  "haptic," 191–92
perceptual discernment, 131–32
personal identity, 266, 267
personality
  as a concept in "Song of Myself," 25–26
  as made up of ordinariness, 36

Index

perspectivism, 334
  notion of the composite self, 48–49
philistinism, 120
philosophical subject, 188, 189
philosophy
  democratic, 269
  of experience, 189–90
Picasso, Pablo, 48–49
"Picasso-like" self, 48–49, 65
Pinero, Miguel, 207
"plantation bloc," 203
Plato, 27, 267, 272
Pliny, the elder, 117
pluralizing masculinities, 232
poems
  homoerotic, 101, 102–5
  negative, 268
  the positive poem of death, 266–69
poetical feeling, 44
poetical perception, 44
poetical speech, 30
poetic language, 328–29
poetic pluralization, 61
poetics of equivalence, 61–62, 87–88
poetics of inclusion, 89
poetic subject, 188–89
poetic voice
  in "Crossing Brooklyn Ferry," 196
  in *Leaves of Grass*, 302
  See also musical voice
poetry
  aesthetic education and, 323
  aesthetic orientation to appearances, 329–35
  angles of aesthetic reflection, 328–29, 337–38
  death as inspiration for, 280–81
  democracy and, 322–23
  democratic, 261–64
  democratic education through, 315–16
  interpretive darkness and, 332–34
  language and, 328–29
  monologic discourse in, 193–94
  nature and, 322
  poeticizing the unknown, 322
  political relevance of, 9–10
  reconciliation and, 320–21, 323, 338

  relationship to scholarship, 4–5
  revising the relationship between God and the world, 335–36
  Whitman on the influence of, 37
  Whitman's belief in the healing power of, 68–69
poets
  democratic, 8–10, 261
  "ethnic," 192–93
  the positive poem about death and, 268–69
  "solar" judging and, 132, 133
  Whitman's criticism of, 260–61
political attachment, 159, 162
political democracy, 249–50
political institutions, 248
political life, 249–50
political science and scientists, 6–8
  scholarship on Whitman, 2–4
political theorists, 5–6
politics
  iconization of democracy and, 238–39
  of the ordinary, 159–60
  of racialization, 78–80
  Richard Rorty on the purpose of, 297–98
polyphony, 194, 195, 197–98
pornography, 119
positive poem of death, 266–69
postmodernism, 297
potentialities, 62
Pound, Ezra, 3
Powers, Richard, 195–98, 199–200, 201–2
preconceptions, 335
premarital sex, 100
presentism, 301, 302
presidential election of 2008
  mass rallies and, 85–88
  Obama and the crisis of race, 80–81
  Obama's poetics of union and, 75, 78–80
  as a political and sensory event, 60, 88–89
  "Whitmanesque" spectacles of diversity in, 61
Price, Leontyne, 205
Princeton University, 102
privatism, 165

"Projection" (Hughes), 205
promiscuity, 119
promiscuous citizenship
   aesthetics of urban encounter and, 170–76
   Whitman's experience of urban life and, 165
   Whitman's notion of, 156, 157–58
property ownership, 257
prosperity, 256–58
prostitutes, 120
prurience, 119–20
psychological distancing, 141
public eros, 163–64
"public" love, 12
Puerto Ricans, 206–7
puritanism, sexual, 119–20

race
   democratic manliness and, 235–36
   Obama and the crisis of, 80–85
   Obama's politics of racialization, 78–80
   Whitman's attitude toward, 67–68, 70, 72, 74, 206
   Whitman's rehabilitation of sexual desire and, 114–18
racial ambivalence
   of Obama, 77–78
   of Whitman, 67–68, 70, 72, 74, 206
racial diversity, 62
racial equality, 68
racial hatred, 97–99
racial identity, 81, 200–203
racialized subjectivity, 62
racial justice, 75
rallies, 85–88
Ramsay, David, 166
reality, poetry and, 335–36, 337
reception-literature, 239
receptivity, 64, 65, 325, 326, 327
"reckless eyeballing," 117
reconciliation
   aesthetic education as a solution to, 323, 324–25
   between identity and difference, 319–21
   between the individual and the mass, 318–19, 323

   the purpose of democracy and, 323–24, 327
   as the task of poetry, 323
   through an aesthetic orientation to appearances, 327–35
   Whitman's three dimensions of, 325–26
"Reconciliation" (Whitman), 73–74
"Recorders Ages Hence" (Whitman), 96–97
reductionism, 270
Reflections on the Revolution in France (Burke), 39
religion
   democracy and, 245
   the democratic body and, 105–8
   Tocqueville on, 266, 267, 270
   Whitman on the purpose of, 267
   Whitman's anti-ecclesiasticism, 270, 311–12
religious soul, 24
resentment, 132
"Return of the Heroes, The" (Whitman), 39
Reynolds, David, 68, 69, 101, 158–59, 163
Riesman, David, 169
rights
   discussed in *Democratic Vistas*, 311
   religion and, 247
   Whitman on the significance of, 19–20
Robbins, Bruce, 196
Roman constitution, 227–28
"romantic utopians," 300
Romer v. Evans, 125–26
Rorty, Richard, 13, 245
   criticism of his interpretations of Whitman, 268
   critique of his future-oriented model for America, 297–307
   death of, 296–97
   notion of Whitmanesque patriotism, 297, 298–99
   notion of Whitman's American imagination, 299–300
   on the purpose of politics, 297–98
   vision of John Dewey, 298
   on Whitman as the prophet of American civic religion, 3
Rosenblum, Nancy, 11, 60–61, 86, 162

Index

Rousseau, Jean-Jacques, 52, 109, 118
runaway slaves, 70
Rush, Benjamin, 167

same-sex love, 101–5
Sanchez-Eppler, Karen, 69
Sartre, Jean-Paul, 42
"Scented Herbage of My Breast" (Whitman), 278–80
scholarship, relationship of poetry to, 4–5
Schoolman, Morton, 13, 201, 273
Secession War. See Civil War
self
   composite, 26–27, 48–49
   as a concept in "Song of Myself," 24–27
   the creation of democratic unity and, 47–57
   George Kateb's characterization of, 48–49, 65
   transmutation of, 300
   Robert Penn Warren on, 51
   Whitman's decentering of, 174
self-affirmation, 273
self-consciousness, 277
self-knowledge, 30, 264, 330–31
self-regulation, 159
self-reviews, 155, 156, 157
"self-trust," 282
sensation, "organic," 188
sex
   premarital, 100
   Whitman's attitude toward, 119–20
   Whitman's rehabilitation of, 108–12
sex industry, 119
sexual desire
   cities and, 150–53, 154
   democratic manliness and, 237
   in "O Hot-Cheek'd and Blushing," 104–5
   the public's fear of, 112–13
   Whitman's attitude toward, 119–20
   Whitman's rehabilitation of, 108–12, 113–20
   See also eroticism
sexual fantasy, 151
sexuality
   cities and, 150–53, 154
   the democratic body and, 108

"sexual liberation," 151
sexual shame, 104
Shakespeare, William, 149
shame, sexual, 104
Shapiro, Michael, 12–13
"shit happens," 140
Simmel, Georg, 169
"singing," 202–3
skepticism, 54
slavery
   Aristotle on, 114
   Lincoln on, 99
   in "Song of Myself," 70, 114–15
   Whitman's attitude toward, 67–68, 236
"Sleepers, The" (Whitman), 42–43
Smith, Rev. Ralph, 102
social cohesion, 161–62
social encounters, 169
social progress, 124–26
social relations, as aesthetic relations, 338
social visibility, 277
Socrates, 272
"solar" judging
   apersonal regard and, 141–43
   middle voice and, 139–41
   notion of material vitality and, 135–36
   Martha Nussbaum's critique of, 136–39
   Whitman's ethos of, 134–35
   Whitman's notion of, 12, 132–34
soldiers, 251–52
solitude, 44–45, 168–70
"So Long!" (Whitman), 38–39
Sommer, Doris, 71
"Song for Occupations, A" (Whitman), 28, 33, 160, 226, 335
song imagery, 202–3
"Song of Myself" (Whitman)
   agnosticism in, 284–85
   catalogs and lists in, 71–72, 134, 173
   city ethnoscape in, 190–91
   connectedness in, 31, 32–33
   the democratic body in, 106–8
   democratic individuality in, 21–45
   democratic receptivity in, 70
   elemental capacities of the subjectified self in, 136
   ethic of action in, 39

"Song of Myself" (Whitman) (*continued*)
  genres in, 29
  Hegelian or Emersonian moment in, 34
  homoerotic imagery in, 105
  interpretive darkness in, 332–34
  material actants in, 134
  "parable" of female sexual longing in, 115–16
  the place of women's issues in, 100–101
  poetic aim of, 27
  "potentiality" in, 64
  racial ambivalence in, 68
  relationship between democracy and eroticism in, 113–16
  self-knowing in, 331
  sequence and texture of, 29–30
  soul, body, and self in, 24–27
  three dimensions of reconciliation in, 325–26
  titling of, 22
  truth and meaning in, 330
  "unconscious ambivalence" toward the self in, 63
  urban poesis in, 193
  vision of death in, 273, 279
  vision of God in, 336, 337
  Whitman's depiction of himself as a "kosmos," 64–65
"Song of the Answerer" (Whitman), 42
"Song of the Broad-Axe" (Whitman), 135
"Song of the Open Road" (Whitman), 20, 34, 38, 68, 334
"Song of the Redwood Tree" (Whitman), 330
"Song of the Rolling Earth, A" (Whitman)
  body/poem analogy in, 278
  detachment in, 141
  earth- and self-affirmation in, 288
  material vitality in, 135
  on the potentiality of the earth, 301
  self-knowing in, 330–31
  "solar" judging in, 139
  on solitude, 44
  on the soul, 39
  sympathy in, 38
  Whitman's consideration of language in, 327–28
"Song of the Universal" (Whitman), 141
"Songs of Parting" (Whitman), 304
soul
  as a concept in "Song of Myself," 24–27
  notion of in *Democratic Vistas,* 35, 36
  religious meaning of, 24
  in "A Song of the Rolling Earth," 39
"Specimen Days" (Whitman), 208
spectacle, 56–57, 61, 87–88, 162
Spillers, Hortense, 200, 201
"Starting from Paumanok" (Whitman), 65, 69, 201, 202, 300–301
Stein, Gertrude, 28
Stendahl, 51
Stevens, Wallace, 44, 303
strangers, 175
subject
  philosophical, 188, 189
  Whitman and Kantian, 188–89
Subjection of Women, The (Mill), 100
subjectivity, racialized, 62
suffrage
  universal, 250
  women's, 100, 101
supernatural, 337
Symonds, John Addington, 102
sympathy
  democratic love and, 100, 107
  identification with others and, 52
  perspectives on the limits of, 41–44
  "universal democratic comradeship" and, 262–63
  virtue and, 264
  Whitman's definition of, 38
  Whitman's encouragement of, 31–32

Thatcher, Margaret, 231
"That Shadow My Likeness" (Whitman), 36
"This Moment Yearning and Thoughtful" (Whitman), 65–66
Thomas, M. Wynn, 71
Thoreau, Henry David, 3
  anti-urbanism and, 168, 169–70
  on *Leaves of Grass,* 170
  the political accompaniment of detachment, 55
  on Whitman as a democrat, 19

"Thoughts—: Visages" (Whitman), 31
time
  "democratic," 201
  Richard Powers's notion of, 199, 201–2
  Whitman's sense of, 198–99, 300–303
Time of Our Singing, The (Powers), 195–98, 199–200, 201–2
Tocqueville, Alexis de
  on the American lack of poetic ideas, 9
  anti-urbanism in, 166
  on aristocracy, 255, 260, 266–67
  Democracy in America, 166, 228, 245
  on democratic greatness, 267
  the democratic poet and, 261
  on the freedom of religion, 270
  on God, 265
  on the modern diffusion of love, 263–64
  pantheism and, 264
  on personal identity and one's perception of immortality, 266, 267
  on philosophic self-respect, 44
  political criticism of democratic individualism, 262
  reductionism of modern science and, 270
  on religion, 266, 267
  on self-understanding, 264
  on sympathy and democratic leveling, 263
  Whitman and, 13, 245
"To Foreign Lands" (Whitman), 233
"To Live in the Borderlands Means You" (Anzaldúa), 82–83
"To Think of Time" (Whitman), 274
"To You" (Whitman), 189
transcendence, 44–45
Transcendentalism, 167–70
Trethewey, Natasha, 68, 74
Turner, Jack, 13

ugliness, 31
understanding, Kant's notion of, 188
"Une passante, A" (Baudelaire), 151
union
  Obama's and Lincoln's legacy of, 59–60
  Obama's poetics of, 74–80
  Whitman and the politics of, 63–74
  Whitman's poetics of, 75

United States
  democracy in, 228–29
  the significance of democratic poetry and, 261–64
  Whitman and the poetic transformation of, 260–61
  Whitman calls the "greatest poem," 106
  Whitman on democratic life in, 258–61
  Whitman's notion of the future of, 298–99
universal suffrage, 250
"unknown," 321–22
Up from Slavery (Washington), 187
urban crowds
  mass merger and, 152–53
  Whitman's aesthetic of urban encounter and, 172–73
  Whitman's notion of democratic citizenship and, 157
urban encounter, Whitman's aesthetics of, 170–76
urban life. *See* cities
U.S. Constitution, 228, 246

virtue
  average identity and, 254–56
  material prosperity and, 256–58
  sympathy and, 264
"Vista" operating system, 296
vitalism, 135–36
voice. *See* musical voice; poetic voice

Wald, Priscilla, 192
Walden (Thoreau), 169–70
"Walt Whitman Strides the Llano of New Mexico" (Anaya), 206–7
war, greatness and, 250–52, 253
Warner, Michael, 171
Warren, James Perrin, 71
Warren, Robert Penn, 51
Washington, Booker T., 187
"When Lilacs Last in the Dooryard Bloom'd" (Whitman), 123–24, 186–87, 203
white guilt, 77
Whitman, Walt
  on the "abnormal libidinousness" of urban populations, 167

Whitman, Walt (*continued*)
- aestheticism of, 40
- aesthetics of urban encounter, 170–76
- agnosticism of, 284–85
- alienation and, 265–66
- anti-ecclesiasticism of, 270, 311–12
- attitude toward sex and sexual desire, 119–20
- on average identity, 252–56
- Charles Baudelaire and, 149
- belief in the healing power of poetry, 68–69
- on the Bible, 269
- calls for a future poetry and, 306–7
- city life and, 12–13, 149–51, 152–54, 165
- as a "conceptual persona," 197
- criticism of poets, 260–61
- on democratic attachment, 155, 159
- on the democratic body, 105–8
- on democratic egalitarianism, 162–63
- on democratic life in America, 258–61
- on democratic love, 96–105
- democratic manliness and, 231–37
- on democratic nationality, 164–65
- on democratic philosophy, 269
- democratic poetry and, 261–64
- on the democratic political principle, 246–49
- on democratic potentiality and connectedness, 63–67
- democratic spectacle and, 56–57, 162
- on democratic union, 86
- on democratic unity and the self, 47–57
- differences between Emerson and Whitman, 33–34
- Betsy Erkkila on the poetry of, 61
- ethnopoetics of New York and, 185–86
- faith and, 265
- frontispiece to *Leaves of Grass*, 78, 176–77, 279
- on "fusing contributions" and social cohesion, 161–62
- on the future of America, 298–99
- on the grace of democracy, 39–40
- the great, positive democratic poem about death and, 266–69
- on greatness, 253
- Hegelianism and, 50, 265
- homosexual love and, 101–5
- as an iconic figure, 78
- iconization of, 223, 225
- indifference to political institutions, 248
- on individual rights, 19–20
- influence of, 185
- on the influence of good poetry, 37
- on the limits of poetical speech, 30
- on Lincoln's death, 123–24, 251
- living the life of equal rights and, 31–32
- on manly friendship, 248–49
- on material prosperity and the ordinary practice of virtue, 256–58
- on moneymaking, 165, 259
- on moral character and political life, 249–50
- musical voice in the New York poems of, 197
- "musico-literary poetics" of the city, 188–95
- on nationalism, 50–51
- "negative receptivity," 55
- noble failure as a democratic poet, 269–70
- pantheism and, 264–65, 285
- as a philosopher of democratic culture, 19
- poetic aim of, 155–56
- poetic pluralization and, 61
- poetics of inclusiveness, 68–74
- poetics of union, 75
- the poetic transformation of America and, 260–61
- poetic trope of "care," 196
- on poetry's relationship to scholarship, 4–5
- on poets of democracy, 8–10
- on political attachment, 162
- political crisis of the 1850s and, 158
- political scholarship on, 2–4
- on the political significance of the "Calamus" sequence, 194–95
- politics of the ordinary and, 159–60
- the politics of union and, 63–74
- polyphony and, 194

racial ambivalence of, 67–68, 70, 72, 74, 206
reclamation of the body, 108–12
recommendations for democracy, 10
rehabilitation of sexual desire, 112–20
religion and, 267, 270
representations of women, 230
Nancy Rosenblum on the significance of, 60–61
secondary literature devoted to, 1–2
self-description as a "great loafer," 172
self-distancing of, 54–55
self-reviews by, 155, 156, 157
slavery and, 236
on "solar" judging, 132–34
temporal sense of, 198–99, 300–303
Tocqueville and, 13, 245
univocal stance of, 193
use of catalogs, 61, 71–72, 73, 74
use of the middle voice, 139–41
vision of death, 13–14, 122–23, 272–73, 302–3, 304–6, 322 (*see also* death)
on *Walden*, 170
on war and greatness, 250–52
women's equality and, 100–101
Whitman the Political Poet (Erkkila), 2
"Whoever You Are Holding Me Now in Hand" (Whitman), 103–4
"Who Learns My Lesson Complete?" (Whitman), 283–84, 285–88
Wihl, Gary, 2
wilderness, 168–70
Williams, William Carlos, 206
"Woman Waits for Me, A" (Whitman), 121–22
women
    democratic manliness and, 230–31, 236
    desiring gaze and, 117–18
    Whitman's reclamation of the body and, 111–12
    Whitman's rehabilitation of sexual desire and, 115–16, 117–18
    Whitman's representations of, 230
women's equality, 100–101
women's rights movement, 100, 101
Woods, Clyde, 203–4
Wordsworth, William, 159
Wright, Rev. Jeremiah, 80, 84, 85

Yau, John, 192–93
"Years of the Modern, The" (Whitman), 306

Ziff, Larzer, 300

www.ingramcontent.com/pod-product-compliance
Lightning Source LLC
Chambersburg PA
CBHW020634230426
43665CB00008B/173